THE ESSENTIAL BOOK FOR MICROSOFT® OFFICE

THE GET-IT-DONE TUTORIAL
FOR PROFESSIONALS

BILL BRUCK

D0791717

PRIMA PUBLISHING

Project Editor: Stefan Grünwedel
Developmental Editor: Joyce Nielsen
Technical Reviewer: Nanci Jacobs
Copyeditor: Matthew Gatheringwater
Book Designer: Prima Design/Production
Indexer: Katherine Stimson
Interior Layout: Marian Hartsough
Cover Designer: Vanessa Wong

ISBN: 0-7615-0430-3
Library of Congress Catalog Card Number: 95-72679
Printed in the United States of America
96 97 98 99 BB 10 9 8 7 6 5 4 3 2

CONTENTS

INTRODUCTION

I've been designing and implementing computer training programs for many years, and I've consulted with organizations on how best to use PCs in a variety of office settings. It seems that as software applications become more complex, fewer people have the time and inclination to learn how to use them effectively.

This isn't a function of "intelligence" or being a "computer whiz." The problem is that more and more features are included with each software release because software manufacturers want to be responsive to clients and stay competitive in the marketplace. Most busy professionals don't have time to keep up with all the improvements and upgrades!

To use software effectively, you must know which features and applications can best be used for a given task; you don't simply learn about every feature that exists. That's where this book can help.

In *The Essential Book for Microsoft Office*, I've distilled my experience to help you learn the most important features of Office 95—the ones that will help you become the most productive in the shortest amount of time.

Office 95 is a tool. For many office workers, it is the most important tool they use. This book will help you appropriate this tool so you can concentrate on the work you're doing, not the tool you're using.

Is This Book for You?

Although Office 95 is easy to use and learn, the sheer number of applications, features, shortcuts, and automation functions suggests that the new user will not be able to take full advantage of Office 95 by solo experimentation. *The Essential Book for Microsoft Office* provides hands-on tutorials, insightful tips, and helpful cautions that will make you glad you didn't try learning all these programs by yourself!

This book is organized around the work you do, not the programs you use. It is not a reference book in the traditional sense; it is a book of solutions to common office problems. The solutions in this book are based on problems found most frequently in offices.

The Essential Book for Microsoft Office is for everyone using Office 95, whether they are administrative support staff who create and organize a variety of documents, professionals who have increasingly less secretarial support, managers who want their offices to work smarter, students who need to write academic papers, or help desk specialists who need not only to know product features, but how products should be used.

Whether you are a first-time Office 95 user or a slightly experienced user of some of the applications, this book is for you:

- Newcomers to Office 95 will learn simple ways to perform basic daily tasks, such as writing letters, maintaining a calendar, creating a spreadsheet, or organizing a presentation

- More experienced users will appreciate discussions on alternative ways to solve common problems, simple ways to customize Office 95, and tips to help you work more efficiently

- Managers or others interested in organizational issues will find discussions on building a solid software infrastructure, along with advice concerning procedures such as building effective electronic filing systems

Conventions

The conventions used in this book should help you learn Office 95 quickly and easily. Most Office commands can be selected with either a mouse or the keyboard. Instructions are written in a way that enables you to choose the method you prefer. For example, if the instruction reads, "Choose File, Open," click the mouse pointer on the File menu to open the menu, and then click again on the Open command. Alternatively, you can press Alt + F to open the File menu and then press O to select Open.

As you can see, menu and dialog box options that are underlined in the program (what you may already know as "hot keys") appear underlined in this book.

When two keys are pressed in sequence, they are separated with a comma. For instance, the [Home] key is often pressed before pressing another key. "Press [End], [Home]" means to press and then release the [End] key, and then press and release the [Home] key.

When two keys are pressed together (i.e., you hold down the first key while you press the second key), a plus sign (+) is used to show this combination: [Alt]+[F] or [Ctrl]+[Z]

Often the quickest way to access a feature is by clicking a button on the toolbar. In this case, the appropriate button is shown in the margin next to the instructions, as the Open button is shown here.

Bold text is used to indicate text that you should type in. On-screen messages appear in "quotation marks."

Special Elements

You will find several special elements that make using this book easier as you read through each chapter.

Hands On: Accomplishing a Specific Task

Occasionally you'll find that it's easier to begin learning an application by following a specific example, rather than learning the general procedure. For example, in Chapter 9 about Excel, you will be taken through the process of creating a specific budget in a *hands-on* exercise.

Sidebars for That Extra Touch

You'll see *sidebars* throughout the text that provide discussions related to how you can best use the program or feature in question. For example, in Chapter 16 about Schedule+, you'll find a sidebar describing four common ways that time-management experts recommend you prioritize your daily tasks.

Whenever a feature is mentioned that is explained in another chapter, you'll see a gray box in the left margin that indicates where you can go for further information.

TIP: *Tips* are short hints that provide shortcuts or recommendations on the best way to use a feature.

NOTE: *Notes* provide further information—often of a more technical nature—on how a feature works, or its uses and limitations.

CAUTION: As you might expect, *cautions* tell you what to watch out for when using a feature.

Acknowledgments

I would like to extend my thanks and acknowledgment to the Prima Publishing staff, including Don Roche, publisher; Nanci Jacobs, technical editor; Joyce Nielsen, developmental editor; Matthew Gatheringwater, copyeditor; Marian Hartsough, layout artist; and Katherine Stimson, indexer, for their support, ideas, and the hard work they put in on this book. A special thanks to Stefan Grünwedel, whose e-mails at literally all hours of the day and night were indicative of the amount of hard work he put in to pull this project together. Also a special thanks to my wife, Anita Bruck, for her support, encouragement, and patience with me during this project.

About the Author

Bill Bruck, Ph.D., is the president of Bill Bruck & Associates, a training and consulting firm in Falls Church, Virginia. BB&A specializes in helping organizations who are upgrading to the latest generations of software suites to maximize the return on their investment in increased productivity. A counseling psychologist by training, Bill has taught at the University of Florida, Seattle University, and West Georgia College. He is currently Professor of Psychology at Marymount University in Arlington, Virginia. Bill can be reached at http://www.bruck.com.

PART I

LEARNING MICROSOFT OFFICE 95

CHAPTER 1

INSTALLING OFFICE 95

IN THIS CHAPTER

- Choosing Office Components to Install
- Installing Office for the First Time
- Adding and Removing Office Components
- Installing Internet Assistants

Whether you're about to open the Office 95 package for the first time, or you have been using the product for months, you may find that you need to run the installation program—either to put it onto your hard drive or to add components that were not installed by default. If you want to integrate Office with the Internet, you may also want to install Office's Internet Assistants—free add-on programs you can download from the Internet.

Deciding Which Components You Need

The first step in installing Office is choosing which applications you'll be using, and which (if any) additional files you might find useful.

Choosing the Appropriate Setup Type

Depending on whether you are installing from disks, CD-ROM, or a network server, Office 95 provides five types of installation setups that you can choose from: typical, compact, custom, run from Network Server, and CD-ROM.

Typical Setup

The *typical setup* of Office Standard (the version of Office 95 that does not include Access) requires 55MB of space. If you are installing Office Professional, you will need an additional 15MB for Access.

The typical setup is probably your best bet for an initial installation. It includes the Office applications, along with other files that help you use the products. For example, the typical setup includes help files, sample files, clip art, additional fonts, wizards to help you with complex tasks, templates to use as "master" documents you can build on, and filters to help you import documents from other programs. It also includes an electronic copy of the *Getting Results* book to help you learn about Office.

Compact Setup

The *compact setup* is an excellent choice if you are using a laptop and hard drive space is at a premium. Like the typical setup, the compact setup includes all the Office applications and the *Getting Results* book. However, it does not contain many of the additional files found in the typical installation to help you use the products. For example, the custom setup does not include help files, sample files, clip art, fonts, wizards, or templates. It contains only the most basic import filters.

Installing additional Office components is discussed further in "Adding Components" later in this chapter.

Custom Setup

Custom setup is the best choice for more advanced users, since you can decide exactly which applications and components you want to install. You also have the opportunity to install all files using this option. If you are loading Office from a CD-ROM or network, you may wish to perform a typical installation first, then come back after you've used Office for a few weeks to install additional components as you need them.

CD-ROM Setup

Choosing the *CD-ROM setup* loads some required files onto your hard drive, but retrieves most of them as they are needed from the CD-ROM. There are several reasons why this is not a good option:

- You must keep the Office 95 CD-ROM in the CD-ROM player whenever you use Office 95
- The programs will operate sluggishly
- You will probably be using Office 95 applications regularly

Run from Network Server

Choosing Run from Network Server also loads some required files onto your hard drive. The main Office program files, however, are stored on the network server, and downloaded to your PC as needed.

This type of installation is typical in large organizations, where an information services (IS) staff is responsible for the care and maintenance of PCs. For IS staff, this type of installation provides several advantages, including:

- Upgrades can be performed once, on the server
- All persons are using the same version of software
- Controls can be put on which Office applications and additional files are available to users

If your network is overloaded, running Office applications from the network server may be somewhat slower than if they were on your local hard drive; moreover, if the network goes down you will not be able to access Office at all. If the network is running well, however, you should notice little if any difference when running office from the network and running it locally.

Adding Components

After you have run Office, there are additional components you may wish to install. Some of these are necessary to access features discussed in this book. Others (like Help for WordPerfect Users) are ones that many people find helpful, but may or may not apply to your particular situation.

Features not included in the typical setup that you may find useful to install later include:

Binder

- All templates

Excel

- All templates
- All add-ins (Report Manager, Solver, View Manager)

Word

- Help for WordPerfect Users
- All Wizards, templates, and letters
- Grammar checker
- Text with Layout Converter

PowerPoint

- All presentation translators

Schedule+

- Additional Importers and Exporters

Additional Office Tools

- WordArt
- Organizational Chart
- Word Clip Art
- Find All Word Forms

Additional Filters and Data Access

- All graphics filters
- All data access options

Installing Office 95 for the First Time

If you are on a network, the system administrator will probably install Office for you. This installation may be customized for your company's needs, and will most likely include only the components that you need for work.

> **NOTE:** You can install Office from CD-ROM or disks. Installing by disk is laborious and time-consuming. Worse, when you want to add components in the future, you'll need to repeat the process of feeding disks into your computer. If at all possible, use the CD-ROM version of Office. Not only is it faster, but the CD-ROM has extras (like additional clip art and templates) that the disks do not. This chapter assumes you are installing from a CD-ROM. If you are not, the same procedures will work, but you will need to insert and swap disks when prompted.

If you are working with Office on a stand-alone computer at home or in the office, you may need to install it yourself. Before doing so, make sure of the following:

- Have the Office CD-ROM and documentation available
- Check the available hard drive space. You will need between 80–120MB free, depending on which Office component(s) you install
- Exit all applications you are running, except for Windows 95 itself
- Load Windows 95 on your system (Office 95 will not run under Windows 3.1)

> **NOTE:** Qualifying products include previous versions of Microsoft Office, Novell's PerfectOffice suite, or Lotus' SmartSuite. You can also install Office 95 if you have a stand-alone word-processor such as WordPerfect on your system. Check the side of the box for a list of all qualifying products. One of them will need to be installed on your system; merely having the installation disks for it will not suffice.

Once you've installed Office, the process of adding and removing components is termed a *maintenance installation.* This is described in the next section.

- If you have purchased an Office 95 upgrade version, ensure that a qualifying product, as listed on the Office 95 box, is installed on your system
- Decide what type of setup you wish to make
- Decide which components you wish to install

When you have completed these tasks, you're ready to install Office 95. You can perform an initial installation as follows:

1. From the Windows 95 desktop, choose Start, Settings, Control Panel. The Control Panel window will become visible.

2. Double-click on Add/Remove Programs to bring up the Add/Remove Programs Properties dialog box shown in Figure 1-1.

3. Choose Install. The first step of the Install Program Wizard prompts you to insert the first floppy disk or CD-ROM.

4. Ensure that the first Office floppy disk or the Office CD-ROM is inserted, then choose Next.

5. After the Wizard looks for the installation program, the Run Installation Program dialog box will appear, as shown in Figure 1-2.

Figure 1-1.
You can install Office 95 using Add/Remove Programs in the Control Panel

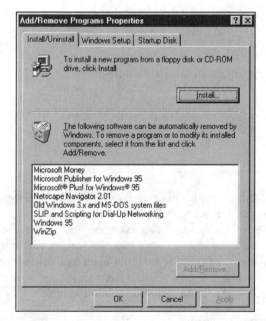

Figure 1-2.
Windows 95
automatically
locates the Office
95 setup program

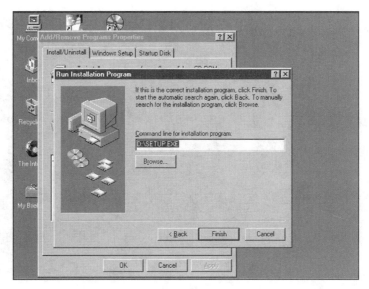

6. If Windows 95 does not find the setup program, make sure the appropriate disk or CD-ROM is inserted, and that the floppy or CD-ROM drive is working. Otherwise, choose Finish. The Office 95 setup program will start.

7. Click Continue at the initial Office 95 Setup screen. Enter your name and the name of your organization and choose OK. Confirm that you have entered the information correctly, then choose OK again. This information is stored in Windows 95 for use in Office 95 applications.

8. If you are installing from the CD-ROM, you will be prompted to enter the CD-ROM key number on the back of the jewel box. After you do this, choose OK. You will see the Product ID number. Choose OK again.

9. If you are installing an Upgrade version, you will be prompted that Setup will locate the qualifying product on your hard drive. If the procedure fails, you can click the Locate button and navigate to the folder where it is.

10. You will be prompted for the folder in which Office 95 should be installed. Unless you have a special location in mind, accept this by clicking OK. You will see the Microsoft Office 95 Setup window shown in Figure 1-3.

Figure 1-3.
You can choose
from four types of
setup when you
install Office 95

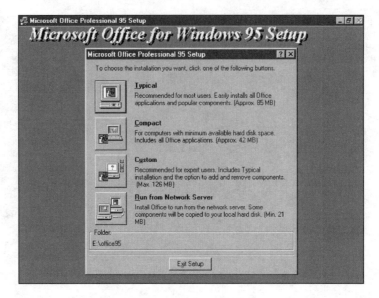

11. Click the button for the type of installation you wish to use. What you see next depends on the choice you make:

    • If you choose Typical, you will be asked if you wish to install the Microsoft Data Map that you can use to chart Excel data geographically. Respond Yes or No.

    • If you choose Compact, the Microsoft Office - Compact dialog box shown in Figure 1-4 will appear. When using this option, you can only install each application in its entirety; you cannot select specific components within each application. Choose the applications you wish to install and choose Continue.

    • Choosing Custom takes you to the Microsoft Office 95 - Custom dialog box shown in Figure 1-5. Choose the components you wish to install, then choose Continue.

    • If you choose Run from Network Server (or Run from CD-ROM), you will see no further dialog boxes from this point onward.

12. Setup checks for necessary hard drive space and starts the installation. If you are installing from disk, you'll begin swapping disks as requested. Otherwise, wait until the necessary files have been copied from the CD-ROM.

Figure 1-4.
You can select which Office components to install if you choose Compact

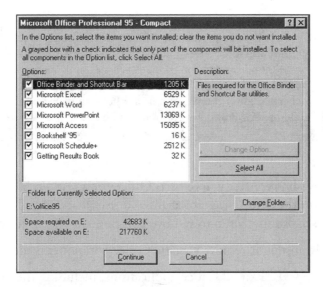

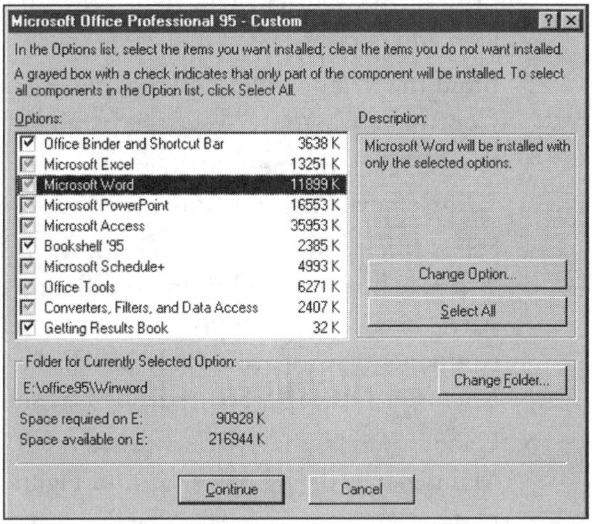

Figure 1-5. The Custom installation allows you to select all or specific components of each Office 95 application

13. You will be prompted to exit Windows and restart your computer. Do so to complete the installation.

Adding and Removing Office 95 Components

The typical and compact installations do not allow you to install every Office component, nor give you access to every feature discussed in

> **NOTE:** If you are running Office from a network, you cannot add and remove individual components. The network administrator chooses which components are available to network users, and generally you have access to all of them. Thus, the following procedure only applies if you are running Office locally.

this book. After you've used Office for a few weeks, you may wish to run the Setup program again and install additional components. You can also use Setup to remove components that you no longer need.

To install or remove specific Office components, do the following:

1. Exit all Office applications, including the Shortcut Bar. (To exit the Shortcut Bar, right-click on the Shortcut Bar icon and choose E~x~it.)

2. From the Windows 95 desktop, choose Start, ~S~ettings, ~C~ontrol Panel. You will see the Control Panel.

3. Double-click on the Add/Remove Programs icon. The Add/Remove Programs Properties dialog box will appear.

4. Select Microsoft Office, then click the Add/~R~emove button. You may be prompted to insert a floppy disk or CD-ROM. After the Office Setup program starts, Setup identifies the components you have already installed and displays the Microsoft Office 95 Setup dialog box shown in Figure 1-6.

5. Choose ~A~dd/Remove. You will see the Microsoft Office 95 - Maintenance dialog box shown in Figure 1-7.

6. Uninstall a component by clicking on it until the check mark goes away.

7. Install a component by clicking on it until the check mark is

> **NOTE:** You can uninstall Office completely at this point by choosing Re~m~ove All. Use ~R~einstall if you have missing or corrupted Office files that are causing errors when you run applications.

Figure 1-6.
You can reinstall
Office 95 at any
time to add or
remove components

Figure 1-7.
When you reinstall
Office 95, you can
select specific
components of
each application to
install or remove

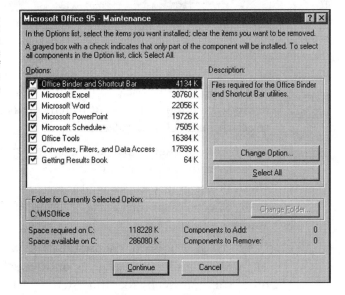

present. If the box is gray, then some part(s) of the component are not selected. Choose Select All to select every part of every component.

8. To change which parts of a component are selected, highlight the component and choose Change Option. A dialog box like the one for Microsoft Excel shown in Figure 1-8 will appear.

Figure 1-8.
You can specify
which part(s) of
a component to
install

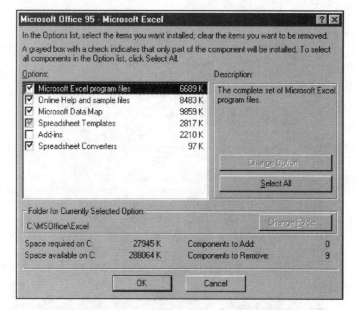

9. Choose the parts of the component that you wish to install by clicking them to place a check mark by them. To uninstall a selected component, click it to remove its check mark. To select all parts, choose Select All.

10. When you highlight a part and the Change Option button becomes active, there are subparts that you can select. If the check box is gray, then some of these subparts are not currently selected. Choose Change Option, if desired, to choose among these subparts.

11. When you are finished, choose OK. You will return to the main Maintenance dialog box. Continue selecting parts of other components by repeating steps 6–10.

TIP: At any point in time, you can see how many components you are adding and removing—and the hard drive space required and available—at the bottom of the dialog box.

12. When you have selected all components and parts of components that you wish to install or remove, choose Continue. Setup checks for necessary hard drive space and starts the installation. If you are installing from disk, you will begin swapping disks as requested. Otherwise, wait until the necessary files have been copied from the CD-ROM.

13. When prompted, restart the computer to complete the installation.

Using the Value Pack

The CD-ROM version of Office includes the Microsoft Office Value Pack—a collection of tools for Office. The Value Pack includes the following:

- **Microsoft Imager** — a utility for converting graphic files that comes with 145 photo images you can include in PowerPoint presentations
- **Microsoft Word Viewer** — a utility for allowing users to view and print documents created in Word 7.0, without actually having to install that program
- **WordPerfect Options** — fonts that make converting WordPerfect documents and a template to make the transition from WordPerfect to Word easier
- **PowerPoint Multimedia** — clip art, templates, photos, sounds, and video that can be included in PowerPoint presentations

There is also a set of demos from companies offering products compatible with Office to make your work easier.

The easiest way to install Value Pack components is via the Value Pack help system:

1. Insert the Microsoft Office CD-ROM in the CD-ROM drive.
2. Choose Start, Programs, Windows Explorer.
3. Double-click on the drive icon for the CD-ROM player. The directory of the Microsoft Office CD-ROM, as shown in Figure 1-9, will appear.

Figure 1-9.
You can access the
Value Pack from
Windows Explorer

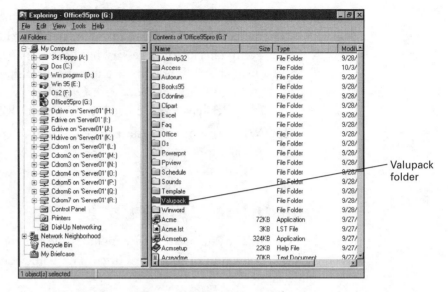

Valupack
folder

Figure 1-10.
The Value Pack
provides several
add on products
for Office

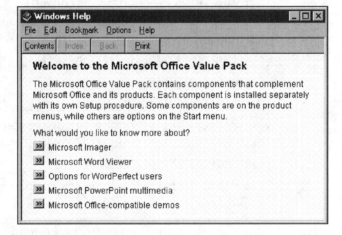

4. Double-click on the Valupack folder, then double-click on the Valupack icon. You will see a Windows Help window for the Microsoft Office Value Pack, as shown in Figure 1-10.

5. Select the Value Pack component you wish to install. You will see some information on that component, and a button you can click for installation instructions, like the information for WordPerfect users shown in Figure 1-11.

Figure 1-11.
The Value Pack includes fonts for converting special characters in WordPerfect documents

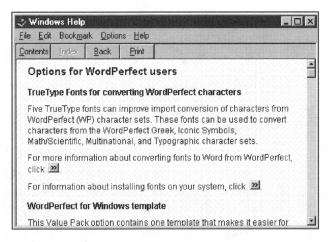

Obtaining and Installing Internet Assistants

Publishing on the Web, including a discussion of basic terminology, can be found in Chapter 26.

Internet Assistants are add-on programs made by Microsoft that work with Word, Excel, PowerPoint, Access, and Schedule+ to enable you to publish documents on the World Wide Web.

These applications are free on Microsoft's Web site; you can download them from the Web and install them into your Office applications.

Installing Internet Assistants is a two-step process. First you download the assistant from the Internet to your hard drive, then you install it.

Downloading Internet Assistants

To download the Internet Assistants, you will need the following:

- Access to the Internet
- A Web browser that allows you to download files, such as Microsoft Internet Explorer, Netscape Navigator, or NCSA Mosaic
- A browser that supports the Tables feature for Web documents so you can view Internet files produced by the Excel, Access, and Schedule+ Internet Assistants

- A browser that supports AnimationX (such as Microsoft Internet Explorer 2.0 or later, or Netscape Navigator 2.0 or later) so you can view files produced with the Schedule+ AnimationX Player

To download Internet Assistants to your hard drive, do the following:

1. Connect to the Internet using a browser such as Microsoft Internet Explorer or Netscape Navigator.

2. Go to the Microsoft Office home page at the following site: http://www.microsoft.com/MSOffice. The command you use depends on your browser. For instance, in Explorer 2.0, it is <u>F</u>ile, <u>O</u>pen. In Netscape 2.0, it is <u>F</u>ile, Open <u>L</u>ocation.

3. Choose Internet Tools. You will see a Web page like the one shown in Figure 1-12.

4. Choose Word, Excel, PowerPoint, Access, or Schedule+. You will see files you can download for the selected product.

5. Choose the linked term for the Internet Assistant. Follow the instructions to download the file.

NOTE: Microsoft changes the look of its Web pages on a regular basis, so the page you see may not resemble the one pictured here exactly.

Figure 1-12.
Internet Assistants can be downloaded from the Microsoft Office site on the Web

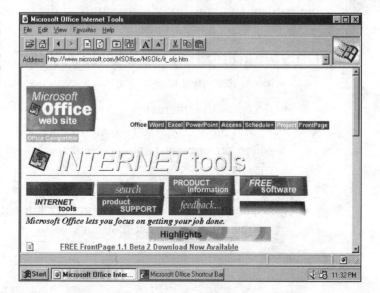

6. When prompted by your browser, choose a temporary folder in which to save the Internet Assistant.

Installing Internet Assistants

Once you have downloaded the Internet Assistant, you can install it as follows (except for the Excel Internet Assistant):

1. Choose Start, Programs, Windows Explorer.
2. Navigate to the folder in which you stored the file you downloaded.
3. Double-click on the file. The compressed file will expand into its component parts. Depending on the specific Assistant, the Setup program may start.
4. If the Setup program does not start, double-click on the Internet Assistant application.
5. Follow the instructions in the Setup program.

The Excel Internet Assistant behaves a little differently. To install it:

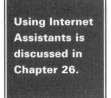

Using Internet Assistants is discussed in Chapter 26.

1. Choose Start, Programs, Windows Explorer.
2. Navigate to the folder in which you stored the file you downloaded—html.xla.
3. Copy this file to the Excel library folder—usually \msoffice\excel\library.
4. Open Excel and choose Tools, Add-Ins. The Add-Ins dialog box shown in Figure 1-13 will appear.
5. Check the Internet Assistant Wizard and choose OK. The Internet Assistant will now appear on the Tools menu.

Figure 1-13.
The Excel Internet Assistant is an Excel add-in

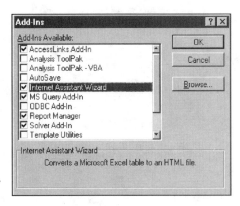

CHAPTER 2

GETTING STARTED WITH OFFICE 95

IN THIS CHAPTER

- **What Is Office 95?**
- **Working with Office 95 Applications**
- **Getting Help**
- **Using the Shortcut Bar**

Microsoft Office 95 is a tool. If you work in an office or need to use several business applications interchangeably, this may be the most important tool you use. This chapter gives an overview of Office 95: what's in it, what common features the integrated applications share with each other, and how to find on-screen help when you need it.

What Is Office 95?

Office 95 is the latest version of Microsoft's productivity suite, designed for Windows 95. It contains all the tools you need to write and edit documents; create spreadsheets, databases, and slide shows; make charts and graphs; send e-mail and faxes; keep a "to-do" list; and even remind you of appointments.

The Standard Edition of Office 95 is comprised of Version 7 of several major applications, including:

- **Microsoft Word** for word-processing
- **Microsoft Excel** for spreadsheets, charts, and simple databases
- **Microsoft PowerPoint** for slide shows and business graphics
- **Microsoft Schedule+** for time management, scheduling, and contact management
- **Microsoft Binder** for combining related documents

The Office 95 Professional Edition includes all of the Standard Edition applications and adds:

- **Microsoft Access** for creating sophisticated databases

> If you have not yet installed Office 95, or if you need to install additional components to try out features discussed in this book, see Chapter 1.

Working with Office 95 Applications

One of the nice things about using Office 95 is the similarity between the applications. It uses common screen elements, menus, toolbars, and dialog boxes throughout. Many tasks—like creating a chart—use the same, small helper applications (sometimes called *applets*) no matter which application you use them in.

A great way to begin using Office 95 is to learn about these common elements.

Starting and Exiting Office Applications

You start and exit all Office 95 applications the same way. To start an application, click the Start button, then choose <u>P</u>rograms. The Office 95 applications will be listed in the <u>P</u>rograms menu by default, as shown in Figure 2-1.

Figure 2-1.
You can open Office
95 applications from
the Programs menu

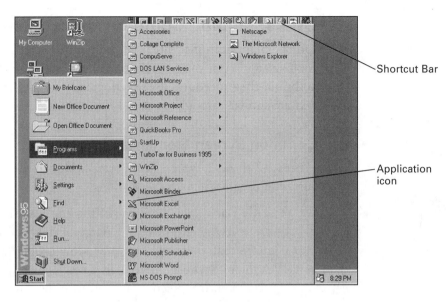

Shortcut Bar

Application
icon

The Shortcut
Bar is
discussed
further at the
end of this
chapter.

There's an easier way to open applications, however. If the Microsoft
Office Shortcut Bar is visible, you can open any Office 95 application
by clicking the appropriate Shortcut Bar button.

Once you have an application open, you can close it with the mouse
or with the menus. If your hand is on the mouse, the easiest way to
close an application is to double-click the application icon on the left
of the Title Bar.

If you prefer to use the menus, you can close Office 95 applications by
choosing File, Exit. (In the Microsoft Binder, this command is File,
Close.)

CAUTION: Never just turn off your computer without
using the Windows shutdown procedure. Not only will you
lose unsaved information in Office programs, but you may
cause fragmentation or other problems on the disk. If you
do accidentally turn off your computer, it's a good idea to
turn it back on run ScanDisk by choosing Start, Programs,
Accessories, System Tools, ScanDisk.

Understanding Common Office Elements

Office 95 applications feature all the familiar screen elements (menus, toolbars, and even some dialog boxes) you expect in Windows 95. In addition, the procedures for selecting and sizing objects and editing text are similar throughout the Office 95 suite.

Common Screen Elements

Figure 2-2 shows a typical Word screen. Notice the following elements common to all Office 95 applications:

- **Title Bar** shows the name of the application with which you are working and often the name of the file that is open. When more than one application window is open, the active window is the one whose Title Bar is dark. If a window is not taking up the entire screen, you can move the window by dragging in the Title Bar, or maximize the window by double-clicking in it.

- **Application icon** is the equivalent of the application Control Menu box in Windows 3.1. Double-clicking on it closes the

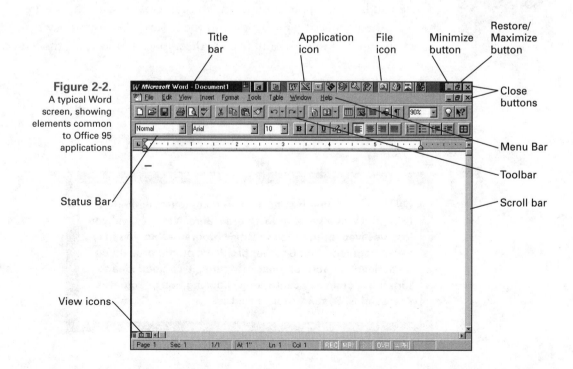

Figure 2-2.
A typical Word screen, showing elements common to Office 95 applications

application. Clicking on it reveals a drop-down menu allowing you to move, size, minimize, maximize, restore, or close the application.

- **File icon** in Word, PowerPoint, and Excel is the equivalent of the file Control Menu box in Windows 3.1. While the application icon controls the application as a whole, the file icon controls the open file. Double-clicking on it closes the file. Clicking on it reveals a drop-down menu allowing you to move, size, minimize, maximize, or restore the file window within the application window, or close the file.

- **Minimize, Maximize, Restore, and Close buttons** appear on the Title Bar of all Office 95 applications, and work as they do in other Windows 95 applications. They also appear in the Menu Bar of applications that allow multiple files to be open at once (Word, Excel, Access, and PowerPoint), and control the size of the file window within the application window.

- **Menu Bar and Toolbars** appear under the Title Bar. These are discussed further below.

- **Status Bar** appears at the bottom of Office 95 applications. It gives different information depending on the application. Frequently, however, you will see warning messages on the Status Bar, information about the state of the application (i.e., Ready versus Edit mode in Excel), your location in a document (i.e., line and column number in Word, cell in Excel, slide number in PowerPoint, record number in Access), and the state of special keys like the Ins key (insert versus overtype mode) or the Caps Lock key.

- **Scroll bars** appear at the bottom and to the right of windows when needed to allow you to scroll through files.

- **View icons** appear to the left of the horizontal scroll bars in some programs such as Word and PowerPoint. They allow you to change the way you are looking at and editing data. (For example, in Word, you can switch between the normal view showing only text, and the page layout view that also shows the top and bottom margins, headers, footers, page numbers, and footnotes.) In other programs such as Excel and Access, you may see buttons that allow you to move between worksheets or records in this same location.

Common Menus and Toolbars

The common elements that will lower your learning curve the most are Office 95's common menus and toolbars, as you can see clearly in Figure 2-3.

MENUS

The first four menu items for all applications are File, Edit, View, and Insert. When appropriate, there is a Format menu and, for applications that allow more than one file to be open, there is a Window menu. There is always a Tools menu and a Help menu on the right. If you understand the basic common structure of menus, you will be able to find the command you want quickly and easily.

The File menu always contains commands that allow you to create and open files, save and close files, print and set printing options, provide information about the file with properties, and exit the application.

The Edit menu also has functions in common with other applications. Many edit functions, however, are unavailable ("grayed out") unless you have selected text or an object. The Edit menu always has the Undo option, along with commands for cutting, copying, and pasting objects. The find and replace function are on the Edit menu, as are the Go To command (if appropriate).

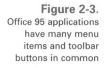

Figure 2-3.
Office 95 applications have many menu items and toolbar buttons in common

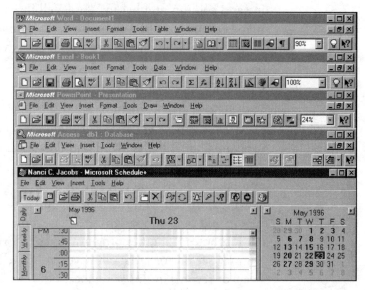

Think of the View menu as controlling how the screen will appear. It contains commands for displaying toolbars, magnifying the display and changing between different modes of viewing data (if appropriate).

The Insert menu, as the name implies, is used to insert objects appropriate to the specific application into the file. Thus, you can insert clip art into many applications with this menu, enter a new record into Access, or add a new appointment in Schedule+.

The Tools menu has widely different tools on it, depending on the application. If a spell-checker is available, it will always be on this menu. One entry that is always on the Tools menu is Options. You use Tools, Options to set program defaults in all Office 95 applications.

The Window menu also shows different options, depending on the application. At the bottom of the Window menu is a list of open files. You can switch between the windows of open files by clicking on the entry for the file you want.

The Help menu, common to all Office 95 applications, is discussed later in this chapter.

TIP: Remember that you can also access a menu with the keyboard by pressing [Alt] and the underlined letter of the menu. Once you see the drop-down menu, you can choose a menu item by pressing its underlined letter—you do not need to hold down the [Alt] key. You will find that the same letters are underlined in all Office 95 applications, so you can use the same keystroke combinations for commonly used commands such as [Alt] + [E], [F] for Edit, Find.

TOOLBARS

Just as menus have similar entries, many of the same buttons appear on the standard toolbars of Office 95 applications. These include:

- The **New button** is used for creating new files. It is the equivalent of choosing File, New and then selecting the default template (document format) on which to base the new file. The difference is that clicking the New button does not bring up the New dialog box.

- The **Open button** is used for opening files on the disk, and is the equivalent of choosing File, Open.

- The **Save button** saves the file that is currently open. If it has already been saved, it overwrites the existing file on the disk. It is the equivalent to File, Save. Schedule+ does not include this button, since your work is saved automatically as you enter it.

- The **Print button** prints your current work. While it is similar to File, Print, it is not identical. Choosing File, Print opens the Print dialog box that allows you to change printing options. Clicking the Print button is like choosing File, Print, then clicking OK without changing any default printing option.

- The **Cut**, **Copy**, and **Paste buttons** are identical to choosing Cut, Copy, or Paste from the Edit menu, or pressing Ctrl + X, Ctrl + C, or Ctrl + V, respectively. The Cut and Copy buttons don't work unless something is selected. The Paste button doesn't work unless something has previously been cut or copied to the Clipboard.

- The **Undo button**, affectionately known as the "oops" button, is the equivalent of choosing Edit, Undo. As the name suggests, it often (but not always) is available to undo your last action.

There are also formatting toolbars that do not appear in every Office program, but do appear in Word, Excel, PowerPoint, and Access as needed to assist you in formatting text. Common buttons you see on these toolbars include:

- The **Bold**, **Italic**, and **Underline buttons** apply the relevant attribute to selected text. These are the equivalent to choosing these attributes from the Font dialog box, accessed by choosing Format, Font.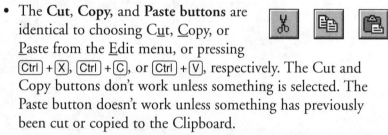

- The **Left**, **Center**, **Right**, and **Justify buttons** align selected text as specified.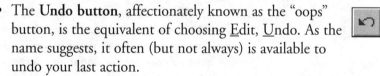

- The **Font** and **Font Size buttons** are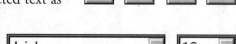

actually drop-down list boxes allowing you to select the font and size you wish for selected text. Alternatively, you can type a specific size in the Font Size box if the size you want doesn't appear on the drop-down list.

Selecting and Editing Text

The methods for selecting and editing text are pretty much the same across applications.

INSERTING AND DELETING TEXT

To insert text in any Office application, follow the same procedure. First, ensure that you are in insert mode rather than overtype mode. Press the Ins (insert) key. Notice that "OVR" appears in the status bar, indicating you are in overtype mode. In this mode, anything you type will overwrite existing text. In the default insert mode, text is pushed ahead to make room for the text as you type. Press Ins again, if needed, to go back to insert mode.

Next, click between the two letters where you want to insert the text. In many applications, you can do this with a single click. In some applications, text is actually contained inside a graphic object—such as the title of a chart or PowerPoint slide. In this case, you may need to click once to select the text object and see a border around it, then click again to position the insertion point. When you're done, you'll see a vertical line—the insertion point—where you want the text to go. Now just type the text!

To delete single characters, position the insertion point in front of or behind the text to be removed. Press Del to delete text to the right of the insertion point, or Backspace to delete text to the left of the insertion point.

CAUTION: Note that the Backspace key is different from the ← key. The latter merely moves the insertion point to the left; the former deletes text to the left of the insertion point.

SELECTING TEXT

To work with a block of text, first select (or highlight) it. Selected text appears in reverse highlight, as shown in Figure 2-4. You can select text with either the mouse or the keyboard. There are two common ways to select text with the mouse. If you drag the mouse over the desired text, it will be selected. Alternatively, you can click at the beginning of the text to be selected, move to the end of the block, and hold down the [Shift] key while you click again.

If you move the insertion point with the keyboard while holding the [Shift] key down, text will also be selected. Thus, holding the [Shift] key down while pressing the [→] key selects text to the right of the insertion point.

Once text has been selected, press the [Del] key to delete it. This is the easiest way to delete large chunks of text. If you type new text while existing text is selected, the new text replaces the existing text.

> For further discussion of selecting text in Word, see Chapter 3.

TIP: Work more efficiently in dialog boxes by typing over filenames or other selected text with the new choice you wish to make. You don't have to delete the default choice if it is highlighted; typing a new choice automatically replaces it.

Figure 2-4.
Selected text appears
in reverse highlight

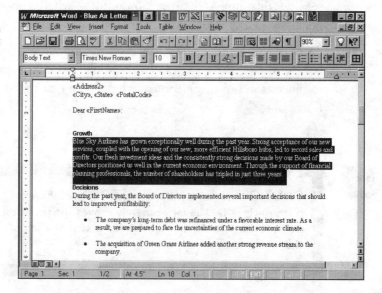

COPYING AND MOVING TEXT

Copy and move text by cutting or copying it to the Windows Clipboard and then pasting it wherever you want it to appear. Start by selecting your text. Then choose Cut or Copy. Move the insertion point to where you want the text to appear. Then choose Paste.

You can choose Cut, Copy, or Paste in any of the following ways:

- Choose Cut, Copy, or Paste from the Edit menu.
- Click the Cut, Copy, or Paste buttons.
- Right-click on the selected text, then choose Cut, Copy or Paste from the pop-up menu, if one appears and the options are available:

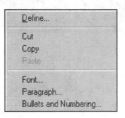

- Press Ctrl+X for Cut, Ctrl+C for Copy , or Ctrl+V for Paste.

Selecting and Manipulating Objects

You may see graphic *objects* in any of the major Office 95 applications. These can be charts, clip art, text art, equations, or even text located in a graphic.

The procedures for creating and inserting graphic objects can be somewhat complex and depend on the application. The basics of selecting existing objects, as well as deleting, moving, sizing, and cutting and pasting them, are more consistent.

SELECTING AND DELETING GRAPHIC OBJECTS

Selecting a graphic object is as simple as clicking on it. When you select an object, eight black (or white) squares appear around it, called *handles*, as seen in Figure 2-5.

Once you have selected the object, you can edit, size, or move it. In addition, you can delete it by pressing the Del key once it is selected.

Figure 2-5.
When you select a
graphic object, you
will see handles
around it

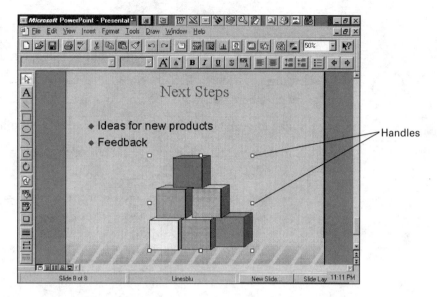

To edit an object, double-click on it. The application that created the object will open, if needed, and you can use that application's editing functions to make the necessary changes.

 TIP: Clip art (in Word and PowerPoint) cannot be edited except to recolor or crop the picture.

MOVING AND SIZING GRAPHIC OBJECTS

Once you have selected an object, you can move it or resize it. To move a selected object, position the mouse pointer inside the object. The pointer changes to a four-pointed arrow—a *move pointer*. While the move pointer is visible, you can drag the object to its new position in the document.

To size an object, position the pointer on one of the eight handles. The pointer changes to a double-headed sizing pointer. While the pointer is a sizing pointer, you can drag the handle to resize the object.

 TIP: Dragging a *corner* handle maintains the original proportions of the object.

CUTTING AND PASTING GRAPHIC OBJECTS

You can copy or move a graphic object from one part of a document to another. Since it is being cut or copied to the Windows Clipboard, you can also paste it in another document, or even into another application.

Copy or move the graphic object just as you would copy or move text: by cutting or copying it to the Windows Clipboard, then pasting it where you want it to appear. To cut or copy the object to the Clipboard, start by selecting it, then choose cut or copy. Move the insertion point to where you want the object to appear, then choose Paste. You can choose Cut, Copy, or Paste in the same ways you choose them for text.

Getting Help

The Help system is the same in all Office 95 applications. You can obtain help in any of several ways: Help topics, the Answer Wizard, context-sensitive help, Tip of the Day, and the Help button.

Help Topics

When you open the <u>H</u>elp menu, there's an entry for Help Topics, such as <u>M</u>icrosoft Word Help Topics, or Microsoft Excel <u>H</u>elp Topics. Picking this selection opens the Help Topics dialog box, such as the Word version shown in Figure 2-6. Each tab in the Help dialog box provides a different way of accessing Help.

CONTENTS

The help contents list is like the table of contents of a book. It's a topical outline of the most common features of the program. This type of help is procedure-oriented. When you know what you want to do, but you really don't have a good idea of how to go about it, this is the place to start. Folders are help topics that contain other subfolders and/or document icons. Document icons are specific help screens.

There are three types of help screens. Text screens, like the one in Figure 2-7, provide detailed information on specific subjects.

Graphical help screens such as the one in Figure 2-8 provide the big picture. They are good for helping you understand how a process works. Click on objects seen on the help screen for more details.

Figure 2-6.
The Help Topics
dialog box allows
you to access help
in any of four ways

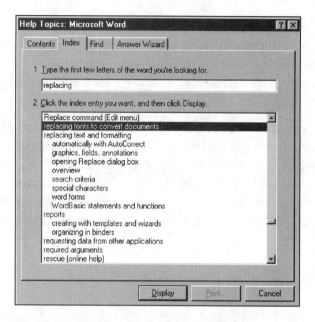

Figure 2-7.
Text screens provide
detailed information
on specific subjects

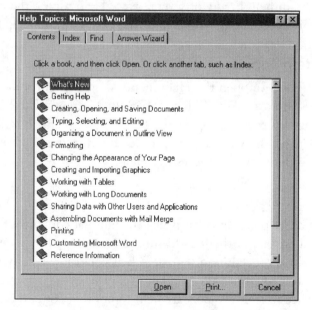

Sometimes when you click a help topic you will see a special type of text screen that can walk you through a desired procedure. It has buttons that you can click to take you through the sequence, step by step.

Figure 2-8.
Graphical help screens are good for understanding processes

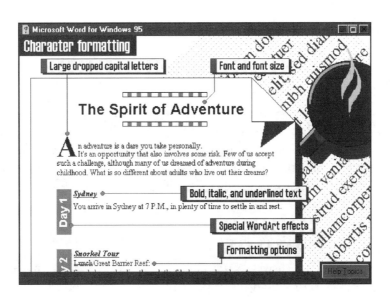

INDEX

Choosing Index is like looking at the index in the back of a book. Many, many terms are listed—far more than the topics in the table of contents, as shown in Figure 2-9.

The index is excellent for intermediate users who know the correct terminology—such as *animation effects* in PowerPoint. There's no point

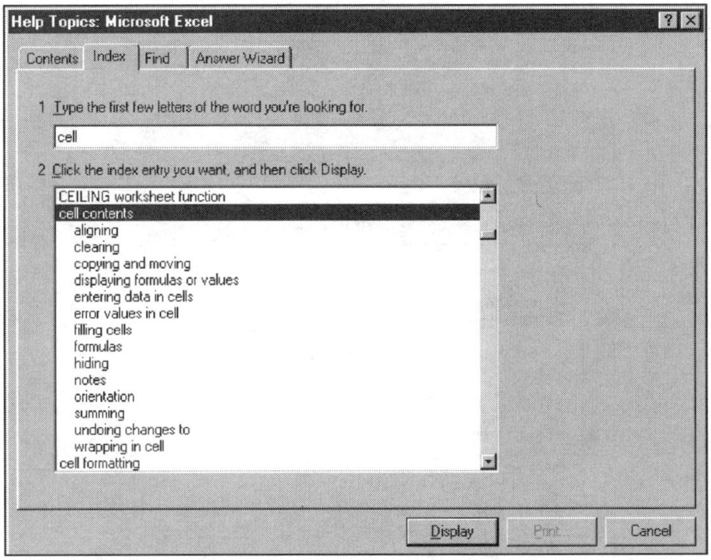

Figure 2-9.
The index is excellent when you know the term under which help will be listed

in going through the contents when you can go directly to the topic of interest.

FIND

However, sometimes you can't find the term you want in the index. Often this is because Office has it listed under a different word. In this case, use the Find feature. The Find feature relies on a small index of all words in the Help system. You can find all help topics containing the desired word—even if the word you want isn't in the topics or the index.

ANSWER WIZARD

The Answer Wizard allows you to ask for help using English syntax. Rather than just typing a word or two, you can type an entire question, like "How do I create mailing labels?" or "How can I chart my data?" The Help system's artificial intelligence reduces this to keywords that the program understands and does a pretty good job of returning just the help you need, as shown in Figure 2-10.

Context-Sensitive Help

Help is available throughout Office 95 applications on specific features that you are using. Many dialog boxes have a Help button—the

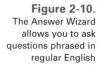

Figure 2-10.
The Answer Wizard allows you to ask questions phrased in regular English

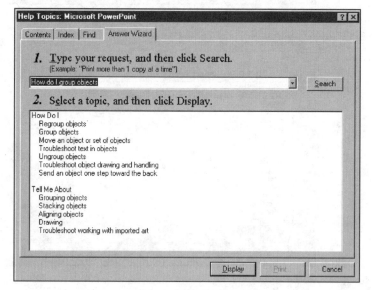

question mark button near the upper-right corner. If there is no help button displayed, you can often press the F1 (Help) key for assistance. It will either provide help on the procedure you are working on or the highlighted option in a dialog box.

Tip of the Day

In Word, Excel, and PowerPoint, you can see a Tip of the Day when you open the application. In Word and Excel, the tip is displayed on a toolbar above the editing window, as shown in Figure 2-11.

The Tip of the Day feature is on by default. If it's off, you can turn it back on. To see a Tip of the Day when you start Word or Excel, choose Tools, Options and click the General tab. In Word, choose TipWizard Active. In Excel, choose Reset TipWizard. In PowerPoint, choose Help, Tip of the Day and check Show Tips at Startup in the Tip of the Day dialog box, as shown in Figure 2-12.

Moreover, in Word and Excel, you can display or hide the Tip Wizard bar at any time by clicking the TipWizard button.

The Help Button

If you see objects on the screen that you do not understand, there are two ways you can find out what they do. The first is to hold the

Figure 2-11.
You can see a Tip of the Day like this one in Excel when you start Word, Excel, or PowerPoint

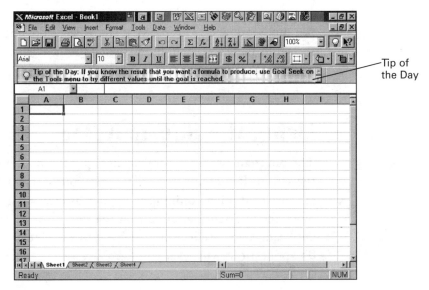

Tip of the Day

Figure 2-12.
PowerPoint shows the tip of the day in a dialog box

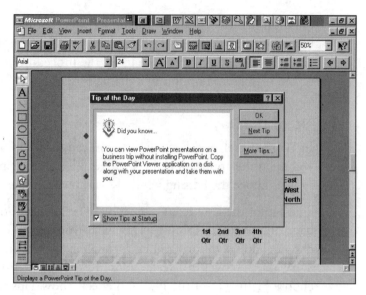

mouse pointer on them without clicking for two or three seconds. You may see a pop-up description or tip that tells you what the object is. If you don't, or if you need more information, use the Help button found in Word, Excel, Access, and PowerPoint.

To use the Help button, click on it. Notice that the mouse pointer now includes a question mark, indicating that Help is active. Click on the object you need help with. You will see a pop-up window explaining what the object does and how to use it, as shown in Figure 2-13. You must click the Help button or press Esc to change the mouse pointer back to normal.

Using the Shortcut Bar

The Shortcut Bar is the toolbar that appears by default at the top of the screen. It contains icons that allow you to start Office 95 programs and perform other common tasks such as creating an appointment. Since the Shortcut Bar appears at the top of the screen no matter what application you are in, you can use it to switch easily between Office 95 applications whenever you need to.

Figure 2-13.
You can obtain help with objects on the screen by clicking the Help button, then clicking on the object

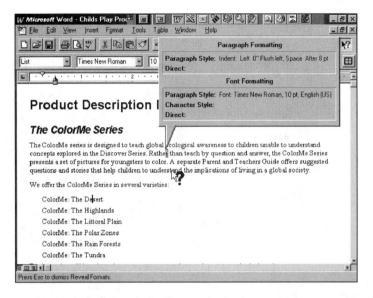

Figure 2-14.
The Office Shortcut Bar offers access to Office 95 applications from whichever program you are in

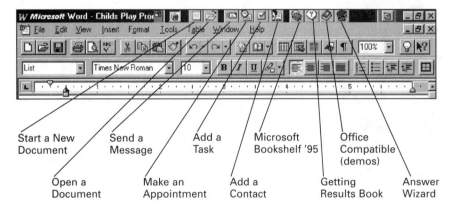

To open an Office 95 application using the Shortcut Bar, just click on the appropriate tool. The tools you may see include the ones in Figure 2-14.

Loading the Shortcut Bar

If you do not see the Shortcut Bar, the Shortcut Bar application may not be loaded. To load it, click the Start button, then choose Programs, Microsoft Office Shortcut Bar. If you do not see it, or if you load it and still can't see the Shortcut Bar, you will need to make further modifications to your setup.

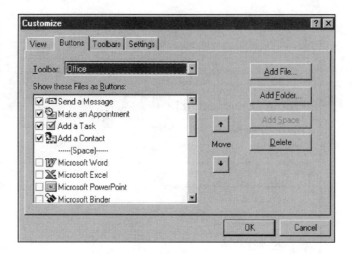

Adding Items to the Shortcut Bar

You may wish to add Office 95 applications or procedures to the Shortcut Bar. To do so, ensure that the Shortcut Bar is visible, then right-click on the Shortcut Bar icon and pick Customize from the pop-up menu. Click the Buttons tab, as shown in Figure 2-15.

Office 95 applications are listed in the list box, along with common procedures such as opening a document or creating a new document. Schedule+ tasks are also listed, including sending a message, making an appointment, adding a task, and adding a contact.

To add an application or procedure to the Shortcut Bar, click in the checkbox to the left of the entry. To remove one, remove the check from the checkbox. Click OK when you have made your changes. The modified Shortcut Bar appears.

Creating
additional
Shortcut Bars
and further
modifying the
Shortcut Bar
appearance
and buttons are
discussed in
Chapter 22.

PART II

WORD

CHAPTER 3

CREATING A SIMPLE DOCUMENT

IN THIS CHAPTER

- Getting Started with Word
- Creating Your First Document
- Saving and Printing Your Work
- Opening Existing Documents
- Editing Your Documents

In this chapter, you will learn the basics of using Word. In the next several chapters, you will learn how to make more complex documents and automate document creation.

Getting Started with Word

Word provides powerful features that allow you to do everything from quickly jot down notes to create complex reports including tables and charts. Word even allows you to automate common tasks such as routine correspondence.

First, however, let's start at the beginning—by opening Word and becoming familiar with its screens.

Learn how to make the Shortcut Bar appear in Chapter 2.

Starting Word

The simplest way to start Word is to click on the Word icon on the Microsoft Shortcut Bar, as shown in Figure 3-1. If the Shortcut Bar is not available, you can access Word by choosing Start from the Taskbar, then Programs, Microsoft Word.

TIP: As you begin to use Office 95 more efficiently, you'll find yourself using several applications in each work session. For this reason, it's smart to make sure that your Shortcut Bar is available so that you can switch between applications with one mouse click, without needing to wade through the Start menu.

Figure 3-1.
The Shortcut Bar allows you to access Microsoft Office applications easily, whether you are at the Windows desktop or in another application

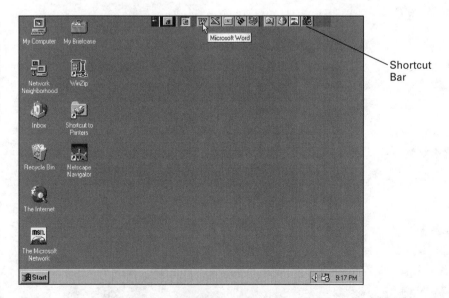

Shortcut Bar

Learning About the Word Window

When you start Word, you will see the window shown in Figure 3-2. This window has many of the elements common to other Office 95 applications.

Elements that are unique to the Word window include the following:

- **Ruler Bar.** This bar is located just below the toolbars. It displays and allows you to set margins, indents, and tabs.

- **Status Bar.** This bar is located at the bottom of the Word window. It displays the page number, section number, current page and total pages, location of your insertion point, and status indicators.

- **View Buttons.** These buttons allow you to switch between three ways of viewing your document: Normal, Page Layout, and Outline. These ways of looking at your document are all discussed in Chapter 4.

> **Common elements in Office 95 application windows are discussed in Chapter 2.**

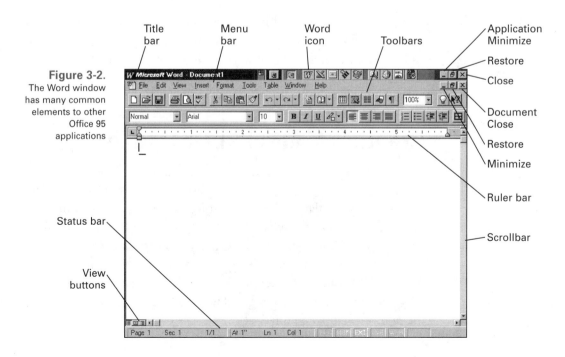

Figure 3-2.
The Word window has many common elements to other Office 95 applications

Title bar   Menu bar   Word icon   Toolbars   Application Minimize
Restore
Close
Document Close
Restore
Minimize
Ruler bar
Scrollbar
Status bar
View buttons

Exiting Word

When you have finished using Word, you can leave by choosing File, Exit.

If you are working on a document which has changes that are not saved, you will be prompted to save your work before you exit Word. Select Yes to save the document, No to not save any changes, or Cancel to continue working on the document.

TIP: If you prefer using a mouse, you can also exit Word by double-clicking on the left end of the title bar (where the symbol for Word is).

You can work more efficiently by keeping the following rule in mind: When your hand is on the keyboard, keep it on the keyboard. When it's on the mouse, keep it on the mouse. If you're a touch typist, it may be more efficient to exit Word by choosing the File menu with Alt + F, then pressing X to choose Exit when your hands are on the keyboard; if your hands are on the mouse, it may be faster to double-click on the Word icon.

You can get overwhelmed if you try to learn five different ways to do every task! For the tasks you do most frequently, however, it may be worthwhile learning the best keyboard method and the best mouse method.

Creating Your First Document

Word processing gives you many helpful ways to format and edit your documents that typing doesn't. The basic process of creating documents is very similar, however. The biggest difference you will need to get used to is *word wrapping*. Word wrapping is a feature that allows you to forget about pressing the Carriage Return key at the end of each line, as you must do on a typewriter. Word determines where the line should break, and takes you to the next line automatically. The only time you need to press Enter while you are typing in Word is at the end of each paragraph.

NOTE: When you use proportional fonts such as Times New Roman, where "W" is much wider than "I," it's almost impossible to get text to line up on different lines by using the spacebar. It's a good idea to get in the habit of using the Tab key.

There are two other keys you may use in creating your first documents. The Tab key moves the cursor to the right half an inch (assuming that you are using the default tab settings). Use Tab rather than pressing Spacebar five times. Similarly, Shift+Tab moves the cursor half an inch to the left.

If you make a mistake, you can easily correct it by pressing the Backspace key. Backspace deletes one or more characters to the left of the *insertion point.* The insertion point is the blinking cursor that appears where you are located in your document. If you start typing, the letters appear at your insertion point. Like all other keys, the Backspace key will repeat if you hold it down for more than a half second or so.

When you reach the end of your page, you can just keep on typing. Word will insert a page break at the appropriate place. If you need to break a page before reaching the end of the page, position the insertion point where you want to break the page and press Ctrl+E. You will see a line across the page; the status bar will also indicate that you are on the next page. Page breaks inserted manually are called *hard page breaks.* You can delete a hard page break by positioning the cursor at the beginning of the new page and pressing the Backspace key. The page breaks that Word inserts automatically at the end of the page are called *soft page breaks.* You cannot delete these, since they occur when you are at the end of a page.

TIP: There are many more sophisticated ways for correcting your errors besides the Backspace key that you'll learn later in this chapter.

Hands On: Creating Your First Document

Perhaps your first document might be a short intraoffice memo asking for another copy of the minutes of last week's staff minutes. You can create this as follows:

1. Start Word as described above. A blank editing screen is the first thing you will see.

2. Type **Memo to:** then press the [Tab] key. Type **James Torrenzano**, then press the [Enter] key. Your insertion point moves to the second line.

3. Type **From:** then press the [Tab] key until your insertion point is under the recipient's name. Type your own name, then press the [Enter] key.

4. Type in the current date, then press [Enter] twice to double-space.

5. Type the text of the memo. Remember not to press the [Enter] key at the end of each line, and use the [Backspace] key to correct any errors you make. The text you should type is as follows: **James, I'd appreciate it if you could send me a copy of the minutes from the last meeting. Somehow I either threw mine away or someone borrowed them. Many thanks.**

That's it. You've created your first document! It should look like the one in Figure 3-3.

Figure 3-3.
Your short memo
should look like this

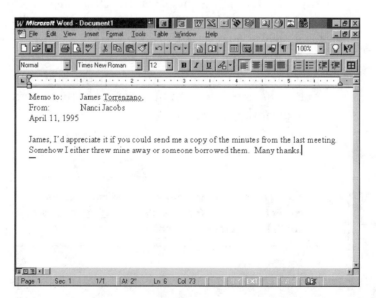

Saving and Printing Your Work

Once you've created your document, you'll want to save it. If you want others to see it, you'll also need to print it. Finally, when you are finished with your document, you will want to close it. Once you've done these things, you'll have all the skills needed to dash off a quick memo or letter whenever you need to.

Saving Your Document

As you compose your document, Word keeps it in your computer's memory. As long as the computer is on, and you are using Word, your document is safe. However, when you exit Word, or if your computer's power is turned off, whatever is in memory is lost. For this reason, you will want to save your work when you are finished with it.

You can save your work to a floppy disk, the hard disk on your computer, or a network drive (if available). Moreover, using Word, you can save files to specific folders on those disks. As you save more and more documents, you will want to create an electronic filing system by putting your documents into different folders on your disk just as you put things into manila folders in your paper filing system.

Creating an electronic filing system is discussed in Chapter 23.

For now, however, we'll just save and retrieve files from the *default* folder—the My Documents folder that Word uses if you don't specify anything different.

Hands On: Saving Your First Document

To save the memo you created, do the following:

1. To save your file, choose File, Save. The first time you save your document, you will see the Save As dialog box shown in Figure 3-4. Depending on how your system has been installed, the default folder may not be the My Documents folder, but you can safely ignore this, since you're just going to save the document to whatever the default folder is.

2. To save your document in the default folder, type the name **Memo - James Torrenzano - 001** in the File Name text box (where your insertion point is already located).

Figure 3-4.
Using the Save As
dialog box, you
can save your file
with a full, English
language name

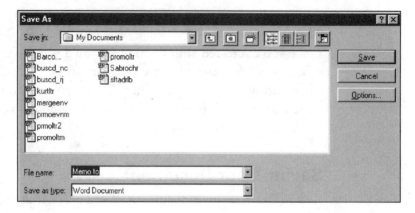

TIP: Windows replaces highlighted text with new text as you type. Since the default filename *Doc1* is highlighted, the new name you type will replace the default filename.

When you edit your work, you will want to save it again, so that further changes to the document are retained. The next time you save your document by choosing File, Save or by clicking the Save button on the Standard toolbar, you will not see the Save As dialog box. Your new version will automatically be saved on top of the previous version, using the existing filename.

CAUTION: When you save your work a second time, the new version overwrites the previous version of the file, and the previous version is lost. You are not warned before this occurs. If you want to save old versions, save the new version with a different name before you start making changes. This ensures that you won't accidentally delete work you want to keep.

If you want to save your work and retain the previous version, use File, Save As and give the file a different name. For instance, you may wish to send a similar memo to the same person and save both versions.

Hands On: Saving Your Document with Another Name

To save your memo document with another name, do the following:

1. Ensure that the memo is on the screen. You will save it under its new name before editing it, so that you don't accidentally lose important information in the original memo.

2. Choose File, Save As. The Save As dialog box appears, with the original name highlighted in the File Name text box.

3. Edit the memo's name to **Memo - James Torrenzano - 002**, by clicking in the File Name box to remove the highlighting, then pressing the End key to position your insertion point at the end of the name.

4. Press the Backspace key to erase the 1, then type **2**.

5. Click the Save button to save your work with its new name.

NOTE: The last four characters of a Word document's filename are .DOC. The last three characters are called the *extension*. A period separates the extension from the rest of the name. The .DOC extension identifies the file as a Word document to your computer. The .DOC extension is automatically appended to the filename when you save the document for the first time. Normally, you will not see ".DOC" at the end of the filename. Windows 95 hides these extensions so you don't have to worry about them.

Previewing and Printing Documents

The final product of your word-processing activities is usually a printed document. An advantage of using a word processor, however, is that you can see how the final product will look by previewing your work on screen before you print it.

Previewing a Document

Print Preview is a special mode that allows you to see your document as it will look when it is printed. You can even see miniatures of several pages of your document. You cannot edit your document in Print Preview mode, but you will find that it is often wise to preview your document prior to printing it.

Hands On: Previewing Your Memo

To preview your memo, do the following:

1. Choose File, Print Preview; or click the Preview button. The Preview window is shown in Figure 3-5.

2. To see your document more closely, click the Magnifier button if it is not already depressed. As you move your mouse pointer on the page, notice that the shape of the pointer has changed to a magnifying glass with a "+" in the middle of it. Click anywhere on the page of your document. You can now read the text of your document, but you cannot see the entire page.

3. Use the scroll bars to move around the page of the document.

4. Since your mouse pointer is still the magnifying glass, click in the document to toggle back to the full page view. Click the Magnify button again to return to a regular mouse pointer.

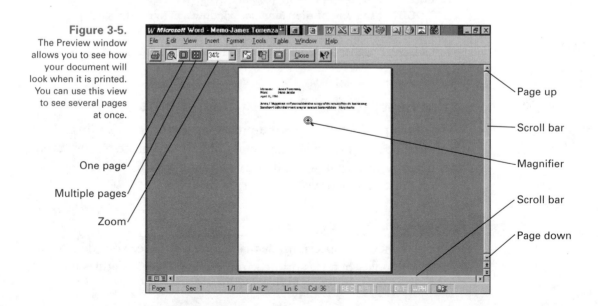

Figure 3-5.
The Preview window allows you to see how your document will look when it is printed. You can use this view to see several pages at once.

One page
Multiple pages
Zoom

Page up
Scroll bar
Magnifier
Scroll bar
Page down

NOTE: When you are in the one-page mode, use the Page Up and Page Down buttons just below the vertical scroll bar to scroll through the document page by page. If you are viewing multiple pages, the Page Up and Page Down buttons will take you to the next set of pages.

PART II   WORD

5. Click the Multiple Pages button. You will see six small page icons. Click the middle in the second row. Your page will shrink to a small size. If your document were longer, four pages would appear simultaneously.

6. Click the One Page button to return to the one-page display.

7. Click the Close button to return to the main editing window.

NOTE: When your font is small or you are showing multiple pages in the window at once, text will be replaced by shaded lines called *Greeking*. Greeking allows you to see how the text as a whole fits on the page, and thus how your page composition looks.

Printing a Document

When you are satisfied with the way your document looks in the pre-view, you are ready to print your document. Word will allow you to continue to work while the document prints.

Hands On: Printing Your Memo

To print out your memo, follow these steps:

1. Choose File, Print. The Print dialog box shown in Figure 3-6 will appear.

2. Choose OK to print the document using the default settings. One copy of the entire document will be printed on the currently selected printer.

Figure 3-6.
The Print dialog box allows you to set printing options, including which pages will print, the number of copies, and the printer to be used

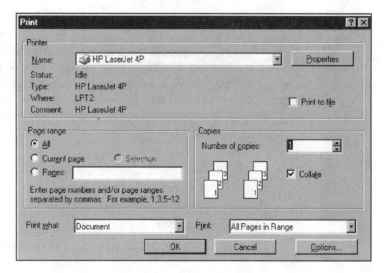

 NOTE: From the Print dialog box, you can also specify the number of copies, print just the current page or a range of pages (e.g., 1-5, 9, 10), or select a different printer.

Closing Documents

When you are finished with your work, close your document. This is not strictly necessary, as the document will close automatically when you exit Word. You can even open another document with the first one still open. However, if you intend to open new documents, keeping old ones open may make your work confusing, unless you need to keep multiple documents open so you can switch between them.

If you have not changed your document since you last saved it, the document will close immediately. If you have made changes, but have not yet saved them, Word will ask if you want to save your changes before you close the document. If you choose <u>Y</u>es, your document will be saved, overwriting any older version of the file. If you choose <u>N</u>o, your recent changes will be lost and the document will close. If you choose Cancel, you'll be returned to your document as it was before you tried closing it.

Hands On: Closing Your Memo

To close your memo, do the following:

1. Choose <u>F</u>ile, <u>C</u>lose.

2. Respond <u>Y</u>es to the question, "Do you want to save changes?" Your document will close.

Working on Your Next Document

You have learned how to get into Word and write a quick memo. Let's work on another document. After you've closed your first document, your Word window should look like Figure 3-7. The menu bar only shows two items: <u>F</u>ile and <u>H</u>elp. This is because you do not have any documents open—not even a new, blank one.

At this point you have two options: create a new document or open an existing document that is already saved on your disk.

Creating a New Document

Word comes with many blank master documents, called *templates*. Some of these templates contain nothing but formatting options

Figure 3-7.
The Word screen with
no documents open

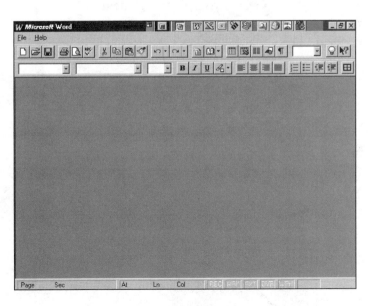

(i.e., specific margin, font, and line spacing settings). Others contain text, such as blank *From:* and *To:* lines for a memo. They may even include *fields* to fill in commonly used information for the document, like the title for your report, the addressee for your letter, or the date of your memo.

You'll learn how to use templates to automate correspondence, write reports, and more in later chapters. For now, however, it's sufficient to know that every document you create is based on a template. When you create a document, you choose which template to base it on.

To create a new document, do the following:

1. Choose File, New. You will see the New dialog box shown in Figure 3-8. The tabs in this dialog box allow you to choose the type of Word document you want to create: letters, faxes, memos, reports, and other types of documents: By default, the General tab is shown.

2. Double-click on the Blank Document template. The default document name will appear in the title bar (e.g., "Document2" if this is the second document you have created), along with the entire menu bar and a blank, white editing window with scroll bars.

3. Type text into your new document, just as you did when you created your first document.

4. Save or print your work as desired, then close your document.

Figure 3-8.
When you create a new document, you can base it on a *template*, which assists you in creating special types of documents, such as letters or reports

Tabs

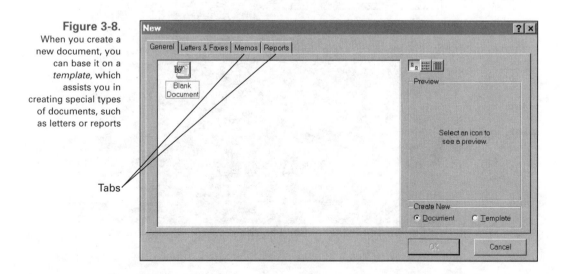

TIP: If you just want to create a new document based on the Blank Document template, there's a shortcut. Instead of choosing <u>F</u>ile, <u>N</u>ew, just click the New button on the Standard toolbar.

Opening an Existing Document

The great thing about word processing is that you can go back and edit a document that you already saved. For instance, you can create a new document based on an existing one. To do this, of course, you have to find the original file.

Windows 95's long filenames should help you from forgetting a file's name. (Previous versions of Windows did not allow a filename to contain more than eight characters, which made it hard to know what to name a file.) In the event that you can't find your file, you can always search through your disk to find it by its name, or even by specific words in the document.

It's important to understand that when you open a document, you are only opening a *copy* of the file. In theory, you could edit it, print it, and close it without affecting the original file on the disk. You only replace the original file when you save the edited file with the same name in the same folder—as you do when you click the Save button.

Finding lost documents is discussed in Chapter 21.

CAUTION: If you are going to save both the original and the edited files, choose <u>F</u>ile, <u>S</u>ave As when you open the file, rather than after you edit it. It's very easy to click the Save button without thinking and accidentally overwrite your original file.

Hands On: Opening Your Memo

To open the memo you created earlier, follow these steps:

1. Choose <u>F</u>ile, <u>O</u>pen; or click the Open button on the Standard toolbar. You will see the Open dialog box shown in Figure 3-9.
2. Double-click on the file *Memo - James Torrenzano - 001*.

Figure 3-9.
The Open dialog
box allows you to
navigate through
folders to find a
document, then
retrieve a copy of
that file to your
editing window

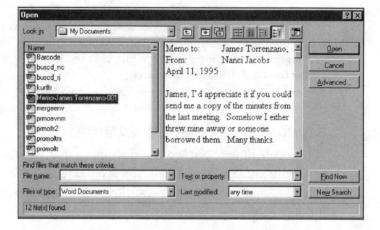

Editing Your Document

To edit a Word document, you need to do four things: navigate to the
appropriate place in the document, insert new text, delete unneeded
text, and move or copy text to new places.

Navigating in a Word Document

To navigate in a Word document, you can use all the keyboard commands that are common to Office 95 programs and use the scroll bars
with your mouse. In addition, you may find Word's Go To function
helpful in moving through longer documents.

To use the Go To command, do the following:

1. Choose Edit, Go To. The Go To dialog box will appear:

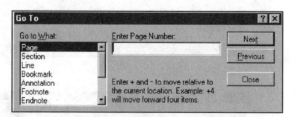

2. Type the number of the page to which you want to go, then
   click Go To. You'll go to the page you specified (and the Go
   To dialog box will remain visible).

3. Press Esc to close the Go To dialog box.

TIP: The shortcut key for the Go To function is $\boxed{\text{F5}}$. This is a function key worth remembering.

NOTE: You can also use the Go To dialog box to move to a specific line, footnote, endnote, graphic, section, or bookmark in your document.

Sections are discussed in Chapter 5. Bookmarks are discussed in Chapter 9.

Selecting Text

In Word, you *select* text to identify it as something that should be edited or formatted. You can easily select text with either the keyboard or the mouse.

Selecting Text with the Mouse

There are two ways you can select text with the mouse: *click-and-drag*, and *click*, $\boxed{\text{Shift}}$-*click*. The former is most useful when all the text you are selecting is visible in the editing window, so you don't have to scroll to see it all. The latter is most useful when selecting larger blocks of text.

USING THE CLICK-AND-DRAG METHOD

The easiest way to select text that is visible on the screen is the *click-and-drag* method:

1. Click to the left of the first word (or letter) you wish to select and continue to depress the mouse button.
2. With the button depressed, drag down and to the right until all the text you wish to select is highlighted.

You can deselect highlighted text by clicking somewhere else in the editing screen that is not part of the highlighted area. You can also select text "backwards" by clicking after the last word you wish to select and dragging up and to the left until the text you wish to select is highlighted. You must start, however, at either the beginning or the end of the text you wish to select.

When you use the click-and-drag method, you can either select text in increments of whole words or individual letters. Experiment with both to determine which works best for you. Select <u>T</u>ools, <u>O</u>ptions; click on the Edit tab; and then choose Automatic <u>W</u>ord Selection.

> **CAUTION:** Clicking and dragging doesn't work well when some of the text lies beyond the screen, because you can easily lose control of how much text you're selecting when the screen scrolls quickly by.

USING THE CLICK, Shift-CLICK METHOD

When you are selecting a large area of text that doesn't fit on the screen, a better alternative is the *click*, Shift-*click* method:

1. Click to the left of the first word (or letter) you wish to select.
2. Scroll through the document (using the scroll bars or the Page Down key) until the end of the text you wish to select is visible on the screen. *Do not click anywhere in the document while you are scrolling to the end of the selection.*
3. Hold down the Shift key and click at the end of the text you wish to select. All the text in between will be highlighted.

You can deselect the text by clicking somewhere else in the document that is not part of the highlighted area. You can also select text "backwards" by clicking to the right of the last word to be selected and then holding down the Shift key and clicking before the first word to be selected.

You can also select text with the mouse by double-clicking and triple-clicking on the text and in the margins, as described in Table 3-1.

Selecting Text with the Keyboard

If you prefer, you can select text with the keyboard. This is useful when your hands are already on the keyboard, as they are when you are entering text. To select text, hold down the Shift key while using any keyboard command that moves the insertion point (such as the arrow keys). This selects the text between the original insertion point and the new one.

For instance, if your insertion point is in the middle of a paragraph, pressing Ctrl + ↓ moves the cursor to the beginning of the next para-

Table 3-1. Shortcuts for Selecting Text with the Mouse

Text to Select	Shortcut
Word	Double-click in the word
Paragraph	Triple-click in the paragraph
Entire line	Click in the left margin to the left of the line
Paragraph	Double-click in the left margin to the left of the paragraph
Document	Triple-click in the left margin

Table 3-2. Shortcuts for Selecting Text with the Keyboard

Text to Select	Shortcut
From insertion point to same position on next line	Shift + ↓
From insertion point to same position on previous line	Shift + ↑
From insertion point to beginning of next paragraph	Shift + Ctrl + ↓
From insertion point to beginning of previous paragraph	Shift + Ctrl + ↑
From insertion point to end of document	Shift + Ctrl + End
From insertion point to beginning of document	Shift + Ctrl + Home

graph. So pressing Shift + Ctrl + ↓ selects the text between the original position and the beginning of the next paragraph.

Some of the most useful selection commands are shown in Table 3-2.

Inserting and Deleting Text

To insert new text, position your insertion point where the new text should appear. Examine the status bar at the bottom of the screen to

> **NOTE:** Word operates in one of two modes: Insert and Overwrite. In Insert mode, new text you type is inserted at the insertion point and existing text is pushed ahead. In Overwrite mode, each character of text that you type replaces a character of existing text. You can toggle between Insert and Overwrite modes by pressing the [Ins] key.

ensure that OVR (*Overwrite* mode) does not appear. If it does, press the [Ins] key to return to Insert mode. Type the text you want to insert. The text following the insertion point will be pushed ahead as your new text is inserted.

You can delete text in several ways. Experienced users learn several ways, finding that each one can be most efficient in different situations:

- Press the [Del] key to delete characters to the right of your insertion point, or press the [Backspace] key to delete characters to the left of your insertion point. These methods are usually the most efficient ones when you are changing text as you type, and have only a few characters to delete.

- If you want to delete a sentence or more, it's most efficient to select the text at once, and then press the [Del] key.

- "Power users" often find it useful to learn two hotkey sequences that speed their editing significantly. Pressing [Ctrl] + [Del] deletes text from the insertion point to the end of the word. This can be quite useful when you are inserting new text into an existing sentence and need to delete the next few words.

If you ever delete text by mistake, you can click the Undo button on the Standard toolbar to undo your deletion, or choose Edit, Undo.

TIP: The easiest way to replace a word or phrase with another one is to select the word(s) and then simply type the new text. The text that is selected will be overwritten by the new text you type.

> ### Hands On: Editing Your Memo
>
> You can practice replacing text by making the following changes to your memo:
>
> 1. Open the memo if it is not already open.
> 2. Double-click on "Torrenzano" to highlight the name. While it is highlighted, type **Johnson**. The name is changed.
> 3. Click before the *t* of "the last meeting." Press Ctrl + Del three times to delete the three words. Type a space, then **March**.
> 4. Click before the word "Somehow." Hold down the Shift key and click after "borrowed them." The sentence is selected.
> 5. Press the Del key to delete it.
> 6. Choose File, Close to close the file. Do not save your changes (this was just practice!). The original document is still intact on the disk.

Moving and Copying Text

There are two very easy ways to move or copy text from one place in your document to another: using the cut-and-paste method and the drag-and-drop method.

Using the Cut-and-Paste Method

The *cut-and-paste* method takes two steps. First the selected text is removed or copied from its original location and placed in the Windows Clipboard. Cutting the text removes it from its original location, whereas copying leaves a copy in the original location. Thus, you use the Cut command to move text and the Copy command to duplicate text.

In the second step, you position your insertion point where you want your text to appear and you "paste" it there. *Pasting* is the term for copying text from the Clipboard to its new destination in your document. This doesn't empty the Clipboard, however; you can paste the same text repeatedly.

So, to move text, select it, cut it to the Clipboard, click where you want it to appear, and paste it. To copy text, select it, copy it to the Clipboard, click where you want it to appear, and paste it.

What Is the Clipboard?

The *Clipboard* is a temporary storage area that Windows 95 reserves for moving and copying things. It is used for everything from moving text from one place to another in Word to copying clip art from PowerPoint to Word.

Remember four basic rules about the Clipboard:

- There is only one Clipboard. It is shared by all Windows programs.
- There can only be one item on the Clipboard at any time.
- Items stay on the Clipboard until they are removed by exiting Windows or putting something else onto the Clipboard.
- Pasting an object from the Clipboard does not empty it. The object can be pasted multiple times.

Since there are several methods for cutting, copying, and pasting, you will find it useful to know the best method to use in common situations:

- If you prefer to use the menus, you can do so by opening the Edit menu and then choosing either Cut, Copy, or Paste. This can be useful when your hands are already on the keyboard, or when the toolbar is not visible.

- If you prefer to use the mouse, you can click on the Cut, Copy, and Paste buttons on the Standard toolbar.

Hands On: Moving and Copying Text in Your Memo

You can practice using the cut-and-paste method as follows:

1. Open your memo, if it is not already open.
2. Select the words "from the last meeting" by clicking in the word "from" and dragging to the word "meeting." Be sure not to include the period following "meeting" in your selection.
3. Click the Cut button. Your text disappears and the period appears directly after the word "minutes."

Working Smarter with Cutting and Pasting

I'm a lazy person—a fact which I freely admit. If there's a way to do something that's even slightly quicker, I like to learn it. If you're like me, you might be interested in these two tricks:

- If your hands are already on the keyboard and you want to cut, copy, and paste most efficiently, use the shortcut keys Ctrl+X for cut, Ctrl+Y for copy, or Ctrl+V for paste. These key combinations save you time, especially if you're a touch typist. Even better, they work in all Office 95 applications, so you only have to learn them once.
- If you want to absolutely minimize your mouse motions—that is, if you're *really* lazy like me—don't move the mouse up to the toolbar; just keep the mouse in the highlighted area after you select your text and right-click it. You'll see the pop-up menu. Now click on Cut, Copy, or Paste.

4. Click after the words "borrowed them," but before the period after "them."

5. Click the Paste button. The words "from the last meeting" will appear in their new position.

6. Click the Undo button two times to undo this cut-and-paste operation.

7. Repeat steps 2 through 6 using Edit, Cut and Edit, Paste, rather than the Cut and Paste buttons.

8. Repeat steps 2 through 6 using the shortcut keys Ctrl+X and Ctrl+V, rather than the Cut and Paste buttons.

9. Repeat steps 2 through 6 using the pop-up menu rather than the Cut and Paste buttons. Which method is easiest for you?

10. Remember to undo your changes when you are finished.

Using the Drag-and-Drop Method

The second method for moving and copying text is the *drag-and-drop method.* This moves or copies the text directly, without using the Clipboard.

To use this method, do the following:

1. Select the text to be moved.
2. Position your mouse pointer anywhere inside the highlighted area.
3. Click-and-drag the text to its new location.

This method works best when you are moving or copying text in the visible editing window. If your mouse wanders above or below this window, the text will scroll—sometimes too quickly to control. Thus for moving large chunks of text, you may find the cut-and-paste method preferable.

> **CAUTION:** Before you get used to the drag-and-drop technique, you may lose control of where the text is going and accidentally deposit it somewhere by mistake. If you do this, click the Undo button to undo the move.

Hands On: Moving Text with the Drag-and-Drop Method

To drag-and-drop text, do the following:

1. Open your memo, if it is not already open.
2. Click in the word "from" of "from the last meeting" and drag it to the word "meeting." The words in the phrase are selected. Be sure not to include the period following "meeting" in your selection.
3. Position the mouse pointer inside the selected text. Notice that the pointer becomes a white arrow.
4. Click and hold down the left button while you drag the text to a new position. As you move it, a vertical line can be seen in the document indicating where the text will be inserted.
5. When you move the vertical line after the words "borrowed them" but before the period, let go of the mouse button. The text will be moved to its new location.
6. Close your document and do not save any changes.

> **TIP:** You can copy text as well as move it by using the drag-and-drop method. Just hold down the Ctrl key while you click-and-drag the text to copy it rather than move it.

CHAPTER 4

FORMATTING AND MANAGING WORD DOCUMENTS

IN THIS CHAPTER

- **Formatting Text**
- **Working with Several Documents**
- **Managing Your Word Environment**

After learning the basics of creating a Word document, discover how easy it is to work with several Word files at a time and improve their appearance considerably. This chapter also shows you how to save time by customizing your Word environment to make it work for you.

Formatting Text

There are many ways to improve a document after you've finished writing it. These changes affect its appearance, not its content. You can modify fonts, emphasize certain words, play with line spacing, change text alignment, and adjust the margins and tab settings.

There's one basic rule to remember when formatting text: *first select the text, then apply the formatting.* If you remember this, all your formatting will be a snap.

There are two ways to make these format changes in Word: using toolbar buttons, or menus and dialog boxes. Toolbar buttons are quicker and easier; menus and dialog boxes offer more options.

Formatting with Toolbars

The fastest way to format your documents is to apply your formatting with the toolbars whenever possible. Reserve the menus and dialog boxes for special cases where you need more sophisticated choices.

Most formatting commands are found on the Formatting toolbar. If this toolbar is not displayed, you can display it as follows:

1. Choose <u>V</u>iew, <u>T</u>oolbars. The Toolbars dialog box shown in Figure 4-1 appears.

Figure 4-1.
You can choose which of your toolbars to display in the Toolbar dialog box

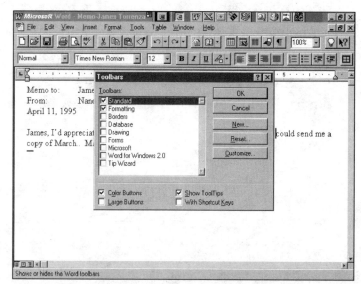

2. Click on the Formatting toolbar checkbox to put a check mark by it.

3. Click OK.

Emphasizing Text

You can emphasize your text easily by applying **boldface**, *italic*, or underline formatting. (You've probably already noticed that this book uses all three.) There are three rules you may wish to keep in mind when emphasizing words:

- Use boldface when you really want to draw the reader's eye to a word, phrase, or head
- Use italics for phrases that would be emphasized when reading a passage, or for foreign words, names of books, etc.
- Try to avoid underlining, unless you're attributing a specific meaning to it. It's somewhat old-fashioned, since it was one of the easiest ways to show emphasis when all we had were typewriters or our own handwriting.

Apply emphasis to text as follows:

1. Select the text to be emphasized.

2. Click the Bold, Italic, or Underline buttons on the Formatting toolbar.

B *I* U

Hands On: Emphasizing Text with the Toolbar

To emphasize text in your memo, you can do the following:

1. Ensure that the memo you created earlier is open.

2. Select the To, From, and Date lines of the memo.

3. Click the Bold button.

4. Click somewhere else in the memo to deselect the first lines. You will see the lines in boldface.

TIP: For faster service, press Ctrl + B for bold, Ctrl + I for italic, or Ctrl + U for underline.

Choosing Fonts

You can change the font (i.e., the typeface) or the font size for all of your document or any part of it with the Formatting toolbar. Your choice includes any of the Windows 95 fonts that are installed on your computer—a fairly large selection.

Be careful, however, not to use too many fonts on a page. Many graphic designers recommend using no more than two typefaces and three sizes per page. Often this is a simple font like Arial for headings and a more readable font like Times New Roman for the body. If you use a large size for headings, a regular size for text, and a small size for footnotes, you will be safe.

To change fonts, try the following procedure:

1. Select the text you wish to change.

2. Click the arrow to the right of the Font drop-down list box on the Formatting toolbar. A list of available fonts will appear, as shown in Figure 4-2.

3. Click on the desired font. You will see the selected text with the new font.

The same procedure can be used to change the size of your text by using the drop-down Font Size box to the right of the Font box on

Figure 4-2.
You can change the fonts used in your document with the Formatting toolbar

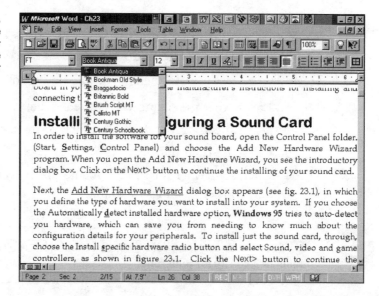

the Formatting toolbar. Let's see how your memo looks with different fonts.

Hands On: Changing Fonts in Your Memo

There are two changes you should make to the fonts in your memo: selecting a new font for the memo text as a whole, then selecting a different font for the heads. You can do so as follows:

1. Ensure that your memo is open.
2. Select all the text in the memo by clicking three times in the left margin. The entire memo should be highlighted.
3. Click the down arrow to the right of the Font drop-down box on the Formatting toolbar. You will see a list of available fonts.
4. Click on the Courier New font. Notice that the text changes to Courier New (unless it already was in this font) and stays highlighted.
5. Click the down arrow to the right of the Font drop-down box again and select the Times New Roman font. Notice that all the text now changes to Times New Roman.
6. Click anywhere in the document to remove the selection.
7. Select the first three lines of the memo (From, To, and Subject).
8. Click the down arrow to the right of the Font drop-down box and select the Arial font. Notice that the text changes to Arial.
9. Click the Save button to save your work.

Changing Text Alignment

Alignment refers to the position of your text on the page. Word offers four types of alignment, which are shown in Figure 4-3.

Body text is almost always left-aligned or justified. Justification gives it a more formal look, and is often used in reports, books, and other desktop published documents (except this book). Correspondence usually looks better left-aligned, as the ragged-right edge gives a more personalized impression for your document. (That's why this book's text is left-aligned: for that hint of informality.) Centered text is most often used for titles, announcements, and the like. Right alignment is often reserved for datelines, letterhead, and specialized desktop publishing jobs.

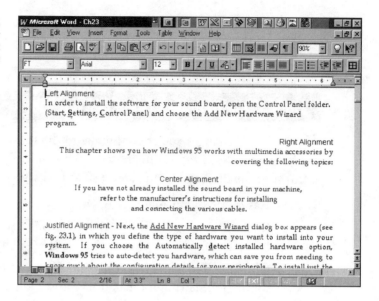

Changing alignment works slightly differently than specifying fonts. You can apply emphasis or fonts to individual characters, words, or sentences, but alignment applies to entire paragraphs. Thus, if any text in a paragraph is selected when you change alignment, the entire paragraph will be affected. If you want to have a line where a few words are left-aligned and a few words are right-aligned on the other side of that line, you will need to set tabs in that line, rather than use the alignment feature. Tabs are discussed later in this chapter.

To change the alignment of your text using the toolbar, do the following:

1. Select the text to be changed.
2. Click the Align Left, Center, Align Right, or Justify button on the Formatting toolbar.

Hands On: Changing Alignment in Your Memo

In your memo, change the alignment of the text from left-aligned to justified, and right-align the date. You can do so as follows:

1. Ensure that your memo is open.

2. Select the entire memo by clicking three times in the left margin. The entire memo should be highlighted.

3. Click the Justify button on the Formatting toolbar. The first lines are unaffected, since they do not span the entire line. The body of the text is now justified, however.

4. Click anywhere in the document to remove the selection.

5. Click anywhere in the line that contains the date.

6. Click the Align Right button. Notice that the date jumps to the right side of the page.

7. Click the Save button to save your work.

Formatting with the Menu

Formatting commands can also be applied by using dialog boxes accessed through the menu commands. While this method is not quite as simple as clicking a toolbar button, you can fine-tune formatting commands in this way.

Using the Font Dialog Box

For the maximum control over the typeface and font attributes of your text, use the Font dialog box to change fonts. You can do so as follows:

1. Select the text to be changed.

2. Choose Format, Font. You will see the Font dialog box shown in Figure 4-4.

Figure 4-4.
The Font dialog box allows you to choose all font attributes, and even displays a preview of what the font will look like

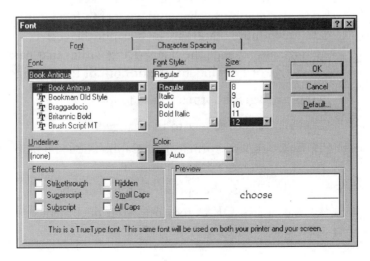

PART II   WORD

3. Choose the options for your fonts as desired. You will see the result of the changes in the Preview window within the dialog box.

4. Click OK to return to your document and see the change(s) take effect.

Use this dialog box when you need to set attributes that cannot be set from the Toolbar, such as ~~strikethrough~~, SMALL CAPS, or ALL CAPS. You can also change the color of your font and apply different styles of underlining this way.

> **NOTE:** You can change the default font for all new documents by clicking on the <u>D</u>efault button. A message will appear, asking if you want to change the default font to the one you have selected. It informs you that all new documents based on the Normal template will be affected by this change. (As was discussed in Chapter 3, all documents are based on templates, which contain formatting information.)

Applying Paragraph Formatting

It is important for your documents to have a consistent appearance. Word helps you achieve this easily with paragraph formatting.

Paragraph formatting determines what happens when you press the Enter key. Normally, the Enter key takes you to the beginning of the next paragraph. By changing paragraph formatting, the Enter key can do much more than that, such as put the correct spacing between paragraphs, change the line spacing within that paragraph, indent the first line, or even indent one or both of the margins.

Apply paragraph formatting as follows:

1. Select the text to be changed.

2. Choose F<u>o</u>rmat, <u>P</u>aragraph. The Paragraph dialog box shown in Figure 4-5 will appear.

3. Choose the options in the dialog box.

4. Click OK to return to your document.

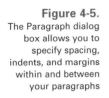

Figure 4-5.
The Paragraph dialog box allows you to specify spacing, indents, and margins within and between your paragraphs

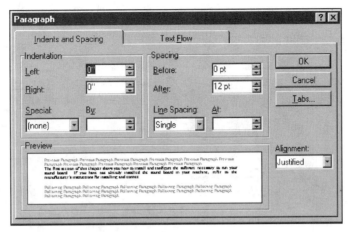

Changing paragraph formatting can help you in several common situations:

- If you prefer your document to be single-, double-, or one-and-a-half spaced, choose Line Spacing and make the appropriate selection.

- If you would like to have a blank line between each paragraph—as is often the case for single-spaced documents—choose After and specify 12 points, or make both Before and After 6 points. (12 points is the equivalent of one line if you are using a 12-point font.) Each time you press the [Enter] key, you will see a blank line between paragraphs.

- If you would like to indent the first line of the paragraph, choose Special, First line and then specify half an inch—the default tab spacing. Each time you press the [Enter] key, the first line of your new paragraph will be indented one tab stop.

- If you want to indent a long quote half an inch from both the right and left margins, make both the Left and Right Indentation half an inch.

- To create attractive bibliographies, choose Special, Hanging and then specify half an inch. The first line of each entry will come to the left margin, and succeeding lines will be indented half an inch.

Figure 4-6.
The Text Flow tab allows you to keep text together on a page

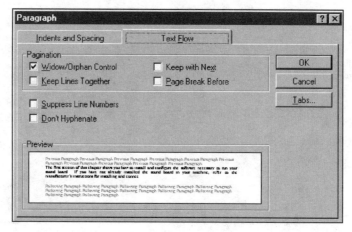

If you click the Text Flow tab, you will see the options shown in Figure 4-6. You can then accommodate other common situations:

- If you want to ensure that a section heading always stays with the first paragraph of the following text, select that heading and then choose Keep with Next. This way the heading will never happen to appear by itself at the bottom of a page.

- To keep the first line and last line of text paragraphs from appearing alone at the bottom and top of pages, choose all your text paragraphs and then select Widow/Orphan Control. You should keep this selected as the default (if it's not set already), since you will want it on most of the time.

- To insert a page break automatically before a major section or chapter heading, select that heading and then choose Page Break Before. You will often use these commands in conjunction with styles that specify all the formatting and appearance attributes of your text and headings.

Styles are discussed in Chapter 5.

Using Borders and Shading

Word can add a variety of borders and shading to selected paragraphs. Overusing this feature is sure to produce an unprofessional-looking document. Used sparingly, however, it can add visual appeal. For instance, you may wish to add a double-line around the subject and author of a report on its title page, or shade a "pull-quote" (common in magazines, a short excerpt displayed by itself) to draw the reader's attention to it.

Figure 4-7.
You can easily
create an attractive
border to emphasize
important points

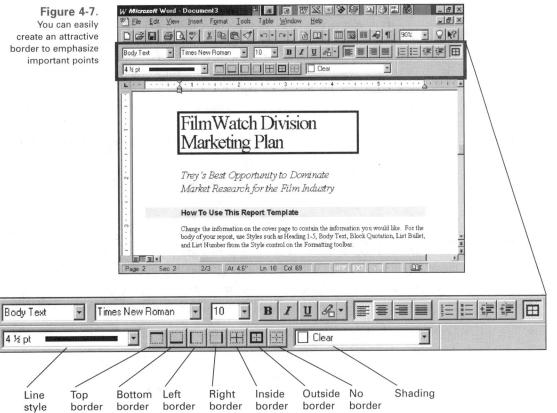

Line
style

Top
border

Bottom
border

Left
border

Right
border

Inside
border

Outside
border

No
border

Shading

If you select several adjacent paragraphs, you can make a border around all of them, as in Figure 4-7.

The easiest way to put borders and shading in your document is by using the Borders toolbar, as follows:

1. Select the appropriate paragraph(s).

2. Click the Borders button at the far right of the Formatting toolbar. The Borders toolbar will appear below it.

3. To insert a border, click the down arrow to the right of the Line Style box and select the appropriate line style and thickness.

4. Click the appropriate button:

   • To put a border at the top, bottom, left, or right of your selected paragraph(s), click the appropriate button

TIP: If you wish to have a thick border around two paragraphs and a thin border between them, create the thick border by following steps 3 and 4, using the Outside Border button. Then repeat steps 3 and 4, choosing a thinner border and clicking the Inside Border button.

- If you want a border all around the paragraph(s), click the Outside Border button
- If you want lines between paragraphs, click the Inside Border button
- To remove borders, click the No Border button

In addition to borders *around* your paragraphs, you may wish to draw attention to a paragraph by filling it with a pattern or shading. For instance, you might want to emphasize your titles by shading the paragraphs they appear in. To add patterns or shading to your paragraph:

1. Click the down arrow to the right of the Shading button and select the appropriate pattern or shading.
2. To remove the Border toolbar, right-click on it. You will see the pop-up menu showing the available toolbars. Click on Borders to remove the check mark by it.

TIP: To create a striking title, make the shading Solid (100%). The text color will automatically change from black to white.

Occasionally you may need more border and shading options, e.g., the ability to create colored borders and shading. You can access these options by selecting the appropriate paragraphs and choosing F̲ormat, B̲orders and Shading to access the Paragraph Borders and Shading dialog box.

Setting Tabs and Indentations

For most documents, you will not need to change the default tabs that Word uses for your documents. Occasionally, however, you may want to set your own. The indentation settings control whether your paragraph appears flush to the margin or indented from it. While these changes can be made using dialog boxes, it's usually easiest to use the *Ruler*—the bar at the top of your editing screen that displays your tabs and margins.

Setting Tabs

Word allows you to set four types of tabs: left, right, center, and decimal. Examples of these can be seen in Figure 4-8. The right and center tabs are especially useful when creating a column in a table, because you'll probably want to center or right-align the column headings. Decimal tabs are appropriate when creating columns of numbers.

To set tabs, do the following:

1. Display the Ruler, if it doesn't already appear on-screen, by choosing <u>V</u>iew, <u>R</u>uler. The Ruler will appear above the editing window.

2. Select the text to which the tab settings will be applied. To have them apply to the entire document, triple-click in the left margin to select all text.

3. Notice the Tab icon to the left of the Ruler. Click on the Tab icon until it toggles to the appropriate type of tab shown in Figure 4-9.

4. Click on the Ruler where the tab should appear.

Figure 4-8.
Word allows you
to set four types
of tabs

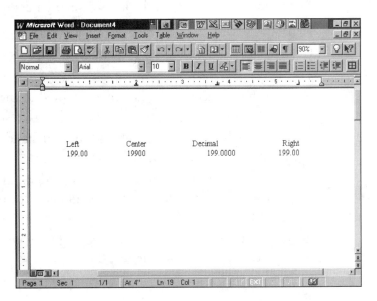

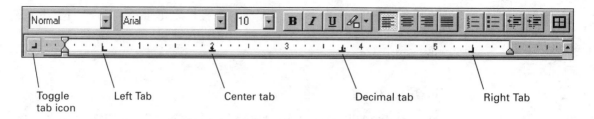

Toggle   Left Tab   Center tab   Decimal tab   Right Tab
tab icon

Figure 4-9.
These are the tab
icons you can
choose from

5. To move a tab, drag it from its original location to the new location.

6. To delete a tab, drag it off the Ruler into the document.

When you set a tab manually in this fashion, any default half-inch tab settings to the left of that tab will disappear.

TIP: You can make more sophisticated changes to tab settings—e.g., tabs with dot leaders before them—by selecting the appropriate text, choosing F<u>o</u>rmat, <u>T</u>abs, and making your choice(s) in the Tabs dialog box.

Setting Indentations

Indentations are the spaces between the margins and your paragraphs. Word allows you to indent the left side of a paragraph, the right side, or just the first line.

There are three times when you may commonly need to indent paragraphs:

- When you want the first line indented ("tabbed in")
- When you use a quote in a document and want to indent both the right and left sides of it to make it stand out from the rest of the text (as in Figure 4-10)
- When you want to create a hanging indent, as in a bibliography, where the first line is at the margin and the other lines are indented

You can set your indents easily by dragging three markers on the Ruler. These are shown in Figure 4-11.

Figure 4-10.
Word allows you to indent the first line of a paragraph or the entire paragraph

Tabbed-in paragraph

Quote

Figure 4-11.
You can set a variety of indent styles using the Ruler

Paragraph-indent

First-line indent

Left-indent

Right-indent

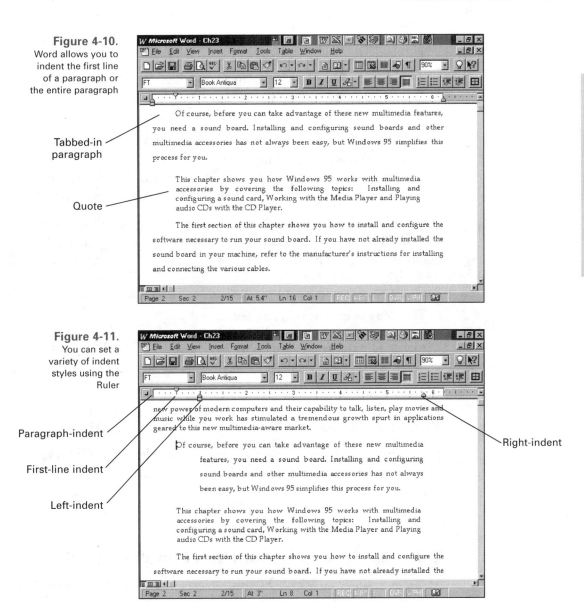

To set indents, do the following:

1. Select the text to be modified.

2. To create a paragraph where the first line is indented half an inch, drag the first-line indent marker half an inch to the right of the left-indent marker.

3. To create a paragraph that is indented on the right and left sides, without the first line being indented further, drag the first-line indent marker until it is directly above the left-indent marker. Then drag both the paragraph- and right-indent markers inward half an inch.

4. To make a hanging indent in which the first line is at the left margin and succeeding lines are indented, move the para-graph-indent marker half an inch in from the left margin, then pull the first-line marker back out to the left margin.

When you drag the paragraph marker, it moves the first-line marker with it. Thus, to change indentation, you must first drag the para-graph marker to its position and *then* drag the first-line indicator.

TIP: You can use the Decrease Indent and Increase Indent buttons on the Formatting toolbar to increase or decrease the left indent of the selected paragraph(s).

Working with Several Documents

Word allows you to open many documents simultaneously. This can be very helpful when combining text from several old documents into a new one or when you want to refer to an old letter as you write a new one.

Opening Several Documents Simultaneously

When you open several documents, each will be in its own document window. You can open, close, and save each window independently. When one document window is maximized, others will be hidden behind it. However, you can easily switch between open documents

NOTE: The maximum number of open windows is determined by your system's memory and what other applications are using system resources. If you cannot open additional document windows, Word will warn you.

or, if you prefer, show several small document windows on the screen simultaneously.

Opening multiple documents is extremely easy. You merely create a new document or open an existing document without closing the original one. You can continue doing this as many times as you want.

> **TIP:** Open several documents at once by holding down the Ctrl key while clicking on additional filenames in the Open dialog box. Alternatively, Shift-click in this list to open several adjacent filenames.

When several documents are open, you can switch from one to the other by using the Window menu. This menu lists all open documents. Select the one you want to display.

Displaying Multiple Documents Simultaneously

You can also display several documents on the screen at once by choosing Window, Arrange All. The active documents will be tiled, as in Figure 4-12.

Figure 4-12.
You can display several documents simultaneously by tiling them on the screen

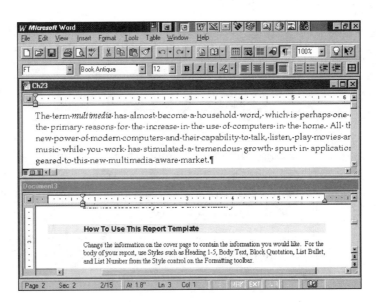

Sizing windows is discussed in Chapter 2.

Once you have tiled your windows, you can size them, maximize them, or minimize them as you would any other window.

Managing Your Word Environment

Before discussing more specialized uses of Word, it would be helpful to learn how to customize your Word environment to help you work more efficiently by using views, zoom, toolbars, paragraph marks, and arranging document windows.

Using Views

Word has three views that you can toggle among while creating and editing your documents. Three buttons at the bottom of your screen allow you to switch between these views. You can always tell what view you are in by looking at which button is depressed.

The default view is the Normal view, which you access by choosing <u>V</u>iew, <u>N</u>ormal. In this view, material that is displayed (and prints) in the top and bottom margins—such as headers, footers, pagination, and footnotes—are not shown on-screen.

The second view is the Page Layout view. This is a WYSIWYG (What You See Is What You Get) view. It does show the material in the top and bottom margins.

The Outline view is discussed in Chapter 6.

The Outline view, accessed by choosing <u>V</u>iew, <u>O</u>utline, is used for outlining your documents. It is discussed later in the book.

Zooming Documents

You can take a closer look at your documents by using the Zoom command. Choose from predefined zoom percentages by using the drop-down list on the Zoom Control button; or else type the specific percentage you want to use in the Zoom text box on the Standard toolbar.

135%

The best zoom percentage for you to use depends on several factors, including the size of your monitor, the font size, and your screen resolution.

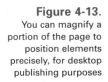

Figure 4-13.
You can magnify a portion of the page to position elements precisely, for desktop publishing purposes

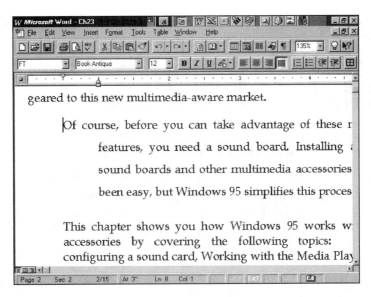

You can increase the zoom factor to magnify a small portion of your page, as shown in Figure 4-13. This can be helpful when you need to place a graphic or text precisely (e.g., for desktop publishing).

Displaying Toolbars

By default, two toolbars appear on-screen: the Standard toolbar and the Formatting toolbar. You can display other toolbars by right-clicking on any displayed toolbar. You will see a shortcut menu listing the available toolbars:

The Borders, Database, Drawing, and Forms toolbars are used when using special operations relating to borders, databases, drawings, and forms. Other ones include the Preview, Header/Footer, Footnote, and

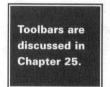
Toolbars are discussed in Chapter 25.

Mail Merge toolbars. The Microsoft toolbar gives you the same access to other Office applications as the Shortcut Bar.

If no toolbar is displayed, you can view them by choosing View, Toolbars. This displays the Toolbars dialog box, which also allows you to create new toolbars and edit existing ones.

Displaying Hidden Codes

You can display certain codes that are usually hidden by clicking the Show/Hide Paragraph button on the Standard toolbar. These codes indicate spaces, tabs, and end-of-paragraph marks, as shown in Figure 4-14.

> **NOTE:** The paragraph mark contains all formatting for the paragraph, including its line spacing, margins, alignment, and indentations. If you include this paragraph mark when copying a paragraph, the paragraph's formatting will also be copied. If you do not include the paragraph mark in your selection, the text will be copied without its accompanying paragraph formatting.

Figure 4-14.
By clicking the Paragraph button, you can see codes for spaces, tabs, and end-of-paragraph marks

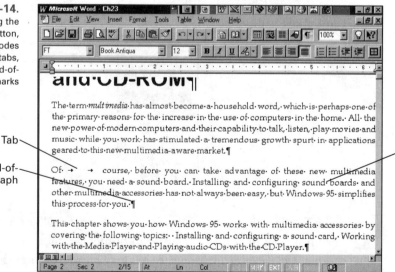

There are other advantages to using this view. For instance, you can tell whether a given indent is tabbed or spaced in. Turning on this view can help you identify other formatting problems and give you a clue as to how to solve them.

Splitting Your Document

Word has one other handy feature that makes working with long documents easy. You can split a single document into two windows that can be scrolled independently. In this way, you can see both the top and bottom of your document simultaneously, and even move or copy text by dragging and dropping it from one window to another.

To split your document, follow these steps:

1. Open the document you wish to split.

2. Choose <u>W</u>indow, S<u>p</u>lit. Your pointer will become a cross with a double horizontal line in the middle of the screen and a gray line will appear, as shown in Figure 4-15.

3. Move the pointer up or down until the split is where you want it, then press (Enter). Your document will become visible in two windows with vertical scroll bars.

4. To remove the split, choose <u>W</u>indow, Remove S<u>p</u>lit. Alternatively, drag the gray bar to the bottom of the screen.

Figure 4-15.
You can split a document into two windows which can be scrolled independently

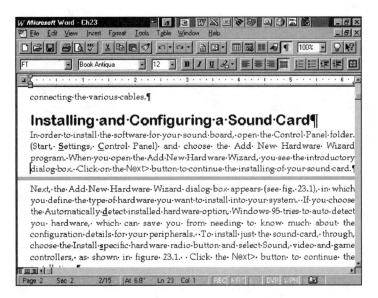

CHAPTER 5

CREATING EFFECTIVE REPORTS

IN THIS CHAPTER

- **Formatting Your Report with Styles**
- **Creating a Consistent Look with Templates**
- **Including Headers and Footers**
- **Incorporating Tables**
- **Documenting Points with Footnotes**
- **Organizing Your Report**

Reports are documents that argue persuasively for a point of view. Some reports consist only of text; others are illustrated with tables, charts, diagrams, and equations.

To write effective reports, you need to be able to create a well-written, well-organized, and well-formatted Word document. In this chapter, you'll learn techniques for writing powerful, persuasive reports.

Formatting Your Report

Effective reports use characteristic style elements to give them a distinct look. For instance, there are often chapter or section heads, then topic and subtopic heads. The body text usually has one style, while quoted text or reference sections have another. The header and footer at the top and bottom of the page may have a line below or above it, and be set in a different point size.

You can use Word's formatting commands to create these elements, but setting complex formatting is time-consuming, and if you forget even one command, you can lose the consistent look of the document. For instance, your level-1 headings may be centered on the page and set in 24-point bold Arial with small caps. Setting these five formatting elements takes time, and it's easy to forget one.

Word enables you to automate the formatting process through the use of styles. A *style* is a group of formatting commands that is saved with a name (like "Heading 1" or "Body Text"). A style may easily be applied to selected characters or paragraphs.

In addition, Word has two other tools that will assist you in formatting your reports: automatic bulleted lists and automatic numbered lists.

Using Styles

While you can easily create styles to customize your report, you may find that the styles that ship with Word satisfy your needs.

Applying Styles

By default, text you type is set in the Normal style. While this is fine for most correspondence and other simple uses, you'll probably want to use other styles that Word supplies for reports.

Word comes with a set of paragraph styles that allow you to format your reports easily. The ones most often used include:

- **Heading 1–9:** Use these styles for your document headings
- **Body Text:** This style should be used for regular text in your document

> **TIP:** While you can use Normal for your body text, you will often find that the text of reports displays some formatting features that normal text does not. For instance, you may want your report text to have a wider left margin, or be double-spaced between paragraphs. For this reason, it's a good idea to use the Body Text style for report text.

- **Block Quotation:** This properly indents and formats quotations in your text
- **Header, Footer, TOC 1–9:** These determine how your header, footer, and table of contents look

To apply a paragraph style to an element in your report, do the following:

1. Place your insertion point anywhere in the paragraph.
2. Click on the down arrow at the right of the Style box on the formatting toolbar. A list of available styles is shown in Figure 5-1.

Figure 5-1.
You can select from a number of predefined styles from the Style box

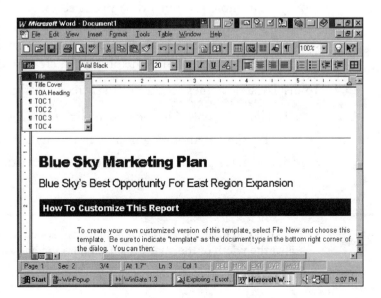

3. Choose the style to be applied. The formatting of the paragraph changes to that of the selected style.

To apply a style to a series of paragraphs, select the appropriate paragraphs before you choose the style.

NOTE: There are two types of styles in Word: paragraph styles and character styles. The most commonly used are paragraph styles. These format entire paragraphs at once. By contrast, character styles format only certain words or groups of characters within a paragraph.

Displaying Styles

You can ascertain the style of any given paragraph by simply clicking in it. The style name will appear in the Style box on the Formatting toolbar.

NOTE: If you select a number of paragraphs that have different styles, the box will be empty.

Since styles are an integral part of report formatting, you may wish to display them more prominently on your editing screen. Word allows you to show the style name for each paragraph at the left side of your screen. This has the disadvantage of taking up screen space, but being able to see style names can be helpful when creating complex reports.

To display style names on the editing screen, do the following:

1. Choose Tools, Options, then click the View tab.
2. Type .5 (or another amount) in the Style Area Width box.
3. Click OK. You'll see the styles at the left side of your editing window, as shown in Figure 5-2.

TIP: You can drag the vertical line that appears on-screen to adjust the width of the style area. Dragging the line all the way to the left removes the style area (sets it back to 0.0).

Figure 5-2.
You can display
document styles at
the left of your
editing window

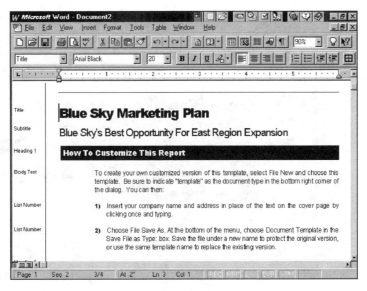

Creating New Styles

While the styles that ship with Word are usually adequate for normal documents, you may wish to personalize your report formats by creating new styles. There are three basic ways to create new styles:

- Redefine existing styles
- Create new styles by example
- Create new styles through the menu

REDEFINING EXISTING STYLES

You should use the names Heading 1, Heading 2, etc., for your headings, since features including automatic tables of contents and outlines depend on your using these names. Sometimes, however, you will want the heading styles to have a different format than they do by default.

To redefine an existing paragraph style, do the following:

1. Apply the style to be redefined to a paragraph.
2. Double-click in the left margin to the left of the paragraph to select the entire paragraph.
3. Change the formatting of that text to reflect how the style should be redefined.
4. Click once in the style box. The style is highlighted.

Figure 5-3.
You can easily
redefine a style
by using the
Reapply Style
dialog box

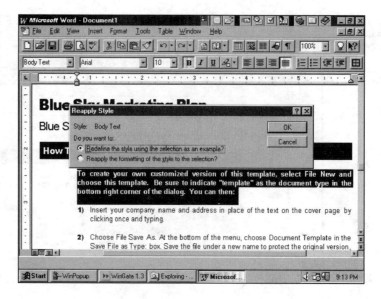

5. Press [Enter]. You'll see the Reapply Style dialog box shown in Figure 5-3.

6. Choose <u>R</u>edefine to change the style. You will notice that all paragraphs that use this style throughout the document have been changed.

CREATING NEW STYLES BY EXAMPLE

On occasion, you may wish to create a new style. This can be useful if your report has callouts, pull quotes, or other unique design elements. You can create a new style by example or from the Style dialog box. Creating a new style by example is similar to redefining an old one.

To create a new style by example, follow these steps:

1. Select the paragraph you wish to format in the new style.

2. Change the formatting of that text as needed.

3. Click in the style box to select the existing style, then type the name of the new style, replacing the name of the old one.

4. Press [Enter]. The new style is created. You'll notice that the entire paragraph now uses this formatting. This style is now on the list of styles, and can be applied to other paragraphs of your document as needed.

CREATING NEW STYLES THROUGH THE MENU

While creating styles through the menu is somewhat more complex, it provides more options than creating styles by example, including the ability to set paragraph options such as spacing within and between paragraphs. Creating styles through the Style dialog box also allows you to base your new style on an existing one. For example, if you change the font of the Body Text style, the font of all styles based on it will change as well.

> **NOTE:** Another thing that a style can do is automatically call the same style (or a different style) for the next paragraph. For instance, your documents might always start with the document title, followed by the subtitle, followed by the author's name, followed by the chapter title, followed by body text. You can specify that when a person types a line in the Document Title style and presses Enter, the next paragraph is automatically set in the Subtitle style. When the Enter key is pressed again, the next paragraph is in the Author style, etc. This is frequently done with heading styles, where the next paragraph after a Heading 1 style is often the Body Text style.

To create a style through the menu, do the following:

1. Choose Format, Style. You'll see the Style dialog box showing a list of existing styles, as shown in Figure 5-4. You can create, delete, and modify styles from this dialog box.

2. Choose New. The New Style dialog box will appear, as shown in Figure 5-5.

3. Give your new style a name in the Name box.

4. Specify the style upon which your new style will be based, if desired, in the Based On box.

5. If appropriate, specify the style for the paragraph that follows it.

6. To set the formatting for your new style, choose the Format button. You'll see a drop-down list showing the different formatting options.

Figure 5-4.
The Style dialog
box allows you
to see what
styles exist in
your document,
as well as create,
modify, and
delete styles

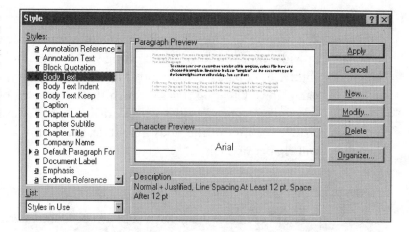

Figure 5-5.
When you define
a new style, you
can base it on
existing styles
and specify a
style for the next
paragraph

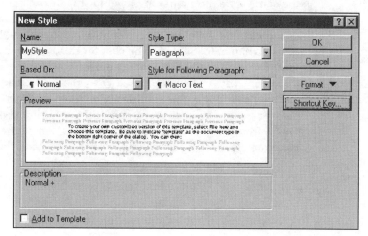

7. Choose the appropriate type of formatting. You will see the same formatting dialog box that you would use to apply formatting directly from the menu. For instance, if you choose Font, you'll see the same Font dialog box you would see if you chose Format, Font from the menu.

8. When you have finished specifying your settings, exit from the appropriate formatting dialog box by choosing OK to return to the New Style dialog box.

9. Choose Format again to make further changes, or click OK to return to the Style dialog box which shows your list of styles.

10. From the Style dialog box, choose Apply to apply the new style to the paragraph containing your insertion point, or

> **NOTE:** You can modify an existing style using these same steps. The only difference is that you should first select the style to be modified from the Style dialog box, then choose Modify rather than New. This can be helpful when you wish to add specifications that cannot be done by example, such as specifying the style for the following paragraph or assigning a shortcut key, as discussed in the next section.

choose Close to exit the dialog box and save the changes you have made to your style list.

Assigning Styles to Shortcut Keys

You can make the process of using styles much more efficient by assigning styles frequently used to shortcut keys. For instance, you can assign your heading styles to Ctrl + 1, Ctrl + 2, etc., and your body text style to Ctrl + B. This way, you don't need to take your hands off the keyboard to apply a style to text as you type.

To assign a shortcut key to a style, do this:

1. Choose Format, Style. The Style dialog box, showing the list of styles, will appear.

2. Select the appropriate style, then choose Modify. You'll see the Modify style dialog box.

3. Click on Shortcut Key. The Customize dialog box shown in Figure 5-6 will appear.

4. Ensure that your insertion point is in the Press New Shortcut Key box, then press the keystroke combination you wish to use as a shortcut key: e.g., Ctrl + 1. The dialog box will display any existing assignment for that keystroke combination.

5. If you want to assign it to the style, click Assign. (Decide first whether you think you'll ever use the preassigned style more than the one you're assigning to this particular keystroke combination.)

6. Click Close to close the dialog box, then choose OK and Close again to close the Modify Style and Styles dialog boxes and return to your editing window.

Figure 5-6.
The Customize dialog box allows you to assign shortcut keys to frequently used styles. This saves you time when formatting reports.

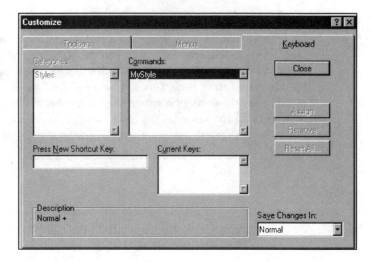

Using Lists

Bulleted and numbered lists are often used in reports. Word allows you to create these lists automatically, and even modify the bullets or numbering systems you use. What's even nicer is that you can add a new item in the middle of your numbered list, and all the following points will be renumbered automatically!

Creating Lists

Use bulleted lists when you want to stress a series of points, and numbered lists to identify steps to follow.

To create a list, do the following:

1. Position your cursor where you want the list to start, or select the existing points that you wish to bullet or number.

AutoFormat is discussed further in Chapter 6.

TIP: You can also create bullets or numbers as you type by starting the line with a small "o" or with "1," followed by a space (or tab) then text, assuming AutoFormat is on. In order for this to work, you need to select Tools, Options, AutoFormat, AutoFormat As You Type. When you start the second line of your list, the "o" will change to a bullet and the "1." will change to Word's code for a number, and you will see a second bullet or the number "2." at the beginning of your second list item.

2. Click the Bullets or Numbering button to make a bullet or number appear. If there is existing text, you'll now have the bulleted or numbered list. As you type new text and press the [Enter] key, a bullet or number appears at the beginning of each new line. Press the [Enter] key twice to stop the list.

Modifying Bullets and Numbers

You can modify the look of your bullets or numbers if you don't like Word's defaults. You can choose any character for bullets, select from among six preformatted numbering schemes, or create your own.

To do so, follow these steps:

1. Select the text that includes the list(s) to be modified.

2. Choose Format, Bullets and Numbering. The Bullets and Numbering dialog box, shown in Figure 5-7, will appear.

3. Click the Bulleted or Numbered tab, as needed. You'll see several preformatted choices for bullets and numbers.

4. If one of the choices is acceptable, click on it, then click OK.

TIP: You can also choose a bullet character from any font supported by Windows 95 by clicking the Bullet button in the Modify Bulleted Lists dialog box. These include characters from the Symbols and the Wingdings character sets, if you want to really add some pizzazz to your document!

Figure 5-7.
You can choose the specific character you want to use for your bullets, or pick from a number of different numbering schemes for your lists

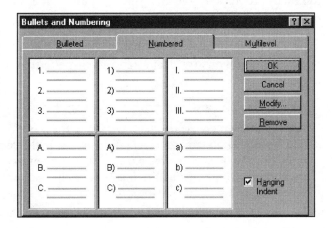

Figure 5-8.
You can specify how bullets and numbers appear in your lists, if you don't like Word's defaults.

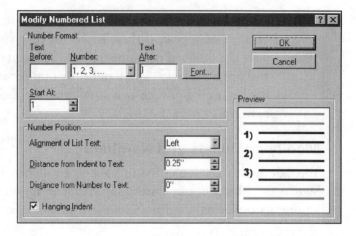

5. Alternatively, if you want to use a bullet character or numbering scheme that is not suggested, click the Modify button. The Modify Numbered List or Modify Bulleted List dialog box like the one shown in Figure 5-8, will appear.

Creating a Consistent Look with Templates

Whenever you create any new document, it is based on a *template*. A template is a "master document" that contains the formatting commands and the list of styles that will appear in your new document. Toolbars, macros, shortcut keys, and abbreviations are also stored in templates. Templates can even have text associated with them. Even the blank document you first open is based on a template—the Normal template.

Templates become useful when you start creating different types of documents. For instance, a report template may have different

> **NOTE:** Lists of styles are also saved in templates. When you modify default styles, changes are saved in the template on which the document was based. You will be prompted to save changes in the default template (usually Normal.dot) when you exit your document after making such changes.

formatting for the Heading 1 style than does a memo template. It might have toolbars that automate processes for report preparation. A customized report template could even contain boilerplate text that appears in all reports—whether it is the title page or a corporate statement.

Word ships with three report templates. One easy way to make your reports look professional is to use them. As you become comfortable with templates, you will want to edit them to suit your personal or organizational style.

Using Report Templates

To create a professionally designed report quickly, use one of the three report templates that come with Word, as follows:

1. Choose File, New. You'll see the New dialog box.
2. Click on the Reports tab. You'll see the three default report templates as shown in Figure 5-9: Contemporary, Elegant, and Professional. Click once on each of them to preview how they look.
3. Double-click on the desired template.

The three default templates already contain text. You can select the text, then type right over it to replace the default text with information that pertains to you. The text in the body of the templates provide instructions on how to use elements of the templates.

Figure 5-9.
Word comes with three default report templates: Contemporary, Elegant, and Professional

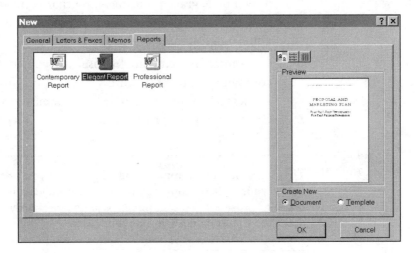

TIP: Print out the template before you delete its text. Keep this printout to help you write your real reports, since these documents have good advice on using styles, making a table of contents, etc.

Modifying a Report Template

The best way to create an attractive report, complete with standard elements like a table of contents, is to customize one of Word's pre-made Report templates.

To customize a report template, you will want to open it, make your modifications, then save it as a template. Opening the template is different than creating a new document based on it, as opening it allows you to modify the template itself. Do so as follows:

1. Choose File, New, then click on the Reports tab.

2. Click on Create New Template at the bottom right corner of the dialog box.

3. Click each of the report styles one by one, and look at the preview of that template on the right side of the dialog box. Double-click on the existing report style that most closely resembles the style you wish to create for yourself. You've now created a new template.

4. Click the Save button. The Save As dialog box shown in Figure 5-10 will become visible. Notice that the Save as Type box is grayed out, meaning that you can't change it, and the file type is Document Template. Give the template a meaningful name and save it.

5. Customize the template by inserting your name and/or your company's name and address where appropriate. Edit the headers and footers if needed, and remove the text that gives advice on report writing.

TIP: Stick with one template and use it for all your reports, unless your style is mandated for you. This builds a certain graphic "presence" so that people will unconsciously associate this style with you or your office.

Figure 5-10.
You can create
templates based
on Word's
default report
templates to
customize report
styles

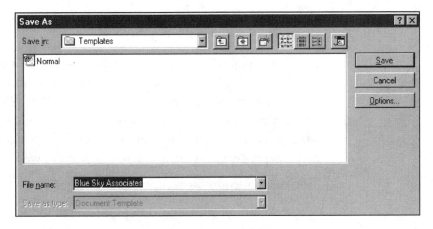

6. Insert information for text elements that the user will need to type in when the template is used, e.g., "Title Goes Here" or "Subtitle Here."

7. Save the edited template.

After you've customized a report template, all your reports will have the same look and feel. To create a new report from Word, choose File, New, and click the Reports tab. Choose your report template from the New File dialog box and click OK.

Including Headers and Footers

A *header* is text that appears in the top margin of every page. A *footer,* as you might expect, is text that appears in the bottom margin of each page. Word allows you to insert headers and footers in your reports with ease. However, before learning how to do this, it is important to understand a new concept: with Word you can divide your file into *sections.* Headers and footers apply either to the whole document, or to a specific section of the document.

Dividing Your Document into Sections

Word divides your document into sections for the purpose of page formatting. A simple document usually contains just one section. If you create a header or footer and your document only has one section, the header or footer will appear throughout your document.

Other functions that work the same way include margins, page numbering, and page layout.

In reports, you will often not wish your header or footer to appear on the title page, table of contents, and other "administrative" pages of the document. To accomplish this, you'll need to place these pages in one section and the rest of the document in another. You may also wish to have a different header or footer in each chapter. In that case, each chapter needs to be a different section as well.

To create a section break, do the following:

1. Position your insertion point where the section break should appear.

2. Choose Insert, Break. You'll see the Break dialog box:

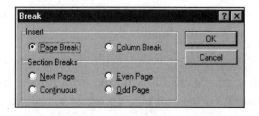

3. Choose whether the new section should start immediately (Continuous), or on the Next page.

TIP: You can even force a section to start on an odd- or even-numbered page. For instance, book chapters or sections in long reports often start on right-facing pages.

Creating Headers and Footers

To make a header or footer, first determine whether it should apply to the entire document or just a part of it. If the first page of a section is to have a different header or footer than the rest of it, you do not need two sections; you're allowed to have different headers and footers on the first page of a section. If you will be using different headers and footers throughout the document, divide it into sections appropriately.

To create a header or footer:

1. Position your insertion point in the appropriate section of your document.

2. Choose <u>V</u>iew, <u>H</u>eader and Footer. Notice the Header and Footer toolbar; your insertion point is in a box in the top margin where you can type the header, as shown in Figure 5-11.

3. Type the text for your header, noting the following:

   • By default, there are two tabs in headers and footers. Tabbing once brings you to the center, where text will be centered. Tabbing again brings you to the right margin, where text will be flush right.

   • Click the Switch Between Header and Footer button to enter footer text.

   • Insert the page number, date, or time by clicking the appropriate button.

   • If you have several sections in your document, you can move between the headers and footers of each section with

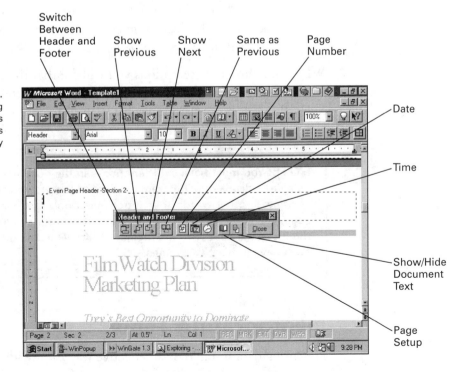

Figure 5-11.
The floating toolbar makes creating headers and footers easy

Figure 5-12.
You can specify whether the first page of a section has a different header and footer than the rest of the section, or whether odd and even pages have different headers and footers

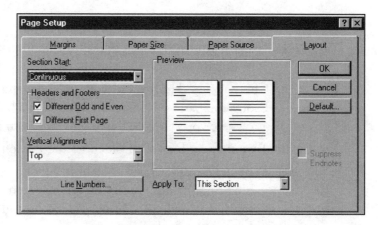

the Show Next and Show Previous buttons. You can also create a new header or footer based on the one in the previous section by clicking the Same as Previous button.

4. If you need to have a different header or footer on the first page of a section, or different ones for odd and even pages, click the Page Setup button. You'll see the Page Setup dialog box shown in Figure 5-12. Click in the appropriate box to specify (or deselect) different odd and even page headers/footers, or different first page headers/footers.

When you choose these options you will see that the text box is labeled first page header, odd page footer, etc. Use the Show Next and Show Previous buttons to move between different headers and footers.

NOTE: You must have sufficient pages in the document to be able to display the different headers or footers you are creating. In other words, if your document only has one page, you cannot use the Show Next button to move from the first page header to the regular header. The document must have at least two pages.

Incorporating Tables

Presenting data in tables is an effective way to provide evidence for the point you are making in your report, and for summarizing a large amount of information. There are two ways you can create tabular data in your report: using a Word table or an Excel worksheet. If it's a simple table, create it in Word. If there are complex calculations, or if the worksheet exists anyway, import it from Excel.

Creating a Word Table

To create a Word table, follow these steps:

1. Position your insertion point where the table should appear in your report.

2. Click the Insert Table button. You'll see a drop-down blank table, as shown in Figure 5-13.

3. Click in the cell that provides the necessary number of columns and rows for your table. For example, to create a table with four columns and two rows, click on the cell that is fourth from the left and second from the top. You will see the table appear in your document.

TIP: Don't worry about having enough rows in your table. If you are in the last cell of a table and press ⎯Tab⎯, a new row will appear. Adding columns, however, is not as easy as adding rows.

Figure 5-13.
You can quickly create a table in a Word document by clicking the Insert Table button

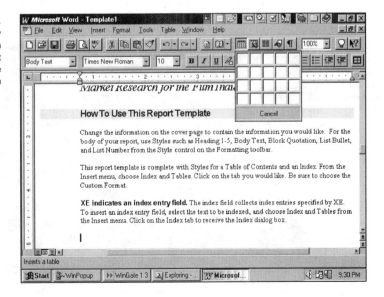

To enter data in your table, click in the appropriate cell. Notice that if what you enter is wider than the cell width, an extra line within the cell will be created. You can press [Tab] to move ahead to the next cell, or [Shift] + [Tab] to move to the previous cell.

Formatting Your Table

You can easily format the table as follows:

1. Position your insertion point inside the table.

2. Choose Table, Table AutoFormat. The Table AutoFormat dialog box shown in Figure 5-14 will appear.

3. Choose the format you desire. If you are basing your report on the Contemporary, Elegant, or Professional template, consider using the table format of the same name that was designed to go with it.

4. When you are done, click OK. You'll return to the main editing window and see the newly formatted table.

You can also apply formatting manually to text within a table or to cells, rows, or columns of the table itself. To do so, select the text or cell(s), then apply formatting using standard Word formatting commands. Make selections within a table as follows:

- Select text in a cell by dragging over the desired text.

- Select an entire cell by moving the mouse pointer until it nears

Figure 5-14.
You can choose from a variety of professionally designed table formats

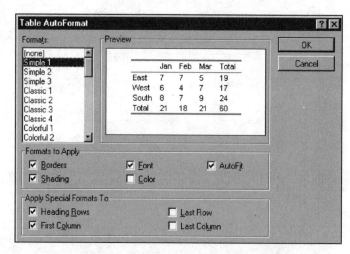

the left edge of the cell, and clicking when the pointer becomes an white arrow pointing up and to the right.

- Select an entire column by moving the mouse pointer to the top boundary of the column and clicking when the pointer becomes a black, downward-pointing arrow.

- Select an entire row by moving the mouse pointer into the margin to the left of the table, at the row you want to select, and clicking when the pointer becomes a white arrow pointing up and to the right.

Commonly used table formatting you may wish to use include aligning text in cells, changing the width of cells, or adding and deleting columns and rows. You may do so as follows:

- To align numbers to the right of the cell, select the appropriate columns, then click the Align Right button on the formatting toolbar.

- To center titles, select the appropriate rows, then click the Align Center button on the formatting toolbar.

- To resize a column width, move the mouse pointer to the column boundary until it becomes a right and left arrow with two vertical lines between them. Drag the column boundary to its new position.

- To insert or delete a row, select the entire row below the one to be inserted (or the row to be deleted) then right-click inside the selected row. Choose Insert Rows or Delete Rows from the shortcut menu.

- To insert or delete a column, select the entire column to the right of one to be inserted (or the column to be deleted) then right-click inside the selected column. Choose Insert Columns or Delete Columns from the shortcut menu.

- To insert a column at the right of the table, ensure that paragraph marks are visible by clicking the Show/Hide button, if needed. Select the paragraph marks at the right side of the table by clicking above the top mark when the mouse pointer is a downward-pointing black arrow. With the marks selected, right-click, then choose Insert Columns from the context menu.

Documenting Points with Footnotes

In many reports, you can write more persuasively by documenting specific points with footnotes or endnotes. You should also use footnotes and endnotes to give proper credit for material that you copy or paraphrase from someone else.

Word's footnotes and endnotes will automatically renumber themselves if additional ones are inserted, or existing ones are moved or deleted. To make a footnote or an endnote, follow these steps:

1. Click after the word where the reference should appear.
2. Choose Insert, Footnote. You'll see the Footnote and Endnote dialog box. This dialog box allows you to specify whether you wish to insert a footnote or an endnote, and whether to automatically number it or use a symbol for it.

TIP: You can choose Options from the Footnote and Endnote dialog box to modify the numbering system for the footnotes or endnotes.

Choosing Where to Put Your Notes

Should you use footnotes that appear at the bottom of the page or endnotes that appear at the end of a section or report?

- If your style is mandated, as it often is for academic papers, follow the required style or take the academic consequences!

- If most readers are not expected to read each note, use endnotes.

- If most readers will be interested in the information, use footnotes so that they don't need to interrupt themselves by finding the endnotes at the back of the report.

- If many of your notes are so long that they take up significant chunks of the page, use endnotes.

- If your notes are lengthy but you think most readers will want to read them, consider including them in the body of the text rather than in a note.

PART II WORD

Figure 5-15.
Type the text of
your footnote or
endnote in a
separate window

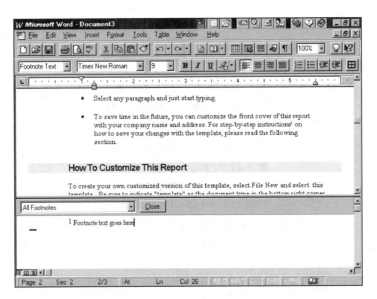

3. Choose Footnote or Endnote, as appropriate, then click OK. A split screen, with your insertion point in the Footnote or Endnote window, will appear as shown in Figure 5-15.

4. Type the text of your footnote or endnote, then click the Close button.

To view footnotes and endnotes, click the Page Layout View button to the left of the horizontal scroll bar. Footnotes appear only in Page Layout view and Print Preview, not in Normal view.

Organizing Your Report

A well-organized report should help the reader find items of interest quickly. With Word, you can easily create a table of contents, table of figures, or an index which will assist readers in finding their way around.

Creating a Table of Contents

It is extremely easy to create and update a table of contents with Word, as long as you use Heading 1, Heading 2, etc. to make your headings:

1. Place your insertion point where you want your table of contents to appear. This should probably be on a page by itself,

two lines under the a title such as "Table of Contents." (The table of contents does not create a title, so you have to do it yourself.)

2. Choose Insert, Index and Tables, then click on the Table of Contents tab. You'll see the Index and Tables dialog box shown in Figure 5-16.

3. Select a format for your table of contents. Each format will appear in the Preview window as you select it. The only other option you normally need to change is how many levels of headings to include in the table.

4. Choose OK to finish. Assuming that you have headings in your report, you will see the new table of contents in your document.

If you are using styles for your headings other than Heading 1, Heading 2, etc., choose Options from the Index and Tables dialog box, then specify which style should be associated with each table of contents level.

CAUTION: If you do not yet have entries for your table of contents, you will see a shaded field saying, "Error! No table of contents entries found." This is normal, and will be replaced by a table of contents when you update the table after entering headings.

Figure 5-16.
Word will automatically create a table of contents from your section headings if you use the Heading styles

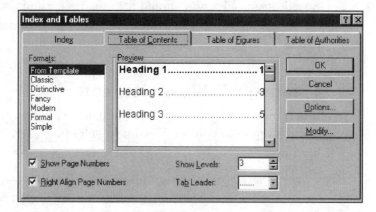

Making Tables of Figures and Lists of Tables

If you have added captions to your figures or tables, you can easily make tables of figures or lists of tables that will assist the reader to find the data they need.

To make such a table or list, follow this procedure:

1. Place your insertion point where you want your table to appear.
2. Choose Insert, Index and Tables, then click on the Table of Figures tab. You'll see the Index and Tables dialog box shown in Figure 5-17.
3. Determine whether you wish to see a list of figures, tables, or equations, and choose the appropriate option from the Caption Label list.
4. Select a format for your table of figures. Each format will appear in the Preview window as you select it. You will not normally need to change any other options in this dialog box.
5. Choose OK to finish. Assuming that you have figures or tables in your report, you will see the new table in your document.

Indexing Your Document

Sometimes your report is so long or complex that it helps to include an index at the back. This allows the reader to find key concepts quickly, even if the concept is not mentioned specifically in the table of contents. Fortunately, Word makes adding an index very easy.

Adding figures and captions is discussed in Chapter 24.

Figure 5-17. Word will automatically create a table of figures from your figure captions

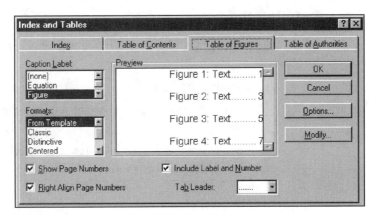

The strategy for building an index is a four-step process, as detailed in the following sections:

1. Create a list of words to be included in the index, called an AutoMark file (this step is optional).
2. Define the index.
3. Mark the entries.
4. Update the index, just as you would update tables and lists.

Building an AutoMark File

An AutoMark file is simply a list of words that you want to make sure are included in your index. This file is saved separately from your document and is checked when the index is created. Any word on the list that is in your document will automatically be included in your index; you don't have to remember to mark words in your AutoMark file individually.

This can be especially helpful if you have a list of names or terms that you always want to include in the index of documents that you create, since you can use the same AutoMark file when you index different documents.

To build an AutoMark file, do the following:

1. Create a new, blank Word document.
2. Type in all words or phrases you wish to include in your index, putting one entry on each line. Figure 5-18 shows an example of an AutoMark file.
3. Save the document.

Defining the Index

Defining an index is similar to defining a table of contents. Do so as follows:

1. Create an AutoMark file, if you are going to use one.
2. Place your insertion point where you want your index to appear.
3. Choose Insert, Index and Tables, then click on the Index tab. You'll see the Index and Tables dialog box shown in Figure 5-19.

Figure 5-18.
An AutoMark file lists all words you want to make sure are included in your index

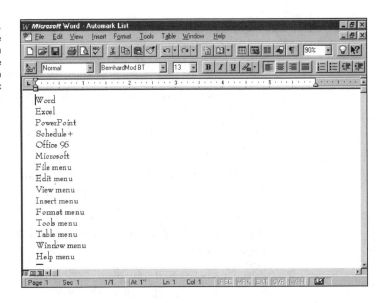

4. Select a format for your index. If you are using an AutoMark file, choose AutoMark, then choose the appropriate file from the Open Index AutoMark File dialog box.

5. Click OK to finish. Assuming that you have index entries in your report, you will see the index in your document.

Marking Index Items

The third step of index creation is marking entries in the text of your document. Even if you have an AutoMark file, you will want to mark

Figure 5-19.
Word will automatically create an index from words you select or a concordance file you create

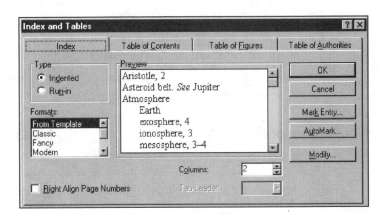

terms that should be included in your index but do not appear in your AutoMark file. To mark entries:

1. Select the word or phrase you want to include in the index.

2. Choose Insert, Index and Tables, then click on the Mark Entry button. You'll see the Mark Index Entry dialog box. The word you selected will be in the Main Entry text box, as shown in Figure 5-20.

3. To mark the selection, choose Mark. To mark every occurrence of the selection, choose Mark All.

4. After choosing Mark or Mark All, the Mark Index Entry dialog box remains open. If you are finished marking entries, choose Cancel.

5. Alternatively, to mark further entries, move the dialog box to the side of the screen, out of the way.

6. Select an additional entry in your document, then click in the Mark Index Entry dialog box. The entry appears in the Main Entry text box.

7. Choose Mark or Mark All as required, then choose Cancel or continue marking entries by repeating steps 6 and 7.

Figure 5-20.
Choosing Mark All marks every occurrence of the selected word or phrase

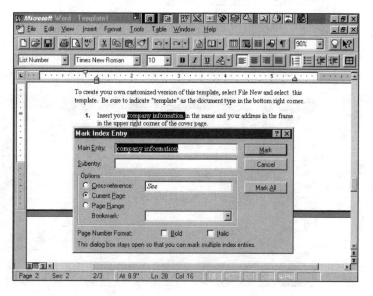

What's the Best Way to Mark Index Entries?

- If you want a single occurrence of a word to be included, mark it as an individual entry. This is seldom preferable. Usually if you want to index a term like "cognitive dissonance," you will want the reader to know every page it appears on, not just one of the pages.

- If you want the index to list every page where a term appears, you will want to mark all occurrences rather than mark a single occurrence. Marking all occurrences is an easy procedure, but has its drawbacks. If you modify the document in the future, new occurrences will not be included in the index.

- Creating an AutoMark file takes a few more steps than marking all occurrences. Including a term in your AutoMark file ensures that every page the term is on will be included in the index, even if you edit the document in the future. Moreover, once you create an AutoMark file, it can be used to index other documents, since it is merely a list of words that should be included in an index only if they appear in the document.

TIP: Choosing Mark All will only mark occurrences that match the same capitalization as the selection. Be careful about words that might occur at the beginning of sentences. For instance, consider the following sentence: "Utilitarianism began in the 1700s with John Stuart Mill." If you select "Utilitarianism" and specify Mark All, only those occurrences of the word with a capital *U* will be marked.

Updating Tables, Lists, and Indexes

Tables, lists, and indexes are actually Word *fields*. A field is a value that Word calculates internally. Some other fields that Word uses are date fields and total number of pages fields. Tables, lists, and indexes, like other fields, can be updated at any time by placing your insertion

Figure 5-21.
You can update the
table of contents at
any time to reflect
new page numbers
or new report
sections

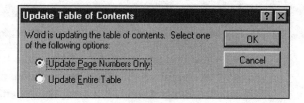

point anywhere in the table or list. Notice that the entire list becomes shaded when you do this. Press the Update Selected Field key, F9 . If you are in an index, the index will be rebuilt and you are done. Alternatively, if you are in a table of contents or figures, Word will need to know if you want to update page numbers only, or look for new headings to be included in the table. You will see an Update Table of Contents dialog box like the one shown in Figure 5-21.

TIP: If you create a table of contents entry in your report template, you can update it when you are finished writing the report; you won't need to do anything else to include the table of contents in the report.

Assuming you are in a table of contents or table of figures, you will normally wish to update the entire table to ensure that any new headings are included. Make your selection accordingly, then click OK to see the updated table. However, if you have changed the formatting or appearance of your table, you can retain these changes only by updating page numbers rather than the entire table.

TIP: You can update all fields in your document at once. Select all text in the document by triple-clicking in the left margin, then pressing F9 .

CHAPTER 6

LETTING WORD IMPROVE YOUR WRITING

IN THIS CHAPTER

- Formatting Documents Automatically
- Organizing Your Thoughts
- Writing Efficiently with the Help of Shortcut Keys
- Making Spell Checking Painless
- Finding Just the Right Word
- Checking Your Grammar

As PCs have become common in offices, professional and technical personnel are increasingly doing without the assistance of secretaries or "administrative support staff." In addition, more people are entering the workforce with existing word-processing skills.

As a result of these trends, it is increasingly common for people to compose documents with a word processor, rather than with pencil and paper. If you are creating documents, Word has a variety of tools that can assist you with document composition.

But don't fall into the trap that computers are just fancy word processors; by letting you concentrate more on writing better, they indirectly become thinking tools, too. Writing effectively on the computer really does require that you use your computer as a thinking tool. Word does this in three ways:

- Worrying about formatting details for you
- Helping you keep your thoughts organized
- Acting as an electronic editor for you

Formatting Documents Automatically

Word has two features that allow you to forget about formatting and concentrate on your writing: AutoFormat and Shrink to Fit.

Letting Word Do the Work with AutoFormat

Word's AutoFormat feature automatically formats your documents. This gives you the freedom to concentrate on what you are writing, rather than how it looks. The easiest way to use AutoFormat is while you type. However, if you are editing someone else's work, you'll have to run AutoFormat on the finished document.

Set AutoFormat options as follows:

1. Choose Tools, Options.
2. Select the AutoFormat tab. You will see the AutoFormat options shown in Figure 6-1.
3. Set options as described below, then click OK.

From the AutoFormat tab, you can choose Show Options For: AutoFormat, or AutoFormat As You Type. You will see slightly different options for each. Options you will see for AutoFormat As You Type include the following:

- Headings: When you type a short line that starts with a capital letter, has no punctuation, and is followed by pressing the (Enter) key twice, it will be transformed into a heading.

- Borders: If you type three or more hyphens, underscores, or equal signs alone on a line, and follow this by pressing (Enter) twice, it will be transformed into a thin, thick, or double line, respectively.

- Automatic Numbered Lists: When you type **1.**, **(1)**, **1)**, or **1-** and then a space or tab, Word will consider this the beginning of a numbered list. When you press (Enter), the next number will appear automatically. You can end the numbered list by pressing (Enter) twice.

- Automatic Bulleted Lists: Type an asterisk, hyphen, or the letter o (*, -, **o**) at the beginning of a line, followed by a space or tab, and Word will consider this the beginning of a bulleted list. When you press (Enter), this character will be replaced by a bullet, and another bullet will appear at the beginning of the line you're typing. End the bulleted list formatting by pressing (Enter) twice.

- Quotes: When you type ", Word will change it to the " character if you are at the beginning of a word, and the " character if

Figure 6-1.
The AutoFormat feature puts a variety of formatting into your document while you type. Its "IntelliSense" technology recognizes headings and bulleted and numbered lists, and automatically inserts the appropriate codes.

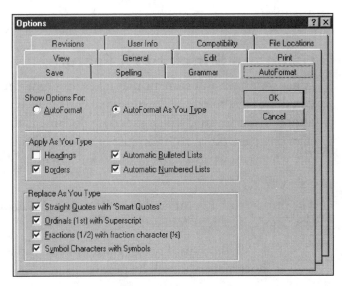

you are the end of a word. Similarly, typing ' will produce
' or '.

- Fractions: When you type a fraction such as "1/2," it will be
  converted into the appropriate special character, i.e., ½.

- Ordinals: Ranks such as "2nd" will be replaced by superscript
  characters, e.g., 2nd.

- Symbols: When you type abbreviations such as ":)", they will
  be replaced by the appropriate symbol, e.g., ☺.

If you use AutoFormat on an existing document, the options will be
slightly different. You will not have the borders option, but you will
have two new options:

- Lists: If you use special styles for your lists, Word will convert
  numbers to the numbering style you are using.

- Other paragraphs: Word converts paragraphs of text to the
  Body Text style. It is even intelligent enough to find the
  address block of a letter, closing, and signature line and
  convert them to the appropriate styles.

> The use of styles is discussed in Chapter 4.

After you've set your AutoFormat options, try them out. In a new
blank document, type **This is a Heading** and press Enter twice. Notice
that the line becomes bold and large. At the beginning of a line, type
1. This is my first point then press Enter once. Notice that the next
line starts with a 2. If you press Enter a second time, the number 2
disappears.

Using the Shrink to Fit Feature

When you have a document that takes up slightly more than a page,
you don't have to edit it down to make it fit. Instead, you can use the
Shrink to Fit feature, which shrinks a document that is slightly more
than one page down to fit on just one page. This is useful, for example, when you write a letter where your signature block extends to the
next page.

The Shrink to Fit command is available when you are in the Print Preview mode. Use it as follows:

1. Click the Print Preview button. This displays your
   document as it will be printed.

When Should You Use AutoFormat?

Consider the following criteria:

- **Choose AutoFormat features that you would like to use all the time. For instance, I always use numbered lists, ordinals, and fractions because there are no types of documents I create where I would not want these turned on.**

- **Similarly, see if there are any features you never want to use. For instance, I dislike the "smiley face" symbol, and there are no other symbols Word uses that I like, so I turn off the feature that replaces certain character combinations with special symbols.**

- **Sometimes it's better to use other shortcuts besides AutoFormat. I use different heading levels in my documents, so I use Word's built-in Heading 1 and Heading 2 styles. Having Word replace short lines with a Heading 1 style is inconvenient for me. Instead, I create shortcut keys for applying frequently used styles.**

- **Determine a time and a place for AutoFormat features. In most of my documents, I use a standard bullet character. Thus, I usually keep AutoFormat turned on. However, in proposals and reports, I use special bullets to enhance the document's appearance. I turn off the Bulleted List AutoFormat feature for these documents. Remember that AutoFormat options are defaults that do not change depending on which template you are using. You must**

Creating Shortcut Keys is discussed in Chapter 4.

2. Click the Multiple Pages button, if needed, so that you can see several pages of your document, as shown in Figure 6-2.

3. If your document extends slightly over a page, reduce it by clicking the Shrink To Fit button, as shown in Figure 6-3.

Figure 6-2.
The Multiple Pages mode within Print Preview allows you to see how your document will look, and whether you should reduce it using Shrink To Fit

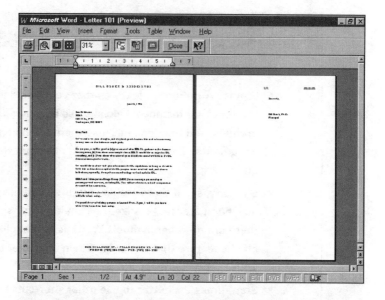

Figure 6-3.
Using Shrink To Fit allows you to shrink a document that extends just barely beyond one page

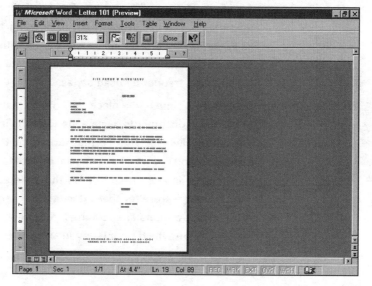

Organizing Your Thoughts

When I was in high school, I was taught to outline my papers before I wrote them. Did I ever hate doing that! Like many schoolchildren, I eventually just wrote my papers, then wrote the outline after the fact.

My writing skills have improved somewhat since my high school days, and I find myself using outlines more and more often to organize my thoughts. Outlines ensure that I don't forget any important points. They help me see the flow of my writing, and show me when I digress from my argument.

Word's Outline view makes it easy and fun to use outlines to organize your work. When you display your document in Outline view, you have the option of just showing your document headings (i.e., the outline of your document), the text for one specific section, or the entire text. In other words, you can see the outline at any desired level of detail. This helps you keep the organization of the document in mind as you write. Even better, you can easily select a chunk of text that pertains to a specific topic (an *outline family*) and move it elsewhere.

To organize your thoughts using the Outline view, you need to be able to do five things:

- Switch to the Outline view
- Create and edit outline text
- Move outline text
- Promote and demote text to different levels
- Show or hide text

Switching to the Outline View

You can switch to the Outline view as follows:

1. Click the Outline View button to the left of the horizontal scroll bar. You'll see your document without much of its current formatting. It shows its heading levels on the left, and has an Outlining Toolbar at the top, as shown in Figure 6-4.

2. To switch to another view, click the Normal View or the Page Layout View button at the bottom of the screen. You can switch back and forth between the Page Layout and Outline views to see how your document will look in final format.

Creating and Editing Outline Text

By default, the first paragraph of text you create in a new document in Outline view will be formatted in the Heading 1 style. You'll see "Heading 1" in the Style box in the Formatting toolbar.

Ten Steps to Improving Your Writing with Outlines

Here's how you can put Word's Outline view to good use in organizing your thoughts:

1. Turn on the Outline view.

2. Write down scraps of thought about your subject, in whatever order they occur to you.

3. As you're writing down these scraps of thoughts, think about a sentence that encapsulates the main point you're trying to make. Write this down at the top of your document.

4. Look over your thoughts and measure them against the central point you are making. Move points that are interesting but don't really fit your topic to another "scrap" document. You might use them later.

5. Figure out which of your thoughts are central points and which ones provide supporting arguments. Move the supporting thoughts below the points they relate to and demote them so that you start forming an outline.

6. Group miscellaneous thoughts at the bottom of the document and decide whether they fit into new main points, can fit into existing points, or should be moved to your scrap document.

7. Think about the order your main points should take. Move families of points (i.e., each point and its evidence) as needed.

8. Start filling in the text of your points and subpoints. Feel free to start anywhere, and jump from point to point as the mood strikes you.

9. When you have a new thought, put it at the bottom of your document immediately.

10. When you finish sections of text, collapse the outline to refresh your mind about the big picture, then expand the outline and reread the text section. Did it accomplish the task it was meant for?

The Heading 1 paragraphs are the first level of your outline. Heading 2 corresponds with outline level 2, etc. All styles, aside from Headings 1–8, are considered text rather than outline levels.

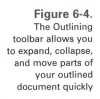

Figure 6-4.
The Outlining
toolbar allows you
to expand, collapse,
and move parts of
your outlined
document quickly

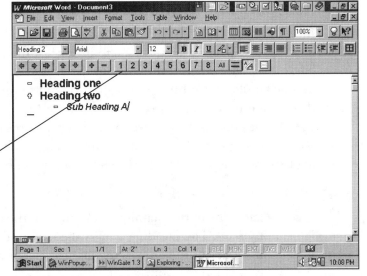

Outlining
Toolbar

Styles are
discussed
further in
Chapter 4.

To enter your outline items, do the following:

1. Switch to the Outline view.

2. Type the points of your outline, pressing Enter after each one. Each new paragraph will retain the outline level of the preceding paragraph.

3. Press the Tab key to demote a point to a "sub-point"—a level-2 heading. Each time you press Enter your next point will also be a level-2 heading.

4. Press the Tab key again to demote the point to a level-3 heading, or press Shift + Tab to promote it back to a level-1 heading. As long as you are in a heading, Tab and Shift + Tab will demote and promote your points, respectively.

5. Change any heading to text by clicking the Demote to Body Text button.

6. You can also change body text to a heading by clicking the Promote or Demote button, depending on whether the new heading should be at the same level as the last heading or a level below it.

TIP: You can also use the Promote and Demote buttons to change a heading to a higher or lower level.

Reorganizing Outline Families

An *outline family* consists of the selected heading, along with all headings and text that are subordinate to it. One of the more helpful capabilities you have when using the Outline view is the ability to move outline families from one spot to another, and to promote and demote them as a unit. For instance, you might have a sub-topic consisting of a level-2 heading and four level-3 headings underneath it, all with the accompanying text. If you promote the entire family, the level-2 heading becomes a level 1, and the level-3 headings all become level 2.

To move an outline family, follow these steps:

1. Select the outline family by clicking on the appropriate Heading Icon. The Heading Icon is the icon to the left of the heading. The entire family is highlighted, as shown in Figure 6-5.

2. To move the outline family, drag the heading icon up or down. As you drag, a light gray arrow and line shows you where the outline family will be inserted when you release the mouse button.

3. To promote or demote an outline family, drag the icon left or right. The outline level for each heading in the outline family is changed. Body text, however, remains the same.

Figure 6-5.
You can move, promote, or demote an entire outline family by clicking on the icon to the left of the family's heading

Heading icon

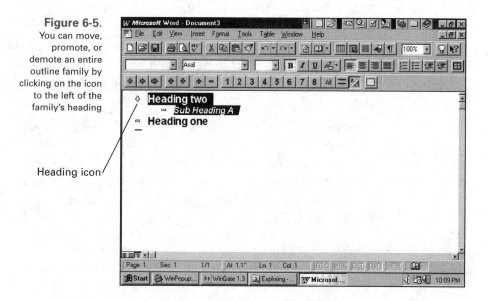

TIP: If you are writing highly structured text where every section needs to have identical subsections, or every point needs three pieces of evidence, copy the required outline points (e.g., Evidence 1, Evidence 2, Evidence 3) from the first point to all others.

PART II   WORD

Showing and Hiding Outline Text

To show the first outline level only (i.e., paragraphs with the Heading 1 style) click the Show Heading 1 button. To see more of the outline, click Show Heading 2, or show the entire outline by clicking Show Heading 8. In all cases, body text will be hidden, and the only thing visible will be the chosen headings. To view the body text, click the Show All button.

[1]

You may wish to show only the full text for the section on which you are working, and keep the text for all other sections hidden. This can help you keep an overview of your document in mind while you work on a particular section in detail, as shown in Figure 6-6.

Do so as follows:

1. Click the Show Heading 1 button to show just the level-1 headings in your document.

Figure 6-6.
You can expand the section you are working on, keeping others collapsed, to help you keep your thoughts organized

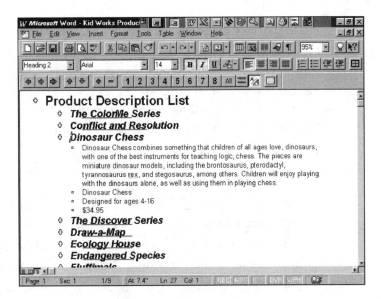

2. Click on the heading of the section you're going to work on in detail.

3. Click the Expand button. You'll see all the subheadings appear under this level-1 heading.

4. Click on any desired level-2 heading, then click the Expand button to see that heading's family.

5. Continue to select each appropriate subheading and click the Expand button until the body text for each section finally appears.

6. You can also contract an outline family by placing your insertion point on its heading, then repeatedly clicking the Collapse button until the desired condensed view is obtained.

Writing Efficiently with the Help of Shortcut Keys

When you are writing, your hands are usually on the keyboard. Thus, it can save you time and effort if you invest some time in creating keyboard shortcuts for things you do often. Some of the best candidates for shortcut keys are styles and commands that use awkward key combinations.

Assigning Styles to Shortcut Keys

One of the best ways to save time when writing is to assign styles to shortcut keys. For instance, I always assign Heading 1, Heading 2, and Heading 3, to Ctrl+1, Ctrl+2, Ctrl+3. That way, no matter what formatting is assigned to the headings in that particular document, I can always insert them with the same keystrokes.

You can assign a style to a shortcut key as follows:

1. Choose Format, Style.

2. In the Styles dialog box, select the style to which you wish to assign a shortcut key, then choose Modify.

3. From the Modify Style dialog box, click on Shortcut Key. You'll see the Customize dialog box shown in Figure 6-7.

4. Press the keystroke combination you wish to use for your

Seven Steps to Avoid

Continually reaching for your mouse when you're typing can mean a lot of wasted motion. For instance, to choose a style from the toolbar, you must do the following:

1. **Look at the mouse (unless you're proficient at groping for it blindly).**
2. **Reach for the mouse.**
3. **Look at the screen.**
4. **Move the mouse pointer to the Style button, then click on the appropriate style.**
5. **Look at the keyboard (unless you're an expert typist).**
6. **Reposition your hands on the keyboard.**
7. **Look at the screen again and begin typing in the new style you've just chosen.**

When you look at it this way, there's an awful lot of wasted time and motion in using the mouse, since your hands were already on the keyboard. One of the best office solutions for saving time can be expressed as follows:

Use the keyboard if your hands are on the keys. Use the mouse if your hands are on the mouse.

shortcut key. For example, for Heading 1 you might press Ctrl + 1. You will see the current assignment for the shortcut key you have pressed.

5. If you would like to assign that keystroke combination to the selected style and remove any current assignment, choose Assign. If you would like to choose another keystroke combination, press the alternate combination, then choose Assign.

6. When you are finished, choose Close to return to the Modify Style dialog box, then click on OK to go to the list of styles. Now you can click on Close to return to the main editing window, or assign a shortcut key to another style by repeating steps 2 through 6.

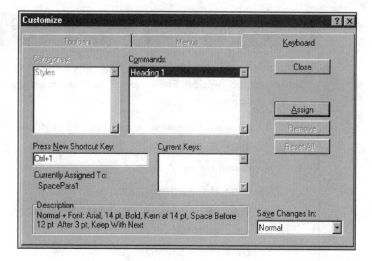

TIP: Good candidates for shortcut keys include the heading styles, the normal or body text style, and a quotation style.

Assigning Word Commands to Shortcut Keys

You can save time by creating shortcut keys for common Word commands that are cumbersome to activate. For example, suppose you often reconsider the word you've just typed. You can erase it inefficiently by pressing the (Backspace) key repeatedly or trying the rather awkward (Ctrl) + (Backspace) combination—since it's very hard to reach the (Backspace) key while touch-typing. Alternatively, you can assign a convenient keystroke combination like (Ctrl) + (W) to erase the previous Word command.

CAUTION: Be careful that you don't accidentally erase a (Ctrl)-key combination that is already programmed into Word when you create new shortcut keys.

To give a Word command a shortcut key, do the following:

1. Choose Tools, Customize. You'll see the Customize dialog box. Select the Keyboard tab if necessary.

2. Choose All Commands from the Categories list box to see all the Word commands listed in the Commands list box.

3. Select the command for which you wish to create a shortcut key. In our example, you might click on DeleteBackWord.

4. Click in the Press New Shortcut Key text box and press the keystroke combination you would like to assign to this command. For instance, you might press Ctrl + W, as is shown in Figure 6-8.

5. The dialog box will show you the current key assignment. Check to make sure that you can safely reassign the key, then click Assign to complete the key assignment.

6. Now you can assign keys to other Word commands if you like, or choose Close to return to the main editing window.

TIP: If you make extensive use of shortcut keys, you may wish to obtain a keyboard that has the Ctrl key to the left of the A, so you can easily use Ctrl combinations while touch-typing.

Figure 6-8.
You can assign shortcut keys to cumbersome Word commands

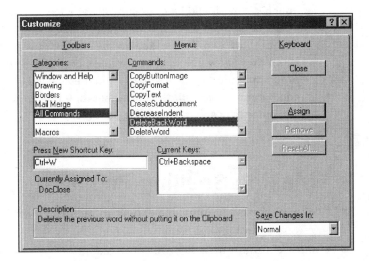

Save Time with an Editing Keyboard

Constructing a custom editing keyboard can cut 25 percent off your editing time because it reduces the movements required to reposition your insertion point.

Almost every editing task involves moving your insertion point. Although you may not realize it, there are six motions involved in moving the insertion point with the mouse:

1. Look from the screen to locate the mouse.
2. Move your hand to the mouse.
3. Look at the screen again.
4. Use the mouse to move the insertion point.
5. Look back at the keyboard to locate home base.
6. Move your hand back to the keyboard.

Using the keyboard arrows requires exactly the same number of motions. If you can move your insertion point by touch typing, you can reduce the number of motions from six to one:

- Use the keyboard to move the insertion point.

The key assignments shown in Table 6-1 are based on the Cursor Control Diamond made popular by WordStar. In addition to having keys for moving the insertion point, there are keys to delete a word or character, and keys to invoke the popular headings.

Your Ctrl key should be in as convenient a location as possible. Many newer computers place the infrequently used Caps Lock key to the left of the A key, and the Ctrl key on the bottom row. Many of these computers allow you to reassign these keys using the CMOS Setup program upon startup. If you're a more advanced (and brave) computer user, consult the documentation that comes with your computer to see whether this is possible.

Making Spelling Painless

One of the most enjoyable things about writing with Microsoft Word 7 is how effortless spelling has become. As you type, many of your most common mistakes are corrected automatically, without any intervention on your part. This is Word's AutoCorrect feature. When Word

Table 6-1. Keyboard Assignments

Key	Assignment
Ctrl + A	Word left
Ctrl + S	Character left
Ctrl + D	Character right
Ctrl + F	Word right
Ctrl + E	Line up
Ctrl + R	Screen up
Ctrl + X	Line down
Ctrl + C	Screen down
Ctrl + T	Delete word
Ctrl + G	Delete character
Ctrl + 1	Level 1 heading
Ctrl + 2	Level 2 heading
Ctrl + 3	Level 3 heading
Ctrl + L	Line numbering on/off
Ctrl + O	Bullets on/off
Ctrl + B	Bold*
Ctrl + I	Italic*
Ctrl + U	Underline*
Alt + C	Copy**
Alt + X	Cut**
Alt + V	Paste**

*These keystroke assignments are already made in Word by default.

**The normal keys for Copy (Ctrl + C) and Cut (Ctrl + X) are used for cursor movement; thus the keystrokes for cut, copy, and paste are transferred to Alt keys.

can't correct a misspelled word automatically (or doesn't recognize it as correctly spelled), the Automatic Spell Checking feature underlines it in red. You can then correct it immediately or go back and make all your corrections when you finish the document (via the standard spell checker) so that your train of thought isn't interrupted.

Using the AutoCorrect Feature

Word 6's AutoCorrect feature has been enhanced with increased IntelliSense technology in version 7. What this means for you is that many more words will be corrected automatically, as you type.

To turn on AutoCorrect and specify its settings, choose <u>A</u>utoCorrect from the <u>T</u>ools menu. You'll see the AutoCorrect dialog box shown in Figure 6-9. AutoCorrect can make the following corrections:

- If a word starts with two capitals, the second one is changed to lowercase.
- If a sentence starts with a lowercase letter, it is changed to uppercase.
- Names of days (such as Tuesday) are automatically capitalized.
- If you have accidentally turned the Caps Lock key on, Word corrects the error and turns the key off automatically. (Word detects this by looking for a sentence that starts with a lower-case letter and continues with uppercase letters. Thus, "wHEN IN THE COURSE" is changed to "When in the course".)
- If you make any of several hundred common misspellings, they'll be corrected immediately after you've typed them. For instance, "hte" is automatically replaced with "the."

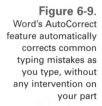

Figure 6-9.
Word's AutoCorrect feature automatically corrects common typing mistakes as you type, without any intervention on your part

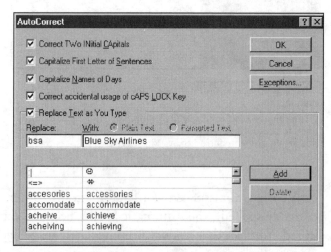

Automatic Spell Checking

Word's Spell Checker has revolutionized spell-as-you-go writing with the addition of Automatic Spell Checking. When Automatic Spell Checking is turned on, Word checks each word against its dictionaries as soon as you press the [Spacebar] after typing the word. Automatic Spell Checking is turned on by default when you first install Word. If it isn't on now, you can turn it on by following these steps:

1. Select Tools, Options; then click the Spelling tab. You'll see the Spelling dialog box shown in Figure 6-10.

2. If you prefer not to see the red wavy lines under spelling errors that cannot be corrected, check Hide Spelling Errors in Current Document.

3. Click OK to return to your document.

What do you do with the red wavy lines? If you don't like to be interrupted, you can simply ignore them. When you run your spell check later, Word will jump only to each misspelled word, thus decreasing the time the spell check takes.

If you prefer to correct your spelling as you go, either correct the spelling of the word manually or right-click on it. When you right-click on a misspelled word, you'll see a pop-up box like the one shown in Figure 6-11, which allows you to select from among alter-

Figure 6-10.
You can opt to turn on Automatic Spell Checking in this dialog box

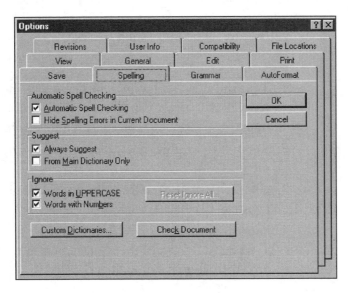

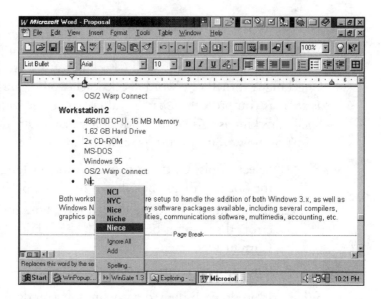

native spellings, ignore the word, or add it to the dictionary (or AutoCorrect list).

Adding Words to Your AutoCorrect List

The misspelled words that Word replaces automatically are contained in the AutoCorrect list. You can add words that you misspell often to this list. You can also add acronyms or abbreviations that you would always like to expand automatically into their full form. This can be handy if you frequently type long names.

To add an abbreviation to your AutoCorrect list, follow these steps:

1. Type the abbreviation in your document. Be sure that Word recognizes it as a misspelled word. A red wavy line will appear under it, since Word considers it a misspelled word.

2. Right-click on this "misspelled word" to bring up the pop-up menu.

3. Choose Spelling. You'll see the Spelling dialog box shown in Figure 6-12.

4. Your abbreviation is now in the Not in Dictionary text box. Type the full form of the abbreviation in the Change To text box, then choose AutoCorrect.

Figure 6-12.
The Spelling dialog box can be accessed from the pop-up menu you see when you right-click on a misspelled word

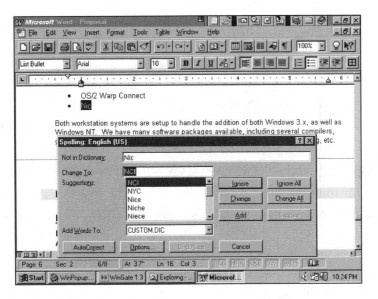

5. Depending on your setup and document, the spell checker may continue to correct misspellings in your document. If this happens, choose Cancel to return to the main editing window.

Your new abbreviation is added to the list of misspellings in Auto-Correct. To use it, type the abbreviation and press the (Spacebar). Notice that the abbreviation expands immediately to its full form.

Finding Just the Right Word

In my work as a consultant, it surprises me how seldom people use the thesaurus feature. I think that it is probably because many people don't really "think electronically" as they write. In "paper thinking," our *Roget's Thesaurus* is a book located on a shelf at the other side of the office. By the time we've fetched it and looked up the word, we've lost our train of thought entirely. In short, it's more trouble than it's worth.

When we keep our electronic tools in mind, however, we should remember that help for finding just the right word is only a keystroke away.

To use the thesaurus, follow these steps:

1. Position your insertion point in the word you wish to replace.

When Should You Use the Thesaurus Feature?

- **When you see the same noun or verb appearing on two consecutive lines, or use it repetitively throughout a page**

- **When you want a more sophisticated or polished tone to your document**

- **When you know you're close, but you really don't have the correct word**

2. Choose <u>T</u>ools, <u>T</u>hesaurus or press Shift + Ctrl. You'll see the Thesaurus dialog box shown in Figure 6-13.

3. The <u>M</u>eanings list box shows you different possible meanings of the word you are looking up. Click on the most appropriate meaning. You'll see a list of synonyms on the right.

NOTE: For some words, you will see Antonyms listed below the different meanings of the word.

Figure 6-13.
The Thesaurus dialog box offers you definitions for the selected word, along with synonyms and antonyms for each definition

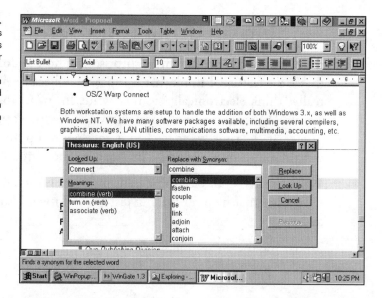

4. Replace your original word with a synonym by double-clicking on it (or clicking on the Replace button). You'll return to the main editing window and the synonym you chose will replace the original word.

5. If none of the synonyms is appropriate, select the closest one and choose Look Up. You'll see a list of synonyms for the chosen word. You can then double-click on the most appropriate synonym for this word to substitute it for the original word in the text.

Checking Your Grammar

Although it's often disconcerting, the best way to improve your writing style is to have someone edit it. That "someone" can be Word's grammar checker. This may be less ego-damaging than using a human editor, since no one sees your work but you. Personally, I find it to be a humbling experience, since the editor makes an unbelievable number of suggestions regarding my writing! Fortunately, you can set the grammar-checking options to ignore specific errors and even whole types of errors.

You should use the grammar checker after you've finished composing your document. It can double as the spell checker, since it includes a spell-checking component.

Before checking your document, you should specify the grammar-checking options to ensure that it uses the appropriate set of rules for the type of document you are writing. To set grammar-checking options, follow these steps:

1. Choose Tools, Options, then click the Grammar tab. You'll see the Options dialog box shown in Figure 6-14.

2. Choose the writing style appropriate for your document.

3. Alternatively, you can find out more about the specific rules that will be used to check your document by highlighting the appropriate style, then choosing Customize Settings. You'll see the Customize Grammar Settings dialog box shown in Figure 6-15.

4. Choose the rules you wish to use in your document, or see an explanation of a rule by choosing Explain.

Figure 6-14.
You can customize Word's grammar checker to use rules appropriate for the type of document you are creating

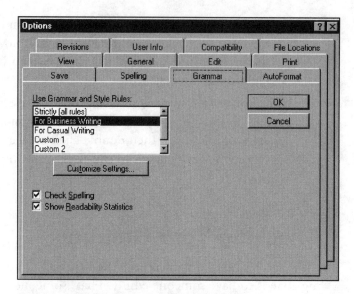

Figure 6-15.
You can see exactly which rules will be applied for the style of writing you have chosen, or choose Explain and see a full description of the rule involved

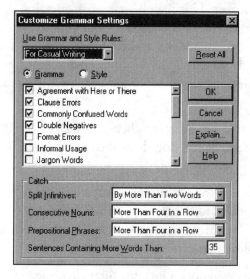

After you've customized the grammar checker, you're ready to let the "electronic editor" check your work:

1. Choose <u>T</u>ools, <u>G</u>rammar. The grammar checking starts. You'll see a word or phrase highlighted, and the Grammar dialog box shown in Figure 6-16. The buttons you see will differ depending on the type of error that is found.

Figure 6-16.
The grammar checker goes through your document phrase-by-phrase and offers suggestions for improving your writing style

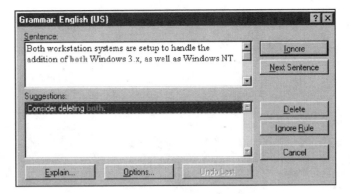

2. Choose from the following options:

   - To accept the suggestion, choose <u>C</u>hange.

   - To skip over the "mistake" one time, choose <u>I</u>gnore.

   - To skip over all other situations in which the same rule is violated, choose Ignore <u>R</u>ule.

   - To see a complete explanation of the rule in question, choose <u>E</u>xplain.

   - To go to the same Options dialog box you accessed earlier, choose <u>O</u>ptions.

3. The checking will proceed to the next questionable word or phrase. Continue with step 2 until you reach the end of the document.

You can cancel the grammar checking at any point by pressing (Esc) or by clicking the Cancel button.

CHAPTER 7

AUTOMATING YOUR CORRESPONDENCE

IN THIS CHAPTER

- Editing a Letter Template
- Automatically Addressing Correspondence
- Automating Letters with a Macro
- Producing Memos and Fax Cover Pages
- Using AutoText

Although computers are most commonly used in offices today for standard business correspondence, they are not often used productively. This chapter will teach you how to create letters, memos, and faxes efficiently. You'll also learn how to find alternative solutions for creating correspondence and choose the best solution for your situation.

Automating Letters

Automating letters can be an organization's single largest time-saver. You can automate the production of letters, memos, or faxes with Word's Wizards, or you can use or modify correspondence templates that ship with Word. Wizards are automated procedures built into Word that step you through often complex tasks in an easy manner.

Hints for Automating Letters

Individuals and small businesses have different needs than large corporations when it comes to automating correspondence.

Hints for Individuals and Small Businesses

Individuals and small businesses can create letterhead based on one of the three letter templates Word provides. They are all attractive formats that were made by professional graphic designers. Unless you're a professional designer yourself, you should build on what's provided. You'll save time and effort if you work with the tool, not against it.

Remember to keep it simple. This applies to your graphic design as well as the operations needed to accomplish a task. Generally, beginners tend to create crowded designs with too many typefaces, font sizes, and graphics.

If you really want to be fancy, use WordArt to make your name, company name, or company initials in a pretty font. If needed, use clip art as a design element.

Buy a laser or inkjet printer. Nothing looks less professional than a letterhead produced on a poor-quality printer.

Consider using color-designed paper stock (Paper Direct is a good source; call 1-800-A-PAPERS) and imprinting your letterhead onto it using a different typeface for the letterhead than for the body of your letters. You'll get a product that looks like you paid for four-color typesetting and printing. You can also get matching envelopes and blank second sheets. Have some of this on hand, but only use it for your most important letters, as it gets a little expensive.

Print your letterhead on regular paper for less important letters. If the letterhead is well-designed, it will still look very nice. Consider pur-

> See Chapter 24 for additional information on adding WordArt and clip art to your documents.

Should You Use Wizards or Modify Templates?

Wizards offer the greatest degree of automation. Unfortunately, you cannot modify the way the Wizard produces the letter, memo, or fax page. You must edit the resulting document manually.

The look of an internal memo or a fax cover sheet is usually not of paramount importance to most organizations. The letterhead, however, projects a corporate image. Thus, controlling the way it looks is very important. To automate your correspondence, you can use Wizards, use or modify an existing template, or create a new template. Which one is for you?

- The letter Wizard produces any of three preformatted letterhead styles. You can decide whether certain elements such as "cc:" and "encl:" should be inserted. However, the appearance of the letter itself cannot be customized. Further, Wizards require you to input things like your company name and your own name on every letter. You can allow the Wizard to write some standard letters for you, and it does offer the option of printing an envelope. Despite this, the letter Wizard is not much more than a toy. Don't use it for serious company correspondence.

- The three letter templates that ship with Word also require that you enter your company name and address, your name, and other items that should be standard in a letter template into each letter you create. They have no capability for importing names and addresses, nor printing envelopes.

- The memo and fax cover page Wizards allow you to create documents quickly and easily. In addition, they allow you to import names and fax numbers from your address books— which you cannot do with a template. You must, however, use one of the three styles provided. For most organizations, these will suffice. You can use the Wizard for memos and fax cover pages unless you need a particular style.

chasing window envelopes that have your return address printed on them. They are fine for most daily correspondence. For $25 or so, you can get 500 of them. This will save you the time and trouble of feeding envelopes into your laser printer.

Hints for Larger Organizations

Larger organizations should consider duplicating the firm's letterhead electronically. This is often "good enough" for 80 percent of the correspondence you send out, and can save *lots* of time in feeding letterhead into printers, unless you have a "correspondence printer."

Consider dedicating a printer as a correspondence printer. This printer should have two paper trays and a power envelope feeder. Load one tray with letterhead and one with second page bond. Be careful of the following, however:

- Don't force people to walk to the other side of the building to get to the printer. You'll lose more time and money than you save.
- Watch out for low-capacity envelope feeders. If there's no paper there, all the print jobs will stack up waiting for someone to feed it.

Some law firms have decided to use a higher quality paper in *all* their laser printers, while totally eliminating imprinted letterhead at the same time. This way they send out everything on laser-printed letterhead—but on the higher quality paper.

In keeping with the automation principle that says "work with the tool, not against it," seriously consider reworking your letterhead, if it cannot be reproduced on a laser printer. For instance, your laser-printed letterhead can include a scanned image, but it should be a logo that scans and prints well. If your current letterhead uses a font that isn't available at your desktop, consider changing the font rather than bemoaning how incapable your computer is. Finally, think about whether you really need to have your letterhead in blue (or some other color) rather than in the standard black that your laser printer can produce.

If you do decide to rethink your letterhead, get professional assistance. Solicit the services of a graphic design specialist who is well versed in working with computers.

Editing a Letter Template

Once you've decided on the look of your letterhead, you're ready to create or edit a template to help you create it automatically. A good letter template should enable you to do several things:

- Print your company letterhead
- Print your signature block
- Select the recipient name and address from a list
- Select different paper for the first and succeeding pages
- Create a second page header with the recipient's name on it

In the following sections, you'll learn to do all five of these automated tasks.

Printing Your Company Letterhead

The simplest way to create a template for your correspondence is to build on an existing Word letter template.

Hands On: Creating Your Own Letterhead

1. Choose File, New, then click Template in the Create New area. You'll see the template folder.
2. Click the Letters & Faxes tab to see the existing letter templates.
3. Click once on each in turn and look at the preview of each template in the preview window, as shown in Figure 7-1.

Figure 7-1.
You can preview existing letter templates to decide which one to use as a basis for your own letterhead

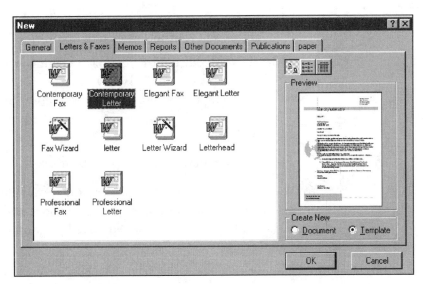

4. Double-click on the Contemporary Letter to open the template.

5. Save your new template by clicking the Save button. Double-click the Letters & Faxes folder in the Save dialog box so that the template will be saved with other letter templates.

6. In the File Name text box, type **Letter** and click Save.

7. Press F11 to move to the first field: "Click Here and Type Return Address." Type your return address. It will replace the field prompt.

8. Select the line that says "Company Name Here" and type your own name or your company's name, replacing the highlighted text.

9. Select the line that says "Click **here** and type your name" and type your name, replacing the highlighted text.

10. Select the line that says "Click **here** and type job title" and type the rest of your signature block, replacing the highlighted text.

11. You are at the "Click Here and Type Recipient's Address field." We will not need this field, because later we'll learn to select our recipient from the address list, so press Del to remove the field. Similarly, press F11 and delete the Recipient's Name field and the envelope icon.

12. Press F11 and insert your name, then press F11 a final time and insert your job title. This completes the fields.

13. To finish editing the text of the template, delete the entire paragraph starting, "Type your letter here." Press Enter twice following the body of the letter (before "Sincerely") to make extra space. Your letter template should resemble the one shown in Figure 7-2.

14. Save the new letter template by clicking the Save button.

You've created a letter template that automatically puts your company or personal information on a letter and includes the date and signature block. If you like, try using the template by choosing File, New and selecting Letter.

Figure 7-2.
Your completed
letter template
contains all the
information about
your organization

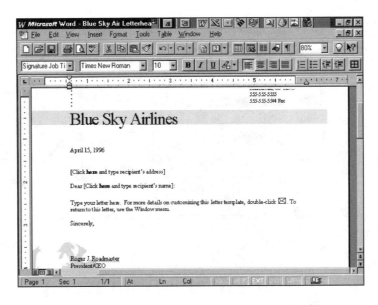

Selecting a Different Paper

This procedure is useful if you are creating a letter template to be used with preprinted letterhead, and you have a printer that uses one bin for letterhead paper and a second bin for blank paper. If you don't have access to this type of printer, you can skip this section.

To have the template automatically select different paper for the first and succeeding pages, do the following:

1. Click the Open button and choose Document Templates.

2. Navigate to the \msoffice\templates folder and double-click on the Letter template to open it.

3. Choose File, Page Setup and click on the Paper Source tab shown in Figure 7-3.

4. Choose Upper Tray for the First Page and Lower Tray for Other Pages. (Obviously, you will need to adjust this for your own paper locations.)

5. Click OK and save the template. Any letters you make using this template will automatically print out using the correct paper bins.

Figure 7-3.
You can use Page Setup
to specify a letterhead
paper for the first page
and plain paper for
following pages

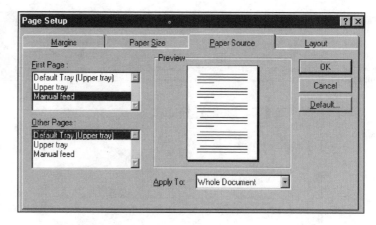

Automatically Addressing Correspondence

Looking up and typing recipients' names and addresses in letters can be a waste of time. Fortunately, Office makes this a quick and simple process. You can access your address book right from within Word and import recipients' names and addresses right into your letters.

Choosing Your Address Book

Depending on which Windows and Office applications you install, you will have a choice of address books from which to select recipient names. Each address book has advantages and disadvantages, so before discussing how to insert names and addresses, it will be useful to understand your address book choices.

If you would like to see the different address books available, click the Insert Address button. In the Select Name dialog box, click the down arrow at the right of the Show Names drop-down list box. Depending on which Windows and Office applications you have installed, you will see different address books, as shown in Figure 7-4.

Schedule+ Contact List

This address book is the contact list stored in Schedule+. If you have installed Schedule+, you will see this option. Here are some of the advantages of using this contact list:

Figure 7-4.
You can automatically insert addresses from your Schedule+ address book or Personal Contact List into your Word document

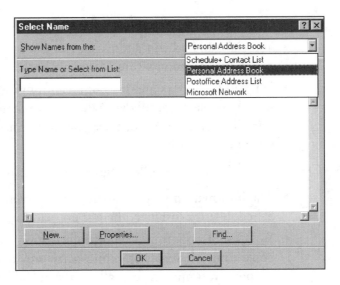

- You can maintain complete information about persons in this contact list, including business and personal information

- You can add and edit address entries from either this Word dialog box or from within Schedule+

- You can use your address book to schedule meetings, and link contacts to appointments and "to do" items

- You can import and export information in ASCII; thus, you can exchange information with Access, Excel, and other Personal Information Manager applications like ACT!, Organizer, Ascend, Contact Plus, etc.

NOTE: You cannot use names and fax numbers from the contact list to send faxes electronically via Microsoft Exchange.

Personal Address Book

This address book is the one maintained via Microsoft Exchange. If you have installed either the fax service or the mail service, you will see this option. Here are some of the advantages of using this address book:

- You can maintain business information about contacts
- You can add and edit address entries from either this Word dialog box or from within Microsoft Exchange
- You can use names and fax numbers from the address book to send faxes electronically via Microsoft Exchange as well as import them into Word; thus, you do not need to maintain separate address books

Disadvantages include the following:

- The information you maintain is not as complete as it is in Schedule+; for instance, there is no field for spouse's name
- You cannot import and export information with this address book; until Microsoft or a third party provides a utility for this purpose, you must type in all names and addresses manually

Postoffice Address List

If you have installed the Microsoft Mail service within Microsoft Exchange, you will see this option. It only maintains the names of persons in your Postoffice, enabling you to send them mail. Although it shows as an option, you can't really use it for correspondence, since it only keeps names and e-mail addresses, not mailing addresses.

The Microsoft Network

If you have installed The Microsoft Network (MSN), you will see this option. You must be connected to MSN to be able to access this address book. Its primary purpose is to enable you to send e-mail to others on MSN; it is not appropriate for use with correspondence.

To learn about using address lists within Word's Wizards, we'll insert a name and fax number into a fax cover page from the Personal Address Book and add a couple of names to the address book from within Word.

Inserting Addresses

To insert an address in a letter, follow these steps:

Open the letter and click where you want the address to appear.

> **Installing Office 95 components is detailed in Chapter 1.**

1. Click the Insert Address button. If Schedule+ and Microsoft Exchange are not currently open, you may be asked for information about them before choosing an address.

How Should You Store Your Addresses?

How you store addresses depends on your needs, and each solution entails compromises. So which should it be—the Schedule+ Contact List or the Microsoft Exchange Personal Address Book? Here are a few suggestions:

- If you intend to send many electronic faxes, you'll need to maintain the Personal Address Book
- If you want to import addresses, you can only do so in the Contact List
- If you want to link "to do" items or appointments to individuals, or if you will be scheduling meetings with Schedule+, you'll need to maintain the Contact List

Unfortunately, some office problems don't have any good solutions. Many users will need to maintain both address books, since each does things that the other doesn't. One compromise you might consider is using the Contact List for names and addresses (which you can import from other applications), and using these for letters and memos. Then you can manually type names and fax numbers in the Personal Address Book and use it for fax cover pages and electronic faxes.

NOTE: This procedure assumes that you have installed Microsoft Exchange and Schedule+. If you have not installed these components, you can skip this section.

2. If you see the Schedule+ Logon dialog box, click OK to accept your default User Name. If you see the Choose Profile dialog box, click OK to accept the default profile.

3. In the Select Name dialog box, choose the address book you want to use: Personal Address Book or Schedule+ Contact List. You'll see the list of names as shown in Figure 7-5.

4. If the name you want appears on the list, select the name and then click OK. The name and address appear in your letter, and you're done.

5. Otherwise, you will need to add the name to your address list.

Figure 7-5.
You can select a
recipient from your
Personal Address
Book or Contact List

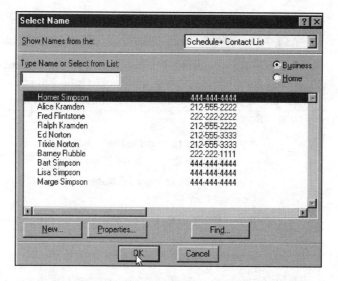

Figure 7-6.
You can add a new
entry to your
Schedule+ database
from within Word

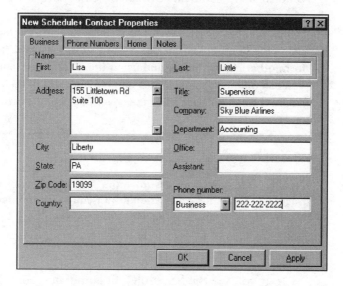

To do this, click <u>N</u>ew. If you are using Schedule+, you'll see the New Schedule+ Contact Properties dialog box shown in Figure 7-6.

6. Enter the appropriate information, then click OK.

NOTE: The procedure for adding entries to the Personal Address Book parallels the one for the Schedule+ contact list.

You can also print your envelopes easily once you've put the recipient's name and address in your letter. Choose <u>T</u>ools, <u>E</u>nvelopes and Labels. Word will insert the address from the letter and print the envelope for you.

Automating Letters with a Macro

You have begun to automate the creation of a letter: a template creates your letterhead and you insert the recipient's name and address from the address book.

You can further automate the process with a macro. A *macro* is like a tape recorder that records the keystrokes you type. Moreover, it can activate menu choices and dialog boxes. Advanced macros can even use logic to perform a variety of tasks, depending on your choices.

Hands On: Creating a Letter-Preparation Macro

You are going to create a macro that will do three things for you: start automatically when you create a letter, insert the recipient's address, and put the recipient's name in a header that starts on the second page. This latter function is particularly helpful, since this is a standard letter format that most of us usually forget to use. Incidentally, you'll learn about how macros work and are created.

1. To start creating your macro, create a new document based on the Letter template. Choose <u>F</u>ile, New and click the Letters & Faxes tab. Double-click on the Letter template.

2. Choose <u>T</u>ools, <u>M</u>acro. You'll see the Macro dialog box shown in Figure 7-7. Type **AutoNew** as the macro name and click on Rec<u>o</u>rd.

3. The Record Macro dialog box appears. Make sure that Make

NOTE: By naming the macro "AutoNew," the macro will automatically run every time you create a new document based on the Letter template.

Figure 7-7.
You can automate your letter template by creating a macro that will fill out information in the letter for you

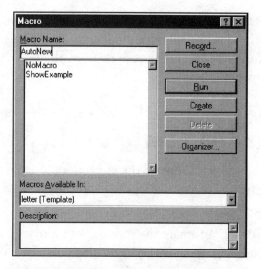

Figure 7-8.
When you record a macro, you can specify the template with which it is associated

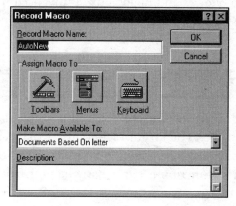

Macro Available To is set to Documents Based On Letter, as shown in Figure 7-8. Otherwise, this macro will run any time any new document is created! Click OK when you are done.

4. The floating Macro Recorder toolbar appears and the shape of the mouse pointer changes to an arrow with a small cassette, as shown in Figure 7-9. These indicate that the macro is recording. Everything you type or click will now be recorded in the AutoNew macro.

5. Make sure that your insertion point will always be at the correct spot to insert the address block by first moving to the top of the letter by pressing Ctrl + Home, then pressing ↓ until the insertion point is on the line above "Dear."

Figure 7-9.
The floating Macro Recorder toolbar indicates that you are recording a macro. You can stop recording the macro by clicking the Stop button on this toolbar.

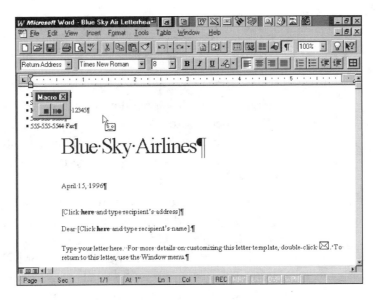

 TIP: You cannot just press ⬆ to move the insertion point, since different addresses may have varying numbers of lines in them.

6. Click the Insert Address button. Follow the prompts and insert an address of your choice from the Contact List. The specific address you insert will not be recorded in the macro, only the fact that you want to insert some address.

7. You need to select the recipient's name. Press `Ctrl`+`Home` to move to the top of the document, then press ⬇ until you get to the first line of the address.

8. Press `Home` to move to the start of the line, then `Shift`+`End` to select the entire line. Finally, Press `Ctrl`+`C` to copy the name into the clipboard.

9. To insert the copied name into a second page header, go to the end of the document by pressing `Ctrl`+`End`, then press `Ctrl`+`Enter` to create a new page. Choose View, Header and Footer. You'll see the Header and Footer toolbar.

10. Press `Shift`+`End` to select the present contents of the header, then press `Del` to delete them. Press `Ctrl`+`V` to paste the

recipient's name into the header. Move to the line underneath the recipient's name. Click the Date button on the Header and Footer toolbar to insert the date.

11. Press [Enter] to move to a new line in the header and type the word **Page** followed by a space. Click the Page Numbers button to insert the page number. Click Close to close the Header and Footer toolbar, then press [Backspace] to erase the page break.

12. To insert the person's name after the word "Dear," move to the top of the document by pressing [Ctrl]+[Home]. Choose Edit, Find and type the word **Dear**. Click Find Next, then click Cancel to close the Find dialog box. The word *Dear* is selected. Press [↓] to move after the word *Dear*. Press [Spacebar], then press [Ctrl]+[V] to insert the name again. Press [Backspace] to eliminate the extra line.

13. Your completed letter template should resemble the document in Figure 7-10. Click the Stop button on the macro toolbar to stop the macro:

Stop

Figure 7-10.
Your macro completes the letter template with sample data. These data will be replaced with actual recipient information when you run the macro.

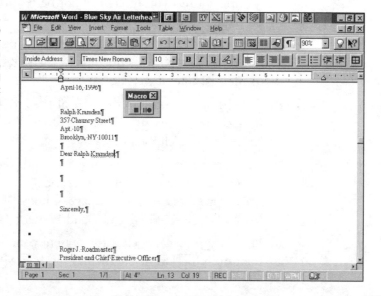

Talk about a lot of work! On the other hand, what we've done is to invest in front end time. Let's see the fruits of our labors.

Hands On: Using the Letter-Creation Macro

Use the letter template by choosing File, New then selecting Letter. Notice that you are immediately prompted for a recipient. Pick one. Notice that Word quickly builds the second page header for you and inserts the person's name in the salutation line. Everything's done for you! Go ahead and type the body of the letter.

Producing Memos and Fax Cover Pages

One of the easiest ways to save time when producing memos and fax cover pages is to use the Memo Wizard or Fax Wizard.

Using a Wizard to produce memos and fax cover pages has a major time-saving advantage—you can easily select recipients' names and fax numbers from your address book.

The alternative to automating memos and fax cover pages is to customize a template as you did for letters. The advantage of this method is that you can put your organization's letterhead on it. The disadvantage is that you need to type names and fax numbers manually. If you absolutely need to use corporate memo forms or fax cover pages, the only way you can insert names and phone numbers automatically is through custom macro programming that is well beyond the scope of this book. Using Word's memo and fax cover page Wizards solves 80 percent of the problem with 20 percent of the effort.

NOTE: The procedure above created a macro by recording keystrokes. You can also program macros using Word's macro programming language to create custom dialog boxes, IF/THEN logic, and a variety of other features.

Creating Your First Memo

To create a memo automatically, use the Memo Wizard from within Word. The first time you create a memo, you need to fill in a few pieces of personal information and indicate some personal preferences. Word remembers these for future memos.

Hands On: Creating a First Memo with the Wizard

1. Choose File, New then click on the Memos tab. You'll see the Memos icons in the New dialog box.

2. Double-click on the Memo Wizard icon. This starts the Memo Wizard. You'll see the first Memo Wizard dialog box, shown in Figure 7-11.

3. If the heading Interoffice Memo meets with your approval, select Yes, Use This Text and click Next. Otherwise, type **Memo** or other text of your choice before clicking Next. You'll see the second Wizard dialog box.

NOTE: You cannot click the New button on the toolbar. You must invoke the command from the menu to access the New dialog box.

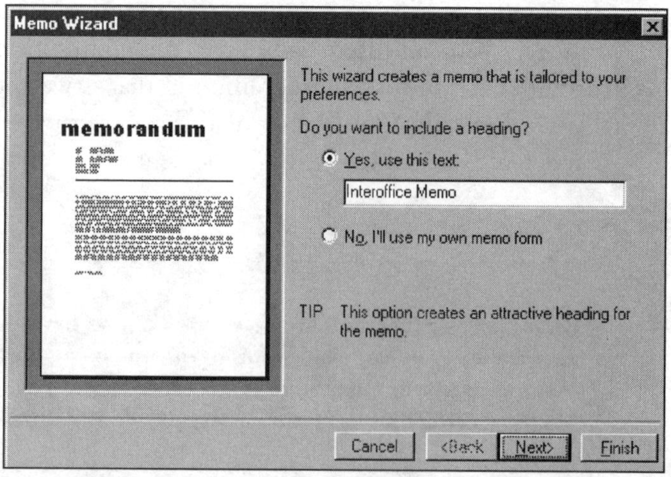

Figure 7-11.
The Memo Wizard takes you through the steps of customizing a memo that you can use for all internal correspondence

Memo Wizard

memorandum

This wizard creates a memo that is tailored to your preferences.

Do you want to include a heading?

● Yes, use this text:

Interoffice Memo

○ No, I'll use my own memo form

TIP   This option creates an attractive heading for the memo.

Cancel   <Back   Next>   Finish

4. This dialog box allows you to opt for a separate page for your distribution list. Generally, you can just click Next here, since memos don't normally use separate distribution pages. You will see the third Wizard dialog box.

5. In the third step, select the elements you want to include in your memo: e.g., Date, To, CC:, From, Subject, and Priority. You can even specify a specific date and person the memo is from.

6. The fourth and fifth steps allow you to specify other elements to include in your memo, such as writer's initials, typist's initials, enclosures, attachments, and the contents of the header and footer. Choose Next when you are finished with each step. You'll see the sixth Wizard dialog box.

7. You can choose any of the three styles for your memorandum. Try clicking on each of the three and viewing how they appear in the preview window at the left of the dialog box, as shown in Figure 7-12. When you have selected the style you prefer, click Next.

8. The final dialog box merely tells you that you are finished. Click Finish to complete the procedure. You'll see your finished memo on the screen.

9. Click in the area that says "[Click here and type names]," as shown in Figure 7-13. Notice that the entire area is selected.

Figure 7-12.
The Preview box allows you to see what each of the three preformatted memo styles looks like

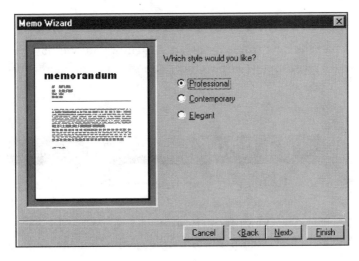

Figure 7-13.
The completed
memo has several
fields that you
must select, then
insert type to finish
your memo

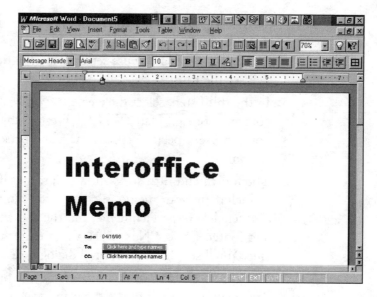

As you type, the prompt gets replaced; there's no need to delete it first.

10. Repeat the procedure for the CC:, RE:, and memo text areas. Now save, spell-check, and print your memo.

Does this seem like a lot of work? Perhaps, but what you're doing is investing time now to save time later. All the preferences you selected were remembered by Word, so the next time you want to create a memo, it will be a lot easier.

Creating Memos Quickly and Easily

The next time you create a memo, you will have made all the decisions regarding its appearance. You can use the memo Wizard quickly and easily.

Hands On: Creating Additional Memos with the Wizard

1. To create your next memo, choose File, New and click on the Memos tab.

2. Double-click on the Memo Wizard icon. This starts the Memo Wizard. You see the first Memo Wizard dialog box.

3. Click on <u>F</u>inish. You see the finished memo on your screen. Press F11 to move to fields and insert memo text.

A little easier this time? We've reduced creating a memo to three simple steps, as indicated above. Later, you'll learn how to reduce this to two steps by putting the Wizard on the toolbar.

Customizing a Fax Cover Page

This procedure assumes that you need to send your faxes via a regular fax machine rather than through your computer, because you either don't have a modem or you need to fax someone a document that's been printed out. The procedure for customizing a fax cover page is similar to that for creating a memo.

Hands On: Creating a Fax Cover Page with the Wizard

1. Choose <u>F</u>ile, <u>N</u>ew and click the Letters & Faxes tab from the New dialog box.

2. Double-click the Fax Wizard icon. You'll see the first dialog box of the Fax Wizard, shown in Figure 7-14.

3. You'll choose the look you want for your fax cover pages in the following dialog boxes. Assuming you want a portrait orientation, click <u>N</u>ext. You'll see the second dialog box.

Figure 7-14.
You customize a fax cover page by using the Fax Wizard, just like you customized a memo using the Memo Wizard

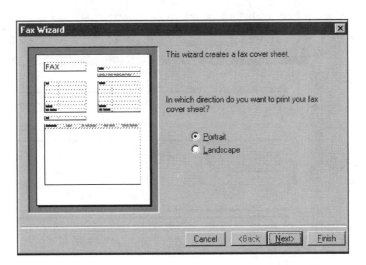

4. Click on each of the three cover page styles, then select the one you prefer. Click <u>N</u>ext when you are finished.

5. Fill in your personal information. You may find that your name and company name are already inserted from when you installed Windows and Office 95. In any case, complete your mailing address then click <u>N</u>ext.

6. Enter your phone and fax numbers and click <u>N</u>ext.

7. In the next step, enter the recipient's name, company name, and address; then click <u>N</u>ext. (You can pick these automatically from your address book just as you did with correspondence above.)

8. Enter the recipient's phone and fax numbers in the next step. Choose <u>N</u>ext.

9. The last dialog box merely informs you that you're done, so you can click <u>F</u>inish. You'll see the completed fax cover sheet on the screen, as shown in Figure 7-15.

10. Fill in any remarks at the bottom of the page and you're done!

As you might be able to guess, making your second fax cover sheet is even quicker. All the settings you chose are saved, and you can quickly go through the steps of the Wizard to produce the same type of fax cover sheet.

Figure 7-15.
The Fax Wizard makes attractive fax cover sheets for you automatically

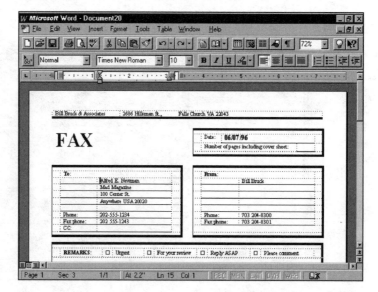

Using AutoText

Although people often don't recognize this fact, many letters use phrases, sentences, and even entire paragraphs repeatedly in letter after letter. There is nothing wrong with this, especially if you write letters repeatedly on the same topic. If you have a way of saying something that you have "wordsmithed" until it reflects you and what you're trying to say, why not use it again?

Word's AutoText feature enables you to indicate easily those phrases you often use, and provides a quick method of inserting this phrase whenever you need to use it again.

Case Study from the Pros

TST, Inc., a small business in the Washington, D.C., area, provides management training to a variety of government clients. A large number of letters are generated each month as responses to requests for information, quotations, and proposals.

In looking at their previous cover letters, a number of phrases seemed to reoccur frequently. These included:

> "TST is pleased to respond to your request for information regarding:"

> "We understand that your situation is characterized by the following critical factors:"

> "The major requirements that vendors must meet include:"

> "We have successfully provided training for new supervisors at agencies including the Department of Agriculture, NHTSA, NIH, and the Department of State."

> "We have successfully provided Senior Executive Service workshops at agencies including . . ."

> "Terms and conditions of payment include . . ."

> "Dr. Sharon Johnson will be the Project Manager for our work with _____. She has successfully managed . . ."

By making AutoText entries of these phrases and paragraphs, cover letter preparation time was cut by 35 percent and the quality of cover letters was made consistently excellent, since TST chose their best text to use in all their cover letters.

You can use Word's AutoText feature as a "glossary" function to insert often-used phrases, sentences, or paragraphs. When using AutoText, it is useful to remember a few rules about how AutoText entries are saved and when they will be available to you:

- When you create an AutoText entry, it is saved in a template
- You can choose to save an AutoText entry in the default template (Normal) or in the template on which the document is based (for instance, Letter)
- AutoText entries saved in the default template are always available to you, no matter what document you are working with
- AutoText entries saved in a specific template (Letter, for example) are available only in documents based on that template

To use AutoText entries effectively, go through existing correspondence and find files that have examples of text that you think you might use repeatedly in future correspondence. Make note of these phrases, then use the following procedure to add them to the appropriate template.

Hands On: Creating an AutoText Entry

1. Create a new letter in which you'd like to create an AutoText entry, based on the Letter template. Choose File, New; select the Letters and Faxes Tab; and double-click on the Letter template.

2. At a blank line in the letter, type your often-used text: e.g., **"Thank you for considering our firm for your training needs."**

3. Triple-click anywhere in the line to select the whole sentence.

4. Choose Edit, AutoText. You'll see the AutoText dialog box shown in Figure 7-16. Choose to make the AutoText entry available to Documents based on Letter.

NOTE: To create an AutoText entry, start from a blank document if you want to store the AutoText in Normal, or use the Letterhead template if you will want it stored in Letter.

Figure 7-16.
You can save
frequently-used
phrases or
paragraphs as
AutoText entries in
the Normal template
or the Letter template

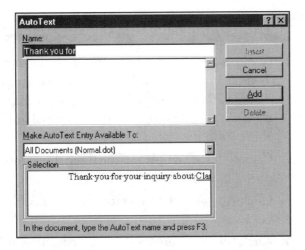

5. Type **Thanks** in the <u>N</u>ame text box and click <u>A</u>dd. Your new AutoText entry will be added to the list saved in the template you selected.

Hands On: Using Your AutoText Entry

1. Click where you want the AutoText entry to appear and type **Thanks**.

2. With your insertion point immediately after the word, press F3 . "Thanks" is replaced with "Thank you for considering our firm for your training needs."

Using an AutoText Entry from Another Template

You can use an AutoText entry from one template in a document based on another template, if you declare the first template to be a global template.

To demonstrate this technique, you can use the "Thanks" AutoText entry you just created above.

TIP: Making a template global also gives you access to shortcut keys and macros stored in the template.

Hands On: Using AutoText Entries from Other Templates

1. Create a new document in Word by clicking the New button. The document is based on the Normal template. Type **Thanks**, then press F3. Nothing happens, since the new document is based on the template Normal and the Thanks abbreviation is stored in Letter.

2. Choose File, Templates. You'll see the Templates and Add-ins dialog box shown in Figure 7-17.

3. Click Add and choose Letter from the Add Template dialog box.

4. Click OK to return to the main editing window.

5. Press F3 again. "Thanks" expands to "Thank you for considering . . ." since your document can now access AutoText entries that are in the Letter template.

Figure 7-17.
The Templates and Add-ins dialog box allows you to use AutoText entries that are stored in other templates

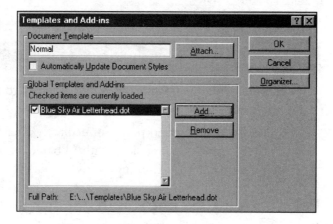

CHAPTER 8

PREPARING DOCUMENTS IN WORKGROUPS

IN THIS CHAPTER

- Preparing a Document for Group Editing
- Creating a Master Document
- Working on Subdocuments
- Consolidating the Group's Work
- Sending Out Documents for Review
- Reviewing Documents

Documents created by individuals are rapidly being replaced by products created by workgroups. These can pose a challenge to both individual workers and to managers trying to coordinate the overall project. In this chapter, you will learn how Word helps you work effectively in groups.

You will learn several ways to distribute documents within your office and with others outside it. You will learn two ways to work on long documents by giving people different "pieces" of it, and three techniques for revising group documents.

Writing Documents in Workgroups

Word provides powerful tools for you to use when you write documents with others. If you have read the previous chapters about Word in this book, you already know many of them. You'll learn some new ones here.

Writing documents in groups offers three challenges:

- Efficiently exchanging documents
- Maintaining consistency of style
- Ensuring completeness of topic coverage without overlap

To exchange documents efficiently, use Office 95's routing feature.

To maintain consistency of style, create a template that contains styles for chapter and section headings, body text, quotations, bulleted lists, or other design elements used in your office. The template might also contain customized toolbars to ensure that people can write the document easily. In addition, organization is especially important in larger documents, which you can accomplish with outlines. If the document contains a variety of files from different applications, you can store them together in a binder.

To coordinate all the documents that different people will use, and to maintain a consistent style, use Word's master document feature.

See Chapter 5 to review creating styles and templates, using outlines to organize your work, and creating tables of contents, lists of figures, and indexes. See Chapter 23 to learn more about binders.

Creating Master and Subdocuments

Edit a document in groups by using Word's master document feature. This feature allows you to create one large document (the *master document*) that can be divided into separate, smaller documents that are saved as separate files (the *subdocuments*). When you open the master document, all subdocument files are also opened and you see the document in its totality. However, people can work on subdocuments individually, since they are separate files.

The general strategy for creating master and subdocuments is to open or create a Word document as you usually do, then decide which sections of this document will be converted into subdocuments. When you create the master document, each of the subdocuments will be saved as a file of its own; thus, group members can work on them individually.

Each section of the document that you split into a separate subdocument must start with the same type of heading—e.g., the Heading 1 style. Word uses the occurrence of this style to determine where new subdocuments should start.

The only rule for converting your document into a master document is that whatever part of the document you select to convert into sub-

Hints for Using Master Documents for Group Editing

To prepare a document for group editing, use the following strategies:

1. **Have a clear idea of the purpose of the document, its intended audience and grammatical style.**

2. **Create the document based on an appropriate template; for instance, base a report upon a report template.**

3. **Use Word's outline feature to break the document into logical components—ones on which various people will work.**

4. **Refine the document's format by modifying styles as needed before breaking it into subdocuments. This way, all subdocuments will have a consistent appearance.**

5. **Create a written style guide that identifies the styles used in the document, along with any other features such as columns or tables.**

6. **If needed, add instructions for the use of graphic elements and any other embedded or linked objects, such as worksheets, to the style guide.**

7. **Build the document framework by creating elements such as the title page, table of contents, lists of figures, and index.**

8. **Convert the document into a master document and subdocuments.**

9. **Distribute subdocuments for individual group members to work on.**

documents must start with the heading you have chosen to determine where subdocuments start.

If you like, you can convert the entire document into subdocuments. In this case, the first line of the document must be in the proper heading style.

Make your master and subdocuments as follows:

1. Create the framework of the document in Outline view by clicking the Outline View button or choosing View, Outline. Use a heading such as Heading 1 for each topic assigned to the different writers. These can be chapters, sections, and the like. Figure 8-1 shows a sample document in Outline view.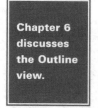

2. Choose View, Master Document. You will see the Master Document toolbar.

3. Select the text in the document containing the headings for the topics in the final document. Make sure that the first selected line is in the style that defines the following subdocuments, as shown in Figure 8-1.

4. Click the Create Subdocument button. The document divided into subdocuments is shown in Figure 8-2.

Chapter 6 discusses the Outline view.

Figure 8-1.
To convert a document into a master document, select the area that should be divided into subdocuments

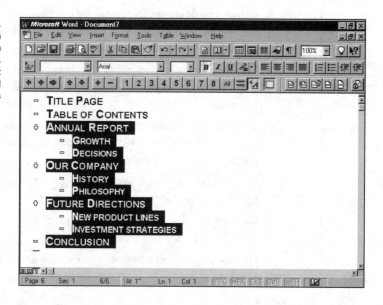

Figure 8-2.
You can divide an
outline into
subdocuments
based on the
heading styles

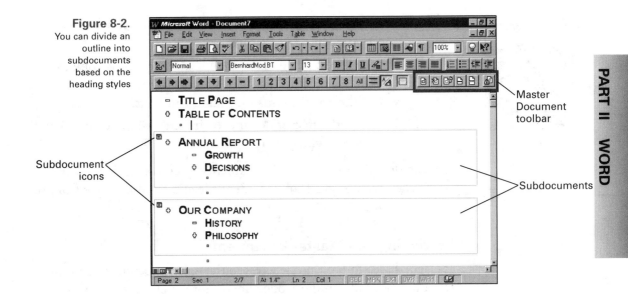

Master
Document
toolbar

Subdocument
icons

Subdocuments

5. Save the master document and give it a name. The status bar will display the filename of the document being saved, and then each subdocument being saved in turn. The subdocuments are named using the first few words of each subdocument—i.e., the heading of each subdocument.

Renaming Subdocuments

When you create subdocuments, Word names each document using the first few words of the heading at the beginning of each subdocument section. If your heading names happen to be long, Word names the document with the first few words of the heading. Before distributing the master document, you may wish to finish preparing it by renaming the subdocuments with more meaningful names.

Rename a subdocument using the Save As dialog box. When you do this, you'll actually have two versions of the subdocument—the one with the original name and the one with the new name. Delete the one with the original name to prevent confusion.

Rename subdocuments as follows:

1. Display the master document in master document view by selecting View, Master Document.

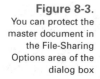

See Chapter 21 for hints on creating and naming files.

2. Open a subdocument by double-clicking the subdocument icon to the left of its first line.

3. Choose File, Save As. Give the file a name that is compatible with your file naming system, then close the document. Repeat this for the remaining subdocuments.

4. Return to the master document (from the subdocument) and save it again when you're finished.

You can delete the original subdocuments by choosing File, Open. Right-click each original subdocument file and choose Delete from the shortcut menu.

Protecting the Master Document

It's a good idea to limit users' access to the master document, allowing them to work only on the subdocuments for which they are responsible. You may protect the master document in a weak or strong way. If you use the weak method, users will see a recommendation that they open the master document in read-only mode whenever they open it. If needed, however, you can protect the master document with a password.

To protect the master document, follow these steps:

1. Open the master document, then choose File, Save As, Options. You will see the Options dialog box pictured in Figure 8-3.

Figure 8-3.
You can protect the master document in the File-Sharing Options area of the dialog box

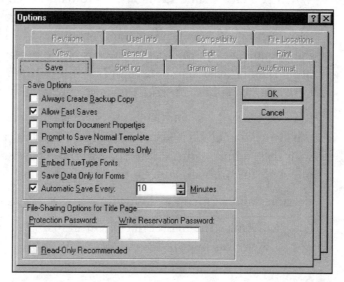

2. Check <u>R</u>ead-Only Recommended, or insert a password in the <u>P</u>rotection Password box, if desired.

3. Click OK to return to the Save As dialog box.

4. Choose <u>S</u>ave to save the master document.

Working on Subdocuments

You can open the subdocument from the master document or directly from the Open dialog box. When a project is active and many people are working on their subdocuments simultaneously, it's usually better to open the subdocument directly from the Open dialog box, so that several people aren't trying to access the master document at once. The only times you will need to work through the master document are when you wish to lock the subdocument, rename it, or delete it. In these cases, open the subdocument by double-clicking on its icon from within the master document.

> **CAUTION:** Only one person should have write-access ("gatekeeper/owner rights") to the master document. Letting many people update the master document can really cause problems.

You may wish to protect subdocuments for which you are responsible so that only you can change them, or so that when others open them, the read-only mode is recommended. You can do this by opening the subdocument and using the same procedure for protecting the subdocument as the one for protecting the master document discussed above.

The main thing you will want to remember when working on a subdocument is to use the same formatting that is used in the master document and other subdocuments. Do this by using styles: make sure the subdocument has the same styles in it that the master document has. You should know what these styles are and when to use them. It's good practice not to create new styles, nor modify existing ones. This should only be done in the master document so that any changes made there will be reflected in the subdocuments automatically.

Consolidating the Group's Work

As the group works on its individual subdocuments, you may need to make modifications in the document as a whole. In addition, you will want to print the entire document periodically, or tie parts of it together. Tasks performed in the master document include:

- Rearranging subdocuments
- Splitting a subdocument into two subdocuments
- Merging two subdocuments into one
- Merging a subdocument into the master document
- Removing a subdocument entirely from the master document
- Creating a table of contents for the entire document
- Making cross references between subdocuments
- Printing the entire document

The following sections show you how to accomplish each of these tasks.

> **NOTE:** You can view the master document in the Normal, Page Layout, or Outline views. When you switch to the Outline View, you see the additional toolbar providing options for master documents, which appears by default to the right of the Outlining toolbar.

Rearranging Subdocuments

To move a subdocument, do the following:

1. Open the master document and click the Outline View button to see the master document in Outline view.

2. Collapse the outline by clicking the button for the top level heading defining each section. For instance, if each major section is defined by a Heading 1, click the Show Heading 1 button. The master document now appears with only these headings.

3. Click on the plus sign to the left of the section to be moved. The mouse pointer changes to a four-pointed black arrow and the section becomes highlighted.

4. Drag the plus sign up or down to its new position. As you drag, the white plus sign turns black and a blue line with a black arrow appears, indicating where the section will move.

5. When you release the mouse button, the heading appears in its new location. Move additional sections or go back to the Normal view to work on the document.

Splitting a Subdocument into Two Subdocuments

Occasionally, a subdocument needs to be split into two or more sub-documents. This can be useful when more than one person is working on a single topic, or a topic grows into two or more topics. Before splitting the subdocument, it's smart to ensure that the document is backed-up by saving it with a different name or copying it to another folder.

When splitting a subdocument into two or more, each new subdocument must begin with a heading like Heading 1, and the text you select to be split must begin with this heading.

NOTE: If you have text in your master document that is not part of a subdocument, you cannot split this text into subdocuments. If you wish this text to be in a subdocument, you must select it and click the Create Subdocument button.

To split a subdocument, follow these steps:

1. Change to the Outline view, if you are not already in it, by clicking the Outline View button.

2. Select the text to be split into one or more new subdocuments, making sure that the text you select starts with the appropriate heading: e.g., Heading 1.

3. Click the Split Subdocument button. The text starting with the insertion point is split off into its own, new subdocument.

4. Save the master document. The new subdocument will be saved in its own file.

5. Rename the new subdocument, if desired, as described earlier.

Merging Two Subdocuments into One

You may occasionally wish to merge two subdocuments into one subdocument. This is often the case when the same person is working on two related, consecutive topics and prefers to work on them as one document.

Merge two subdocuments as follows:

1. Ensure that the master document is backed up by saving it with a different name or copying it to another folder.
2. Change to Outline view, if you are not already in it.
3. Move the subdocuments so that they are adjacent to each other, if necessary. Select the first subdocument by clicking its subdocument icon.
4. Hold down the (Shift) key and click the icon of the next subdocument to select it as well. The editing window should resemble Figure 8-4.
5. Click the Merge Subdocuments button. The subdocuments are merged into one.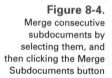
6. Save the master document. The new merged subdocument is saved with the first subdocument.
7. To prevent confusion, delete the second subdocument that was merged into the first one from the disk. Do this by right-

Figure 8-4.
Merge consecutive subdocuments by selecting them, and then clicking the Merge Subdocuments button

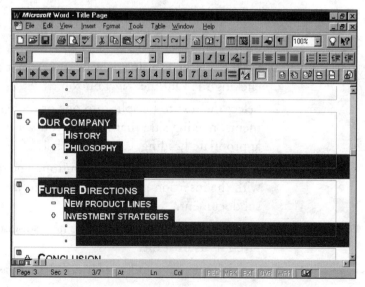

clicking on it in an Open dialog box and choosing <u>D</u>elete from the shortcut menu.

Merging a Subdocument into the Master Document

On occasion you may wish to merge a subdocument into the text of the master document itself, rather than into another subdocument. If you use Heading 1 for your subdocuments, for example, and you also use this for the Table of Contents, List of Tables, and Index pages, you will inadvertently create subdocuments for these pages, when they should be part of the master document.

> **NOTE:** Merging a subdocument into a master document is different than merging two subdocuments together.

To merge a subdocument into the master document, follow these steps:

1. Ensure that the master document is backed up by saving it with a different name or copying it to another folder.
2. Change to Outline view, if you are not already in it.
3. Select the subdocument by clicking its subdocument icon. Click the Remove Subdocument button. The sub-document icon disappears, as does the blue box surrounding the text. The text is now part of the master document.
4. Save the master document.
5. To avoid confusion, delete the subdocument from the disk.

Removing a Subdocument from the Master Document

If you decide that a certain topic should not be included in the final document at all, remove it from the master document entirely, as follows:

1. Select the subdocument by clicking its icon.
2. Press the [Del] key. The subdocument is deleted from the master document.

> **NOTE:** Removing (deleting) a subdocument from a master document is different than removing the subdocument definition box.

3. Save the master document.

4. The subdocument still exists as a separate file on the disk. To avoid confusion, delete it as well.

Printing the Master Document

To print the document, open the master document and update fields such as the Table of Contents or Index. To do this, triple-click in the left margin to select the entire document and press [F9] to update all the fields in the document.

When the fields are all updated, choose File, Print to print the file, or click the Print button. The printed master document will have the styles of the master document, even if styles have been modified in subdocuments.

Printing a document's outline—including chapter, section, and topic headings—can help collaborators see the organization of other sections, without wading through all the text. To print an outline of the document, first view the outline, then click the appropriate Show Heading button (1–8) which provides the level of outline detail you want to print. Print the document as you would normally.

Reviewing Documents in Workgroups

Once you have created a Word document, either alone or with others, you will often need to have it reviewed. This process can now be done electronically, saving time and avoiding transcribing multiple generations of hand-written comments. The electronic review process contains three steps:

1. The primary author prepares and sends the document out for review.

2. Reviewers comment on the document.

3. The primary author consolidates the comments.

Thankfully, Office 95 provides easy-to-use tools for each step of the process.

Sending Out Documents for Review

Before you send the document, you need to decide what reviewing strategy to use. In some cases, it is better to permit reviewers unrestricted access to a document. An example of this is when a memo goes up a chain of command. At other times, it is better for reviewers' changes to be marked in the document, so that each reviewer can easily see what changes others have made. Sometimes, you don't want reviewers to be able to change the document at all, but merely highlight specific areas of concern or make annotations that do not change the body of the document.

Once you have decided on your strategy, you can send the document to reviewers via a routing slip, or by placing the document in a specified network location. Routing documents is the most frequently used document-distribution method during the review process.

Routing Documents

You can route Word documents (or an Excel workbook) to reviewers so that each person gets the document, one after another. When each person finishes reviewing the document, he or she sends it to the next person on the list. You can also route it so that everyone gets it at once. This is often faster, and better when you don't wish reviewers to see what others have said (as in a blind review process for academic journals).

Route a document as follows:

1. Open the document.
2. You may set password protection options as described earlier.
3. Choose File, Add Routing Slip. The Routing Slip dialog box will appear.
4. Type any text you'd like to send with the file in the Message Text box and choose whether you wish to have it returned when it has completed its route, and whether you wish to be notified when each person finishes the document.

TIP: Use the Message Text box to specify a due date so that the document doesn't sit with one person for too long.

5. Choose the routing method: <u>O</u>ne After Another sends it to each recipient in turn. The second recipient won't see the document until after the first recipient is finished with it. A<u>l</u>l at Once sends it to all reviewers simultaneously.

6. Check Return <u>W</u>hen Done if you want the document back when the last reviewer is finished with it. This way you don't have to add yourself as the last person on the routing list.

7. Check Trac<u>k</u> Status to be notified via e-mail when each person is finished with it.

8. Select an option in the <u>P</u>rotect For drop-down list box. If you select Revisions, reviewers can revise the document, but revision marks will be turned on so that you can track additions, deletions, and moved text. If you select Annotations, reviewers cannot change the document, but can add comments to it. You can also select None if you choose not to protect the document.

9. Click the A<u>d</u>dress button. You will see the Address Book dialog box. Double-click on each person to which you wish to route the document, in order. When you are finished, click OK. You will return to the Routing Slip dialog box, as in Figure 8-5.

10. Choose <u>R</u>oute to send the document immediately or choose <u>A</u>dd Slip to store the routing information, but not send the document at this time.

Once you have made a routing slip, you can always edit it. Open the <u>F</u>ile menu to see the Edit <u>R</u>outing Slip option. Select it to reopen the Routing Slip dialog box, then click on <u>R</u>oute to send the file.

Sending Documents for Review on a Network

When the number of reviewers makes it impractical to route a document to everyone, save it in a public folder on a network so that they can read it at their convenience. In this case, you may still limit the reviewers to simply making annotations or marking revisions.

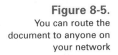

Figure 8-5.
You can route the
document to anyone on
your network

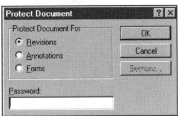

To do this:

1. Choose <u>T</u>ools, <u>P</u>rotect Document. The Protect Document
   dialog box will appear:

**Modifying
toolbars is
discussed in
Chapter 22.**

2. Choose to protect the document for revisions or annotations,
   as preferred. Since reviewers could access this dialog box and
   turn off protection, you may wish to include a password in
   the <u>P</u>assword box to protect the choices you make.

3. Choose OK when you are finished.

NOTE: You can make it easy for reviewers to accomplish
the tasks you set for them by customizing toolbars.
Consider creating a Reviewer toolbar that has tools for
Send, Highlight, Add Annotation, Add Sound Object, and
Show/Hide.

Reviewing Documents

When you're on the receiving end of a routed file, you'll receive it as an item in your In Box. Double-click on the Word document icon to open it in Word.

Depending on which permission(s) the creator has given you, you may be able to highlight the document, annotate it, or make changes in it, as described below.

After you have added your comments, you can send the document to the next person on the route by choosing File, Send. Since the document has a routing slip, you will see the Send dialog box. Choose Route Document to [Next Person] to forward the document.

Using Revision Marks

If the primary author has protected the document for revisions, revision marks will automatically be added to the document as you edit it. Inserted text is usually underlined; deleted text is struck out. Moved text appears as both inserted at its new location and deleted at its old location.

When revising a document that has been transmitted by a routing slip, revision marking may be turned on for you and you won't be able to turn it off. You can, however, change the appearance of the revision marks, or even choose not to display them if they are distracting.

TIP: Revision marks are not just for routed documents; they can be turned on at any time for any document.

To turn revision marks on or off, or to modify them:

1. Choose Tools, Revisions. The Revisions dialog box will appear:

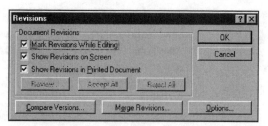

Figure 8-6.
You can change the appearance of revision marks and highlighted text in the Revisions tab of the Options dialog box

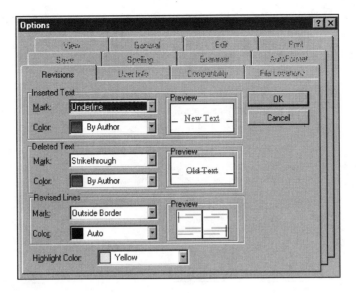

2. Choose the revision options:

   • To turn revision marking on, choose <u>M</u>ark Revisions While Editing. (This option is grayed out if the document is locked for revisions.)

   • Uncheck Show Revisions on <u>S</u>creen to turn off the display of revision marks. The revision marks are still recorded, however. You just don't see them.

   • To change the color or style of the revision marks, choose <u>O</u>ptions. This brings up the Options dialog box, as in Figure 8-6. When you are finished setting revision marking options, choose OK.

Adding Annotations

Reviewers can also add *annotations*—nonprinting comments—in a document. These are notes that other reviewers and the document author can read. You can even add a voice annotation, if your computer is equipped with a microphone and sound card.

To add an annotation:

1. Open the document.

2. Move the insertion point to the part of the document you'd like to comment on, or select all the appropriate text. If you

Figure 8-7.
Reviewers can
insert annotations
to a document that
will remain hidden
until viewed later
on-screen

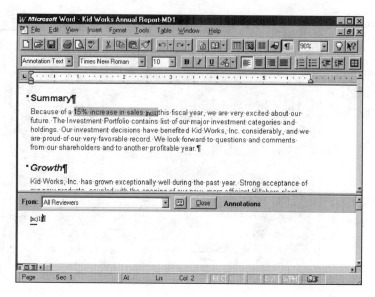

select text, the author will see this text highlighted when he or she reads your annotations.

3. Choose <u>I</u>nsert, <u>A</u>nnotation. An annotation window will appear at the bottom of the screen, as in Figure 8-7.

4. Type the text of the annotation and click <u>C</u>lose when you are finished.

TIP: To change your initials as they appear in the annotation marks, choose <u>T</u>ools, <u>O</u>ptions and click the User Info tab. The initials found in the Initials box are used for annotations.

To insert a voice annotation, do the following:

1. Insert an annotation as described above, but do not click the <u>C</u>lose button in the Annotations window.

2. Click the Insert Sound Object button to the left of the Close button. This opens the Sound Object dialog box shown in Figure 8-8.

3. Click the Record button to record a comment, or use the other buttons as you would on a regular tape recorder.

4. Close this dialog box when you are done.

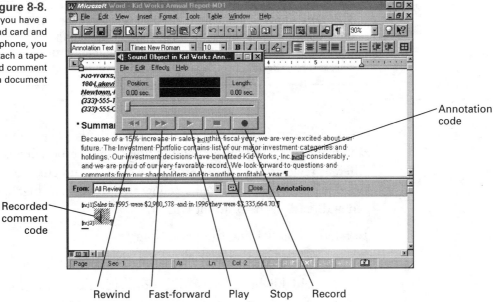

Figure 8-8.
If you have a
sound card and
microphone, you
can attach a tape-
recorded comment
to a document

Recorded
comment
code

Annotation
code

Rewind   Fast-forward   Play   Stop   Record

NOTE: The Sound Object dialog box appears only if the
appropriate sound equipment is installed on your computer.

You will not normally see annotations as you review a document. If you would like to see where comments have been
added, click the Show/Hide button on the Standard toolbar.
This reveals the codes for each comment in the document. To view an
annotation, double-click on its code.

Highlighting Points of Interest

Another way to draw attention to points of interest is to highlight
them. This is often done by both the author and reviewers, so that
they can make sure an important or controversial point in a document
is noticed by other reviewers.

To highlight part of a document:

1. Select the appropriate text.
2. Click the Highlight button on the Formatting toolbar.

PART II   WORD

> **TIP:** Here's how you highlight multiple text selections at one
> time: Click the Highlight button (*without* preselecting any
> text); select each text section you want to highlight; then
> click the Highlight button again to turn this feature off.

If you click the down arrow to the right of the Highlight button, you
can change the color of the highlighting. This is especially useful when
different reviewers are highlighting the same document. The result
looks just as if you had taken a yellow (red, blue, etc.) highlighting
pen and marked the printout with it.

To remove highlighting from a section:

1. Change the color of the highlighter to clear (none).
2. Rehighlight the colored section with the clear highlighter.
3. Change the highlighter color back to its normal shade.

Consolidating Reviewer's Suggestions

When the review cycle is finished, incorporate the changes that reviewers have made into the final document and integrate the annotations
that have been offered. Word offers several tools for easily accomplish-
ing both these tasks. In fact, you can even incorporate changes that
have been made to a draft of the document when the reviewer did not
use revision marks by comparing versions of the document.

Comparing Versions

Sometimes a reviewer will make changes to a document without turning on revision marks. You can insert these revision marks automatically by comparing the reviewer's version with the original.

To do so:

1. Open the reviewer's copy of the document.
2. Choose Tools, Revisions. The Revisions dialog box will
   appear.
3. Choose Compare Versions. You will see the Compare Versions
   dialog box shown in Figure 8-9.
4. Change the File Name to that of the original document and

Figure 8-9.
The Compare
Versions dialog box
allows you to
compare documents
that did not use
revision marks and
inserts these marks
for you

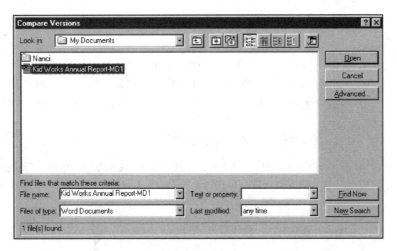

choose Open. Revision marks are added to the revised document, wherever differences between it and the original exist.

5. You can now accept or reject the revisions as described below.

Merging Revisions

As you receive copies of the document from reviewers, merge all the
suggestions that they make.

TIP: Save all reviewers' revisions in separate files that start
with the same name, but end with their initials. For instance,
the Urschel Industries proposal and its two reviewed versions
might be named "Proposal Urschel," "Proposal Urschel - BB,"
and "Proposal Urschel - AT."

To merge revisions of documents stored on your disk, do the following:

1. Open the original document.

2. Choose Tools, Revisions. You will see the Revisions dialog
box.

3. Choose Merge Revisions. The Merge Revisions dialog box
resembles an Open File dialog box.

4. Navigate to the correct folder and double-click on the revised
document to be merged with the original.

5. Repeat steps 2 through 4 to merge additional revised documents.

At the end of the process, you have a document that shows all the revisions by different reviewers, identified with different colors. You can now choose to accept or reject the revisions as described next.

Consolidating Revisions

After you have incorporated all the reviewers' suggestions with your document, consolidate them into a final document and accept or reject the proposed revisions.

Consolidate revisions as follows:

1. Open the document with the revision marks.

2. Move the cursor to the beginning of the document if you want to review the document's changes from beginning to end.

3. If necessary, use the procedures described above to compare documents or merge revisions.

4. If the document was protected for revision during routing, unprotect it by choosing Tools, Unprotect Document.

5. Choose Tools, Revisions. The Revisions dialog box will appear.

6. Choose Review to accept or reject each revision individually. The Review Revisions dialog box will appear.

7. Check Find Next After Accept/Reject to speed the acceptance process.

8. Click on the Find button. The first revision will be highlighted in the document and the Review Revisions dialog box will show you who made it and when.

9. Choose Accept or Reject. Word will move to the next revision.

TIP: If you know you want to accept or reject all revisions without reviewing them individually, choose Accept All or Reject All.

10. Repeat step 9 until you reach the end of the document.

11. When you are finished, exit the dialog box, then save your work—preferably with a different name. This way, you can return to previous versions if needed.

Integrating Annotations

If there are annotations from reviewers in a document, you can display them, print them, or even copy them into the document.

To display annotations:

1. Choose View, Annotations. You will see the Annotations window at the bottom of the screen.

2. To view the annotations from only one reviewer, select that reviewer's name from the From box.

3. Voice annotations are denoted by a sound icon. To listen to a voice annotation, double-click on the icon.

4. If an annotation relates to a specific selection of text, that portion of text will appear in gray in the main window. It is not actually selected, however. To select it press [Alt] + [F11]. Now you can copy it to the Clipboard, delete the text, or whatever you want.

You may include annotations when you print the document. Choose File, Print and click the Options button. In the Options dialog box, check Annotations in the Include with Document group, then choose OK. Annotations print at the end of the document.

Annotations cannot be directly converted into document text. However, you can copy them easily enough. Highlight the part of the annotation you wish to include as document text, then hold the [Ctrl] key while you drag the highlighted section to the appropriate place in the main text window. (Or else copy the annotation to the Clipboard and paste it elsewhere.)

PART III

EXCEL

CHAPTER 9

CREATING A SIMPLE WORKSHEET

IN THIS CHAPTER

- Getting Started with Excel
- Creating a Simple Worksheet
- Editing a Worksheet
- Formatting a Worksheet
- Printing a Worksheet

Excel 7 is arguably the best spreadsheet software for PCs today. Its power is unsurpassed, and its ease of use has set a model for its competition. Whether you need to create a simple budget, maintain a database, or conduct what-if analyses using several scenarios, Excel is for you.

Getting Started with Excel

In this chapter, you will learn the basics of using Excel to create a simple worksheet, such as a budget. In the next chapter, you will learn about Excel databases and analyses.

First, however, let's start by getting into Excel and becoming familiar with its screens.

Starting Excel

The Shortcut Bar is introduced in Chapter 2.

The simplest way to start Excel is to ensure the Programs Shortcut Bar is visible, then click on the Excel icon on the Microsoft Shortcut Bar.

If the Shortcut Bar is not available, you can also start Excel by clicking on the Start button, then choosing Programs, Microsoft Excel.

Basic Spreadsheet Concepts

Electronic spreadsheets are also very useful for creating databases. Excel databases are discussed in Chapter 10.

A spreadsheet is a matrix made up of cells arranged in rows and columns. The arrangement provides a convenient way to work with numbers such as those appearing in a budget. Excel uses the term *worksheet* to refer to an electronic spreadsheet.

Each worksheet cell has an address, which is the intersection of its row and column. For instance, the address of the active cell in Figure 9-1 is B5. *Cells* can contain text (called labels), numbers, or formulas.

As people use Excel regularly, they often find that they work on several worksheets that are related to each other. For instance, branch budgets may be maintained together, and combined into a departmental budget. To assist you in keeping related items together, Excel organizes related worksheets into *workbooks*. Workbooks can even contain charts on chart sheets that relate to the worksheets.

See Chapter 11 for a discussion of Excel charting.

When you open an Excel file, you are actually opening a workbook that contains 16 sheets, unless you change this option. You can use just the default sheet (Sheet1), or you can move between sheets.

Learning About the Excel Window

When you open Excel, you will see the window shown in Figure 9-2. The window has some elements common to other Office 95 applications.

Figure 9-1.
A spreadsheet is
made of cells
arranged in rows
and columns

Cell Address

Active Cell

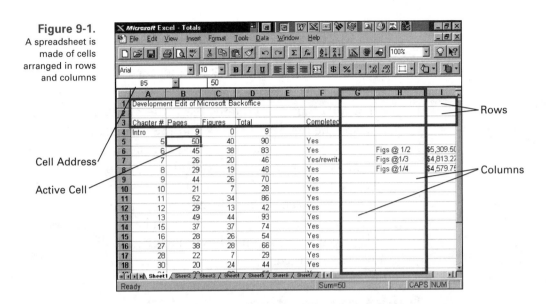

Rows

Columns

Figure 9-2.
The Excel
window, with
elements labeled

Active Cell

Row
Headings

Formula
Bar

Sheet Tabs

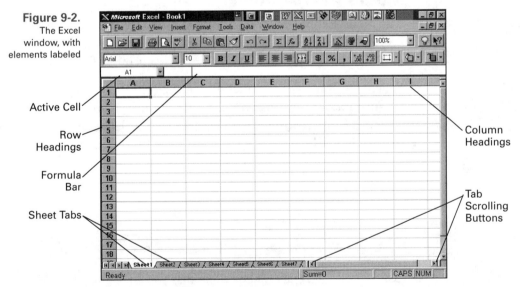

Column
Headings

Tab
Scrolling
Buttons

Elements that are unique to the Excel window include:

- **Cell Selector.** The active cell is the cell that is selected—the one you have clicked on. The active cell has a dark border around it, called the *cell selector*.

- **Column and Row Headings.** These letters and numbers appear at the top and to the left of the worksheet window, respectively. They provide the addresses for the cells in the worksheet.

- **Sheet Tabs.** Sheet tabs are used to switch between the sheets in the workbook.
- **Tab Scrolling Buttons.** If you cannot see all the Sheet Tabs, you can use the tab-scrolling buttons to see additional sheet tabs.
- **Formula Bar.** The Formula Bar is the row that appears just below the toolbars. At the left of the Formula Bar is the address box. If the active cell has a name, it is displayed in the address box, otherwise the cell address is shown. The right side of the Formula Bar is the formula box, showing the actual contents of the cell. If the cell contains a formula, it is displayed in the formula box. If it contains a number, the actual number is displayed in the formula box, while the cell displays the number as formatted.

Modes of Operation

The mode Excel is in appears at the left end of the status bar at the bottom of the screen. When you first start Excel, you are in *Ready* mode. In this mode, Excel is ready to accept input from you.

When you start typing something into a cell, the word *Ready* changes to *Enter* mode—because you are entering information. When you press Enter or an arrow key to complete your data entry, you return to the Ready mode.

Another common mode you will see is the *Edit* mode, seen when you are editing a cell's contents.

> **NOTE:** When you are not in Ready mode, many of the menu commands will not be available to you. If, for instance, you try to copy a cell and you cannot, ensure that you are in Ready mode by looking at the bottom of your screen. If you are not in Ready mode, you can return to it by pressing the Esc key repeatedly until *Ready* becomes visible at the bottom of your screen.

Navigating in an Excel Workbook

To navigate in your workbook, you need to know how to move to the appropriate sheet, and then move to the desired cell within that sheet.

Figure 9-3.
Move between
sheets using the
sheet tabs or tab
scroll buttons

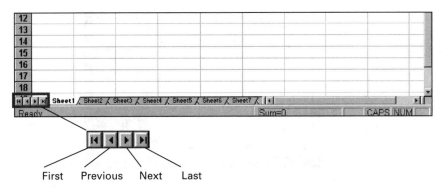

First   Previous   Next   Last

You can move between cells within a worksheet by using either the
mouse or the keyboard.

Moving Between Sheets

To move to another sheet, click one of the sheet tabs at the bottom of
the screen, as shown in Figure 9-3. If you cannot see the tab for the
desired sheet, click the Next or Previous scroll buttons. You can also
move directly to the first or last sheets by clicking the First or Last
button.

Moving Around a Worksheet with the Mouse

Once you are at the desired worksheet, you will want to move to a
specific cell. Moving to a cell selects it, making it the active cell (i.e.,
the cell that you can enter data into). To select a cell that is visible in
the worksheet window, click on it. If the cell is not visible, use the
scroll bars at the right and bottom of the screen to scroll down or
across the worksheet. To move a large distance, drag the scroll button
as needed.

Moving Around a Worksheet with the Keyboard

When using larger worksheets, you will want to learn some simple
shortcut keys to assist you in quickly moving to the desired cell.

If you press the F5 key (or choose Edit, Go To), the Go To dialog
box shown in Figure 9-4, becomes visible. Type the cell address in the
Reference text box and click OK to go directly to the specified cell.

Figure 9-4.
The F5 Go To key
enables you to
move quickly to
any specific cell

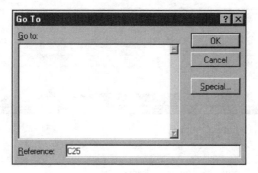

Alternatively, you can use the keystrokes in Table 9-1 to move around the worksheet.

Exiting Excel

When you are finished using Excel, you can exit the program by choosing File, Exit.

If you are working on a workbook which has changes that are not saved, you will be prompted to save your work before you exit Excel. Select Yes to save the workbook or select No to continue working on the workbook.

Table 9-1: Simple Navigation Keystrokes	
Keystroke	**Action**
Arrow keys	One cell in direction of arrow
Tab	One cell to the right
Shift + Tab	One cell to the left
Enter	One row down
Page Up / Page Down	One screen up/down
Ctrl + Home	Top of the worksheet (cell A1)
Ctrl + End	Last cell of the worksheet

TIP: **If you prefer using a mouse, you can also exit Excel by double-clicking on the Control icon at the left of the title bar.**

Creating a Simple Worksheet

The first step in creating a worksheet usually involves entering the labels that identify the rows and columns of data. Then, you enter the worksheet data. You also can enter formulas that total or average numeric data.

One of the best ways to learn to create simple worksheets is by creating a household budget. A budget worksheet can demonstrate many basic Excel features. The sample budget you will create in this chapter is shown in Figure 9-5.

Entering Worksheet Labels

Entering the labels that show where data and calculations go in your worksheet is an easy process. Just follow the steps in the section below.

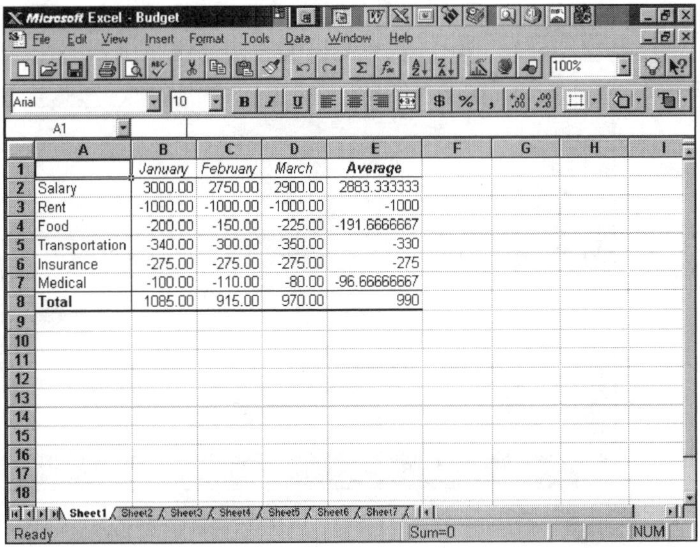

Figure 9-5.
Excel is ideal for creating budgets that include labels, data, and formulas

	A	B	C	D	E	F	G	H	I
1		January	February	March	Average				
2	Salary	3000.00	2750.00	2900.00	2883.333333				
3	Rent	-1000.00	-1000.00	-1000.00	-1000				
4	Food	-200.00	-150.00	-225.00	-191.6666667				
5	Transportation	-340.00	-300.00	-350.00	-330				
6	Insurance	-275.00	-275.00	-275.00	-275				
7	Medical	-100.00	-110.00	-80.00	-96.66666667				
8	**Total**	1085.00	915.00	970.00	990				

Hands On: Entering Labels for a Budget Worksheet

To begin the creation of a worksheet:

1. Start Excel. You will see a blank worksheet.
2. Click on cell B1. It becomes the active cell.
3. Type **January** in this cell, then press Tab. You move to cell C1.
4. Type **February** in this cell, then press Tab again.
5. Similarly, type **March** in cell D1, and **Average** in cell E1.
6. Click on cell A2. Type Salary then press Enter. You are in cell A3.
7. Type **Rent** and press Enter again. You are in cell A4.
8. Type the words **Food**, **Transportation**, **Insurance**, **Medical**, and **Total** in cells A4, A5, A6, A7, and A8, respectively. Your worksheet looks like the one in Figure 9-6.

TIP: Notice that the word "Transportation" extends into the next cell. We will correct this in a later section.

Figure 9-6.
A worksheet with labels indicating where data and calculations will appear

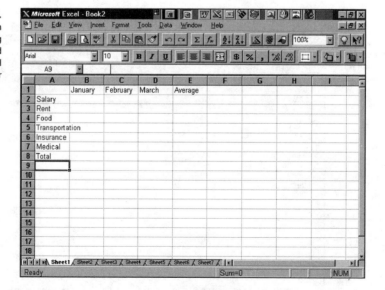

Entering Numeric Data

The next step in creating a worksheet is to enter the numeric data you need. When you enter numeric data, you don't need to worry about formatting it by typing dollar signs, decimals, etc. You'll learn how to format your data later. Right now, the important thing is to get the numbers into your worksheet.

Hands On: Adding Budget Data to Your Worksheet

To add numeric information to your worksheet:

1. Click on cell B2 and type the salary for January: **3000**.

2. Enter figures for the other budget categories: **–1000** for rent, **–200** for food, **–340** for transportation, **–275** for insurance, and **–100** for medical expenses. Remember to put the minus sign in front of the numbers, since they are expenditures. Your worksheet looks like the one in Figure 9-7.

The numbers in a worksheet may not exactly match the numbers you type. What appears in a cell is the formatted number, not the raw value. Thus, if the cell's formatting calls for a number to be displayed

Figure 9-7.
After you enter the worksheet labels, add numeric data as needed

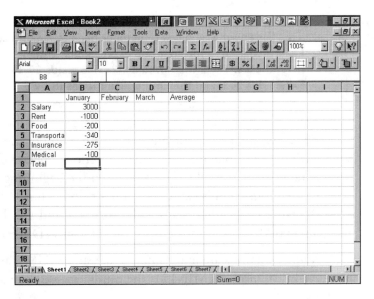

TIP: An easy way to display numbers as percentages or currency is to type them in with a % or $, e.g., 5%, or $23.

as an integer, typing **1.8** it will mean the number is displayed as "2." The actual figure (1.8, in this example) will be used for calculations, however. Similarly, if a cell is formatted as a percent, a number typed as .23 will be displayed as "23%." You will learn more about formatting numbers later in this chapter.

Using Formulas and Functions

Formulas are calculations made up of numbers, cell values, and operators. In Excel, all formulas start with an equal sign (=). For instance, a cell can contain the formula =1033-82. This can be helpful when you are entering totals into your worksheet and don't want to use a calculator. More commonly, however, formulas will reference particular cells. For instance, the formula =A1-B1 puts the difference between the value of A1 and B1 in the active cell. This is especially handy for totaling budgets, because when the budget item in A1 changes, the total automatically reflects this. The most common operators are addition (+), subtraction (-), multiplication (*), and division (/).

TIP: For anyone who can remember back to algebra class, Excel also allows you to group expressions with parentheses. Thus, the formula =(2+3)*6 yields 30. First, Excel adds 2+3, and then multiplies the result by 6.

Functions are special formulas in which many of the calculations have already been done for you. Many functions operate on a *range* of cells. A range of cells is all the cells between the beginning and ending cell of the group, and is expressed with a colon. Thus, A1:E1 designates the range containing cells A1, B1, C1, D1 and E1. The function =SUM(A1:E1) is a shortcut for =A1+B1+C1+D1+E1.

Many functions are fairly simple, like sum (SUM), average (AVERAGE), minimum (MIN) for the minimum value in a range of

Functions are discussed further in Chapter 10.

numbers, and maximum (MIN) for the maximum value. For instance, if you type =MAX(A1:E1) in cell B5, cell B5 will contain the largest value from cells A1 through E1.

Many functions, however, are much more complex. Excel comes with over 300 functions that cover financial, mathematical, scientific, and statistical calculations. There are even functions that work on text, and logical functions that provide IF/THEN logic.

The best way to put calculations such as totals in your worksheet is to use the SUM function.

Hands On: Entering a Formula in Your Worksheet

To insert the SUM function in your worksheet:

1. Click on cell B8—the cell that will receive the total.
2. Type =**SUM(B2:B7)** and press [Enter].
3. Click on cell B8 again to make it active and the result of the calculation—1085—appears in cell B8. The formula bar will display =SUM(B2:B7) which is the formula that was used to calculate the result.
4. Save your worksheet by choosing <u>F</u>ile, <u>S</u>ave or clicking the Save button on the Standard toolbar, then giving your worksheet the name Budget.

TIP: Another advantage of using the SUM function is that, since it totals all the cells between B2 and B7, any new rows (budget categories) inserted between rows 2 and 7 will automatically be included in the total.

Editing a Worksheet

After you create a simple worksheet, you will want to add and edit its contents. Editing a worksheet involves changing cell contents, copying and moving data, and inserting and deleting rows and columns.

Changing Cell Contents

There are two common ways of editing the cell contents. As you become more familiar with Excel, you will probably find yourself using both.

Using Edit Mode

One way of editing cells is to select the cell you want to edit, then press the F2 (Edit) key. When you press this key, Edit appears on the status bar. Cancel, Confirm, and Function buttons appear on the formula bar as shown in Figure 9-8. You also see an insertion point at the end of the cell entry.

A second way of editing cells is to click on the cell, then click on the formula bar. You will see the same, except that the insertion point appears in the formula bar rather than in the cell.

Editing Cell Contents

While you are in Edit mode, certain keys will work differently. The left and right arrows move you backward and forward through the cell entry, rather than between cells, and the Home and End keys take you to the beginning and end of your cell entry.

Figure 9-8.
The formula bar
changes when you
are in Edit mode

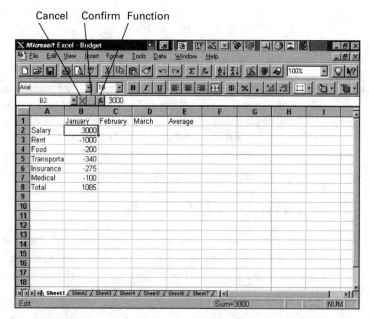

While in Edit mode, you can insert characters just as you would in Word—by placing your insertion point at the spot where you want to enter text then typing the new characters. The [Backspace] and [Del] keys can be used to delete characters to the left or right of the insertion point, respectively.

When you have finished editing the cell contents, press [Enter] or click the Confirm button (the check mark) on the formula bar. To cancel the editing process and return the cell to its original contents, press [Esc] or click the Cancel button (the X) on the formula bar. When you finish editing, Excel returns to the Ready mode.

Copying and Moving Data

As you create worksheets, you will find that you often need to repeat numbers and formulas. Excel's ability to easily copy cells will make your work much easier. To continue our earlier example, the budgets for February and March will be similar to the one we created for January. The easiest way to add budget amounts is to copy the values from January to February and March, then edit any cells to make necessary changes.

A very useful feature of Excel allows cell references in a formula to change relative to the location to which it is copied. For instance, if you copy the January total to the February column, it will sum the February data without your needing to adjust the formula.

When you move a cell, in contrast, cell references do not change. Thus, if you moved the January sum to the February column, it would still display the sum of the January data, not the February data.

You can select, then copy or move one cell or a range of cells. If you are copying, you can copy one cell such as the January Salary cell (B2) to a range of cells—such as February and March (C2:D2)—all at once. You can copy a range of cells such as all budget categories (B2:B7) to a specific cell such as the first February cell (C2), in which case all the January budget cells will be copied to their February counterparts. You can even copy one range to another range. For instance, you can copy all the January budget categories (B2:B7) to February and March (C2:D2), and both months will be filled out at once!

There are three basic ways to move or copy cells in Excel: copy-and-paste, drag-and-drop, and (for copying) the AutoFill feature. They all start with the selection of the cell(s) to be copied or moved.

Selecting Cells

To select one cell, click on it. To select a range of cells, do one of the following:

- To select a range of cells with the keyboard, click on the first cell. Hold down the ⎡Shift⎤ key, then use the four direction arrows. The selected cell range grows as you move further from the starting cell, as long as you hold the ⎡Shift⎤ key down.

- You can do the same thing with the mouse. Click on a corner cell of a range, then hold the ⎡Shift⎤ key down while you click on the last cell (the opposite corner). The range can be part of a row, a column, or even a rectangle.

- You can also position your mouse pointer in the first cell, then drag to the last cell. This is the quickest and easiest way to select cells when you can see them all in the worksheet window.

- To select non-contiguous cells, click on the first cell, then hold down the ⎡Esc⎤ key while you click on the additional cells.

- Select all cells in the worksheet by clicking the Select All button, which is the blank button above the row indicators and to the left of the column indicators.

- Select a row or column by clicking in the appropriate row or column heading.

TIP: The first selected cell will be white, the remaining ones black. A heavy border will appear around the entire selection.

Copying and Pasting

The easiest way to move or copy data is to cut or copy it, and then paste it. This is most familiar because the procedure is similar to cutting and pasting in Word or other Office 95 applications. To cut or copy and then paste data, follow these steps:

1. Select the cell(s) you want to move or copy.
2. Choose <u>E</u>dit, Cu<u>t</u> or <u>E</u>dit, <u>C</u>opy. You will notice that there is a revolving dashed line around the selected cell(s), called a *marquee*, as shown in Figure 9-9.

Figure 9-9.
A marquee designates cells being moved or copied

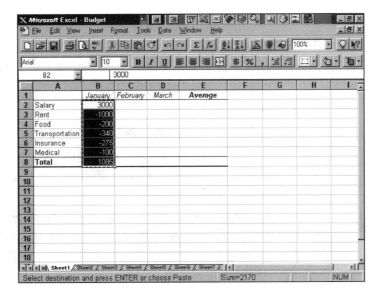

PART III EXCEL

3. Click on the destination cell(s).

4. Press (Enter). The cells are moved or copied, and Excel returns to Ready mode. Alternatively, if you wish to paste data repeatedly, choose Edit, Paste instead of pressing (Enter). You are still in the move data mode and you can keep pasting data until you press (Enter) to paste it one last time or press (Esc) to return to Ready mode.

NOTE: There is one important difference in cutting and pasting with Excel and other Windows applications. Even though the cut/copy operation places the cells in the Windows clipboard, when you paste data by pressing (Enter) you return to Ready mode, the Clipboard contents are cleared, and you cannot paste it again. However, if you choose Edit, Paste instead of pressing (Enter), you will still see Select destination in the status bar, and you can continue to paste the data to different locations until you press (Enter) a final time or (Esc) to return to Ready mode.

Dragging and Dropping

Alternatively, you can copy or move data by dragging and dropping it, similar to the way it is done in Word. This method does not use the Windows Clipboard, so the data can only be copied once.

To drag and drop cells:

1. Select the appropriate cell(s).
2. Position your mouse pointer on the heavy border of the cell or selection. Notice that the pointer changes from a white cross to an arrow.
3. Ensuring that the mouse pointer is an arrow, click on the border, then drag the cell or selection to its new destination.
4. Alternatively, to copy it, hold down the [Ctrl] key, then drag the cell or selection. Notice that when you press [Ctrl], the pointer changes to an arrow with a plus sign.

> **TIP:** The drag and drop method is the easiest and fastest way to move or copy data, but works best if you are only moving or copying cells within the visible worksheet window.

Using AutoFill

Excel provides a useful feature that makes copying cells even easier than the methods described above. At the bottom-right corner of the active cell or range of selected cells a black dot, called the *fill handle,* is visible. If you position your mouse pointer on it, the pointer becomes a black cross, as shown in Figure 9-10. If you drag the fill handle down or to the right, you are automatically filling the cells over which you drag.

If the source cell contains text, a number, or a formula, the AutoFill process copies the source cell to the destination cells—just as if you cut and pasted them.

If, however, the source cell contains a day or month, the AutoFill feature recognizes this and fills the destination cells with the next day or month in the sequence. Thus, if we clicked on January (B1) and dragged it from C1 to F1, the months February through June would appear.

Figure 9-10.
The fill handle can
be used to copy
cell contents

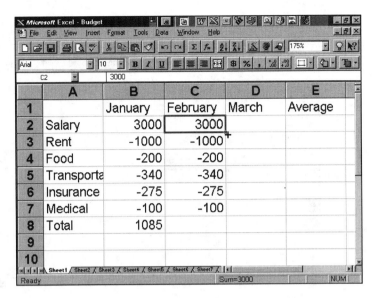

Moreover, if you select two or more cells containing data as the source cells, the AutoFill feature will fill the destination cells with the sequence defined by the source cells. Thus, if you select two cells containing the numbers 1 and 2, the remaining cells will contain 3, 4, 5, etc.

Thus, the easiest way to fill in the rest of our sample budget would be to use the AutoFill feature.

Hands On: Using AutoFill to Fill in Your Budget

To use AutoFill in your worksheet:

1. Drag over the January budget categories and total (B2:B8) to select them.

2. Position your cursor on the fill handle at the bottom-right of cell B8.

3. Click and drag the fill handle through C8 to D8. The budget amounts and totals for January are copied to February and March, as shown in Figure 9-11.

4. Edit any amounts, as desired, in the February and March columns.

Figure 9-11.
You can easily
copy one column
of data to other
columns with the
AutoFill procedure

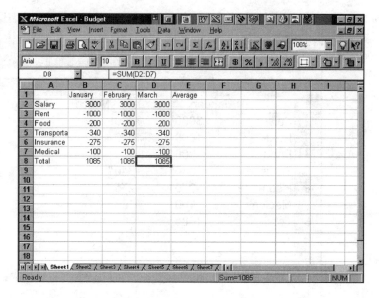

5. Create an average in E2 by clicking in E2 and typing **=average(B2:D2)**.

6. Copy this formula by clicking in cell E2, positioning your mouse pointer on the fill handle, then dragging the fill handle down to E8.

Inserting and Deleting Rows and Columns

Occasionally, you may need to insert an additional row or column in your worksheet. This might happen when you create or delete a budget category, or when you want to add additional months.

To insert a row:

1. Select the entire row (where you want the new row to be inserted) by clicking on the row number at the left of the row. The entire row is highlighted.

2. Position the mouse pointer inside the selected area, then right-click. A shortcut menu, as shown in Figure 9-12, will become visible.

TIP: You can also right-click directly on the row number to select the row column and show the shortcut menu at once.

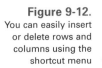

Figure 9-12.
You can easily insert or delete rows and columns using the shortcut menu

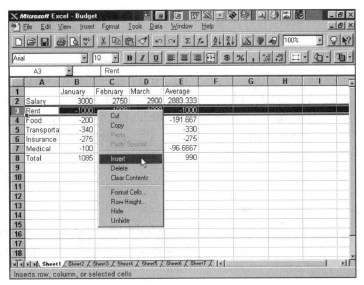

3. Choose Insert to insert a row, or Delete to delete it. Inserted rows will appear above the selected row.

TIP: Remember that you can click the Undo button on the standard toolbar, or choose Edit, Undo if you make a mistake.

NOTE: The procedure for inserting or deleting a column is similar to the procedure for rows. Click the appropriate column letter to select the entire column. Then, right-click inside the selected column and choose Insert to insert a column, or Delete to delete the selected column.

Formatting a Worksheet

Now that you've created your worksheet, the next step is to make it look attractive. Excel has several tools for doing this effortlessly. To format cells, you'll need to select them, then apply formatting commands. In addition, you will want to be able to change the width of cells or, occasionally, the height of rows to make the worksheet more attractive.

Formatting Cells

The format of a cell determines how text and numbers will be displayed—not how Excel will store them. For example, a cell containing the number 1.2 formatted as an integer will display the number as "1." However, 1.2 will still be stored and used for calculations. Formatting changes the look of existing data in cells. In addition, you can format empty cells, and the data typed later into them will be appropriately formatted.

To access the Format Cells dialog box, follow these steps:

1. Select the cell or cells to be formatted.

2. Choose Format, Cells. You will see the Format Cells dialog box. This dialog box has tabs for formatting numbers, alignment (i.e., justification), fonts, borders, patterns, and setting cell protection.

3. Choose the appropriate tab and options as described in the following sections.

TIP: You can also access the Format Cells dialog box by right-clicking inside selected cells, then choosing Format Cells.

Formatting Numbers

Number formatting determines such things as how many decimal places will be displayed, whether negative numbers are displayed with a minus sign or parentheses, and whether currency and percentages are expressed with the appropriate symbol. In addition, dates are considered numbers, and number formatting determines how dates are displayed.

To format numbers:

1. Select the cell(s) containing the numbers you want to format.

2. Choose Format, Cells to access the Format Cells dialog box.

3. Click the Number tab (if necessary).

4. Choose the appropriate number format category from the Category list.

5. Options will appear in the center of the dialog box that are

Figure 9-14.
Predefined
categories make
formatting numbers
easy with Excel

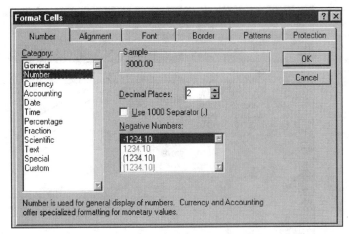

appropriate for the category you pick. For example, options for the Number category are shown in Figure 9-13.

6. Choose the desired option(s), then click OK. The formatting is applied to the selected cells.

TIP: You can select an entire row or column by clicking the appropriate row number or column letter in the worksheet frame, or by selecting multiple rows or columns by holding down the Ctrl key as you select them. This is an easy way to format a column of numbers all at once.

Setting Alignment

The alignment feature allows you to set the justification and orientation of your numbers or text within the cells. After you select a cell or group of cells, simple alignment can be set using the Left, Center, and Right buttons on the Formatting Toolbar shown in Figure 9-14. These buttons allow you to align the text or numbers within their respective cells.

For more sophisticated alignment options, you will want to use the Cell Format dialog box:

1. Select the appropriate cells, and then choose Format, Cells.

2. Click the Alignment tab. The alignment options, as shown in Figure 9-15, appear.

Figure 9-14.
Alignment options can be set from within the Format Cells dialog box or from the Formatting Toolbar

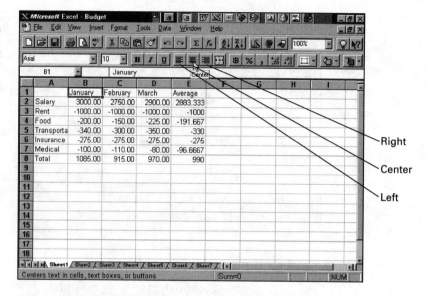

Right

Center

Left

Figure 9-15.
You can set a variety of vertical and horizontal alignment options

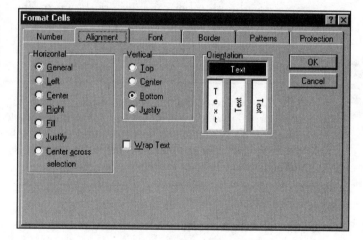

3. Select alignment options including:

• *Center Across Selection* allows you to center a title across the width of your worksheet. To use this option, place the title in the leftmost cell (e.g., A1), then select not only A1 but all other cells across which the title should be centered (perhaps A1:E1). When you choose Center Across Selection, the title in A1 will center across all the selected cells.

• *Wrap Text* is used when you have one column heading that takes up a lot of horizontal space, and you don't want to widen the column. By choosing Wrap Text, the cell contents will expand vertically and show the contents on several lines.

- *Vertical Alignment* is used when some cells in a row have more lines of text in them than do others. For instance, if one cell might have three lines of text in it, and other cells have only one. In this case, you need to decide whether the text of one-line cells should be aligned at the top of the cell, middle of it, or bottom of it.

- *Orientation* can be helpful as another option for long column titles—especially when there are many column entries and the column entries are fairly short (like True/False, or checked v. unchecked). In these cases, you may wish to have the column label run vertically rather than horizontally.

4. Click OK after making your selection.

Formatting Fonts

You can select the typeface, size, and weight of fonts used in your Excel worksheet just as you do in Word. In fact, you may wish to coordinate the typeface you use in Excel with the one you choose for your Word documents—producing an integrated look for your work products.

To specify font information:

1. Select the appropriate cells, and choose Format, Cells.

2. Click the Font tab. The font options will appear, as shown in Figure 9-16.

3. Select font options including:

    - **Font, Font Style, and Font Size** change the typeface, style (regular, bold, italic, or bold italic) and/or size of the font in selected cells by selecting the appropriate option in the Font, Font Style, or Size list.

    - **The Underline drop down box** allows you to choose from four different types of underlining.

    - **Effects** include Strikethrough, Superscript, and Subscript.

    - **Specify Font Color** using the Color drop down box.

Alternatively, you can set simple font options from the toolbars. To do so, select the appropriate cells, then use the Font, Font Size, Bold,

Figure 9-16.
Excel offers the
same font
formatting options
you found in Word

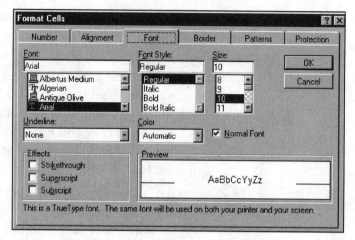

Figure 9-17.
You can set simple
text formatting from
the Formatting
toolbar

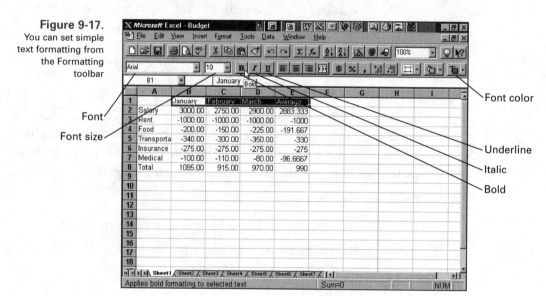

Italic, Underline, and Font Color buttons on the Formatting toolbar, as shown in Figure 9-17.

Creating Borders

You can also set options for the lines around selected cells. These surrounding lines are called the cell *borders*. This can be helpful to highlight summary lines, or to make a border around a cell to which you want to call attention.

Figure 9-18.
Draw attention to
important cells by
creating borders
around them

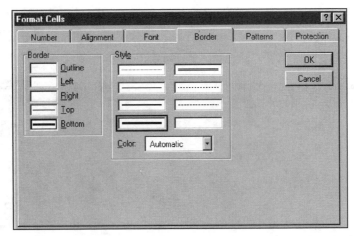

To create a border around a cell:

1. Select the cell(s) around which you wish to make borders.
2. Choose Format, Cells.
3. Click the Border tab. The Border tab shown in Figure 9-18 will appear.
4. Choose the Style you prefer, then in the Border area click the side(s) of the cells it should apply to.

NOTE: When applying borders it is important to select all the cells around which you wish to have borders, since the border will go around or on the side of the entire selection.

Using Patterns

Another way to emphasize a cell is to fill it with a pattern or color. While this feature should be used sparingly, it can emphasize your worksheet title or a cell containing the grand total to call the viewers' attention to it.

To set cell colors and patterns:

1. Select the cell(s) to which you wish to apply colors or patterns.
2. Choose Format, Cells.

Figure 9-19.
You can choose
colors or even fills
for selected cells to
draw attention to
titles or important
points

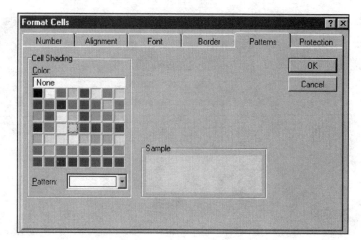

TIP: You can also set the color of cells by clicking the Color button on the formatting toolbar.

3. Click the Patterns tab. You will see the Patterns tab shown in Figure 9-19.

4. Click the desired color in the Color area, then click the down arrow to the right of the Pattern box to choose the fill pattern for the cells, if you don't want a solid color.

NOTE: If you want to lock cells such as formulas or titles so that users can only go to cells they need to change, click the Protection tab in the Format Cells dialog box and choose Locked. You will then need to turn the protection on by choosing Tools, Protection, Protect Sheet.

TIP: The Format Painter button allows you to take the formatting of one cell and quickly apply it to others. Click on the sample cell whose formatting you want to copy, then click the Format Painter button. The mouse pointer changes to a paintbrush. With the paintbrush pointer, select the cell or range you wish to reformat.

Formatting Columns and Rows

There's one last thing you may need to do before completing your worksheet: ensure that all your columns have the proper width. If your columns are too wide, you will have unnecessary white space in your worksheet, and it may print on an unnecessary number of pages. If the columns are too narrow, you will find that some text is truncated. You will also see number signs (#) in any cells where there is not enough space for the entire number.

While it is less often problematic, you may also find that you would like to adjust the height of various rows. For instance, you may wish to leave more white space between your titles and data. It is preferable to make a row taller rather than adding an extra blank row.

Adjusting Column Width and Row Height

While you can make row and column adjustments with the menus, most people use the mouse.

To change the width of a column:

1. Move your mouse pointer to the border between two column letters, as shown in Figure 9-20. The mouse pointer becomes a vertical line with two black arrows.

Figure 9-20.
You can drag with the mouse to adjust column widths

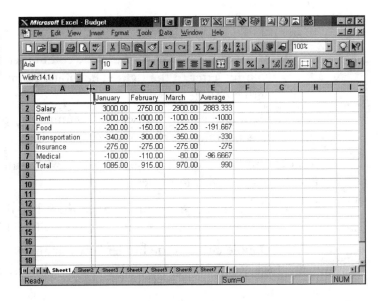

> **CAUTION:** It is very easy to make mistakes when pointing to row numbers in the worksheet frame. When you are in the middle of a row number, your mouse pointer is a white cross. If you click and drag at this time, you are selecting multiple rows. Many people don't notice that they are too close to the border between two row headings, and accidentally resize a row when they are trying to select multiple rows. You can avoid this problem by noticing the shape of your mouse pointer before you drag it.

2. Drag the pointer right or left to make the column wider or narrower.

You can make rows taller or shorter by using the same method. When you move your mouse pointer between two row numbers, it becomes a horizontal line with two black arrows. You can then drag up or down to adjust the row height.

Using AutoFit

While you can resize a column manually, it is often easier to let Excel resize the columns to fit the widest cell entry in the selected columns with AutoFit.

To use AutoFit to resize a column:

1. Move to the border between the column letter and the next column letter to the right. The mouse pointer becomes a line with a double arrow.

2. Double-click the mouse. The column is automatically resized to accommodate the widest entry in the column.

You can also resize several columns at once with AutoFit by selecting all columns you wish to resize:

1. Click on the first column letter, then drag the mouse pointer to the last column. All the columns will be highlighted.

2. Double-click on the border between any two columns in the selection. All columns are automatically resized.

You will probably find much less need to use AutoFit to resize rows, since they usually are sized to accommodate the largest font size in them automatically. If you need to change the row height, however, the AutoFit feature works exactly the same with rows as it does with columns.

You can also resize all rows and columns of the worksheet at once:

1. Click the Select All button—the blank button above row number 1 and to the left of column letter A. All cells in the worksheet are selected.

2. Double-click on the boundary between any two row or column headers.

There is one circumstance where the AutoFit feature will give you results that you probably don't want. If you have one cell that contains an especially long entry, you will find that AutoFit makes the column wide enough to accommodate the long entry. This can make for an awkward looking worksheet.

To solve this problem, you will want to wrap the text in the offending cell. This causes the row height to increase, and the text in this cell wraps to two or more lines. When you use AutoFit, this cell will be ignored, and the column width will be set to accommodate the next-longest cell entry in the column. To wrap text, select the cells to be wrapped. Then choose Format, Cells, click the Alignment tab, and select Wrap Text.

Hiding Rows and Columns

You can hide rows or columns in an Excel worksheet. This can be very useful when you want to hide columns containing information such as wholesale costs and markups, or salary information. The data will still be used for calculations in visible rows, but users will not be able to see the source data.

Hide columns or rows by resizing them until they totally disappear:

1. Drag the border between the appropriate column letters or row numbers as described above until the row or column totally disappears.

2. To unhide a column, select the columns on either side of the hidden column, as shown in Figure 9-21.

Figure 9-21.
You can unhide
columns by
selecting
surrounding
columns then using
the AutoFit feature

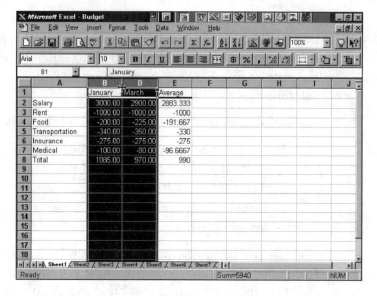

3. Double-click on the border between the column headings. Since all selected columns (including the hidden ones) are resized by the AutoFit feature, the hidden columns become visible.

Using AutoFormat

Sometimes, the complexity of Excel's powerful formatting features can become time-consuming and overwhelming. There is an easier way, however, to format your worksheets quickly and professionally. If your data is arranged in a table, you can use Excel's AutoFormat feature to apply any one of over a dozen pre-designed formats to your worksheet.

To use AutoFormat:

1. Select the range to be formatted.

2. Choose Format, AutoFormat. The AutoFormat dialog box will appear:

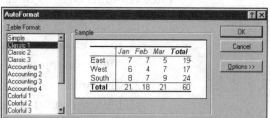

3. Click on each of the <u>T</u>able Formats and see how they look in the Sample window.

4. When you find one you like, double-click on it.

Printing a Worksheet

Printing a worksheet is similar to printing a Word document:

1. Select the area of your worksheet you wish to print, if necessary.

2. Choose <u>F</u>ile, <u>P</u>rint. You will see the Print dialog box shown in Figure 9-22.

3. Choose whether you want to print your whole worksheet with Selecte<u>d</u> Sheet(s) or the <u>E</u>ntire Workbook (collection of related worksheets). Alternatively, if you have selected a specific area you want to print, choose Selectio<u>n</u>.

While the print command is fairly straightforward, there are two additional print options you may want to explore: Page Setup and Print Preview.

TIP: If you want to print one copy of your worksheet to the default printer, you can click the Print button in the Standard toolbar.

Figure 9-22.
You can print your entire worksheet or just a portion of it

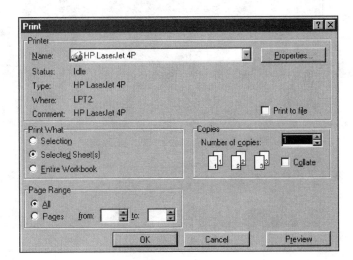

Defining Print Options

Printing worksheets does not automatically lead to a nicely printed product. Often, worksheets look better when oriented sideways (landscape) rather than up and down (portrait), and centering them on the page can often improve their appearance. You will sometimes find that there are one or two columns that don't fit on the page, and you'd like to make the printout fit on one page. The Page Setup dialog box can assist you with all these tasks, and more.

Access the Page tab of the Page Setup dialog box shown in Figure 9-23 by choosing File, Page Setup and clicking the Page tab. You will see several options that can improve the appearance of your printout:

- Choose the orientation of your printout by clicking Portrait or Landscape. Portrait is the default setting.

- Make your worksheet fit on one page by choosing Fit to. Sometimes your worksheet is very long and may take many pages, but you want all the columns to fit on one page across. In this case, specify 1 page wide by 100 pages tall. When you specify "fit to page" the fonts used to print the worksheet will often reduce in size. You can also reduce them manually by choosing Adjust to.

To determine where the printout appears on the page, click the Margins tab. This is especially important when you have a small work-

Figure 9-23.
In the Page tab of the Page Setup dialog box, you can print your worksheet on exactly one page

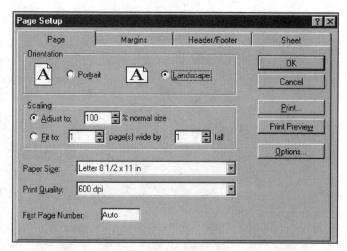

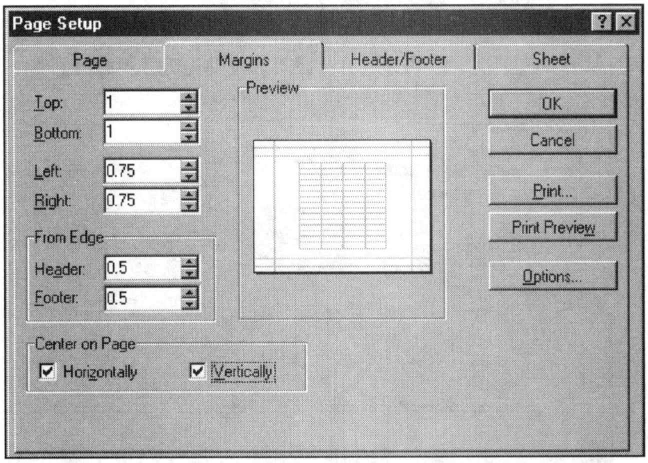

Figure 9-24.
You can specify margins and center your printout on the page using the Margins tab

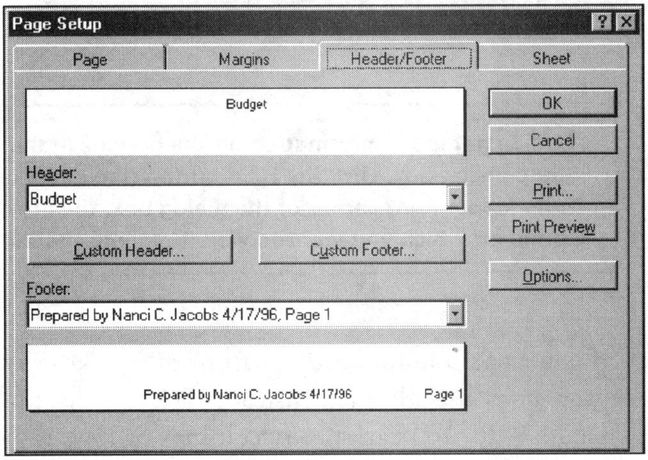

Figure 9-25.
You can select from a number of pre-defined headers and footers

PART III   EXCEL

sheet, that may not look good when printed only at the top-left of the page. The Margins tab options shown in Figure 9-24 will appear. Set your margins and the location of the header and footer, if desired. More importantly, you may specify that the printout be centered on the page either Horizontally, Vertically, or both.

Click the Header/Footer tab to insert a header and footer, as shown in Figure 9-25. You can select from a number of predefined headers and footers, by clicking the down arrow to the right of the Header or Footer drop-down list box. You can also create a custom header or footer by clicking the Custom Header or Custom Footer buttons.

Figure 9-26.
You can specify
columns and rows to
be repeated at the top
of every page

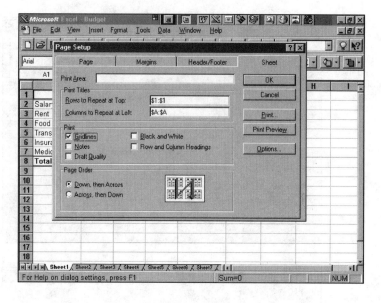

TIP: To get more information on the options in the Page
Setup dialog box, click the Help button (the question mark)
in the upper-right corner of the dialog box, then click the
option on which you want to view Help information.

If you want column headings from the worksheet to appear on every
page, don't use a header. Instead, click the Sheet tab, as shown in
Figure 9-26. You can specify columns or rows to be repeated at the top
or left of every page. You can also determine whether you want to
print the gridlines of your worksheet.

Previewing the Printout

You can also preview how your worksheet will look before you print it
out, and set many print options from the preview mode.

To preview your printout, choose File, Print Preview, or click
the Print Preview button. You will see the print preview window
shown in Figure 9-27. Click the Zoom button to see more
detail, or choose Setup to access the Setup dialog box. After
you select your print options, you will return to the print
preview window.

Figure 9-27.
You can preview how
your printout will look
before you print it

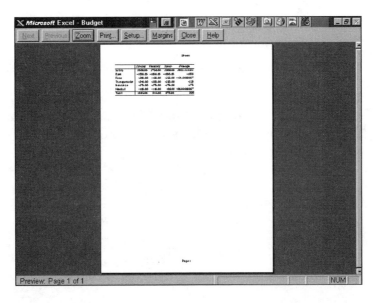

Figure 9-28.
You can change your
margins and column
widths by dragging
the indicators in
print preview

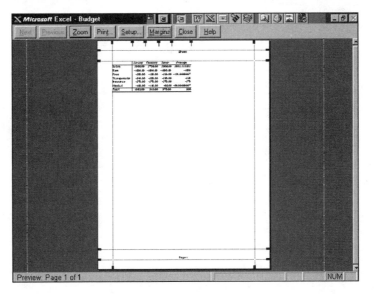

You can also set your margins and column widths in the print preview
mode. This gives you a visual guide to how the worksheet looks as you
make your changes. To do so:

1. Click the Margins button in the preview window. You will see
   indicators where your margins and columns are, as shown in
   Figure 9-28.

2. Drag the margin and column indicators to change their location.

This can be an effective way of ensuring that your worksheet will look just the way you want it when it's printed out.

Click the Print button in the preview window if you want to print your worksheet while in preview mode. Click the Close button to return to the worksheet.

CHAPTER 10

MAINTAINING AN EXCEL DATABASE

IN THIS CHAPTER

- Familiarizing Yourself with Excel Databases
- Creating an Excel Database
- Entering and Editing Data
- Sorting, Selecting, and Grouping Records
- Importing and Exporting Data

A database is simply data organized in a systematic fashion. Databases don't even have to be computerized. A Rolodex is a good example of a paper database. Each card has information on one person, and every card has the information arranged in the same way—perhaps with the name in the top left, phone in the top right, and address information underneath.

Most databases are organized using fields and records. A *record* is all the information on one item. In a Rolodex, everything related to one person is on a Rolodex card, so the card is the record. A *field* is an item of information. In a Rolodex, name, phone, and address are three fields.

The way a worksheet organizes information makes it ideal for creating simple databases. In an Excel database, each row represents one record, and each column is a field. This can be seen in the simple database shown in Figure 10-1. All the information for a single person is in one row. All the first names are in a single column. In addition, the top row of the database contains the names of the fields, rather than data. This is called the *header row*.

There should not be any blank lines between the header row and the data, or within the data itself. This is because Excel will automatically ascertain the boundaries of the database for various operations, looking down through the rows until it reaches a row that is blank.

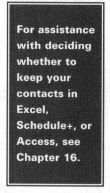

For assistance with deciding whether to keep your contacts in Excel, Schedule+, or Access, see Chapter 16.

An address list or contact system is a common type of database that everyone understands, and is often kept in Excel. For this reason, an address list will be used as an example throughout the chapter. Everything that is said here about contact lists applies to other databases, however.

Figure 10-1.
Excel's rows and columns serve as records and fields for your database

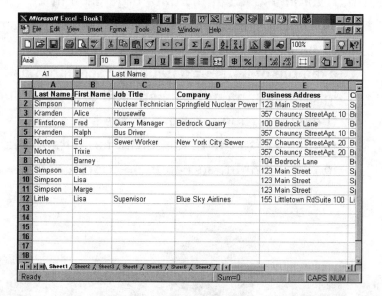

Creating an Excel Database

The first step in creating your Excel database is to decide what fields you wish to maintain for each record. If your database is a contact management list, you might consider whether you wish to include business and personal information on your contacts, and how many different phone numbers you will need to store. One easy way to decide this is by using the same fields that are in the Schedule+ Contact List. Creating the database is then only a matter of setting up a header row, formatting it, then entering data.

For information on maintaining a contact list in Schedule+, see Chapter 15.

Create your database as follows:

1. Decide on the fields you wish to maintain in your database.
2. Click the New button in the Standard toolbar to create a new workbook.
3. Type your field names in Row 1, one name per cell. Then select all field names and apply boldface (or another type of) formatting to emphasize them.
4. If you want to be able to always see your column headings, no matter how many rows are in your database, click in the row underneath your header row then choose <u>W</u>indow, <u>F</u>reeze Panes. Now no matter how many data records you have, when you scroll down, you will still be able to see your titles.
5. Click the Save button and save your Excel database.

Entering and Editing Data

Once you have created your Excel database, you need to be able to enter and edit data in it. If you like, you can enter data by scrolling down to the first blank row and entering data directly into the cells.

NOTE: If you have over 30 fields in your database, you cannot use the data form feature. If your database is complex, you may wish to store the data in Access. Otherwise, if you want to keep it in Excel, you can move to the bottom of the database and enter information directly into the worksheet.

PART III   EXCEL

> **NOTE:** If you're an advanced user who has a large, existing Excel worksheet, you may wish to create an Access data form to use with that worksheet. To do so, choose <u>D</u>ata, <u>A</u>ccess Form. Follow the prompts in the Wizard to create the Access data form. This process can be rather lengthy, even for a simple Excel database.

<aside>
Creating an Access database is discussed in Chapter 18.
</aside>

As the database grows larger, however, you may find it more convenient to use a data entry form that Excel will create for you.

Using a Data Form to Enter Records

Excel provides the data form feature to help you enter, find, and edit data in Excel databases that have fewer than 30 fields. The data form is a dialog box that has text boxes for each field in your database, along with command buttons to help you find and edit your data. Only one record is visible on-screen at a time.

To create an Excel data form, do the following:

1. Click on any cell in the database. If there is no data in the database yet, select a cell in the header row.
2. Choose <u>D</u>ata, <u>F</u>orm.
3. If this is the first time you've done this, you will see a message saying "No headers detected. Assume top row of selection is header row?" Respond with OK. A data form, as shown in Figure 10-2, will appear.
4. If the fields are blank, as they will be the first time you use the form, enter data in the appropriate fields.
5. You can save the new record in two ways. Select Ne<u>w</u> to enter additional records or choose <u>C</u>lose to save your work and close the form.

Editing Records with the Data Form

You can also use the data form to find existing records and edit them:

1. Select any cell in the database.
2. Choose <u>D</u>ata, <u>F</u>orm. You will see the data form for the database.

Figure 10-2.
Excel's data form
makes it easy to
enter new data,
find records, and
edit information

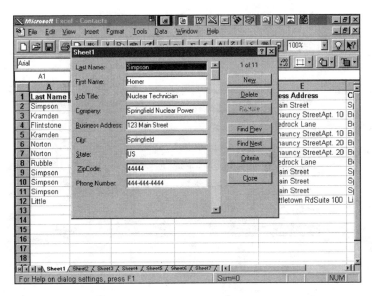

3. Choose Criteria. A blank form will appear, as shown in Figure 10-3.

4. Type the criteria in the blank data form boxes. For instance, to find anyone named Smith who lives in Virginia, type **Smith** in the Last Name box and **VA** in the State box. Click Find Prev or Find Next until you see the desired record appear in the data form.

TIP: You can also move between records by using the scroll bar that's part of the data form.

5. Edit the record by changing the data in the text boxes.

6. If you change your mind after you've edited some of the fields, choose Restore before you save the record.

7. You can also delete the selected record by choosing Delete. (This, however, deletes the record permanently.)

8. When you are finished, choose Close.

9. Save your workbook.

PART III   EXCEL

Figure 10-3.
You can find
specific records
by entering the
criteria for the
search in the
data form

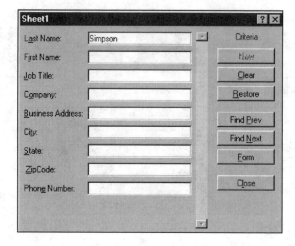

Organizing Your Data

One of the advantages of using Excel for your database needs is the ability to sort, select, and group records whenever you want.

Sorting Records

Sorting your database will help you to find records in it more easily. Furthermore, you must sort your database before performing more advanced operations on it, like creating subtotals.

To sort your database:

1. Click in any cell in the database.
2. Choose Data, Sort. This selects the entire database and brings up the Sort dialog box shown in Figure 10-4.
3. In the Sort By box, use the down arrow to select the field you want to sort.
4. Select the Ascending or Descending option to specify the sort order for that field.
5. Repeat the process, if needed, by using one or both of the other text boxes in the Sort dialog box for additional sort criteria to be used in case of a tie. For example, if you have several records with the same entry in the Last Name field, your secondary sort might be by First Name.

Figure 10-4.
You can sort your
Excel database by
up to three criteria

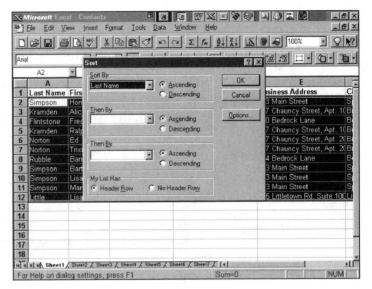

 TIP: You can also quickly sort a database by clicking in the
column to sort by, then clicking the Sort Ascending or Sort
Descending button on the Standard toolbar:

6. Choose OK. Your contact list is sorted by the criteria you specified.

Selecting Records

Sometimes you will wish to see a list containing only a subset of your records. For instance, you may wish to only see people who live in a specific state, or prospective versus actual customers. Using the data form, you can select specific records and move between them.

To select records by using a filter:

1. Select a cell in the database.

2. Choose Data, Filter, AutoFilter. You will see a down arrow to the right of each of the field names in the header row, as shown in Figure 10-5.

PART III EXCEL

3. Click the right arrow to the right of the column on which you wish to apply a filter, and choose the desired filter option. You may pick from among several choices:

- Each value that a field has in the database is listed in the drop-down box. For instance, every last name that is in the database is listed in the Last Name field's drop-down box. To pick only the records with a specific value, choose the appropriate entry.

- You may also pick only records that have blank values in this field, or non-blanks, by choosing (Blanks) or (Non-Blanks).

- You may choose the records that have the most common values by choosing (Top 10...). This would pick contacts from the top ten states, top ten ZIP codes, etc.

- You may choose (All) to remove any filters from this field, and pick records without regard to what this field contains.

- You may choose (Custom...) to display the Custom Auto-Filter dialog box. This allows you to specify multiple criteria for advanced selections:

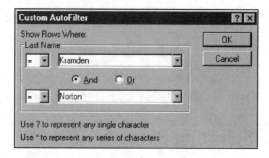

4. You will see the selected records in the database, and can view, print or edit them.

5. To remove the filter, choose <u>D</u>ata, <u>F</u>ilter, Auto<u>F</u>ilter again.

Grouping and Subtotaling Your Database

You can also group your records, so that you can calculate counts of people from each state, for example. This can be very helpful as a first

Figure 10-5.
You can view
subsets of your
database by
clicking the right
arrow to the right
of the column on
which you wish to
apply a filter

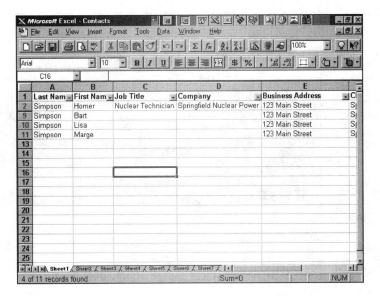

step in making sense of your database and getting summary information on its contents.

To group records:

1. Select a cell in the database.

2. Choose Data, Subtotals. The Subtotal dialog box shown in Figure 10-6 will appear.

3. In the At Each Change In drop-down list box, select the field by which you wish to group, such as Company Name, State, or Zip Code.

4. In the Use Function drop-down list, choose the function you want to perform (such as Count). In the Add Subtotal To list, select the same field that you picked to group.

5. Choose OK. Your database is subtotaled and outline symbols appear at the left of the worksheet, as shown in Figure 10-7.

6. By default, you see all information. To hide the details and just see the totals for each category, click the Level 2 button. To see only the grand total, click the Level 1 button. To see all information again, click the Level 3 button.

7. To remove the grouping, choose Data, Subtotals, Remove All. Your database is restored to its original form.

PART III   EXCEL

Figure 10-6.
You can view and
count the number
of contacts in each
company, ZIP code,
state, or other
category by using
the Subtotal
command

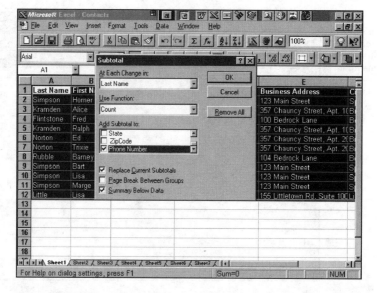

Figure 10-7.
A grouped
database shows
subtotals and
outline symbols

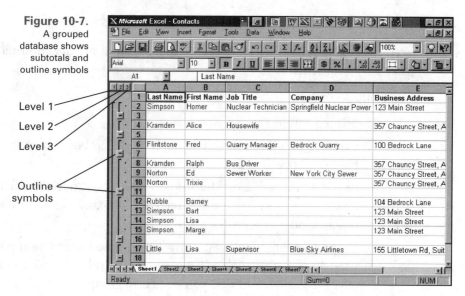

Importing and Exporting Data

In today's office environment, it is quite common to find some staff
using Excel, some using Access, and some using data from a mainframe computer. It is increasingly important to be able to translate
data to and from the various systems in which it may be maintained
by learning to import and export it.

Importing Data

While Excel has powerful features for adding and editing data, you will often want to populate your database with data that already exists in another database. (This is particularly true for contact lists.)

The easiest way to import most databases is by converting them to a simple format that almost all modern databases and spreadsheets understand. While there are several of these formats, the most common is *CSV* (Comma Separated Value). In this format, database records are saved as ASCII text files, with no special control codes. A CSV file containing two records, each having a first name, last name, and phone number field looks like this:

> "John","Smith","234-9939"
> "Sam","Delaney","303-9399"

Notice that each record occupies one line. Each field is surrounded by quotation marks, and separated from the next field by a comma. (Hence the name "comma separated value".)

If Excel cannot import files made by another database, you will want to convert the database file into a CSV file. The commands for doing this are a function of the database program you are using; see your instruction manual for the particular program.

There are certain database formats that Excel can import directly. These include files created in Lotus 1-2-3, dBASE, QuattroPro, and MS Works 2.0. Import these files from an Open dialog box by choosing the appropriate file type, then opening them as you would any other file. You can also import Access data directly, as described below.

Importing CSV Files

To import a CSV file into Excel, follow these steps:

1. Export the database into CSV format using the procedures appropriate in that program. It must be saved as a text file.

2. Open Excel, then click the Open button. You will see the Open dialog box.

3. In the Files of Type box, select Text Files. Navigate to the folder containing the CSV file, then double-click on it. The Text Import Wizard Step 1 appears, as shown in Figure 10-8.

Figure 10-8.
The Text Import
Wizard allows you
to import CSV,
delimited, and
fixed-length text
files into Excel

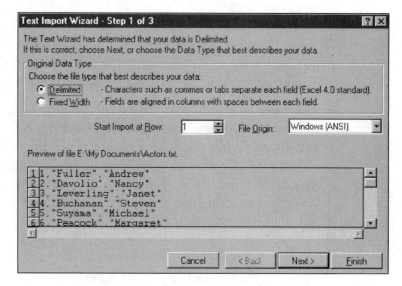

4. Select <u>D</u>elimited and choose Next. You will see Step 2 of the Wizard.

5. Ensure that <u>C</u>omma is specified under Delimiters, and " (quote mark) is specified as the Text <u>Q</u>ualifier, then choose <u>F</u>inish. (You are skipping the last step that allows you to format your data, which is usually not necessary.) Your text file is brought into Excel, with each field in a separate column.

6. Format the file as desired.

7. Choose <u>F</u>ile, Save <u>A</u>s to save your file.

8. In the Save as <u>T</u>ype drop-down list, select Microsoft Excel Workbook (rather than Text File), if you wish to convert the text file into an Excel workbook. Give the file a name, then choose <u>S</u>ave.

Importing Access Databases

Microsoft Access has a feature that allows you to export Access tables or queries directly into Excel. This makes it very easy to transfer your contact list from Access into Excel when needed.

Figure 10-9.
You can export a table or query directly to an Excel worksheet by clicking on the OfficeLinks button

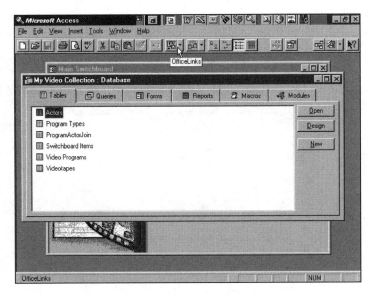

To export Access tables or queries into Excel:

1. Open the database in Access.

2. Click the Tables or Queries tab, depending on whether you wish to import a table or a query.

3. Select the Table or Query you wish to import by clicking on it, as shown in Figure 10-9.

4. Click the down arrow to the right of the OfficeLinks button and choose Analyze It with MS Excel.

5. Excel opens, and you will see the table or query converted into an Excel worksheet.

6. Format the worksheet as desired.

7. Save it in Excel.

Exporting Data

On occasion, you may wish to export data for use in Schedule+ or another database program. (You can import Excel worksheets directly into Access, so you do not need to export it for this purpose.) Since

Figure 10-10.
You can save Excel worksheets as CSV files directly from the Save As dialog box

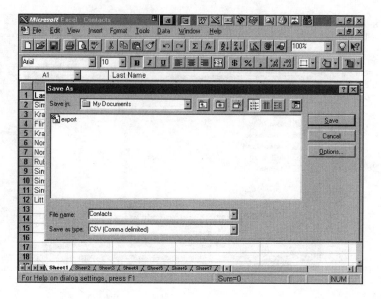

most database programs can import CSV files, the first step of exporting your data is normally to convert it into a CSV file.

To save your data as a CSV file:

1. Open your Excel database.

2. Choose File, Save As.

3. In the Save as Type box, choose CSV (Comma delimited). The Save As dialog box looks like the one in Figure 10-10.

4. Give the file a name, and choose Save. You can now import or open the file in the other database program.

CHAPTER 11

ANALYZING YOUR DATA

IN THIS CHAPTER

- Using Excel Functions
- Summarizing Data with Pivot Tables
- Conducting "What-If" Analyses
- Applying Statistical Functions
- Charting Your Results

When you need to analyze data, you can't pick a better program than Excel. Excel provides several tools that allow you to make sense of a disorganized volume of data and turn it into useful information.

These tools include:

- **Functions** that help you process various types of data, including statistical, date and time, and text
- **Pivot tables** that provide summary information and cross tabulations
- **What-If analyses** that allow you to create scenarios and solve problems such as maximizing profits while maintaining certain constraints
- **Statistical functions** that allow you to test the validity of your data
- **Charting capabilities** that permit you to see the results of your data analyses

Using Functions

In Chapter 9 you learned that Excel has built-in formulas called *functions* that assist you in making complex calculations. These mathematical, statistical, and financial equations make solving complex problems easy.

Functions do much more than just mathematical calculations, however. They can process different types of data, including numbers, dates, text, and databases. They can even provide conditional IF/THEN logic.

While it is impossible to discuss thoroughly the hundreds of functions that Excel offers, this chapter discusses many of the most frequently used, and most helpful, functions.

Entering a Function Manually

Very simple functions, such as the SUM function, can be entered in much the same way as a value is entered into a cell. For instance, you might have a series of numbers in cells E2 to E7 and wish to put the formula =SUM(E2:E7) in cell E8. One way to do this is to simply type the formula in cell E8.

Many Excel users are not comfortable typing a range address. They prefer to use the mouse to ensure that they specify the correct cells. In this case, you can type the function and then use the mouse to select the range to which it applies. In the example above, you would do so, as follows.

Hands On: Selecting a Range with the Mouse

1. Click on cell E8.
2. Type =SUM(.
3. Click on cell E2 to start the range and drag to cell E7 to select the entire range. The formula bar will say "=SUM(E2:E7."
4. Click the button with the green check mark on it, called the Confirm button. Excel completes the formula by putting in a closing parentheses.

The same thing can be done with the keyboard, as follows.

Hands On: Specifying a Range with the Keyboard

1. Use the arrow keys to move to cell E8.
2. Type =SUM(.
3. Move to cell E2 with the arrow keys.
4. Hold down the (Shift) key while you use the arrow keys to move down to cell E7. The cells are selected as you move and you will see "=SUM(E2:E7" on the formula bar.
5. Press (Enter). The formula is complete.

Using the Function Wizard

You can also select a function using the Function Wizard, rather than typing the name—i.e., =SUM(. The Function Wizard is helpful in three ways:

- It categorizes functions, allowing you to find the one you need quickly
- It provides information about the function and what it does
- It helps you supply the information that the function needs

Most functions require information (called *arguments*) to make them work. For instance, the SUM function requires a range of numbers to total. The Loan Payment (PMT) function requires the amount of the loan, the number of payments, and the interest rate to tell you how much the periodic payments will be.

TIP: If you need a quick sum of all numbers in the column directly above a cell, or in the row to the left of it, click on the cell, click the AutoSum button, and press Enter.

You can enter numbers or cell references as arguments for functions. In the example above, the PMT function has three required arguments (plus two optional ones that, for simplicity, we will ignore). It is expressed as =PMT(*rate,nper,pv*). The *rate* argument is the interest rate, *nper* is the number of periods, and *pv* is the present (initial) value of the loan.

If you want to determine the payments on a $100,000 loan given at 12 percent interest over 30 years, you would first convert the rate and periods to 1 percent and 360 months, since you will be making monthly payments.

To enter this function, you could type **=PMT(.01,360,100000)** or **=PMT(A1,C3,B2)** (supposing those cells contained the appropriate values).

As functions become more complex, you will find it easier to use the Function Wizard to enter them, rather than typing them manually. To do so, follow these steps:

1. Click on the cell that should contain the formula.

2. Click on the formula bar. You'll see (from left to right) the Cancel, Confirm, and Function Wizard buttons:

3. Click the Function Wizard button. You'll see the Function Wizard's first step, shown in Figure 11-1. At the left of this

Figure 11-1.
The Function Wizard categorizes Excel's functions and assists you in entering them

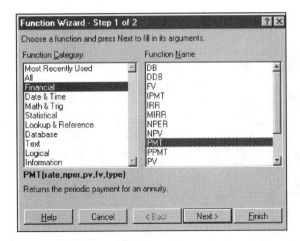

dialog box is a list of all function categories. In the list on the right are all functions in each category.

4. Select the category containing the type of function for which you are looking. In our example, we're looking for PMT, which is in the Financial category. If you don't know the category, choose All to see all the functions.

5. Select the appropriate function. You'll see two pieces of information under the list boxes. The first is the function's arguments—the information the function needs to do its work. The second is a brief description of what the function does. In our example, we see that PMT provides information on how much a loan payment will be. We can also see that the arguments include the loan rate, the number of periods, the present value (amount of loan), future value (amount at the end of the loan), and loan type.

6. Click Next. You'll see a dialog box that prompts you to supply a value for each of the arguments in the function, as shown in Figure 11-2. A description of each argument appears when you click in the text boxes.

TIP: If you don't understand what any of the arguments mean, click the <u>H</u>elp button for assistance with the highlighted function.

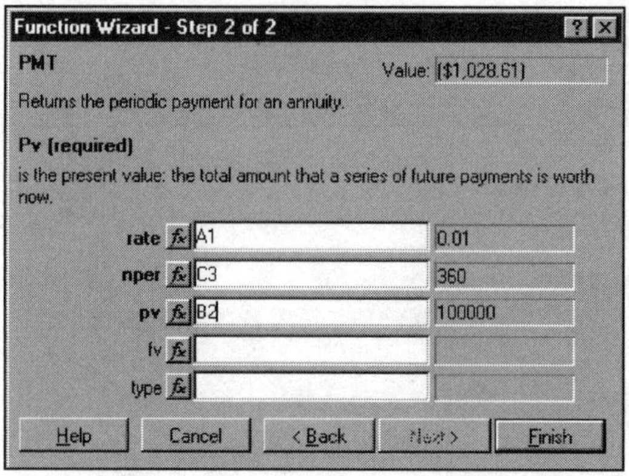

Figure 11-2.
The Function Wizard
prompts you for each
value you need for the
function

7. For each argument, type a number, type the address of the cell(s), click in the appropriate cell, or drag across the range of cells to select them. You may need to drag the dialog box to the edge of the screen in order to see the cells you need.

8. After you have entered the arguments, click Finish. Your function appears in the worksheet.

Calculating Simple Statistics

Excel makes it easy to calculate simple statistics, such as summing and averaging a column of numbers, or finding out what the largest or smallest number is in it. These calculations are simple when you use Excel. The necessary functions work similar to the SUM function you're already familiar with. The only argument they take is the range of numbers on which they operate. Examples of common statistical functions include:

- **SUM(***range***)** gives you the total of the range
- **AVERAGE(***range***)** provides the numerical average of the range
- **MAX(***range***)** and **MIN(***range***)** return the maximum or minimum value in the range
- **COUNT(***range***)** tells you how many non-zero cells are in the range

Working with Dates and Times

One of the types of data that can be entered into cells are dates. Whether you type **1/1/96**, or **January 1, 1996**, or **01-Jan-96**, Excel

Formatting cells is discussed in Chapter 9.

interprets it as a date for you. Similarly, **13:30** or **1:30 PM** are interpreted as times. You can even choose how dates will be formatted, just as you format other data.

There are several functions that may come in handy when working with dates. These include the following:

- **TODAY( )** returns the current day's date
- **NOW( )** returns the current date and time
- **MONTH**(*date*) returns the month of the specified date; similarly, **YEAR**(*date*), **DATE**(*date*), and **DAY**(*date*) return the year, day of the month, and day of the week for the specified date

You can also add and subtract dates. For instance, assume that today's date is September 1, 1996. If you put **TODAY( )** in cell A1, **9/15/96** in cell B1, and **=B1–A1** in cell C1, C1 would display "14." This can be useful to show project deadlines as they approach.

Using Financial Functions

While many of the financial functions are rather complex for non-accountants, there are a few that can be useful for home and small business use.

- **PMT** (*rate,nper,pv*) is the Payment function, which shows the payments necessary to make on any given loan
- **PV**(*rate,nper,pmt*) is the Present Value function, which allows you to start with the amount of money you can afford to pay and add the prevailing interest rate to determine how much you can afford to borrow
- **FV**(*rate,nper,pmt*) is the Future Value function, which tells you how much money you will have if you keep investing it at a given rate
- **NPER**(*rate,pmt,pv*) is the Number of Payments function, which can be very helpful if you are weighing different loan options to decide which one you can pay off the soonest

These financial functions use some or all of the same four arguments: *rate* is the interest rate, *nper* is the number of periods, *pv* is the present value, and *pmt* is the payment amount. For instance, to calculate a monthly payment on a loan, the rate would be the yearly interest rate divided by 12 (to obtain the monthly interest); *nper* is the number of months of the loan and *pv* is the loan amount.

Manipulating Text Strings

If you are working with text, you may occasionally need to manipulate text entries as you do numbers. For instance, you might include a first name in cell A1 and a last name in cell B1, and want to show the full name in cell C1. You could try to do this by entering the formula **=A1&B1**. This would work, but the result would be something like "JohnSmith." The ampersand *concatenated* (strung together) the two cells; you need a space between the names. Anything that you put in quotes will be taken as a literal string of text to be added, so you can do exactly what you want by entering **=A1&" "&B1** to get "John Smith" in C1.

If you wanted only to use the person's first initial, or if you wanted to know the length of his last name, you could use other text functions, such as the following:

- **LEFT**(*string, number of characters*) returns the specified number of characters at the left of the string. Similarly, **RIGHT**(*string, number of characters*) returns the specified number of characters at the right of the string. The string can be the actual text in quotes—e.g., LEFT("John")—or a cell reference—e.g., LEFT(A1).

- **MID**(*string, starting point, number of characters*) provides a subset of the characters in a string. To obtain the first initial of the person's name in cell A1, you would enter **MID(A1,1,1)**.

- You can even convert a string to uppercase with the **UPPER**(*string*) function, to lowercase by using **LOWER**(*string*), or to initial caps with **PROPER**(*string*).

Using Logical Functions

You can make formulas more powerful when you incorporate conditional logic into them.

For instance, your database contains invoice information and you want to have a column that helps you target invoices that are overdue by 30 days or more. You can use the IF function to do this.

Figure 11-3.
An IF function can
make a spreadsheet
more powerful by using
conditional logic

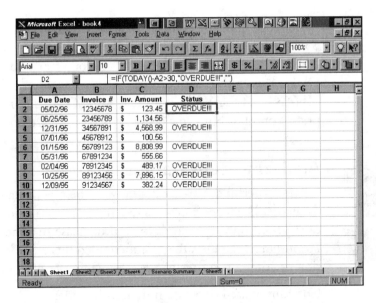

Using the IF Function

The structure of the IF function is IF(*test, cell contents if true, cell contents if false*). Therefore, you need three things for an IF function: a test (is the invoice overdue by 30 days or more?), contents if true ("OVERDUE!!!"), and contents if false (blank).

Such a worksheet is shown in Figure 11-3. Cell A2 contains the due date of the invoice. Cell D2 contains the formula =IF(TODAY( ) –A2>30,"OVERDUE!!!"," "). Everything in the parentheses before the comma is the test: TODAY( )–A2>30. TODAY() gives today's date and A2 contains the due date of the invoice. If today's date minus the due date is more than thirty, then we have a problem. "OVERDUE!!!" is what appears if the test is true. Two quotes in a row serve to indicate a blank—there's nothing between the quotes.

Using the AND and OR Functions

Conditional logical is even more powerful when combined with the AND and OR functions. For example, you might want to target only persons with invoices that are over 30 days old and over $500.

The structure of the AND command is AND(*condition 1, condition 2*). The first condition in the example is TODAY()–A2>30, since the invoice date is in cell A2 and it must be over 30 days ago. The second

PART III
EXCEL

is C2>500, since the invoice amount is in cell C2 and it must be over $500. If you want both of these to be true, you would have AND(TODAY()–A2>30,C2>500). If you want to display "OVER-DUE!!!" when they are both true, the entire formula is then =IF(AND(TODAY()–A2>30,C2>500),"OVERDUE!!!"," "). This looks pretty complex, but it makes sense is you analyze how it's built up.

Analyzing Your Database

Excel's powerful database functions can help you analyze data in your databases. Database functions resemble statistical functions, but they do calculations only on records in your database that meet specific criteria. For instance, the DCOUNT function counts records that meet a criterion or criteria you specify—e.g., the number of invoices over $500.

Commonly used database functions include:

- **DCOUNT**(*database, field, criteria*) counts the number of records in the database that meet the specified criteria
- **DSUM**(*database, field, criteria*) totals the specified field for all records that meet the specified criteria
- **DAVERAGE**(*database, field, criteria*) returns the average value of the specified field for all records that meet the specified criteria
- **DMAX**(*database, field, criteria*) and **DMIN**(*database, field, criteria*) provide the maximum and minimum values of the specified field for all records that meet the specified criteria

Database functions all use the same three arguments:

- The range that encompasses the database
- The cell address of the field to which the function is applied
- A criterion or criteria to select records

Criteria are entered into worksheet cells, rather than being typed into the formula. Put the field name that is being compared in a blank cell, and put the criterion underneath it. For instance, Figure 11-4 shows a criterion that looks for all invoice numbers greater than 96000. The field being compared is typed in cell F1; the criterion (>96000) is typed in cell F2. The range of the criterion used in the formula is F1:F2.

> Databases are defined and discussed in Chapter 10.

Figure 11-4.
Database functions
require a field and
criterion

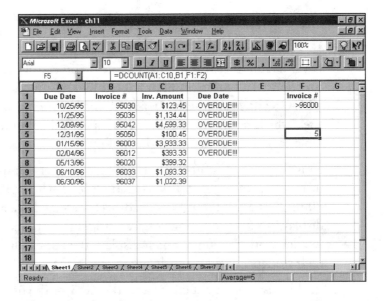

Figure 11-5.
You can use multiple
criteria for database
functions

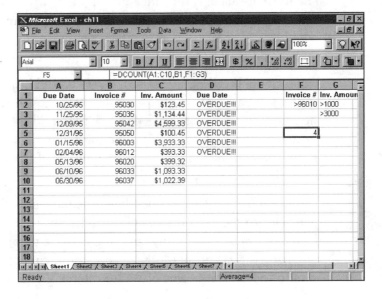

You can even specify multiple criteria that the records must meet by putting AND criteria on the same row and OR criteria on different rows. This can be seen in Figure 11-5. In the example, records will be chosen that have an invoice number over 96010 *and* are over $1,000, or any invoice over $3,000.

Categorizing Data with the VLOOKUP Function

Excel has another feature that can help you categorize data: the lookup functions. The most commonly used lookup function is **VLOOKUP**(*lookup value, reference table, column in reference table to use*), which returns a value from the specified column in the reference table that is associated with the lookup value.

This may sound complex, but it's actually a very simple concept. For instance, a teacher may have a grading scale where 90 to 100 is an A, 80 to 90 is a B, etc. In his spreadsheet, he may have a column which displays a numeric average of each student's test grades. He may wish to add another column which displays the appropriate letter grade for each student, based on their numeric average.

In this case, he would create a worksheet like the one in Figure 11-6. The reference table is the range that specifies which letter grades are associated with numeric ranges—G1:H5. The numbers are ordered from lowest to highest, and the lowest number associated with each grade is specified.

The formula is cell F2 is VLOOKUP(E2,G1:H5,2). To analyze this, let's look at each part. The first argument, E2, is the lookup value—the student's numeric average of 87. The second argument is the range for the reference table, G1:H5. The third argument, 2, is the column in the reference table that should be returned. In this case the letters are in the second column.

The VLOOKUP function goes down the reference table, comparing each value to the lookup value of 87. When it finds a value greater than the lookup value (90, in this case), it goes back up one row to G4, the row that has 80. The VLOOKUP function then looks in the second column to return the value of B into the cell the formula was in.

Absolute references are discussed in Chapter 12.

CAUTION: When copying a VLOOKUP function from one cell to another, the range of the reference table will adjust for it, which you do not want. Use absolute cell references such as $G$1:$H$5 to prevent the range of the reference table from changing as you copy the formula to other cells.

Figure 11-6.
Numeric grades can be
converted to letter
grades with the
VLOOKUP function

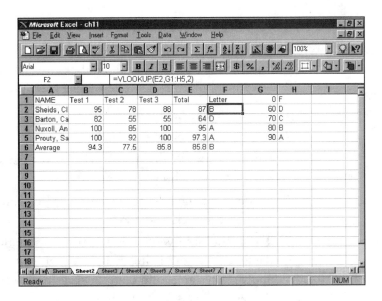

Summarizing Data with Pivot Tables

Pivot tables show a summary of data categorized by field. For instance, you may wish to view a summary of sales organized by department, by state, or both, such as the one shown in Figure 11-7.

Figure 11-7.
Pivot tables show a
summary of data

Database

Pivot table

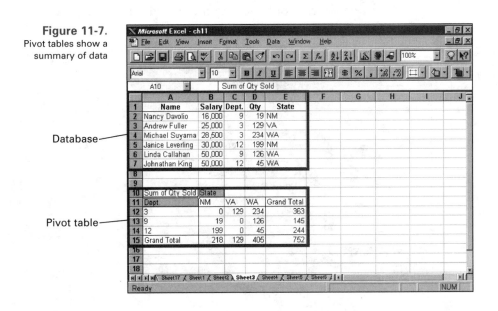

Creating a Pivot Table

When you create a pivot table, you can see the summary in a selected empty area of the worksheet, or on a different worksheet if you so specify. To create a pivot table, follow this procedure:

1. Open the database you wish to use.

2. Click on any cell in the database.

3. Choose Data, PivotTable. You'll see the first step of the Pivot-Table Wizard, shown in Figure 11-8.

4. Specify that the data comes from a Microsoft Excel List or Database and choose Next.

5. The PivotTable Wizard asks you to specify the range for the database. It should already be selected. If it is not, select the appropriate range and choose Next. You'll see the third step of the Wizard, as shown in Figure 11-9.

6. Notice that on the right side of the dialog box there is a button for each field in the database. Drag the button for the field that should be summed or counted to the Data area. If it is a non-numeric field, the pivot table will count occurrences by default. If it is a numeric field, the pivot table will summarize the field by default. Figure 11-10 shows the Sum of... button in the data area.

7. If you wish a different calculation performed on the field in the data area, double-click on the field button in the data

Figure 11-8.
You can make a pivot table from your Excel database or external data sources such as Access

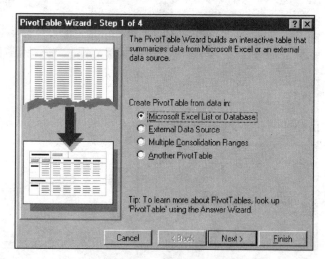

Figure 11-9.
You can select the fields for the data area, row, and column headings

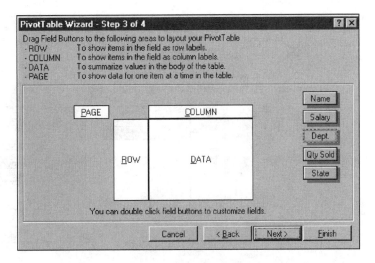

Figure 11-10.
When you drag a field, it will appear in the appropriate area of the pivot table

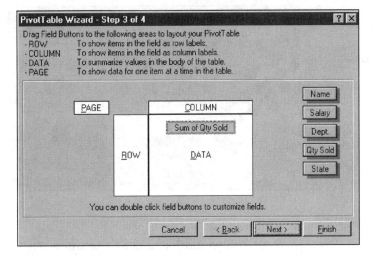

area. You'll see the PivotTable Field dialog box. Choose the calculation (such as COUNT or SUM) that you wish to use from the Summarize By list, and choose OK. You'll return to Step 3 of the Wizard.

8. You will often wish your pivot table to show subtotals for each value of a field. For instance, you may wish to see the total amount sold for each state. To show subtotals, drag the appropriate field button to the Row or Column area of the pivot table. In this example, drag the State button to the Column area.

Figure 11-11.
You can subtotal by
fields in both rows and
columns

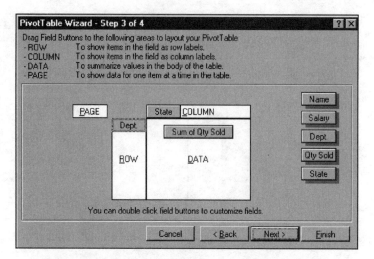

Figure 11-12.
You can place your
pivot table in the active
worksheet or in a new
worksheet of its own

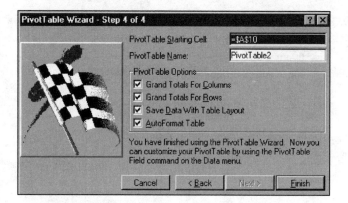

9. If you would like a table that subtotals your data by one field in rows and an additional field in columns, drag the appropriate field button to the Row or Column area that you have not yet used. For instance, you could drag the Dept. button to the <u>R</u>ow area. The Wizard would look like the one in Figure 11-11.

10. Choose Next when you have finished setting options for rows, columns, and the data area. You'll see the last step of the Wizard, shown in Figure 11-12.

11. If you would like your pivot table to appear in a new worksheet, leave the PivotTable <u>S</u>tarting Cell text box blank. If you want it to appear in the active worksheet, enter the cell address where the pivot table should start.

NOTE: You can filter your data so that it only shows records with one specific value in a selected field by dragging that field button to the <u>P</u>age area. Doing so creates a pivot table with a drop-down list box providing all values of the selected field. When you select a value in the drop-down list box, the pivot table subtotals records with the specified value in the Page field.

12. Give the pivot table a name, choose whether or not totals should appear for rows and columns, and check whether or not you want Excel to use AutoFormat to format the pivot table automatically.

13. Choose <u>F</u>inish when you are done. The pivot table will appear in the worksheet, as shown before in Figure 11-7.

Editing a Pivot Table

After you have created the pivot table, you need to recalculate its values as data in the source database change, since pivot tables do not recalculate data automatically. You may also wish to edit the way the pivot table displays the data.

To recalculate the pivot table:

1. Click on any cell in the pivot table.

2. Make sure that the Query and Pivot toolbar is displayed and click the Refresh Data button.

NOTE: The toolbar should be displayed when you are viewing the pivot table. If it isn't, display it with <u>V</u>iew, <u>T</u>oolbars.

To edit rows or columns in a pivot table, do the following:

1. Click on any existing row heading or column heading, or any cell containing the data of the pivot table.

2. Click the Pivot Table Field button. You'll see the Pivot Table Field dialog box shown in Figure 11-13.

Figure 11-13.
You can change the
way data are totaled in
rows or columns by
editing the pivot table

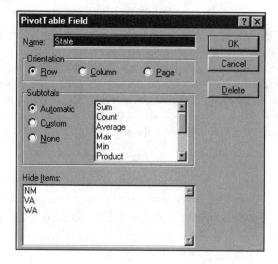

3. If you wish to change where on the pivot table the field is subtotaled, choose Row, Column; or Row, Page.

4. To change the type of calculations used in the pivot table, choose Custom and highlight the calculation(s) you wish to use.

5. To hide specific values of the field, click on the values to be hidden in the Hide Items box.

6. Choose OK. The pivot table will be recalculated based on the new options you chose.

NOTE: You can click in the data area of the pivot table and click the PivotTable Field button to set display and calculation options for data in the pivot table.

Conducting What-If Analyses

Excel can help you analyze data in other ways, as well, by conducting What-If analyses for you:

- **Goal Seek** solves problems where you want a formula to evaluate to a specific value, and you vary the value in one cell that the formula depends on to reach that value

- **Scenarios** provide the ability to try several different alternatives and display the results of all of them at once

Using Goal Seek

The Goal Seek feature is extremely useful when you need to "guess" at the appropriate contents of one cell in order to make another cell have a certain value. For instance, you may know how much you can afford in house payments and want to know the maximum total price you can afford for your new house.

The PMT function only tells you how much your payment will be for a certain loan amount. One way to find out how much you can afford is to keep changing the total loan amount and see how it affects the payment amount, until you reach the maximum amount you can spend. This can be time-consuming as you keep entering different values in the worksheet.

Use the Goal Seek feature instead. It automatically "guesses" at values until it comes up with the solution. Use Goal Seek as follows:

1. Create a worksheet that has a cell you want to change (the loan amount) and another cell whose value you want to determine (maximum payment). The second cell must be a formula that depends on the first cell, like the one in Figure 11-14.

Figure 11-14.
A typical goal seek problem is finding the most you can borrow for a given payment

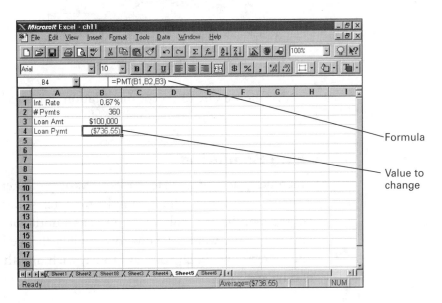

Formula

Value to change

2. Choose <u>T</u>ools, <u>G</u>oal Seek. You'll see the Goal Seek dialog box:

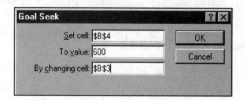

3. Choose <u>S</u>et Cell and click on the cell whose value you want to set to a specific value. In our example, it would be the Loan Pymt cell, B4.

4. Choose To <u>V</u>alue and type in the value you wish to achieve. In our example, it is the amount of the maximum payment you wish to make, $600.

5. Choose By <u>C</u>hanging Cell and click on the cell you will be making "guesses" at—the Loan Amount cell in the example, B3.

6. Choose OK. You'll see the Goal Seek Status dialog box, showing the solution that Goal Seek found:

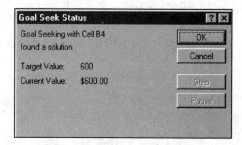

7. Choose OK to accept the solution or Cancel to return the worksheet to its original condition.

Using Scenarios

Sometimes you may want to present a variety of alternatives in your what-if analysis. In our first example, the interest rate could change over the months you look for a house, and until you lock in your loan. You would want to know how much a change in interest rate would affect how much you have to pay each month for the house you are buying.

The current worksheet shows a monthly interest rate of 0.67 percent. This is an 8 percent yearly interest, divided by 12 months. You might want to know the effect of the yearly interest going up to 8.5 percent per year (0.71 percent monthly) or down to 7.5 percent (0.63 percent monthly).

The Scenario Manager permits you to try out alternative solutions and save each solution as a *scenario*. You can then create a report that summarizes the results from each one.

To create scenarios:

1. Determine the different values you'll use for your scenarios. In our example, these might be interest rates of 0.63, 0.67, and 0.71 percent.

2. Create a worksheet that arrives at a solution using any one of these values. For example, the procedure above arrived at the solution for a 0.67 percent interest amount.

3. Choose Tools, Scenarios. You'll see the Scenario Manager dialog box.

4. Choose Add. You'll see the Add Scenario dialog box shown in Figure 11-15.

5. Give the scenario a descriptive name. Often if you have three alternatives, you might name them "Low," "Mid," and "High." In our example, 0.67 percent is the middle value, so we could name this scenario **Mid**.

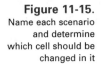

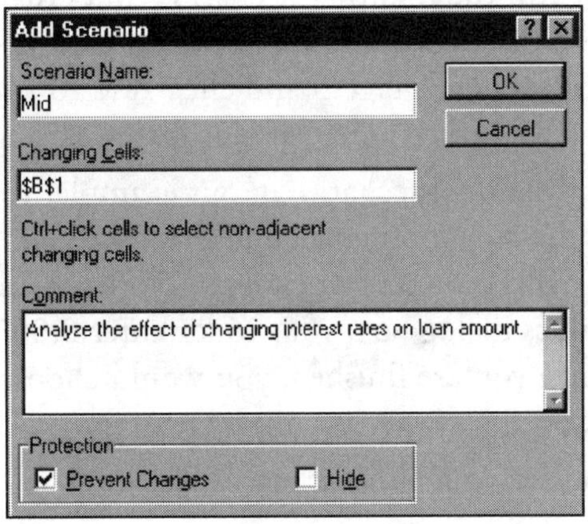

Figure 11-15.
Name each scenario and determine which cell should be changed in it

Add Scenario

Scenario Name:
Mid

Changing Cells:
$B$1

Ctrl+click cells to select non-adjacent changing cells.

Comment:
Analyze the effect of changing interest rates on loan amount.

Protection
☑ Prevent Changes   ☐ Hide

OK
Cancel

TIP: The dollar signs you see in the cell name ($B$1) indicate that it is an absolute address.

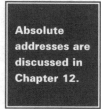

Absolute addresses are discussed in Chapter 12.

6. Click in the Changing Cells box to specify which cell(s) will be changed in the scenario. In this case, you will be changing the interest rate, so click in cell B1.

7. Choose OK. You'll see the Scenario Values dialog box:

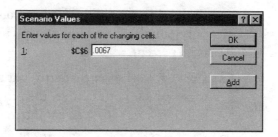

8. This dialog box enables you to enter the value that each changing cell has in this scenario. In this case, there is only one cell that changes—the interest rate. The value that is already there is appropriate for the Mid scenario. Choose Add to add another scenario. You'll see the Add Scenarios dialog box again.

9. Repeat steps 4 through 7 for additional scenarios. In our example, you would enter **Low** as the scenario name. The changing cell is already specified as $B$1, so you can choose OK. In the resulting Scenario Values dialog box, you would enter **0.0063** as the value (watch your decimal places to express percentages!) and click Add to add the third scenario. You'll see the Add Scenarios dialog box again.

10. For the final scenario, in our example, you would enter **High** as the scenario name. The changing cell is already specified as $B$1, so you can choose OK. In the resulting Scenario Values dialog box, you would enter **0.0071** as the value. Since you are finished, you would choose OK.

11. You now return to the Scenario Manager dialog box, where you see your three scenarios listed, as shown in Figure 11-16.

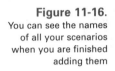

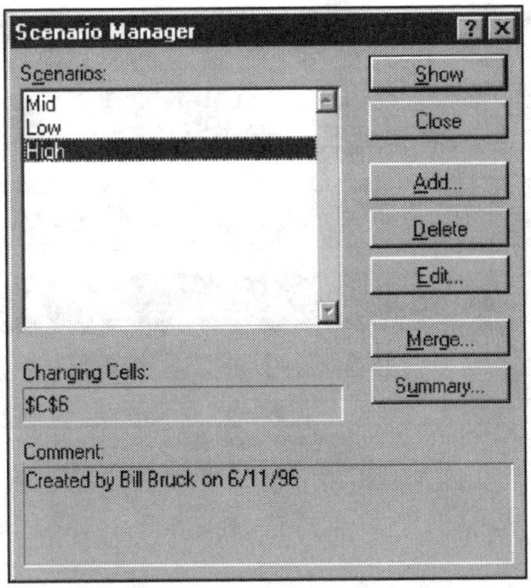

PART III EXCEL

Figure 11-16.
You can see the names of all your scenarios when you are finished adding them

12. At this point, you have several options to manage your scenarios:

- To delete a scenario, highlight it and choose <u>D</u>elete.

- To add a new scenario, choose <u>A</u>dd and follow steps 4 through 7 above.

- To edit a scenario, highlight it and choose Edit. You'll see the Edit Scenarios dialog box, which is exactly like the Add Scenarios dialog box, displaying the existing name of the scenario. Change the name and choose OK. You'll see the Scenario Values dialog box. Edit the value of the changing cell, if desired, and choose OK to return to the Scenario Manager dialog box.

- To see the results of a scenario, highlight the desired scenarios and choose <u>S</u>how. The values in your worksheet will change as specified in the scenario.

- To see a summary of the scenarios, choose S<u>u</u>mmary. You'll see the Scenario Summary dialog box, which asks whether you want to show a Scenario S<u>u</u>mmary or a Scenario Pivot Table. If you choose Summary, you'll see an attractively formatted report in a new worksheet, as shown in Figure 11-17.

13. Choose Close to return to the main editing screen when you are finished with the Scenario Manager.

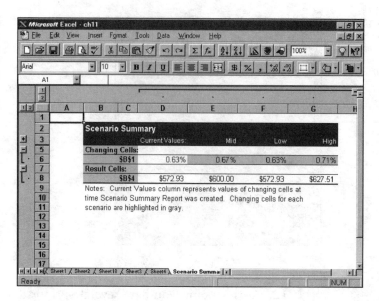

NOTE: Many people are not aware that Excel also provides a full range of statistical analysis functions, including Anova, correlation, covariance, exponential smoothing, F-Test, Fourier Analysis, Moving Averages, T-Test, and Z-test.

Although a discussion of these functions presupposes a statistical background that is beyond the scope of this book, if you are interested in them, you can use them by loading the Analysis Toolpak into Excel. Do this by choosing Tools, Add-Ins and checking Analysis Toolpak. After they are loaded, you can choose Tools, Data Analysis to see the Data Analysis dialog box containing the statistical functions.

Charting Your Results

You will often want to present data by using charts. Excel offers a variety of charting methods to produce attractively formatted charts, including three-dimensional (3-D) charts that can enhance the visual impact of your analyses.

Creating a Simple Chart

The easiest way to create a chart from data is by using the Chart Wizard. The Chart Wizard assists you in creating

15 different types of charts by answering a few simple questions. To use it:

1. Open the file containing the data to be charted in Excel.

2. Click the Chart Wizard button. Your mouse pointer changes to a black cross.

3. Drag the mouse pointer over the area in the worksheet where you wish the chart to appear. You'll see the first step of the Chart Wizard shown in Figure 11-18.

4. Specify the range of data to be charted. The data do not need to be continuous; you can specify A1:A10, C1:10, D1:D10 if the labels are in column A and the data are in columns C and D. Choose Next when you are done.

5. In the second step, choose from among several chart types, as shown in Figure 11-19, then choose Next.

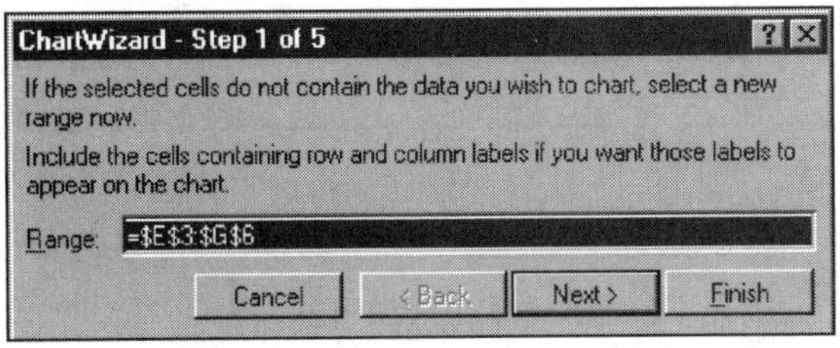

Figure 11-18.
The Chart Wizard automates the process of creating charts

Figure 11-19.
Excel offers you 15 different basic chart types

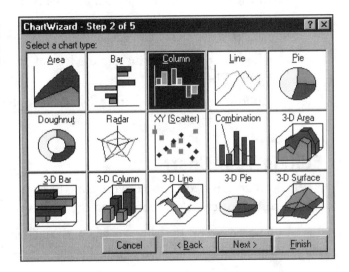

Figure 11-20.
For each type of chart, several different formats are provided

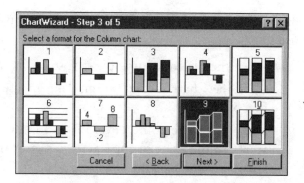

Figure 11-21.
You can specify where labels and legend text is located

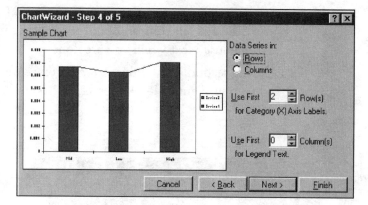

6. In the third step, choose the format of the chart, as shown in Figure 11-20. Choose Next when you are done.

7. In the fourth step, specify which cells contain labels and legend text, as shown in Figure 11-21.

8. Provide optional titles for the chart if you like, and determine whether you want to display the legend or not, as shown in Figure 11-22.

9. Choose Finish. Your chart is displayed in the specified area, as shown in Figure 11-23.

Editing Your Chart

After the chart has been created, you can edit its elements easily. You edit the different chart components in the same way:

1. Click once on the chart to select it. You'll see handles around the chart, as shown in Figure 11-23.

Figure 11-22.
You can provide optional titles, and choose whether or not to display a legend

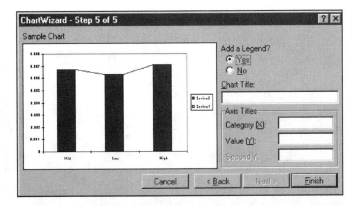

Figure 11-23.
Your chart is displayed in the area you selected when you started the Chart Wizard

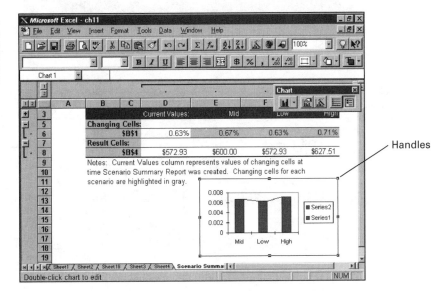

Handles

2. Double-click on the component you wish to edit. You'll see the appropriate dialog box and can make the changes you desire:

   • If you double-click on a bar, line, or pie slice, you will see the Format Data Series dialog box shown in Figure 11-24. The tabs of this dialog box allow you to specify color and pattern, location in the worksheet of the data series, labels, and data series name.

NOTE: Your dialog box will show slightly different options depending on the chart type you have selected.

Figure 11-24.
You can format the data in a chart by double-clicking on data series elements

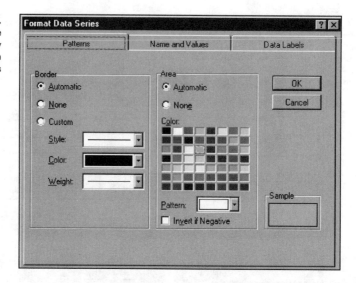

Figure 11-25.
Set axis options by double-clicking on an axis of a chart

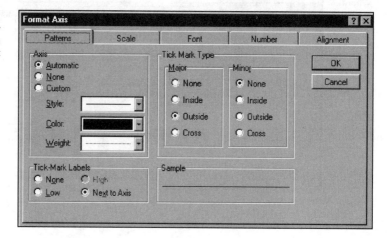

- When you double-click on an axis, the Format Axis dialog box shown in Figure 11-25 will appear. By choosing among the tabs of this dialog box, you can select the format of the axis line, as well as its starting and ending points (the *scale*), the font, number format, and alignment of its values.

- Similarly, double-clicking on the legend, the area outside the chart (the *chart area*), and the area inside the chart (the *plot area)* will set other chart options.

3. When you are finished editing your chart, click in your worksheet outside the chart area to deselect the chart.

CHAPTER 12

USING WORKBOOKS FOR LARGER PROJECTS

IN THIS CHAPTER

- Working with Workbooks
- Linking Cells Together
- Naming Cells
- Adding Cell Notes
- Protecting Cells
- Allowing Multi-User Editing

Large projects often require more than one worksheet. For example, you may need to create a divisional budget out of several departmental budgets, or perhaps you have a large database and need to perform a series of summary analyses on it. Larger projects often involve both more than one worksheet and more than one person.

In this chapter, you will learn about using workbooks that combine worksheets, how to combine information from different worksheets together, and how several people can work together effectively with Excel.

Working with Workbooks

A *workbook* is a collection of worksheets or other types of sheets that are saved as a single file. There are actually five different types of sheets that can comprise a workbook. The first is a *worksheet*. This is Excel's term for an electronic spreadsheet. You can also have a *chart sheet*, a sheet containing nothing but a chart. Similarly, you can have a *macro sheet*, which is a sheet containing an older Excel 4–style macro. There are also *modules*, which are programmed macros, and *dialog sheets*, which are sheets containing custom dialog boxes that you create.

When you open an Excel file, you are actually opening a work*book*, not a single work*sheet*. Now that you have learned to create simple worksheets, make databases, and analyze data, you can begin to work with workbooks containing more than one worksheet.

You select a single sheet by clicking on its tab. You can select several adjacent sheets by clicking on the tab of the first one, then holding down the (Shift) key and clicking on the tab of the last one. Select several nonadjacent sheets by clicking on the first tab, then holding down the (Ctrl) key while you click on additional tabs.

The easiest way to insert, delete, copy, move, or rename sheets is to select them, then right-click on one of the selected tabs. Right-clicking on a tab reveals the shortcut menu shown here:

Inserting a Worksheet

To insert a worksheet, do the following:

1. Right-click on the tab of the sheet *after* the one you wish to insert, then select Insert from the shortcut menu. You'll see the Insert dialog box shown in Figure 12-1.

2. Insert a blank worksheet by double-clicking on the Worksheet icon.

There are other choices to make in this dialog box:

- You can insert a Chart sheet by double-clicking the Chart icon. This starts the Chart Wizard.

- Double-click the MS Excel 4.0 Macro icon to create macros in Excel 4 format. Newer macros are written like a Basic program, whereas old macros had one command in each cell and looked like worksheets. You can still use the old macro-writing format if you're more comfortable with it.

- Double-click the Module icon to create modules, the newer, programmed type of macros.

- Double-click on the Dialog icon to include a custom dialog box in your macros.

- If you do a standard installation, you will also see a Spreadsheet Solutions tab that contains many helpful templates for solving common problems. If you save worksheets in the Spreadsheet Solutions folder, you can click on the Spreadsheet Solutions tab to insert them into your current workbook. This can be very helpful if you have a worksheet like an amortization table that you find useful in a number of different workbooks.

PART III   EXCEL

Figure 12-1.
You can insert a worksheet, chart, macro, module or dialog box sheet into your workbook

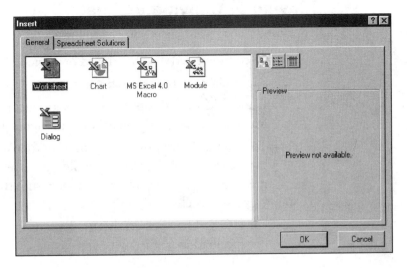

Deleting or Renaming a Worksheet

Right-clicking on a worksheet tab also allows you to delete or rename the selected worksheet. To delete the worksheet, right-click the tab of the worksheet you want to delete and choose Delete from the shortcut menu. You will be asked for confirmation; if you choose OK, the worksheet will be permanently deleted.

You can also rename your worksheet by choosing Rename from the shortcut menu. The name you enter in the resulting Rename Sheet dialog box will be displayed on the sheet tab. Make it a habit to name your worksheets if you have more than one in the workbook, so that it's easy to navigate around the workbook. Try to make the name descriptive, but not too long, since the tab will expand to accommodate it and you won't be able to see as many tabs on-screen at one time. For instance, if you have budgets for several months in your workbook, name the tabs "Jan," "Feb," "Mar," etc. You needn't name them "January Budget," "February Budget," etc. if they are all budgets.

TIP: You can also rename a worksheet by double-clicking on its tab and entering the new name in the Rename Sheet dialog box.

Moving or Copying a Sheet

To move or copy your sheet, do the following:

1. Select the sheet(s) to be moved or copied.

2. Right-click on the selected sheet(s).

3. Choose Move or Copy from the shortcut menu. You'll see the Move or Copy dialog box shown in Figure 12-2.

4. To move a sheet within the same workbook, select the sheet in the <u>B</u>efore Sheet list that it should be moved *in front of.* If you prefer to copy rather than move it, ensure that the <u>C</u>reate a Copy box is checked.

5. Click OK. The selected sheet(s) have been moved or copied to the specified location.

Figure 12-2.
You can move or
copy sheets
within or between
workbooks

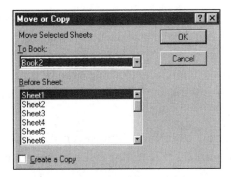

TIP: You can also move sheets within a workbook by dragging their tabs to a new location. Copy sheets by holding down the Ctrl key while dragging them to their new location.

You can use a similar procedure to move or copy the worksheet to another workbook, as follows:

1. Open both the source and destination workbook.

2. Activate the source workbook.

3. Select the sheets to be moved or copied.

4. Right-click on one of the selected sheet's tabs, then choose Move or Copy.

5. Click the down arrow in the To Book box. You'll see the names of all open workbooks, as well as a "(new book)" option, to move the worksheet to a new workbook.

6. Choose the appropriate workbook, then click OK.

Linking Cells Together

When you begin working with multiple worksheets, you will often find that they contain formulas that rely on values contained in cells in other worksheets. On occasion, you may even find that values in one workbook feed values into another workbook.

For instance, branch office budgets may be kept as separate workbooks maintained by the branch chiefs. The departmental budget may be a compilation of the branch budgets, stored in a departmental budget worksheet maintained by the department manager. If the manager has access to the network workspaces where the branch budgets are stored, he or she can build references to these branch budgets into the departmental budget—linking the branch values into the departmental worksheet.

Before learning how to link cells, however, it's important to learn about two new worksheet features: cell references and named cells.

Understanding Cell References

Normally, when you copy a formula from one cell to another, the formula changes as needed. For instance, in Figure 12-3, the formula in cell B5 is the sum of B2:B4. If you copy the formula in B5 (=SUM(B2:B4)) to C5, the formula will change to =SUM(C2:C4). This is because the cell addresses B2:B4 are relative.

A *relative address* is relative to the cell it is in. It's like giving the directions, "Go up the street and take your second right. The house you want is the third one on the left." The accuracy of these directions depends on where you're standing. Excel uses relative addressing by default because this makes it very easy to move formulas around the spreadsheet.

Figure 12-3.
Normally, cell references are relative rather than absolute

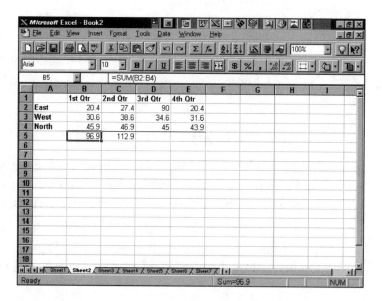

Figure 12-4.
Absolute addresses
don't change when
a cell is copied

	A	B	C	D	E
1		1996	1997	Goal	106%
2	**Region 1**	20,000	=B2*E1		
3	**Region 2**	25,000	=B3*E1		
4					
5					
6					
7					
8					
9					
10					
11					
12					

PART III   EXCEL

There are times, however, when you need an *absolute address.* In giving directions, one might say, "The house you want is at 321 Center Street." These directions are independent of where you are standing.

The need for absolute addressing can be seen in Figure 12-4. The 1997 sales goals for Region 1 are 6 percent greater than the 1996 actual sales. Thus, the formula in cell C2 is =B2*E1. However, if we copy this formula down to C3, the formula becomes =B3*E2, which is a problem because there's nothing in cell E2. What we really want is cell B2 to change to B3, but cell E1 to be held constant. In other words, we need the reference to cell E1 to be an absolute address.

In Excel, a cell's address in a formula is indicated as absolute by putting a dollar sign in front of each element that should be held constant. Since we want both the row (1) and the column (E) to be held constant, our formula in cell C2 should be =B2*$E$1. Then, when we copy it down, the B2 will change to B3 (since it's relative), while the $E$1 will stay as it is (since it's absolute).

TIP: While entering a formula, you can make a cell address absolute by typing the dollar signs yourself, or by repeatedly pressing F4 while the insertion point is in front of the cell address until the appropriate order of dollar signs appears.

Naming Cells

When you are including references to cells within formulas, you often cannot see the cell you are referencing. If the cell is in another worksheet, you can't even see it while you are writing the formula.

When you come back after the fact and try to decipher a formula such as =F192*(1+C1), you have to navigate to each cell to figure out what it refers to. Errors creep in. On the other hand, isn't it easier to understand the formula =Sales95*(1+Percent_Increase)?

You can name cells in Excel as follows:

1. Select the cell(s) to be named.

2. Choose Insert, Name, Define. You'll see the Define Name dialog box shown in Figure 12-5.

3. Type the name and choose Add. Be sure to start your name with a letter (not a number) and don't include any spaces in the name. Underscores are fine, however (so use "Total_96," not "Total 96"). Your name will be added to the list of names. Click OK to close the dialog box. (You can also use this dialog box to delete names by using the Delete button.)

NOTE: At the bottom of the dialog box is the cell that the name refers to. Notice that the cell is actually made up of the sheet name, an exclamation point, and the cell reference. Cell B5 in Sheet2 is actually Sheet2!$B$5, for example, since named cells use absolute references. This is how Excel distinguishes cells in different worksheets of the same workbook.

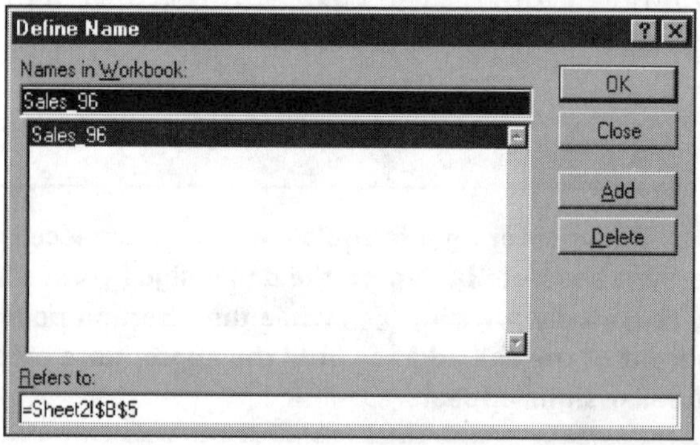

Figure 12-5.
You can assign names to cells in your worksheet for easy reference

Define Name	? X
Names in Workbook:	OK
Sales_96	Close
Sales_96	Add
	Delete
Refers to:	
=Sheet2!$B$5	

Linking Cells in a Workbook

When cells are linked, a change in one cell is reflected in the other cell. The formulas discussed so far have included linked cells. If cell C1 has the formula =A1+B1, a change in A1 or B1 is reflected instantly in C1. Thus, C1 is linked to the two other cells.

You can link cells between worksheets within a workbook just as you would link them inside the same worksheet. You do it by typing the appropriate address (which is often the harder way to do it), by typing the cell's name (if it has one), or by using a point-and-click method.

Hands On: Using a Cell Name in a Formula

1. Type **500** in cell A1 of Sheet1 in a blank workbook.

2. Choose Insert, Name, Define.

3. Name the cell **Total**.

4. Click in the Sheet2 tab, then click in cell B2.

5. Type =**Total** and press Enter. You'll see "500"—the value in the Total cell of Sheet1.

6. Click in Sheet1 and change 500 to **600**.

7. Click in Sheet2. You'll see that the value has changed there as well.

When you are writing a formula involving a cell in another sheet, you can also refer to it by pointing and clicking on it, as follows:

1. Click in the cell where the formula should appear.

2. Type = or click in the Formula Bar to start the formula, then begin to type the formula.

3. When you get to the place in the formula where the cell reference should appear, click on the tab of the sheet containing the cell, then click on the cell you want to reference. Notice that the address of the cell (including the sheet name) appears on the formula bar, as shown in Figure 12-6.

4. When you press Enter to complete your formula, you'll return to your original cell and worksheet.

Figure 12-6.
You can refer to
the cells of other
worksheets in your
formula by
pointing and
clicking on them
while you type
your formula

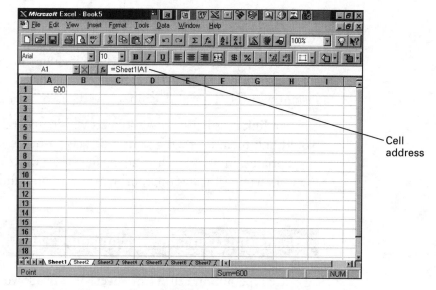

Cell
address

> **NOTE:** Alternatively, you could actually type in the appropriate cell reference such as =Sheet1!A1. Since you can't usually see the appropriate sheet and cell, it's easy to misspell the cell reference, so avoid this method.

Linking Cells between Workbooks

You can also link cells between workbooks. When you do this, you will often want the cell to actually be linked to a cell in the destination worksheet, rather than just be referenced in a formula. The principle for creating these links is the same, although the keystrokes are a little different.

To link a cell from one workbook to another, do the following:

1. Open both workbooks.

2. Navigate to the source cell in the source workbook and click on it.

3. Click on the Copy button. You'll see the "Select destination and press ENTER or choose Paste" message on the status line.

4. Switch to the other workbook by choosing <u>W</u>indow, then clicking on the name of the destination workbook.

TIP: You can also switch between open workbooks
by pressing `Ctrl`+`F6`.

---

5. Click in the destination cell, then choose Edit, Paste Special. You'll see the Paste Special dialog box:

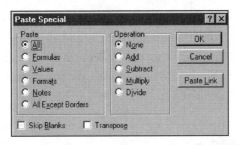

6. Click the Paste Link button. This closes the dialog box and shows the value of the source cell. As the value of the source cell changes in the source workbook, this change will be reflected in the destination cell.

7. Press `Esc` to return to the Ready mode.

Whenever you open the destination workbook, you will see the dialog box shown here if any entries in the source document have been changed since the last time you opened the destination workbook:

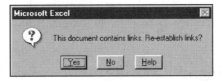

You will want to answer Yes to ensure that you are using the latest values from the source workbook(s).

NOTE: You can insert a cell reference from another workbook in a formula using the same method that was described above in "Linking Cells in a Workbook." A cell reference from another workbook consists of the workbook name in brackets, the sheet name, an exclamation point, and the cell address: e.g., =[Workbook]Sheet1!$A$1.

Working in Workgroups

Just as you may collaborate with others on Word documents, there may be times when you want to collaborate on the preparation of an Excel worksheet. Excel provides several tools that:

- Attach notes to specific cells that provide instructions to collaborators
- Protect specific cells and worksheets so that collaborators focus on their specific areas and don't inadvertently (or deliberately) modify the wrong section
- Share the workbook, allowing several collaborators to open and edit it simultaneously

NOTE: You should provide access to your worksheet by placing it in a shared folder on a network before you consider any of the steps detailed below.

Preparing Your Workbook

The first step in collaborating with others on workbooks is planning. Before you share your work, decide what data you will be entering into the workbook and what you want others to enter. Create the skeleton of your workbook with individual worksheets, row and column titles, and appropriate formulas. Format the workbook as needed. Now you're ready to proceed by adding workgroup features.

Adding Cell Notes

Once your workbook has been created and is ready to share, you may wish to add instructions for your collaborators so they'll understand their tasks. This is easy to do with *cell notes*. Cell notes are pop-up notes that appear whenever your mouse pointer moves over cells to which the notes are attached.

To add a cell note:

1. Select the cell to which a note will be added.
2. Choose Insert, Note. You'll see the Cell Note dialog box in Figure 12-7.
3. Type your note in the Text Note box, then choose OK.

Figure 12-7.
You can provide instructions to workbook collaborators by attaching notes to specific cells

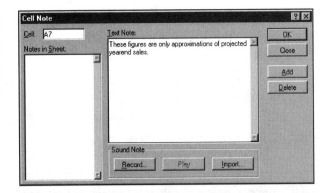

Figure 12-8.
You can attach notes to your cells that will pop up when you move your mouse pointer over them

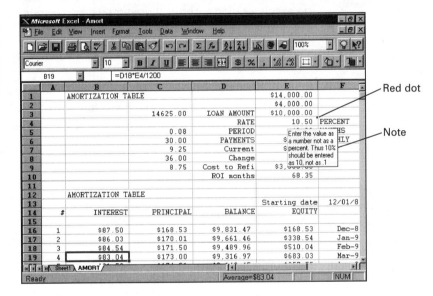

You will see a small red dot in the upper-right corner of cells that have notes attached to them, as shown in Figure 12-8. When you move your mouse pointer over a cell that has a note, you will see the note in a small pop-up window.

If you have a sound card and microphone, you can even attach a sound note, as follows:

1. Choose <u>I</u>nsert, No<u>t</u>e to access the Cell Note dialog box.

2. In the Sound Note area, choose <u>R</u>ecord. You'll see the Record dialog box:

3. Click the Record button to record your comment, or use other buttons as you would a tape recorder. Click the Stop button when you are finished.

4. Click OK twice to close both dialog boxes and return to the worksheet.

All notes in your workbook will be listed in the Cell Note dialog box, where you can review or delete them.

TIP: You can only add cell notes when you are editing the workbook in exclusive mode, not in shared mode, as described below.

Protecting Cells

After you have constructed and annotated your workbook, you will probably want to protect it in a way that allows users to add information only in the cells for which they are responsible.

When you protect a worksheet or entire workbook, other users cannot change any cells in it. So before you protect a worksheet, you should specify which cells collaborators *can* edit.

1. Open the workbook and move to the appropriate worksheet.

2. Select the cells that users should be able to edit.

3. Right-click on the selected cells and choose Format Cells from the pop-up menu that appears.

4. Click on the Protection tab. You'll see the Format Cells dialog box shown in Figure 12-9.

5. Remove the check from Locked to unlock the cells, then choose OK.

6. Repeat this procedure (steps 2 through 5) until all cells that you wish collaborators to have access to are unlocked.

7. Activate the cell locks and protect the workbook by choosing Tools, Protection, Protect Sheet. You'll see the Protect Sheet dialog box:

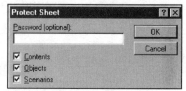

8. Choose the desired protection options, add a password if desired, then choose OK.

Figure 12-9.
This dialog box allows
you to unprotect cells
that collaborators
should be able to edit

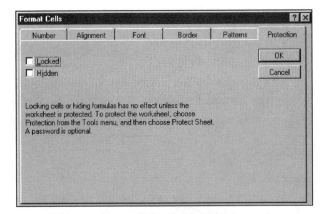

NOTE: Adding a password offers an additional level of protection for your worksheet. If you don't use a password, anyone can unprotect the worksheet.

If you would like to protect your work further, choose Tools, Protection, Protect Workbook. You'll see the Protect Workbook dialog box. As before, choose the protections required, add a password if desired, then choose OK:

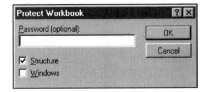

Allowing Multi-User Editing

The last step you will want to take in preparing your workbook for others is to set file-sharing options. These options are only relevant if more than one person will be editing the workbook at the same time. So if you are sending a workbook out via a routing slip, you will not need to set these options. Similarly, if the file is in a shared folder, but there is no danger that people will work on it simultaneously, you do not need to worry about setting file-sharing options.

File-sharing is very useful, however, when you want to place a workbook in a shared directory so that collaborators can look at it whenever they want. When a workbook is shared in this way, people can view it, edit it, add rows and columns, and even sort the workbook. They cannot, however, alter formulas or add notes to cells.

To share an Excel workbook, do the following:

1. Choose File, Shared Lists, and click the Editing tab. You'll see the Shared Lists dialog box:

2. Check Allow Multi-User Editing, then click OK.

3. You will need to save the file to activate this feature, so respond to the prompt, "This action will now save the file. Do you want to continue?" by clicking OK.

4. Ensure that the folder in which the workbook is saved is shared among the workgroup, and you're done!

To remove the sharing feature, follow the same procedure, but deselect the Allow Multi-User Editing option.

TIP: You can see who else is editing the workbook by selecting the Status tab in the Shared Lists dialog box. All users who have the file open will be listed.

Editing Shared Workbooks

Once it has been set up correctly, working on a shared workbook is easy. You just open it as you normally would, then enter and edit data as usual. On the title bar, you'll see the name of the file, with "[Shared]" after it to indicate that several people can edit the workbook simultaneously.

Cells you cannot access are locked, so you will not accidentally disturb the data of others. If you try to enter information in a locked cell, you will see a warning message stating that locked cells cannot be changed.

Whenever you save the document, you will update the shared workbook with your changes; you'll also be able to see the changes that others have made. If the changes conflict with yours, the latest person to save the workbook will be shown the conflict and asked which version to save.

CHAPTER 13

CUSTOMIZING YOUR EXCEL ENVIRONMENT

IN THIS CHAPTER

- Choosing Display Options
- Setting Editing Options
- Changing the Look of the Excel Window
- Exploring Default Templates
- Using Workbook Templates
- Using Sheet Templates

Now that you have some experience in creating worksheets, maintaining databases, analyzing data, and working with workbooks, you should go a step further and begin to customize your Excel environment.

There are four ways that you can do this:

- Choosing your display options
- Setting editing options
- Changing the way your Excel window looks
- Using templates

Choosing Display Options

Excel allows you to change virtually all of the elements you see in your display. You can change the display options by choosing Tools, Options, and clicking the View tab. You'll see the Options dialog box shown in Figure 13-1. Options in the Show area which you can set in this dialog box include:

- **Formula Bar** toggles the display of the formula bar. Keep this bar displayed whenever you are editing a worksheet; it provides valuable information about what is actually in the active cell, as opposed to what is displayed in the cell itself.

- **Status Bar** toggles the display of the status bar. Keep this bar

NOTE: This chapter concentrates on the options that most users will have reason to change. This keeps you from having to wade through extraneous material to find the information you need.

Figure 13-1.
The View tab allows you to choose which screen elements you wish to see

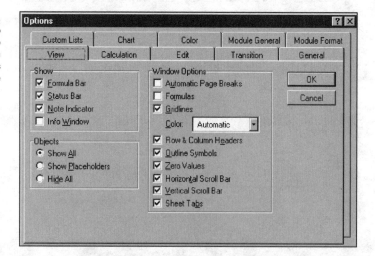

Figure 13-2.
The Information
window shows
information
about the active
cell in a full-
screen mode

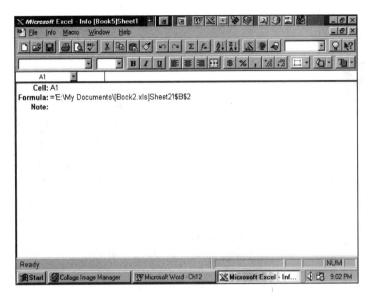

displayed whenever you are editing a worksheet; this is the only way you will know whether you are in the Ready mode or some other mode.

- **Note Indicator** is only important if you use cell notes. If you use them, you'll probably want the indicators to appear.

- **Info Window,** when active, opens a second window that has information about the active cell, shown in Figure 13-2.

There are also three options for your objects that will appear in your worksheet. Objects are charts, text boxes, and graphic elements like circles or lines that can be added to an Excel worksheet. You may choose to display them as follows:

- **Show All** displays all objects in your worksheet. You will usually choose this option.

- **Show Placeholders** shows a symbol where the object will appear. Use this option if you are short on computer memory.

- **Hide All** hides all objects in your worksheet.

There are several window options you may want to change from time to time, and many that you'll probably never touch. The window options include the following:

- If you want to see where your page breaks will occur when you print your worksheet, choose Automatic Page Breaks. This can

The Fit to Page feature is discussed in Chapter 9.

be helpful when designing your worksheet, although the Fit to Page feature in Page Setup allows you to adjust your printing as needed.

- If you want to see the formulas that you type into cells, rather than their results, you can choose Formulas. This can be helpful when you are debugging your worksheet.

- You can toggle your gridlines, row and column headers, scroll bars, and sheet tabs on and off. These features can be very helpful if you want to use a worksheet in a presentation, or give it to senior management for reviewing summary data. In these cases, you'll want as much of a "clean screen" as possible, so consider toggling this feature off, as well as the formula bar, status bar, etc., as shown in Figure 13-3.

- You may wish to toggle your Zero Values on or off, too, depending on your application. If the Zero Values box is checked, the number zero or a formula that evaluates to zero will be displayed. Otherwise, it will appear blank. This can be very helpful when you want to copy a formula into cells where data won't be entered for a while, as shown in Figure 13-4. There's no point in showing that the total sales are zero for months still in the future, as shown in the figure, but it was easier to copy the formulas into all the month cells when the

Figure 13-3.
You can turn off extraneous screen elements when you want to display a "clean screen" look

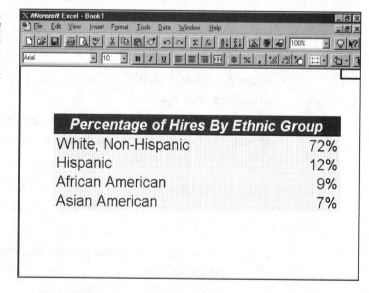

Percentage of Hires By Ethnic Group	
White, Non-Hispanic	72%
Hispanic	12%
African American	9%
Asian American	7%

Figure 13-4.
The more attractive worksheet (left) does not display zeros for upcoming months

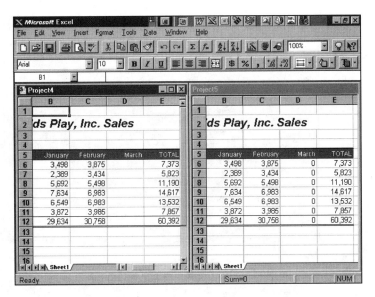

spreadsheet was created. Eliminating the zeros makes the worksheet look better.

CAUTION: Hiding the display of zero values does not work when cells are formatted as accounting. Accountants like to see zero amounts!

Setting Editing Options

There are a few other options that you may wish to specify for your Excel worksheets that control Excel's appearance.

If you choose Tools, Options, and select the Edit tab, you'll see the dialog box shown in Figure 13-5. By default, the active cell in a worksheet moves one cell down when you press the (Enter) key. For most applications this is useful, since the active cell moves down upon pressing (Enter) and to the right upon pressing (Tab). Sometimes, however, you may find this inconvenient. You may wish the active cell not to move upon pressing (Enter), or have it move in a different direction. Set this option with the Move Selection after Enter option.

Figure 13-5.
The Edit tab allows you to control options such as how the Enter key works

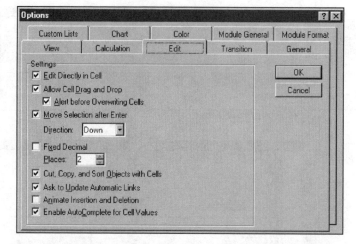

Figure 13-6.
The General tab allows you to specify your default directory

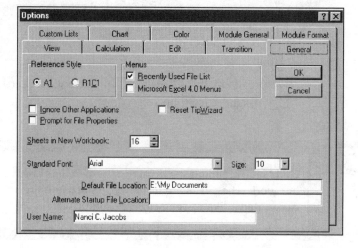

If you find that you cannot move or copy cells with the drag-and-drop method, this option may not have been selected in this dialog box.

You can also change two other commonly used options by clicking the General tab. You'll see the Options dialog box shown in Figure 13-6. This tab allows you to specify your default data directory, as well as how many sheets you want by default in new workbooks.

TIP: If your pointer is too near a cell's edge, you may accidentally move cell data when you think you are simply selecting cells. In that case, turn drag-and-drop off until you gain more accuracy with your mouse.

Changing the Look of the Excel Window

There are several ways that you can change the look of your Excel editing window. These can be very helpful when you are working with larger worksheets and either need to see more information on the screen or need to see the titles of your rows and columns.

Freezing Window Panes

Perhaps the most useful way to modify your editing window is by using the freeze panes feature. This allows the row and column titles to appear on the screen at all times, no matter how far down or to the right you scroll when viewing the worksheet.

To ensure that you can always see your row and/or column titles, do the following:

1. Click on the first cell that you do *not* want frozen. This is usually the first cell under the row containing your column headings and to the right of the column containing your row headings. In a typical worksheet such as the one shown in Figure 13-7, this would be cell C2, since the headings are in row 1 and columns A and B.

Figure 13-7.
You can freeze the row and column headings of your worksheet so they always appear on the screen no matter how far you scroll away from them

Frozen columns A and B

Frozen row 1

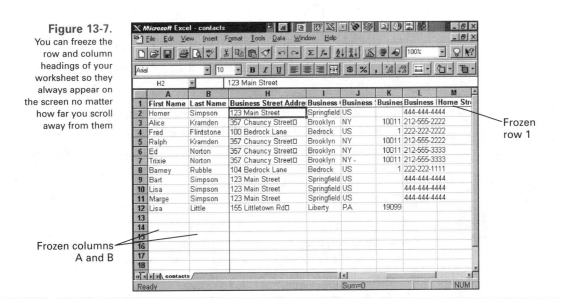

2. Choose <u>W</u>indow, <u>F</u>reeze Panes. You'll see an underline under the heading row(s) and to the right of the heading column(s). As you scroll, notice that the heading row(s) and column(s) remain on the screen.

If you do not need to freeze the row headings, but only the column headings that are in row 1, you would click on cell A2 in the example, rather than C2. This way, no column containing row headings is frozen.

If you have a number of title rows before your column headings, freezing panes may pose a special problem: the area of your worksheet that is not frozen may be so small that you cannot see much data. In this case, before you click on the first cell to be unfrozen, scroll down until your titles are on the first row that you can see in the editing window. Then freeze the panes as you normally would.

While panes are frozen, you can still click directly into a row or column heading cell to edit it. However, if you need to unfreeze your window panes, open the <u>W</u>indow menu. Notice that the <u>F</u>reeze Panes command has been replaced by the Un<u>f</u>reeze Panes command; choose this to unfreeze your window.

Using Zoom

While freezing headings is useful, there are times when you just need to see more data on your screen. You can easily do this by adjusting the Zoom factor: [100% ▼]

1. Click on the Zoom Control button in the Standard toolbar.
2. Type the new zoom percentage in or select it from the drop-down list.

Depending on your eyesight, monitor size and resolution, and font size, you may be able to read worksheets that are zoomed to 60 to 75 percent, which can easily double the number of rows of data you are looking at, as shown in Figure 13-8.

TIP: You can also select a cell or group of cells, then choose Selection from the drop down Zoom list to zoom the worksheet to the area you have selected.

Figure 13-8.
Using Zoom can double the amount of information you see on the screen

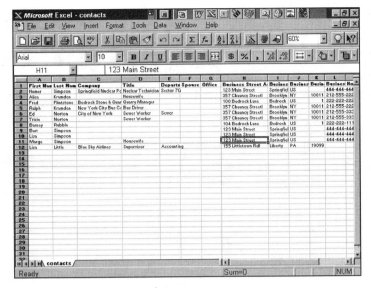

Splitting the Window

Excel offers one other feature that allows you to work simultaneously in more than one area of your worksheet. By splitting your window into two or four panes, you can add data to the bottom of a database and simultaneously see how it affects a formula contained in another area of the worksheet.

To split the window into two windows horizontally, drag down the *split box* at the top of the vertical scroll bar (just above the up arrow). You'll see two separate areas of your worksheet, each having its own scroll bar, as shown in Figure 13-9.

To switch from window to window, simply click inside the one you want to work in. Scroll through each window independently until you see the area of the worksheet you want.

You can similarly split your worksheet vertically into two windows by dragging over the *split box* to the left of the horizontal scroll bar.

TIP: To remove a split, double-click on the line that denotes the split in the worksheet.

Figure 13-9.
You can split your worksheet into two separate windows by dragging the split box

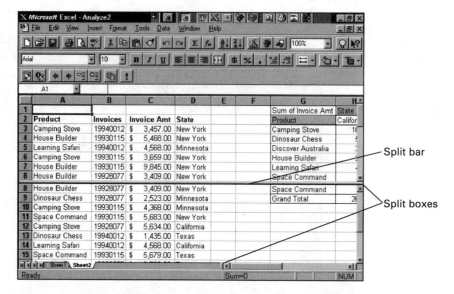

Split bar

Split boxes

Figure 13-10.
You can split your window into four separate panes, if desired

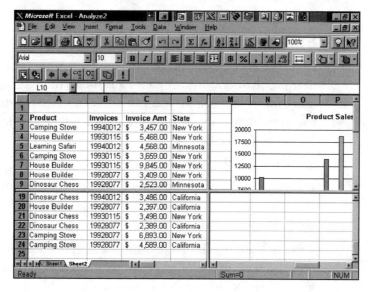

You can also split your worksheet into four windows, as follows:

1. Click on the cell below and to the right of where the split should occur.

2. Choose <u>W</u>indow, <u>S</u>plit. You'll see your window split into four smaller windows, as shown in Figure 13-10. By using the two vertical and two horizontal scroll bars, you can scroll through the four windows.

3. To reposition the split, move the mouse pointer to the intersection of the split until the pointer becomes a four-pointed arrow, then drag the split to its new location.

4. To remove the split, choose Window, Remove Split.

Using Templates

Using Excel efficiently means learning not to reinvent the wheel each time you create a spreadsheet. You must learn how to build upon your previous work. You do this in Excel just as you would in Word. In fact, what you use is the same: templates.

There are two common situations in which you will want to build upon your previous work. The first is when an entire analysis is repeated periodically. For example, an annual departmental budget may be a workbook consisting of several branch worksheets consolidated into a departmental worksheet, with two or three charts added. In this case, you will want to build this year's budget on last year's workbook, substituting this year's figures for last year's.

The second common situation involves inserting an individual worksheet into a variety of workbooks. For instance, you might have a simple amortization table that you would like to use in a number of different workbooks.

Exploring Default Templates

All Excel worksheets are based on templates. Excel templates store information about the toolbars, formatting, settings, and default cell contents of each worksheet. A new Excel workbook is based on a template that contains no information in its worksheets. However, your templates can contain existing data; this is how you'll build upon your previous work.

To see the possibilities, start by looking at the templates that ship with Office 95 in the Spreadsheet Solutions tab. You'll see templates for creating a business plan, deciding on whether a car lease is good for you, managing a loan, creating a personal budget, and creating business documents like invoices, sales quotes, purchase orders, expense statements, and change requests.

To start understanding some of the possibilities that templates offer to casual, intermediate, and advanced users, let's look at the template for creating a personal budget.

Hands On: Using the Personal Budgeter Template

To create a new template:

1. Choose File, New. You'll see the New dialog box.

TIP: You cannot click the New button in this situation. The New button creates a new workbook based on the default template; it does not allow you to choose a template.

2. Click on the Spreadsheet Solutions tab. You'll see the Excel templates that ship with Office 95.

3. Double-click on the Personal Budgeter template to create a new workbook based on this template. You'll see the Budget Summary worksheet shown in Figure 13-11. Notice the following:

   • The template created a new workbook that has several named worksheets

   • The new workbook automatically opens to a specific worksheet

   • This worksheet contains well-formatted labels and formulas

   • If you click on the Total Monthly Income cell (also known as cell G19), you'll see that it contains the formula ='Income Data'!G23; thus, a template can contain cells that are linked to cells in other worksheets in the workbook

   • There is a Customize button on the worksheet, which runs a macro that helps you insert a logo and personal information on all worksheets in the workbook

4. Click on the Customize button. You'll see the Customize Your Budgeter worksheet. Notice the cell that says "Hover your Pointer HERE for useful tip." Try it, and notice the tip that pops up.

5. Fill out the information on the worksheet, then click on the

Figure 13-11.
Worksheets in new workbooks based on templates can contain forms you fill out, macro buttons, and summary information linked to other worksheets

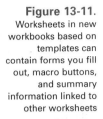
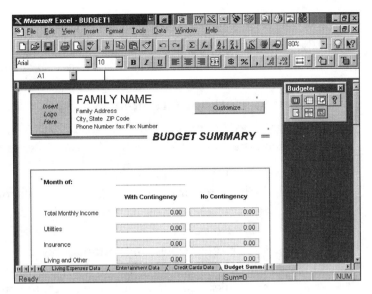

Lock/Save Sheet button. Lock the customize information and/or save your workbook.

6. Click on the Income Data worksheet tab. The Customize tab disappears and you cannot use the Previous Sheet button to access it again. The only way you can get back to it is to click the Customize button on worksheets that have it.

7. Click on the Last Sheet button, then on the Budget Summary, then on the Budget Graph tab. Notice that your personal information has been entered on both worksheets.

This template illustrates several things that you can include in your own templates:

- Casual users can create templates containing a group of simple worksheets and charts. These can be formatted with the appropriate headings, so that users will fill in the data as needed.

- Intermediate-level users can also provide links between these worksheets, so that a summary worksheet is created automatically as data are entered into subordinate worksheets.

- Advanced users can use Visual Basic to create buttons that accomplish advanced tasks and make totally automated applications from Excel workbooks.

Utilizing Workbook Templates

By now, you already know how to create a simple worksheet. You can build on this knowledge to create *workbook templates* for yourself.

Creating Workbook Templates

The easiest way to create a workbook template is by building on a workbook that you use frequently. You can do so as follows:

1. Open the existing workbook.
2. Include one or more worksheets that will contain the data you will use. These worksheets may include databases, budgets, or other tables of data.
3. Create titles, labels, and formulas, but delete all the data that will be changed when the worksheet is used. Create the necessary links, and format the worksheets to your satisfaction.
4. Lock all cells that do not contain data that the user will input. This way, it will be easy for you or others to enter data without accidentally erasing formulas or labels.
5. Create worksheets that analyze the data. Since these will primarily contain labels and formulas, you will not need to delete much, if any, data. Format the worksheets and lock the cells.
6. Create any charts or pivot tables that display summary information about your data.
7. Arrange the worksheets in a sensible order and label the sheet tabs appropriately.
8. Choose File, Save As. You'll see the Save As dialog box.
9. Specify Template in the Save as Type box. Notice that Excel automatically changes the active directory to the Templates folder.
10. If you want the template to be in the folder that you see when you choose File, New, save it in the Templates folder. If you want it to be in the Spreadsheet Solutions folder, double-click on this folder.
11. Give your template a name, then choose Save.

Creating folders is discussed in Chapter 21.

TIP: You can also create a subfolder of your own under the Templates folder and save all your Excel templates there. This subfolder will appear as a tab in the New dialog box when you create new files.

Using Workbook Templates

Once you've created a template, it's very easy to use it. To use a workbook template:

1. Choose File, New. You'll see the New dialog box in Figure 13-12.
2. Click on the Spreadsheet Solutions tab, if needed.
3. Double-click on your Excel template.

Since you are creating a new document rather than opening an existing one—even though it is based on a template—you will be prompted for a name when you save the document. There is no danger of accidentally overwriting your template.

Utilizing Sheet Templates

The other type of template you may find useful is the *sheet template* and it functions in much the same way as a Word "scrap document." It is a single worksheet, like an amortization table, that you can insert into any other workbook that you are creating.

Creating a Sheet Template

To create a sheet template, follow these steps:

1. Create a new, blank Excel workbook or open an existing Excel workbook containing the worksheet.

Figure 13-12.
Templates you create will be available to you whenever you choose File, New

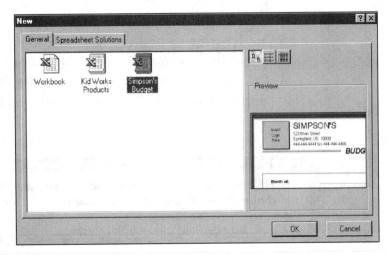

2. Navigate to the sheet you want to save as a sheet template.

3. Put any necessary labels, values, and formulas in the work-sheet, and remove any data that you don't want to appear when you open the template.

4. Format the worksheet and rename it, if desired.

5. Delete all other worksheets in the workbook.

TIP: You can select sheets 2 through 16 by clicking on Sheet2 to make it active, clicking the Last Sheet button to move to the last sheet, and holding down the [Shift] key while you click on Sheet16. Then right-click and choose Delete to delete all the other sheets at once.

6. Choose File, Save As and specify Template in the Save as Type box.

7. Navigate to the folder in which you wish to save the template and choose Save.

Inserting a Sheet Template in a Workbook

Once you have created a sheet template, you can easily insert it in a workbook you are working on:

1. Open the workbook in which you want to insert the sheet template.

2. Right-click on the worksheet *after* the point where you want the new one to be inserted, then choose Insert.

3. You'll see the Insert dialog box. Here you choose the template on which the new worksheet will be based.

4. Double-click on the sheet template on which you wish to base the new worksheet. The sheet template will be added to the workbook.

CAUTION: This procedure only works if you right-click and choose Insert. It will not work if you select Insert, Worksheet from the menu bar.

PART IV

POWERPOINT

CHAPTER 14

CREATING A SIMPLE PRESENTATION

IN THIS CHAPTER

- **Getting Started with PowerPoint**
- **Creating Your First Presentation**
- **Editing Presentations**
- **Including Data in Presentations**

This chapter shows you the basics of using
PowerPoint. The next chapter explains how to
"spice up" your presentation with animation
effects and other graphic objects. For now,
let's start at the beginning—by learning about
basic PowerPoint concepts, starting
PowerPoint, and becoming familiar with
its screens.

Getting Started with PowerPoint

PowerPoint provides you with sophisticated presentation software designed to help you easily create on-screen presentations, overhead transparencies, 35mm slides, or paper printouts of slide shows that can be used for demonstrations, briefings, or other presentations.

A *presentation* is a PowerPoint file that consists of one or more *slides*, along with information on any special effects you have selected. A slide is like a page of your presentation. It consists of text, graphics, clip art, charts and/or multimedia effects like sound or animation.

PowerPoint allows you to build slides from scratch using basic drawing tools, but few people use PowerPoint in this way. Instead, most people use professionally designed slide backgrounds called *design templates*. PowerPoint's 27 design templates provide professionally-designed graphics and color schemes like the slide with multiple colored bars shown in Figure 14-1, so all you need to do is add text.

Most presentations combine a number of different types of slides: title slides, bullet slides, and slides with paragraphs of text, tables, graphs, or organizational charts. PowerPoint provides layouts for each of these types of slides. In fact, PowerPoint provides 24 different slide layouts for each of its 27 design templates. Twelve of the 24 slide layouts can be seen in Figure 14-2.

Figure 14-1.
PowerPoint's professional design templates allow you to create finished presentations just by adding text

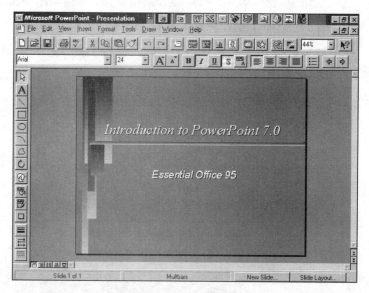

Figure 14-2.
PowerPoint
provides layouts
for many common
types of slides

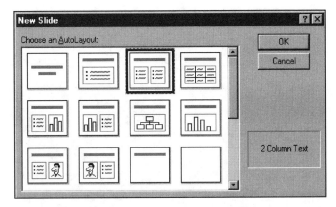

All of these features mean that you won't often need to draw figures, apply colors, or insert graphic lines manually. If you do, however, PowerPoint's drawing features make it a snap. If you need to add other graphic elements, you can insert charts, text art, organizational charts, and even equations!

Starting PowerPoint

Switching
between
Shortcut Bars
is introduced
in Chapter 2.

When you start PowerPoint, you see a Tip of the Day, then an initial window that gives you options for three ways to create a new presentation, or the ability to open an existing one.

To familiarize yourself with the PowerPoint window, start PowerPoint and create a blank presentation. To do so, do the following:

1. Click on the PowerPoint icon on the Office Programs Shortcut Bar. You can also start PowerPoint by clicking on the Start button, then choosing Programs, Microsoft PowerPoint.

2. When you start PowerPoint for the first time, you will see the Tip of the Day dialog box. Click OK after you read it. You'll then see the PowerPoint dialog box shown in Figure 14-3.

TIP: If you do not want to see the Tip of the Day when you open PowerPoint, uncheck Show Tips at Startup in the Tip of the Day dialog box.

PART IV POWERPOINT

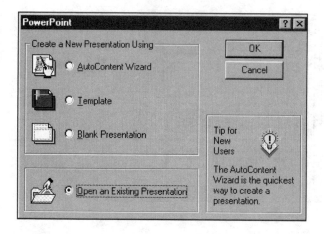

Figure 14-3.
The PowerPoint
dialog box is where
you decide what
kind of presentation
to create

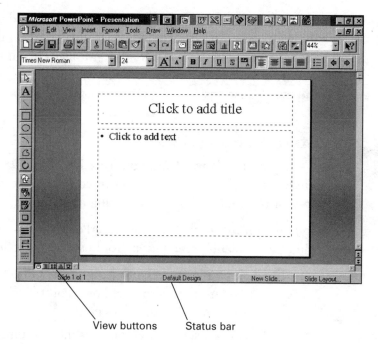

Figure 14-4.
A blank slide ready
for you to enter text

3. To learn about the PowerPoint screens, create a blank presentation. Choose Blank Presentation and click OK. You'll see the New Slide dialog box.

4. Click OK. You'll see a blank slide like the one in Figure 14-4.

Learning about the PowerPoint Window

Figure 14-4 highlights some features of interest to the PowerPoint user:

- **Status bar** is located at the bottom of the PowerPoint window. In the default Slide View, it displays the slide number, design template name, and buttons to create new slides or change the slide layout of the current slide.

- **View buttons** allow you to switch between four ways of viewing the presentation. In addition, a button is provided to run the slide show.

Learning about the PowerPoint Views

PowerPoint uses different representations of your slide show—called *views*—to make it easy for you to accomplish different tasks while creating your slide shows. These are the Slide View, the Outline View, the Slide Sorter View, and the Notes Pages View.

Slide View

The Slide View shows one slide at a time, as shown in Figure 14-5. This view is used to edit or add objects such as text, graphic elements

Figure 14-5.
Use the Slide View to add or edit graphic objects

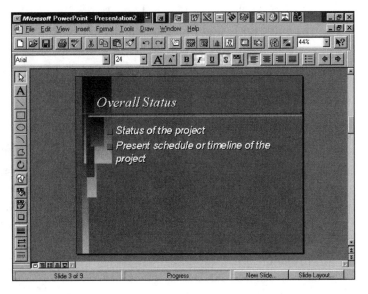

Figure 14-6.
Use the Outline
View to create the
text of the
presentation easily

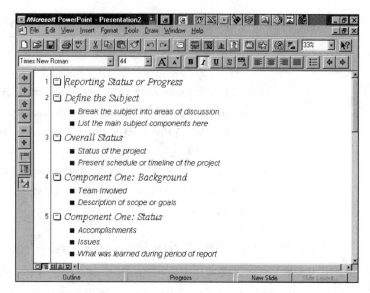

(lines and rectangles), charts, or clip art. The Slide View is the only view that allows you to select individual objects for editing. It is also the only view that allows you to change the slide layout.

Outline View

The Outline View displays the text of the presentation in an outline format, as shown in Figure 14-6. Using the Outline View is the easiest way to insert slide titles, as well as text for bulleted lists. Because you can see all of the presentation's text, you get an overview of what you are saying in the presentation. You can also import text from Word in this view.

Slide Sorter View

The Slide Sorter View shows each slide in miniature, as shown in Figure 14-7. The Slide Sorter View is used to arrange slides and add transitions and animation effects to them. PowerPoint provides a variety of transitions like fades and wipes that make it easy to move from one slide to another. The Slide Sorter View is also useful when you wish to select an entire slide and copy or move it from one presentation to another.

Figure 14-7.
Use the Slide Sorter
View to arrange
slides and add
transitional effects

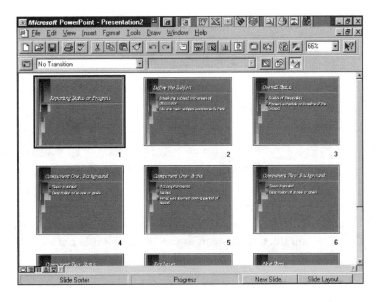

Figure 14-8. The
Notes Pages View
allows you to add
speaker's notes to
each slide

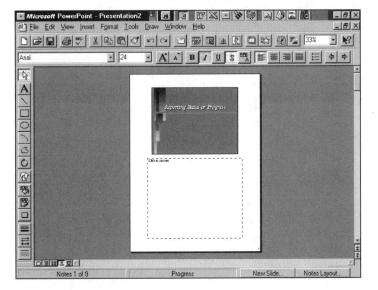

Notes Pages View

The Notes Pages View shows one slide at a time with speaker's notes at the bottom, as shown in Figure 14-8. This view is used to create notes that can accompany the presentation, or be distributed to participants.

Exiting PowerPoint

When you are finished using PowerPoint, you can exit the program as follows:

1. Choose File, Exit.

2. If you are working on a presentation which has changes that are not saved, you will be prompted to save your work before you exit PowerPoint. Select Yes to save the presentation or select No to exit PowerPoint without saving the presentation.

 TIP: You can also exit PowerPoint by double-clicking on the Control icon at the left of the title bar.

Creating Presentations

PowerPoint provides four ways to create presentations, depending on your needs:

- Creating a **Blank Presentation** makes a presentation based on the Blank Presentation template—by default, a design template with a blank background. This is useful when you want to create slides starting with a "clean slate" and add your own design elements.

- You can create a presentation using **Presentation Designs**. Doing so creates an empty presentation based on one of 27 professionally designed backgrounds and color selections. This option is useful when you want to add the text of your presentation yourself.

- You can create presentations using **Presentations**—templates that include not only a presentation design, but sample text written for common situations like communicating bad news, recommending a strategy, or selling a product or idea. This sample text can give you a head start and make sure that you include important elements in your presentation.

- The **AutoContent Wizard** helps you choose the appropriate presentation template, and additionally chooses the best presentation template depending on the medium you will use to make your presentation (electronic slide show, transparencies, etc.).

The commands you use and the dialog boxes you see when you create presentations differ depending on whether or not you are already in PowerPoint when you create your new presentation.

The easiest way to create your first presentation is by using the Auto-Content Wizard. After that you can insert your own text to customize the presentation, see how it looks, and print it.

Creating Presentations with the AutoContent Wizard

The AutoContent Wizard is designed to help you select a presentation design and provide sample slides for the type of presentation you're making. You will start the Wizard differently, depending on whether you are already in PowerPoint or not.

If you are not in PowerPoint, do the following:

1. Start PowerPoint.
2. Click OK if you see the Tip of the Day dialog box. You'll see the initial PowerPoint dialog box.
3. Choose AutoContent Wizard, then click OK. The first step of the AutoContent Wizard appears.

Alternatively, if you are already in PowerPoint, start the Wizard as follows:

1. Choose File, New and select the Presentations tab. You'll see the New Presentation dialog box shown in Figure 14-9.
2. Double-click on the AutoContent Wizard icon to see the first step of the AutoContent Wizard.

Once you have started the Wizard, you can create your presentation as follows:

1. From the introductory screen of the AutoContent Wizard, choose Next to move to the second screen, shown in Figure 14-10.
2. The second step of the Wizard asks for your name, the title of

Figure 14-9.
Select from any of
these presentations to
get started, or use the
AutoContent Wizard

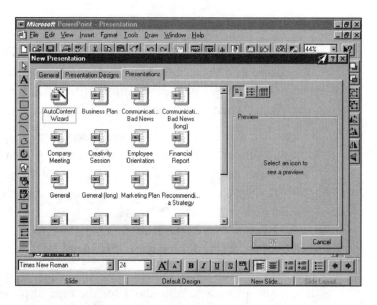

Figure 14-10.
The second step of the
Wizard asks you for
information to display
on the title slide of your
presentation

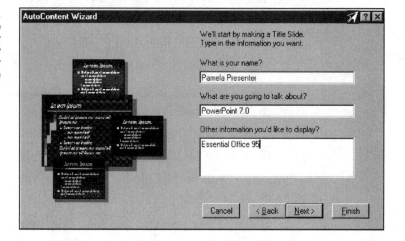

the presentation, and any other information you'd like to display on the title slide. Choose <u>N</u>ext after entering this information.

3. The third step, shown in Figure 14-11, asks what you're going to talk about and offers a few suggestions that are appropriate for briefings and presentations. By choosing <u>O</u>ther, you'll see a list of other subjects. Some of these are especially appropriate for meetings, such as Company Meeting and Creativity Session; others are useful for talking to a friendly or hostile audi-

Figure 14-11.
The third step of the Wizard selects the subject of your presentation.

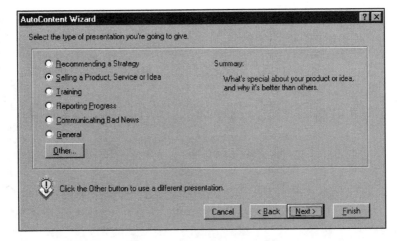

Figure 14-12.
The fourth step of the Wizard allows you to pick the visual style and length of your presentation

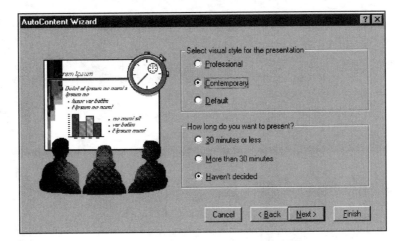

ence about an idea. Select the most appropriate topic and choose OK. Choose <u>N</u>ext to continue.

4. The fourth step, shown in Figure 14-12, allows you to select the style for your presentation and its length. These determine the design that is chosen for your presentation and the amount of sample text you will see. Choose <u>N</u>ext to continue.

5. In fifth step, shown in Figure 14-13, you determine whether you will be making black and white overheads, color overheads, an on-screen presentation, or 35mm slides. Each of these formats has its own design templates that are optimized for the size and color of the medium. You can also determine

Figure 14-13.
The fifth step of the Wizard allows you to determine the medium for your presentation

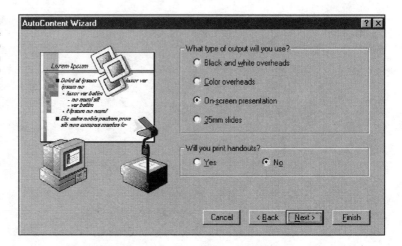

Figure 14-14.
The Wizard prepares an attractively formatted presentation for you

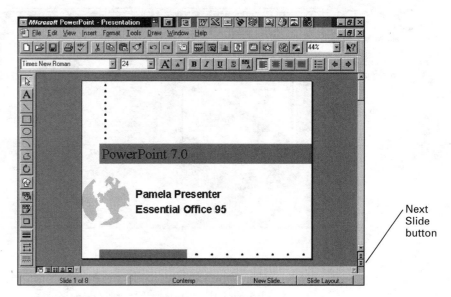

Next Slide button

whether or not you wish to prepare handouts. Fill in the options and choose <u>N</u>ext to continue.

6. Click <u>F</u>inish to construct the presentation.

The Wizard will create a presentation consisting of several slides and leave you in the Slide View to look at the first slide, as shown in Figure 14-14. Click the Next Slide button under the right scroll bar to move from slide to slide and view the sample presentation.

Send Us
YOUR COMMENTS

Dear Reader:

Thank you for buying this book. In order to offer you more quality books on the topics *you* would like to see, we need your input. At Prima Publishing, we pride ourselves on timely responsiveness to our readers' needs. If you complete and return this brief questionnaire, *we will listen!*

Name (First) _____ (M.I.) _____ (Last) _____

Company _____ Type of business _____

Address _____ City _____ State ____ ZIP ____

Phone _____ Fax _____ E-mail address: _____

May we contact you for research purposes? ☐ Yes ☐ No

(If you participate in a research project, we will supply you with the Prima computer book of your choice.)

---

❶ How would you rate this book, overall?

☐ Excellent   ☐ Fair
☐ Very good   ☐ Below average
☐ Good   ☐ Poor

❷ Why did you buy this book?

☐ Price of book   ☐ Content
☐ Author's reputation ☐ Prima's reputation
☐ CD-ROM/disk included with book
☐ Information highlighted on cover
☐ Other (please specify):_____

❸ How did you discover this book?

☐ Found it on bookstore shelf
☐ Saw it in Prima Publishing catalog
☐ Recommended by store personnel
☐ Recommended by friend or colleague
☐ Saw an advertisement in:_____
☐ Read book review in:_____
☐ Saw it on Web site:_____
☐ Other (please specify):_____

❹ Where did you buy this book?

☐ Bookstore (name):_____
☐ Computer store (name):_____
☐ Electronics store (name):_____
☐ Wholesale club (name):_____
☐ Mail order (name):_____
☐ Direct from Prima Publishing
☐ Other (please specify):_____

❺ Which computer periodicals do you read regularly?_____

_____

_____

❻ Would you like to see your name in print?

May we use your name and quote you in future Prima Publishing books or promotional materials?

☐ Yes   ☐ No

---

❼ Comments & suggestions: _____

_____

_____

8 **I am interested in seeing more computer books on these topics**

- ❏ Word processing
- ❏ Desktop publishing
- ❏ Databases/spreadsheets
- ❏ Web site development
- ❏ Networking
- ❏ Internetworking
- ❏ Programming
- ❏ Intranetworking

9 **How do you rate your level of computer skills?**

- ❏ Beginner
- ❏ Intermediate
- ❏ Advanced

10 **What is your age?**

- ❏ Under 18
- ❏ 18–29
- ❏ 30–39
- ❏ 40–49
- ❏ 50–59
- ❏ 60–over

SAVE A STAMP

Visit our Web site at **http://www.primapublishing.com**

and simply fill out one of our online response forms.

PRIMA PUBLISHING
Computer Products Division
701 Congressional Blvd., Suite 350
Carmel, IN 46032

Creating Presentations with Templates

If you do not use the Wizard, you will be creating presentations with templates, whether you create a blank presentation, use presentation designs, or presentations with sample text.

The procedure for creating new presentations based on templates is, again, slightly different depending on whether or not you are in PowerPoint. If you are not, do the following:

1. Start PowerPoint.

2. Click OK if you see the Tip of the Day dialog box. You'll see the initial PowerPoint dialog box.

3. What you do next depends on how you want to create your presentation:

   • To create a blank presentation, choose <u>B</u>lank Presentation and click OK. You'll see the New Slide dialog box.

   • To create a presentation based on a presentation design, choose <u>T</u>emplate and click the Presentation Designs tab. You'll see the New Presentation dialog box shown in Figure 14-15. Double-click on the template you wish to use. This brings up the familiar New Slide dialog box.

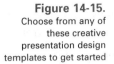

PART IV POWERPOINT

Figure 14-15.
Choose from any of these creative presentation design templates to get started

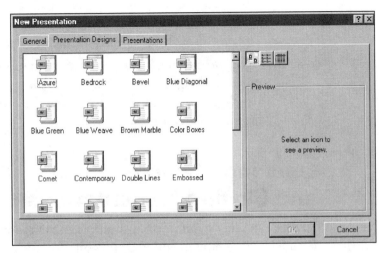

- To create a presentation based on a presentation template with sample text, choose Template and click the Presentations tab. You'll see the New Presentation dialog box shown earlier in Figure 14-9. Double-click on the template you wish to use. After seeing the presentation on your screen, you are finished.

4. If you are creating a blank presentation or one based on a presentation design, choose the layout you wish to use for your first slide and click OK. After seeing the presentation on your screen, you are done.

Alternatively, if you are already in PowerPoint, your procedure will be slightly different:

1. Choose File, New. You'll see the New Presentation dialog box.

2. What you do next depends on how you want to create your presentation:

   - To create a blank presentation, ensure you are at the General tab. Choose Blank Presentation and click OK to bring up the New Slide dialog box.

   - To create a presentation based on a presentation design, click on the Presentation Designs tab. Double-click on the template you wish to use to see the New Slide dialog box appear.

   - To create a presentation based on a presentation template with sample text, click on the Presentations tab. You'll see the New Presentation dialog box. Double-click on the template you wish to use and see the presentation. You're done.

3. If you are creating a blank presentation or one based on a presentation design, choose the layout you wish to use for your first slide and click OK. After seeing the presentation on your screen, you are done.

Opening, Saving, and Closing Presentations

PowerPoint allows you to open multiple presentations simultaneously. Before learning how to edit your presentations, it's smart to review how to open and close them.

Opening an Existing Presentation

You will open an existing presentation differently, depending on whether you are in PowerPoint or not. If you are not in PowerPoint, do the following:

1. Start PowerPoint.
2. Click OK if you see the Tip of the Day dialog box. Now you see the initial PowerPoint dialog box.
3. Choose Open an Existing Presentation to see the File Open dialog box shown in Figure 14-16.
4. Choose the presentation you wish to work on and choose Open.

If you are already in PowerPoint, the procedure is slightly different:

1. Choose File, Open or click the Open button on the Standard toolbar. You'll see the File Open dialog box shown in Figure 14-16.

2. Choose the presentation you wish to work on and click Open.

Saving and Closing a Presentation

As you compose your presentation, PowerPoint saves it in your computer's memory. When you exit PowerPoint, or if your computer's power is turned off, this work may be lost. For this reason, save your work on your hard drive when you are finished with it.

PART IV POWERPOINT

Figure 14-16.
The File Open dialog box allows you to navigate to the appropriate folder and open an existing presentation

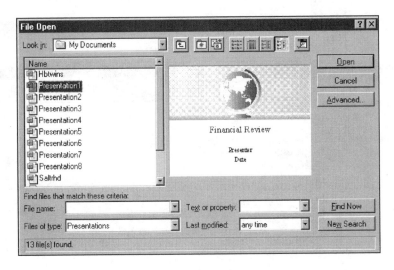

When you're ready to learn all about electronic file management, see Chapter 21.

When you save files on your hard drive, you can direct them to specific folders, just as you do with a paper filing system. For now, however, just save and retrieve files from the default folder called My Documents.

To save a presentation file:

1. Choose <u>S</u>ave from the <u>F</u>ile menu or click the Save button on the Standard toolbar. The first time you save the presentation document, you'll see the File Save dialog box shown in Figure 14-17.

2. To save the document in the default folder, type the name you wish to use in the File <u>N</u>ame box (where the insertion point is already located) and choose <u>S</u>ave.

As you edit your work, save it again so that your changes to the document are retained. The next time you save the document, you will not see the File Save dialog box. The new version will automatically be saved without your needing to name it again.

CAUTION: When you save your work a second time, the new version overwrites the old one and the old one is lost. You are not warned before this occurs. If you want to save old versions, save the new version with a different name before you start making changes. This ensure that you don't accidentally delete work you want to keep.

Figure 14-17.
Using the File Save dialog box, you can save a presentation with long filenames in any disk or folder on your system

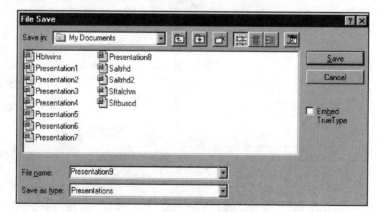

You often build new presentations based on existing ones, retaining certain "stock" slides about your organization. When you want to save your work under a different name, do the following:

1. Choose File, Save As. You will see the File Save dialog box again.

2. The original name is highlighted. To replace it with a new name, just type over it and choose Save.

Editing Presentations

Once you have created your initial presentation, you will have one or more slides that are either blank or have sample text in them. Editing your presentation involves several activities. You need to be able to add and remove slides, change the slide layout (i.e. the *type* of slide—bullet, title, chart, etc.), enter text into your slides, and add graphical objects to support your points.

Adding and Deleting Slides

If you start with a blank presentation or a presentation template, your presentation will have only one slide in it. To add slides to your presentation, do the following:

1. Click the Slide View button, if needed, so you are in the Slide View.

2. Move to the slide before the slide to be added using the Previous Slide and the Next Slide buttons (or pressing Page Up and Page Down).

3. Click the New Slide button. The New Slide dialog box will appear.

4. Select the appropriate layout for your new slide and choose OK. You will see the new slide appear in the presentation.

If you use the Presentations with sample text to create your presentation, you may find yourself with slides you don't need. To delete a slide, do the following:

1. Click the Slide View button, if needed, so you are in the Slide View.

2. Move to the slide to be deleted.

3. Choose Edit, Delete Slide. The slide is deleted from your presentation.

Changing a Slide Layout

You may occasionally change your mind and decide that a slide should have a different layout than the one you originally chose. You can easily change the layout of a slide as follows:

1. Click the Slide View button, if needed, so you are in the Slide View.

2. Move to the slide to be changed.

3. Click the Slide Layout button. You'll see the Slide Layout dialog box.

   > Slide Layout...

4. Select the layout you wish to use and choose Apply. The slide's layout will be changed to the chosen type.

Adding Text to Slides

The next step in creating your presentation is to replace the sample text with your own text. An excellent way to ensure that you give an organized presentation is to outline your thoughts. These thoughts are usually presented in Bullet Slides—slides with a title, followed by a number of bulleted points. These slides often constitute the bulk of the text of a presentation; they are supplemented with charts or figures to emphasize particular points.

Adding Text in the Outline View

PowerPoint provides you with the Outline View to make creating Bullet Slides quick and easy. Using this view, you can see all the text of your presentation in one place, and add and delete points as needed. To create the text of your presentation using the Outline View:

1. Switch to Outline view by clicking the Outline view button. The screen should resemble the one shown in Figure 14-18.

2. To replace text, select it and then type the new text over the selected text. You can select text by dragging the mouse over

Figure 14-18.
The Outline view is best
for replacing sample
text with your own

Promote

Demote

Move Up

Move Down

Outline View
button

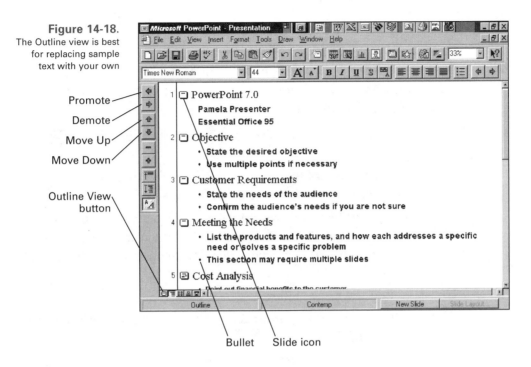

Bullet   Slide icon

it. To select an entire bulleted item, click on the bullet. To select an entire slide, click on the slide icon just to the left of the slide title.

3. Insert and delete text as you normally would in Word. To promote a bulleted item to a new slide title, highlight it and click the Promote button. Similarly, use the Demote button to change a slide title into a bulleted point, or a bulleted point into a sub-bulleted point.

4. Move slides up and down by clicking on the slide icon to select the entire slide, then using the Move Up and Move Down buttons.

5. Create a new slide by moving to the end of the presentation. As you move to the last blank line, a new slide is created.

6. If you need to insert a new slide in the middle of the presentation, click at the end of the previous slide and press [Enter] to add a bulleted point. Promote the new bulleted point to a new slide.

PART IV   POWERPOINT

Adding Text in the Slide View

Once you have created your text, see how it fits on each slide. You can then edit slides as needed if any of them contain too much text. Try to keep each slide to six points or fewer, and summarize the points on one line. To view and edit your slides:

1. Switch to the Slide View by clicking the Slide View button.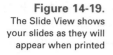

2. Use the Next Slide and Previous Slide buttons to move between slides. A Bullet slide is shown in Figure 14-19.

3. To edit the text of your slide, click in the text area to select the text box. You'll see a box around the text area and a vertical bar (the insertion point) in the text, as shown in Figure 14-20.

4. Edit the text as follows:

   • Move to the appropriate spot by clicking in it or using the arrow keys.

   • Select text, if desired, by dragging the mouse pointer over it.

   • Delete text by selecting it then pressing the Del key, or by clicking in front of it and pressing the Del key repeatedly.

   • Insert text by moving to the appropriate position and typing the new text.

Figure 14-19.
The Slide View shows your slides as they will appear when printed

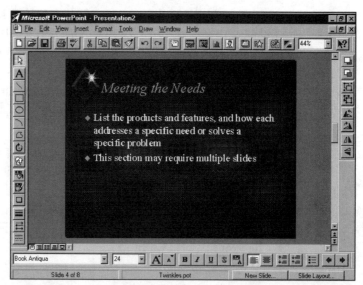

Figure 14-20.
When you select text, a border appears around it. You can then edit the text.

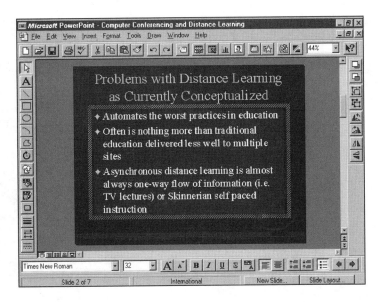

- Insert a new bulleted point by clicking at the end of the previous line and pressing (Enter).
- Insert a sub-bullet by moving to the beginning of a bulleted line and pressing (Tab).
- Toggle a bullet on and off by clicking the Bullet On/Off button.

5. When you are finished editing text, click in the slide outside the text box to deselect it.

Creating Speaker's Notes

Speaker's notes are pages with a miniature version of each slide, with space underneath for you to write notes about what you will say while the slide is being shown.

PowerPoint makes it easy to create speaker's notes that you can print and keep with you during your presentation. To do so, follow these steps:

1. Click the Notes Pages View button. You will see your slide in Speaker Notes view, as shown in Figure 14-21.

2. Use the Next Slide and Previous Slide buttons to move to the slide to which you wish to add notes.

Figure 14-21.
Speaker's notes allow
you to keep key points
in front of you while
you give your
presentation

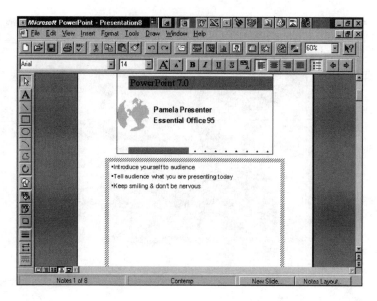

3. Click in the text box at the bottom of the screen and type the speaker's notes.

4. Repeat steps 2 and 3 to add notes to additional slides.

TIP: Click the Zoom button to magnify the notes page. That way, you can read the notes as you type them.

Including Data in Presentations

Powerful presentations include more than just text. Tables and charts can show data in a compelling way to help persuade your audience about the points you are making.

Adding Tables

There are three ways to include data tables in the presentation. You can type them into a table slide, create an Excel worksheet, or import an existing Excel worksheet.

Which Method Should You Use to Create Data Tables?

You cannot display very much data in a slide. In fact, a slide containing a table can only hold a maximum of seven rows of information. With this in mind, consider the following thoughts:

- If you aren't putting very much data in the table, it's probably just as easy to make the slide in PowerPoint
- If the data in the slide come from Excel and you wish your PowerPoint slide to reflect changes in the Excel workbook, create a link from the Excel workbook to the slide

Adding a Table Slide

A table slide is one of the slide layouts in PowerPoint. When you use it, it actually creates a Word table (using OLE) in the PowerPoint slide. When you create and edit the table, you will see Word menus rather than PowerPoint menus.

To add a table slide to a presentation:

1. Create a new slide in your presentation and choose Table as the slide layout, as described above. You'll see a new slide like the one in Figure 14-22.

2. Double-click the icon in the center of the slide. The Insert Word Table dialog box appears:

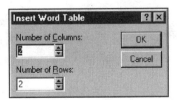

NOTE: OLE stands for *Object Linking and Embedding*. It's just a fancy term for the technology used to link data from one application to another in Windows.

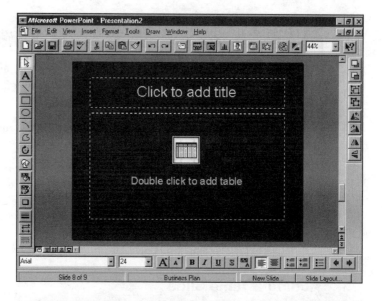

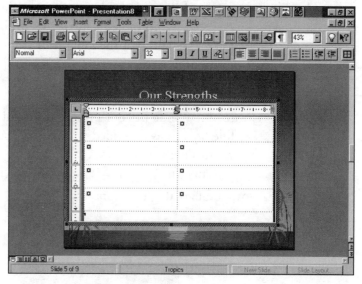

3. Specify the number of rows and columns for the table and choose OK. You will see the blank table in the slide. Notice that the menus are now Word menus rather than PowerPoint menus, as shown in Figure 14-23.

4. Enter the data you want in the table and choose Table, Table AutoFormat.

5. Select a format for the table and choose OK.

6. When you are finished adding data and formatting the table, click anywhere in the slide, *outside* the table. You'll return to the PowerPoint menus.

Any time you wish to edit the table, simply double-click on it to open the Word menus and edit the data or change the formatting.

Adding an Excel Table

If you wish to link an existing Excel worksheet to a slide, do the following:

1. Open the PowerPoint presentation.

2. Click the Slide View button, if needed, so you are in the Slide View and move to (or create) the slide into which you wish to link the Excel worksheet.

3. Choose Insert, Object. You will see the Insert Object dialog box shown in Figure 14-24.

4. Select Create from File and select the Link checkbox that appears.

5. In the File text box, type the name of the workbook, or choose Browse and choose the Excel workbook from the Browse dialog box.

6. Click OK. The Excel worksheet appears in the slide, as shown in Figure 14-25. Resize it as needed.

Figure 14-24.
You can create a new Excel worksheet in a slide, as well as embed or link an existing one

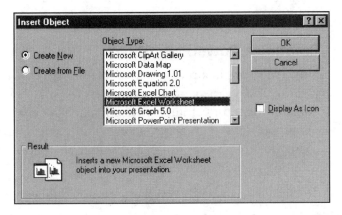

Figure 14-25.
Your Excel appears in
your PowerPoint slide

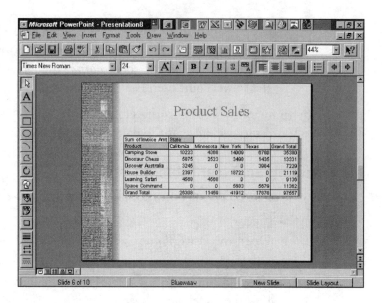

TIP: Depending on your presentation template, the inserted object may be difficult to read. Select the object and select Format, Colors & Lines; choose a fill color to offset the background, such as white. For a touch of class, add a shadow. (Adding a shadow before filling doesn't work.)

Inserting Charts

Inserting a chart in a slide is very similar to inserting a table. You can create it with PowerPoint itself, or you can copy, embed, or link it from Excel.

Creating a PowerPoint Chart

Using MS Graph, a program available in many Office 95 programs, you can add a variety of types of charts to your PowerPoint slides. Some of the most commonly used include pie charts (useful for showing proportions), bar charts (showing differences between groups), line charts (for trends over time), and scatter charts (for displaying the distribution of individual responses).

To create a chart with PowerPoint, do the following:

1. Open the PowerPoint presentation.

2. Click the Slide View button, if needed, so you are in the Slide View. Move to the slide before the one to be added.

3. Click the New Slide button. The New Slide dialog box will appear.

4. Select the MS Graph layout—the fourth layout in the second row—and choose OK. You will see the new slide in the presentation.

5. Double-click on the icon in the middle of the slide. You are now in Microsoft Graph. You will see some sample data already in the datasheet, as shown in Figure 14-26.

6. Select all the cells by dragging over them, then press ⌐Del⌐ to delete the sample data.

7. Type your own data in the datasheet, using the first column and row for headings.

8. Click the View Datasheet button to switch between looking at the data and looking at the graph.

9. Click the down arrow at the right of the Chart Type button to change from a column chart to a pie, line, area, or other type of chart.

10. If desired, display a legend by clicking the Legend button.

PART IV POWERPOINT

Figure 14-26.
When you create a graph in PowerPoint, you start with sample data already in the datasheet

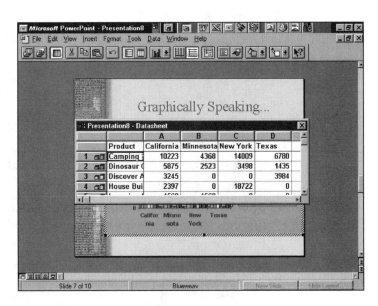

Figure 14-27.
The finished chart appears on your PowerPoint slide

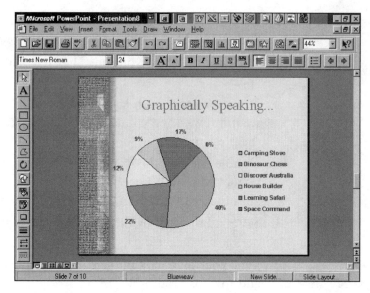

11. Format the chart as needed by right-clicking on the chart element you want to format, then choosing the appropriate formatting command from the pop-up menu.

12. When you are finished, click anywhere outside the chart. The chart will appear in the slide as shown in Figure 14-27 so you can move or size it as needed.

Importing an Excel Chart

You can also import an Excel chart into a PowerPoint slide. This is often done when the chart already exists as part of an Excel worksheet and is to be used in a presentation. Do so as follows:

1. Open the PowerPoint presentation.

2. Click the Slide View button, if needed, so you are in the Slide View and move to the slide before the slide to be added.

3. Click the New Slide button. The New Slide dialog box will appear.

4. Select the MS Graph layout—the fourth layout in the second row—then choose OK. You will see the new slide in the presentation.

5. Double-click on the icon in the middle of the slide. You are now in Microsoft Graph.

Figure 14-28.
You can import
charts from Excel 4.0
through 7.0

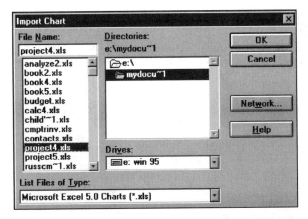

6. To import an Excel chart, click the Import Chart button. The Import Chart dialog box shown in Figure 14-28 will appear.

7. Double-click on the chart you want to import. You will see the chart appear and then return to the PowerPoint slide.

TIP: To import Excel 7.0 charts, choose Excel 5.0 as the file type.

CAUTION: MS Graph 5.0 is not compatible with some Windows 95 features. Notably, it does not use the same Open File dialog boxes and does not support long filenames. Be sure to save the Excel workbook with a short, eight-character (or less) filename before importing it into Excel; otherwise, the long filename will be truncated to something unintelligible. Also, be sure that any chart you want to import from Excel 5.0 or 7.0 is the first chart sheet in the workbook, since this is the only chart MS Graph will be able to find.

You can also import an Excel worksheet to use as data for the chart that is created with MS Graph. To do so:

1. Access MS Graph as described above.

Figure 14-29.
You can import data
from text files as well
as Lotus 1-2-3 and
Excel files

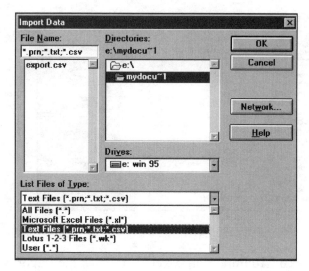

2. Click the View Datasheet button. You will see the data for the chart.

3. Click the Import Data button. The Import Data dialog box shown in Figure 14-29 will appear.

4. Choose List Files of <u>T</u>ype and specify whether the data is text or an Excel workbook.

5. Select the file to be imported, noting that you will only see the short DOS filenames, not the Windows 95 long filenames.

6. If desired, choose R<u>a</u>nge and specify the range of data.

7. Choose OK. You will be asked to verify that the imported data will overwrite the current data. Then you'll see the new data in the datasheet.

Cutting and Pasting Excel Charts

There is another way that you can import an Excel chart into a Power-Point slide. It is often the easiest, and allows you to link the file rather than just copy it. You can use the Windows Clipboard, by following these steps:

1. Open the Excel workbook containing the chart and click once on the chart to select it.

2. Click the Copy button to copy it to the Clipboard.

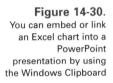
Figure 14-30.
You can embed or link
an Excel chart into a
PowerPoint
presentation by using
the Windows Clipboard

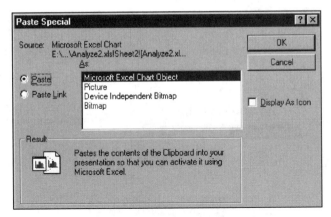

3. Switch to PowerPoint and move to the slide in the PowerPoint presentation that will receive the chart. (You do not need to create a chart or go into MS Graph.)

4. To copy the chart into the presentation, click the Paste button. Alternatively, to embed or link the chart, choose Edit, Paste Special. The Paste Special dialog box shown in Figure 14-30 will appear.

5. Select Paste to embed the chart or Paste Link to link it; then choose OK. The chart will be placed into the PowerPoint slide. If you chose Paste Link, changes you make to the Excel chart (in Excel) will be reflected on the PowerPoint slide.

Importing Word Documents into a Slide Show

An interesting way to construct a slide show is to import data from Word into PowerPoint. For example, you might want to import your agenda into a PowerPoint presentation, where each agenda item is the title of a new slide.

You can easily import a Word document, or a portion of one, into a PowerPoint slide show by using the Clipboard:

1. Open the Word document containing the text you wish to export into PowerPoint.

2. If you wish to have the text automatically formatted for bulleted list slides, make sure that the slide titles are at the left margin and that each point is indented by one tab space.

Figure 14-31.
The headings of
Word documents
copied into
PowerPoint slides
appear as bulleted
items

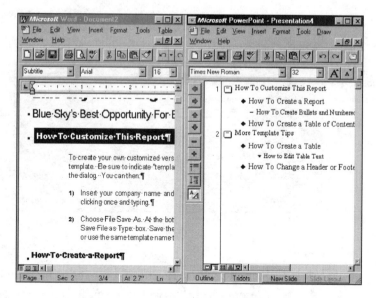

Alternatively, use the Heading 1 style for slide titles and the Heading 2 style for bullet points.

3. Select the text, then click the Copy button to copy it to the Clipboard.

4. Switch to PowerPoint and open the presentation into which you wish to paste the text.

5. Click the Outline View button.

6. Position the insertion point at the point in the presentation where you wish to import the text.

7. Click the Paste button to paste the text. The new slides will be created in the PowerPoint presentation, as shown in Figure 14-31.

Printing in PowerPoint

There are several ways to deliver your presentation. If you decide to print it, you can do so on paper or overhead transparencies. If you have the right equipment, you can even give it as an electronic (or traditional film) slide show. You may also want to print handouts for the attendees, and speaker's notes for yourself.

TIP: Even if you are going to give your presentation electronically, make a printout on transparencies for backup purposes. You never know when electronics will fail!

Printing the Presentation

When you are satisfied with the way the document looks, print it as follows:

1. Choose File, Print. The Print dialog box shown in Figure 14-32 will appear.

2. Choose the appropriate range of slides to print: All, Current Slide, or Slides. If you choose Slides, specify the range of slides to be printed (e.g., "1-5, 9, 10").

3. Ensure that Slides appears in the Print What box.

4. Check Black & White unless you have a color printer.

5. Choose the Number of Copies to be printed.

6. Choose OK.

Alternatively, if you know you wish to print simply one copy of all slides on the currently selected printer, just click the Print button.

Figure 14-32.
The Print dialog box allows you to set printing options, including which pages will print, the number of copies, and the printer to be used

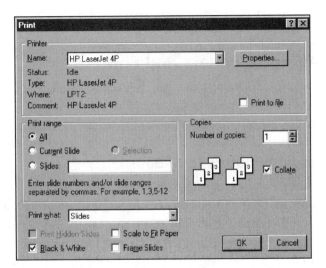

Printing Handouts and Speaker's Notes

Presentation attendees often find it useful to get printouts of the slides, so that they can take notes during the presentation.

> **NOTE:** Since handouts are merely miniature representations of the slides in your side show, you do not "create" handouts. You need to create speaker's notes, however, since you must add the text of the notes to each slide.

Speaker's notes always print the same way: one slide per page, with the slide at the top of the page and the notes at the bottom.

You can print handouts in three different formats: with two, three, or six slides per page. Since slides use large fonts, the printout will be easily readable with six slides per page; besides, you can save paper this way. Alternatively, you may wish to print two or three slides per page to leave space for participants to take notes.

To print speaker's notes and handouts, do the following:

1. Choose <u>F</u>ile, <u>P</u>rint. The Print dialog box will appear.
2. In the Print <u>W</u>hat drop-down list, select Notes Pages, Handouts (2 slides per page), Handouts (3 slides per page), or Handouts (6 slides per page).
3. Choose OK to print the handouts.

Adding Headers and Footers

You can add footers to your slides, and headers or footers to your handouts and speaker's notes. Most commonly, the printing date, author, or originating office are included in headers and footers.

Adding Footers to Slides

You can add either the date the slides are printed, or a date that you enter manually in your footer. In addition, you can add the slide number and extra text of your own. You can even prevent the footer from appearing on your first slide. To add footers to all your slides, do the following:

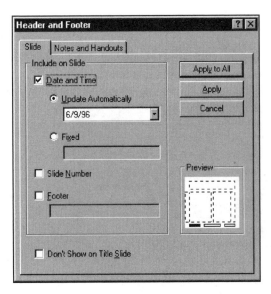

Figure 14-33.
You can customize
your slides by
including information
in the footer

1. Choose View, Header and Footer.
2. Click the Slides tab. You will see the Header and Footer dialog box shown in Figure 14-33.
3. Choose Date and Time, if desired. To enter today's date, select Update Automatically. To enter the date yourself, choose Fixed and enter the desired date.
4. Choose Slide Number, if desired.
5. Choose Footer, if needed, and type in some text.
6. If you wish to prevent the footer from showing on the first slide, choose Don't Show on Title Slide.

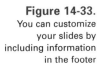

Using the
Slide Sorter
view is
discussed in
Chapter 15.

TIP: You can add footers to only selected slides by selecting the appropriate slides in the Slide Sorter view and using the procedure above.

Adding Headers and Footers to Handouts and Notes

PowerPoint uses the same headers and footers for both handouts and speaker's notes. You have the same options as with slide footers, except that you can opt to print the page number rather than the slide number. To add headers and footers, do the following:

PART IV POWERPOINT

Figure 14-34.
Customize your
handouts and
speaker's notes by
including information
in the header and
footer

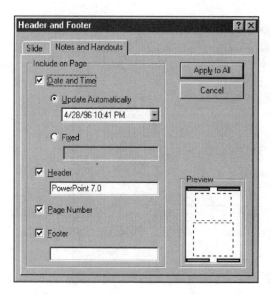

1. Choose <u>V</u>iew, <u>H</u>eader and Footer.

2. Click the Notes and Handouts tab. You will see the Header and Footer dialog box shown in Figure 14-34.

3. Choose <u>D</u>ate and Time, if desired. To enter today's date, select <u>U</u>pdate Automatically. To enter the date yourself, choose Fi<u>x</u>ed and enter the desired date.

4. Choose Header, if desired, and type in some text.

5. Choose Page <u>N</u>umber, if desired.

6. Choose <u>F</u>ooter, if needed, and type in some text.

7. Choose Appl<u>y</u> to All. You'll return to the PowerPoint main window. The header and/or footer will now print on all handouts and speaker's notes.

NOTE: You can send a presentation to a slide service and have them create 35mm slides out of it. To do so, select Send to <u>G</u>enigraphics from the <u>F</u>ile menu. If this option does not appear on the <u>F</u>ile menu, you can reinstall PowerPoint and add it. Once you have made arrangements with the service, you will be able to send the slide show directly from PowerPoint to Genigraphics via a modem.

Customizing Your Presentation

After you've created a few presentations, you'll probably decide on a style that you'd like to use for all your future ones. You can customize your presentations by changing the design template it is based on. If you find yourself using similar slides in all your presentations, you can even create a customized template so you don't need to keep recreating the same slides.

Changing the Appearance of a Presentation

As a rule, pick one design for most of your presentations and stick with it. This gives your audiences a chance to associate a certain look with you or your office, and gives you a certain personal graphic "style."

Occasionally, however, you'll need to change the design of a presentation on which you are working. For instance, if you are presenting to a conservative audience, select a design template that reflects the participant's tastes.

To change the design of a presentation:

1. Choose Format, Apply Design Template, or click the Apply Design Template button. The Apply Design Template dialog box shown in Figure 14-35 will appear.

2. Select a template to see it previewed on the right of the dialog box.

Figure 14-35.
You can alter the design of a presentation you are working on at any time

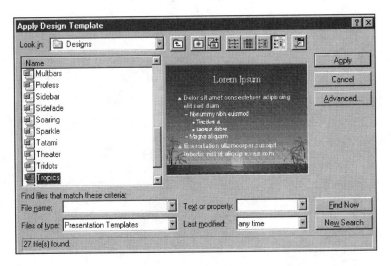

3. Double-click on the design of your choice. The existing slides will be reformatted with the new design.

Creating Customized Templates

As a time-saving measure, save the slides you use over and over as a template. For instance, you may find that a title slide, description of services, or disclaimer appears in all your presentations. By saving these slides as a template, you can build on previous work.

To create a customized template:

1. Create or open a presentation that uses the template design you prefer.

2. Enter the text for any slides that will appear in all your presentations.

3. Choose File, Save As. You will see the File Save dialog box.

4. Choose Presentation Templates in the Save as Type box. The default folder changes to the Templates folder.

5. If you want the template to be saved in a subfolder, so that it appears in the Presentations tab rather than the General tab, double-click the Presentations folder.

6. Type the name of the presentation template in the File Name box and then click Save.

CHAPTER 15

MAKING PROFESSIONAL SLIDE SHOWS

IN THIS CHAPTER

- **Working with Slide Objects**
- **Creating Slide Shows**
- **Showing the Presentation**
- **Taking Your Show on the Road**

The key to captivating and persuading an audience is often in the visual aids that accompany a presentation. One way to make your presentations more visually appealing is to get away from simple text and use the medium more effectively by including other visual design elements, such as clip art, shapes, and lines.

You can make a another quantum leap in visual effectiveness, however, if you present a presentation electronically rather than with transparencies or 35mm slides. Increasingly, corporate and government conference rooms are equipped with technology that makes this possible. Some facilities have portable overhead projectors and LCD panels, while others have projectors built into the ceiling. If you want to stay abreast of the technology power curve, you will want to learn to project your aids electronically.

Working with Slide Objects

While standard presentations made with PowerPoint can clearly state the points you are making, you can enhance the power of a presentation by including other types of objects in your slides. These include clip art, specially formatted text, shapes, and lines.

Adding Clip Art

PowerPoint comes with an entire gallery of clip art that can be used to illustrate your points. This clip art gallery makes it easy to organize and find the clip art you need. You can insert clip art from other sources into your slides, but you will not then be able to take advantage of some of the features that the gallery provides. You can, however, add other clip art to the gallery.

Inserting Clip Art from the Gallery

Inserting a piece of clip art into a slide from the gallery is very easy. To do so, follow these steps:

1. Switch to the Slide View, if necessary, and navigate to the target slide.

2. Choose Insert, Clip Art or click the Insert Clip Art button on the Standard toolbar. You will see the Microsoft ClipArt Gallery 2.0 dialog box shown in Figure 15-1.

3. Click on one of the clip art categories at the left of the dialog box. You will see previews of the images in that category.

4. Scroll through these images to find the best one for your presentation, then double-click on the most appropriate one. The image is inserted into the slide.

Figure 15-1.
PowerPoint's clip art
is organized by
categories and
descriptions to help
you quickly find
appropriate images
for a presentation

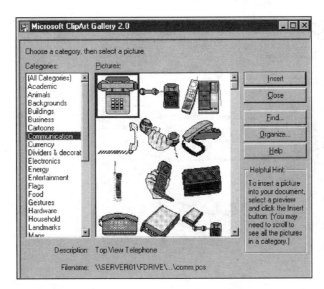

5. Move and resize the image to fit the application as described below.

Finding Clip Art

Clip art images are stored with both a filename and a description. If you don't see the image you want, you can search for it by using keywords. This can be very helpful when you have a subject for the slide, but don't know exactly what image might be appropriate.

To search for clip art:

1. Switch to the Slide View, if necessary, and navigate to the target slide.

2. Choose Insert, Clip Art. The Microsoft ClipArt Gallery 2.0 dialog box will appear.

3. Click the Find button. You will see the Find ClipArt dialog box shown in Figure 15-2.

4. Type the search keywords in the Description box. You may also search for a filename in the Filename Containing box, or limit the search to a specific category by specifying the Picture Type.

5. Choose Find Now. The images that match your criterion appear.

6. Double-click on the one you wish to insert into the slide.

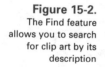

Figure 15-2.
The Find feature
allows you to search
for clip art by its
description

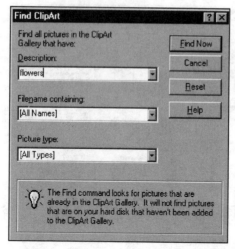

Adding Clip Art to the ClipArt Gallery

In order to take advantage of the features of the ClipArt Gallery when using clip art that isn't already part of the clip art gallery, you must first add the new clip art to the ClipArt Gallery. For instance, you may wish to use clip art from Microsoft Word.

To do so, follow these steps:

1. From the Slide View, choose Insert, Clip Art or click the Insert Clip Art button on the Standard toolbar. You will see the Microsoft ClipArt Gallery 2.0 dialog box.

2. Click the Organize button. You will see the Organize ClipArt dialog box.

3. Choose Add Pictures. If you see the Add New Pictures dialog box, click Other Pictures. Otherwise, go to the next step.

4. You will see an open file dialog box titled Add Pictures to ClipArt Gallery. Navigate to the folder containing the pictures, e.g., \msoffice\clipart for Word clip art.

5. Highlight all pictures you wish to add and click Open. You will see the Picture Properties dialog box shown in Figure 15-3.

6. Type in a description for the picture, and click the check boxes for any categories with which it should be associated.

7. Click OK. You will be prompted to specify the properties for the next picture you selected.

Figure 15-3.
When you add images to the ClipArt Gallery, you have the option of including a description of them and assigning them to one or more categories

8. Continue this process until you have inserted all the selected pictures.

Letting PowerPoint Find Clip Art for You

PowerPoint comes with an AutoClipArt feature that will find clip art appropriate for your presentation. It does so by looking at the text of the presentation, then matching it with the descriptions of clip art in the organizer.

To use the AutoClipArt feature:

1. Create the presentation, including all its text.
2. Switch to the Slide View, if necessary.
3. Choose Tools, AutoClipArt. You will see a message which says that AutoClipArt is scanning the text of the presentation. The AutoClipArt dialog box shown in Figure 15-4 will then appear.
4. You will see the word that was found on the slide, and the slide number containing it.
5. To view the associated clip art, choose View Clip Art. You will see the ClipArt Gallery, with the appropriate image selected.
6. To insert it into the slide, choose Insert.
7. If you don't want this piece of clip art, choose Close. In either case, return to the AutoClipArt dialog box.

Figure 15-4.
The AutoClipArt feature
scans the text of a
presentation and
chooses appropriate
clip art automatically

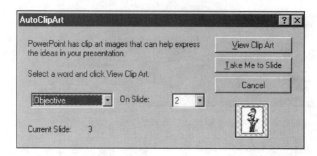

8. When you are finished, click Cancel. You will return to the slide show and can move and resize clip art as discussed below.

Using Drawing Objects

Generally, you will find that the design templates supplied with PowerPoint provide you with slides that have graphic design elements that meet your needs. Occasionally, however, you may need to include a drawing object on a slide in order to emphasize a point. PowerPoint provides you with tools to create basic objects such as lines, rectangles, circles, ellipses, arcs, and other shapes. You can also use these drawing tools to modify existing clip art.

Creating Basic Shapes

To insert a basic drawing shape on a slide, do the following:

1. Ensure that you are in the Slide View.

2. Notice the Drawing toolbar that is on the left of the screen. If you do not see the Drawing toolbar, choose <u>V</u>iew, <u>T</u>oolbars, and select the Drawing check box.

4. To insert a shape such as a line, click the Line tool. The mouse pointer changes to a crosshair.

5. Click at the point where the line should start, then drag the pointer to where the line should end and release the mouse button.

TIP: If you hold the (Shift) key down as you are dragging the pointer, it constrains the line to a vertical, horizontal, or 45 degree line.

TIP: Double-clicking the Line tool keeps it selected until you click the Line tool again, allowing you to easily add many lines to the slide.

6. The pointer changes back to a arrow—a selection pointer—when you are finished drawing the line.

Inserting rectangles, ellipses, and arcs is similar to inserting lines. Holding down the Shift key will transform rectangles into squares and ellipses into circles.

When you click the AutoShapes tool, you will see a pop-up AutoShapes window, shown in Figure 15-5. You can click on any of the shapes to insert them into the slide.

Editing Drawing Objects

You can edit drawing objects by changing their line or fill attributes. It is even possible to add text inside a drawing object that will move and be resized along with the drawing object. To edit a drawing object, you will first want to select it. If it is a complex object, you may need to ungroup it before you can edit it. Very complex objects can be ungrouped several times before the simple components they are made of are revealed.

PART IV   POWERPOINT

Figure 15-5.
The AutoShapes window allows you to insert a variety of drawing shapes into a slide

Drawing shapes

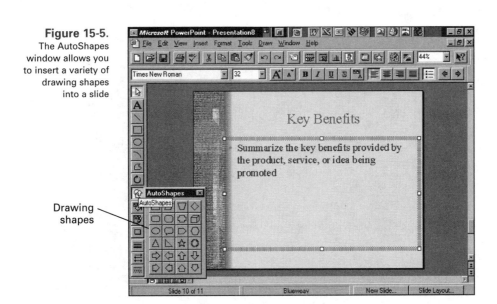

EDITING LINE ATTRIBUTES

A line is the visible border that separates an object from the rest of the slide. An object can have no visible line, or it can have a line of a specified width. You can also specify the color of a line, and whether the line is solid, dotted, etc. Edit line attributes as follows:

1. Select the object or objects that should be changed.

2. Click the Line Color button. You will see a pop-up menu showing line colors, as shown in Figure 15-6.

3. Choose No line, Automatic or select from among some basic color choices. Alternatively, choose Other Color to select from a virtually infinite color palette.

4. To change the thickness of the line or whether it is a single versus a double line, click the Line Style button, then click on the desired line style in the resulting pop-up window.

5. To choose from a variety of dashed line types, click the Dashed Lines button, then select the type of line from the pop-up window.

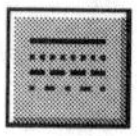

6. Add a shadow to figures like rectangles and ellipses by clicking the Shadow On/Off button, and add arrowheads to lines by clicking the Arrowhead button.

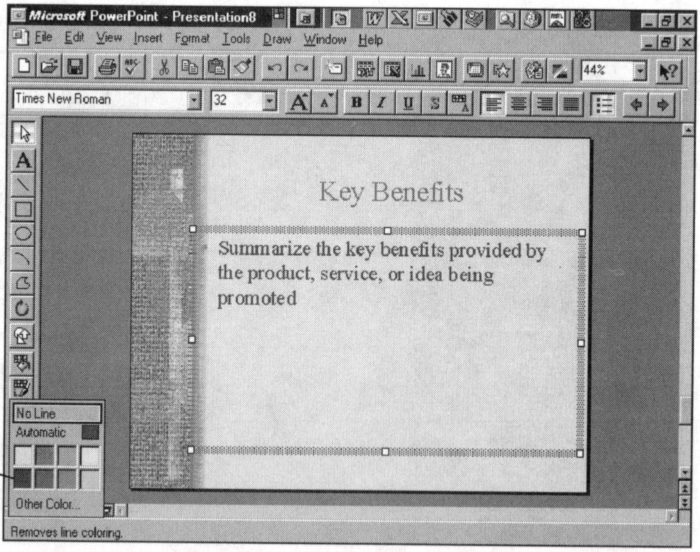

Figure 15-6.
A pop-up menu allows you to choose the line color of drawing objects

Line colors

NOTE: **To change the default line style for new objects, choose Colors and Lines from the Format menu after you have selected an object. Select all options listed in the Colors and Lines dialog box, then check Default for New Objects.**

EDITING FILL ATTRIBUTES

An object's fill is the color and/or pattern that occupies the space inside its border. Certain objects, like lines and arcs, do not have fills. Editing fill attributes is similar to editing line attributes:

1. Select the object or objects that should be changed.
2. Click the Fill Color button. Select from among the basic colors for this presentation in the resulting pop-up window, or choose Other Color to select from a virtually infinite color palette.
3. To apply shading, patterns, or textures to a fill, click the Fill Color button, then click on Shaded, Patterned, or Textured. You will see a dialog box such as the Textured Fill dialog box shown in Figure 15-7.
4. Select the desired texture and click OK. You'll see a filled object like the one in Figure 15-8.
5. Change shading and patterns just as you change textures.

Figure 15-7.
The Textured Fill dialog box allows you to create sophisticated fills for drawing objects

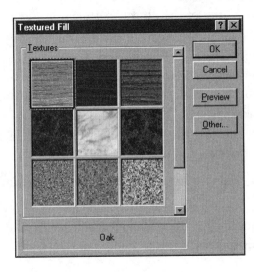

PART IV   POWERPOINT

Figure 15-8.
Textures can add
dimension to your
presentations

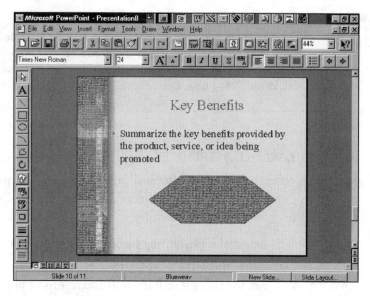

ADDING TEXT TO DRAWING OBJECTS

You can also add text to a drawing object. This allows you to create titles that have unique borders, or flow charts that incorporate a variety of shapes. You can add text to any drawing objects except for lines and arcs.

Add text to an object as follows:

1. Double-click the object. You will see handles around it and an insertion point in the middle of the object.

2. Type the desired text. The text will appear centered within the boundaries of the object, as shown in Figure 15-9.

3. To align the text within the drawing object, choose Format, Alignment; then choose Left, Center, or Right. Alternatively, click the Left Alignment or the Center Alignment buttons on the Formatting toolbar.

4. Click in the slide outside the object to deselect it when you are finished entering text.

You can edit text you have already put into a drawing object as well. To do so:

1. Double-click the object. You will see handles around it and an insertion point in the middle of the object.

Figure 15-9.
You can place text
inside PowerPoint
drawing objects

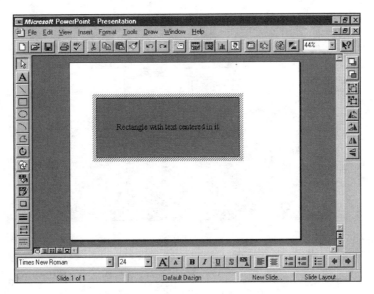

2. Edit the text as follows:
   - To insert new text, click where you want text to appear and type the text.
   - To select text, drag the mouse pointer over it.
   - To delete text, select it and press the [Del] key.
   - To move or copy text, select it and click the Cut or Copy button. Click where you want it to appear and click the Paste button.

3. Click in the slide outside the object to deselect it when you are finished editing text.

Changing Font Attributes

Once you Once you have selected text, you can change its font attributes. Be aware, however, that the text will still be positioned in the text box. If you make the text too large, it may not fit.

To format text:

1. Select the text to be formatted as described above.

2. Choose Format, Font. The Font dialog box shown in Figure 15-10 will appear. Note that it is similar to the Font dialog box in Word.

Figure 15-10.
The Font dialog box
allows you to change
font attributes, as well
as set new font
attribute defaults

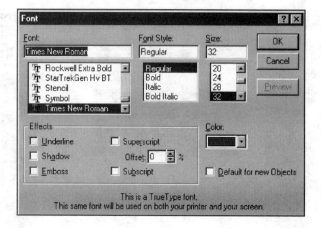

3. Choose the appropriate typeface, size, and style, as well as the color and any effects you wish to use.

4. If you wish all new text to share these attributes, click Default for New Objects in the Font dialog box.

5. Click the OK button. You will see the changed text on the slide.

If you want to apply these changes to other text in the presentation, click in the changed text, then click the Format Painter button. The mouse pointer changes to a paintbrush. Drag the paintbrush over other text to be changed. The new text takes on the new format.

TIP: If you want to use the Format Painter repeatedly, double-click on the button. It will stay selected until you click on it again, allowing you to reformat several areas of text.

Moving and Copying Objects

You can cut and paste graphic objects between slides within a slide show, between different slide shows, or from PowerPoint into a Word document. The procedure is identical to moving and copying text in Word or cell data in Excel. To do so, follow these steps:

1. Ensure that you are in the Slide View.

2. Select the object(s) to be moved or copied.

3. Choose <u>E</u>dit, Cu<u>t</u> to move the object to the Clipboard, or Edit, <u>C</u>opy to copy it to the Clipboard; or click on the Cut or Copy buttons in the Standard toolbar. Since the object is now in the Clipboard, you can paste it on the same slide, to another slide in the same presentation, to a slide in a different presentation, or even into a Word document.

4. Switch to the appropriate presentation and slide, or to the Word document.

5. Choose <u>E</u>dit, <u>P</u>aste, or click the Paste button on the Standard toolbar. The object is moved or copied to the appropriate destination. The object also stays in the Clipboard until you replace it with something else, and can thus be pasted many times if desired.

Selecting and Positioning Objects

When you have inserted clip art into a slide, it will usually not be in the correct position, and often is not the right size. You can move and resize it after you select it. These same procedures work for other objects on slides, such as charts and drawing objects. You will do all your selecting and positioning in the Slide View, as this is the view that is meant for working with slide objects.

Selecting Objects

You can select objects as follows:

1. Ensure that you are in Slide View.

2. Click on the Selection Tool, if it is not already active.

3. Click on the appropriate object. You will see handles (8 squares) around the perimeter of the object.

4. To select an additional object, hold down the [Shift] key, then click on the second object.

TIP: You can tell if your selection tool is active because the selection tool button will be pressed.

TIP: You can also select a group of objects by positioning the selection tool above and to the left of any of the objects, then dragging a box around all the objects to be selected.

Once an object or objects are selected, you can delete them by pressing the Del key.

If the object you are trying to select is behind another object, you may move the object in front to the side, or you can put it behind the desired object. Do so as follows:

1. Select the object in front.
2. Choose <u>D</u>raw, Send to Ba<u>c</u>k to move it behind all other objects.
3. Choose <u>D</u>raw, Send <u>B</u>ackwards to move it backwards by one object.

Grouping Objects

If you will be working with several objects, you may wish to group them together to make one object. This can be very helpful when you want to be able to move or size several objects. To do so:

1. Select all the necessary objects.
2. Choose <u>D</u>raw, <u>G</u>roup. The handles of each object are replaced by one set of eight handles that extends around the perimeter of the group.

You can now move, resize, copy, or delete the group as if it were one object. Before you move the parts of the object in relation to each other, however, you must ungroup them by selecting the grouped object then choosing <u>D</u>raw, <u>U</u>ngroup.

Moving and Resizing Objects on a Slide

Once you have inserted clip art or other graphic objects into a slide, you may wish to move them or resize them to the appropriate position on the slide.

MOVING OBJECTS

To move objects on a slide:

1. Select the object or objects.

Figure 15-11.
You can move a
group of objects by
selecting them and
dragging them to
their new location

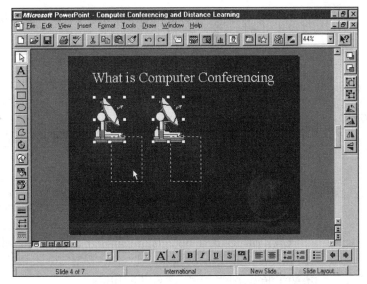

2. Place the mouse pointer inside the selected object and drag it
to its new position on the slide, as shown in Figure 15-11.

3. To copy an object, hold down the [Ctrl] key, place the mouse
pointer inside the selected object, then drag the copy to its
new position on the slide.

TIP: You can also move several objects at once by selecting
all of the objects you want to move and dragging them to
their new position.

The procedure for moving *text* is slightly different. When you select a
text box by clicking on it, you will see a thick border with handles
around the selection. To move the selected text box, position the
mouse pointer on the border and drag the block to its new position.

RESIZING OBJECTS

You can also resize objects on a slide, as follows:

1. Select the object or objects to be resized.

2. Place the pointer on one of the handles, and drag the handle
to resize the object:

- Dragging a side handle allows you to resize an object in one direction only.
- Dragging a corner handle allows you to resize an object both vertically and horizontally at once.
- Hold down the [Shift] key while dragging the corner handle to resize the object and maintain its *aspect ratio* (i.e., its proportions). PowerPoint calls this *scaling objects.*

Editing Objects

When you add text to a PowerPoint slide, it appears inside a *text object.* The text object is the box that appears around your text when you click on it. Text objects are similar to drawing objects in that they can be deleted, moved, copied, or resized. By default, a text object has no visible border, and no visible fill.

You can also edit text within the text object by changing its font, color, and size. Usually, you will not need to edit the appearance of text, because the color and font that PowerPoint's templates use for text is most often appropriate. However, there are occasions when you need to make a font smaller to get a few more words on the slide, or add impact to a presentation by putting a word in a large font and contrasting color.

Editing Text

To change the attributes of text, you need to first select the text to be changed within the text box. This is slightly different than selecting the text object as a whole. Do so as follows:

1. Ensure you are in the Slide View.
2. Click on the appropriate text object. A heavy border will appear around the text box.
3. Drag the mouse pointer over the specific text to be selected. The text that you select becomes highlighted in a contrasting color to the slide background, as shown in Figure 15-12.

Editing Text Objects

In a slide, text is positioned within a text object. This object is the area defined by a thick border when you click in the text. The text object defines how long each line of text will be, and where the text will wrap. It also defines the area within which text will be aligned. For

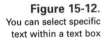

Figure 15-12.
You can select specific
text within a text box

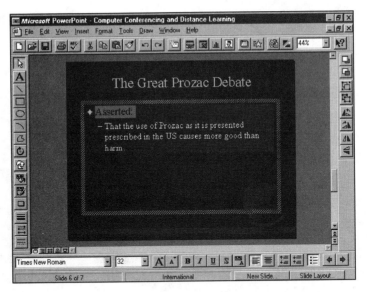

instance, text that is centered is centered in the text object, not centered on the slide itself.

There are two common times when you will want to edit a text object: when you have made the font size of the text larger, and need to resize the text object to accommodate it, and when you need to move the text object.

To resize and move a text object:

1. Click once in the text to select the object.
2. Click once in the thick border around the text object. You will see handles in the border, as shown in Figure 15-13.
3. Drag a handle to resize the objectbox, just as you would any other graphic object.
4. To move the text object, position the mouse pointer in the thick border around it, but not on the handles. Drag the object to its new position.

TIP: Moving a text object can be a little confusing, since it's different than moving a drawing object. If you position your mouse pointer in the middle of the text object to move it, like you would a drawing object, you'll find that when you click and drag the mouse, it selects text rather than moving the text object.

PART IV   POWERPOINT

Figure 15-13.
Resize a text objectbox
by selecting it, then
clicking in its border

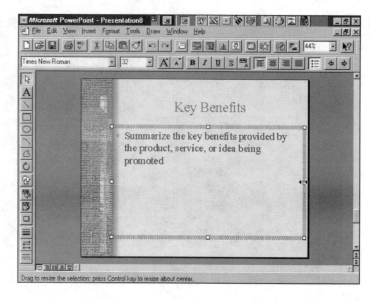

Showing the Presentation

You can display a presentation as a series of electronic "slides" on a computer. By attaching your computer to an LCD panel with an overhead projector, you can display a slideshow to an audience.

To show slides as a presentation:

1. Choose <u>V</u>iew, Slide Sho<u>w</u>. The Slide Show dialog box shown in Figure 15-14 will appear.

2. Specify the slides to be displayed, and whether to advance slides manually or use pre-programmed timing. You can also

Figure 15-14.
The Slide Show dialog
box allows you to set
options for the
electronic display of a
presentation

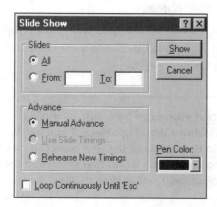

specify that the presentation should repeat continuously. This feature can be very useful during unattended displays.

3. Click <u>S</u>how to start the presentation.

While you are presenting a slide show, you have several viewing options:

- To advance to the next slide, click the left mouse button, press [Enter] or press [N].

- To advance to the previous slide, click the right mouse button and select Previous from the pop-up menu, or press [P].

- To terminate the presentation, press [Esc].

- To go to a particular slide, click the right mouse button, and select Go To, Slide Navigator. You will see the Slide Navigator dialog box shown in Figure 15-15, listing all the slides in the presentation. Select the appropriate slide and choose <u>G</u>o To.

- You can also go to a specific slide by typing the number of the slide and pressing [Enter].

- Create an electronic "pen" to highlight points of interest by clicking the right mouse button and choosing Pen, or press [Ctrl]+[P]. You can then click and drag to draw on the slides, as shown in Figure 15-16. Pressing [E] erases your drawing.

- Pressing [B] or [W] makes the screen go completely black or white, respectively. Pressing the key again shows the current slide.

PART IV   POWERPOINT

 TIP: You can also click the **Slide Show** button to automatically display the slide show starting at a selected slide.

Figure 15-15.
The Slide Navigator allows you to move directly to a specific slide in a presentation

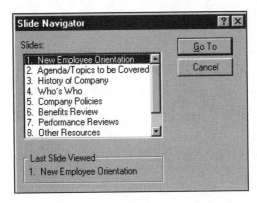

Figure 15-16.
You can draw on slides
with an electronic pen
to emphasize your
points

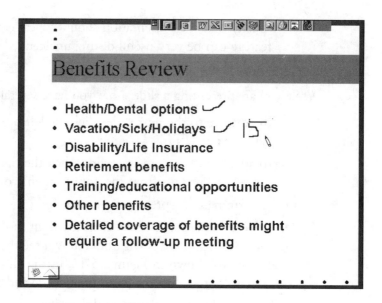

Formatting Electronic Slide Shows

Electronic slide shows can be "formatted" with transition and animation effects, sound, and movie clips that make them much more effective than transparencies. You can jump from one point in the
presentation to another, and even have hidden slides that you can use
when asked tough questions.

To format an electronic slide show, you will want to know how to
arrange slides, copy slides from one presentation to another, and
include multimedia special effects for the slide show.

You will use the Slide Sorter View for all these tasks, shown in
Figure 15-17. This view has toolbars with buttons for transitions
and other special effects.

Rearranging Slides

The first step in making an electronic slide show is to ensure that the
slides are arranged in the order you wish to present them. To rearrange
slides:

1. Switch to Slide Sorter View. You will see a small representa-
    tion of each slide, called a *thumbnail.*

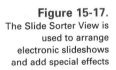

Figure 15-17.
The Slide Sorter View is
used to arrange
electronic slideshows
and add special effects

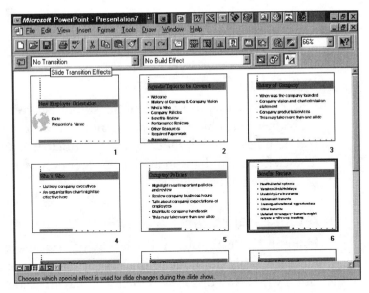

2. To move a slide, click on it, then drag it to its new position in the slideshow. As you drag it, you will see a vertical line that indicates where the slide will be moved when you release the mouse button.

Copying Slides between Presentations

You may find that you use one or more slides repeatedly in several presentations. This may be a standard corporate title slide, a company overview, or a disclaimer slide.

To copy slides between presentations:

1. Open the presentation containing the slides.
2. Switch to Slide Sorter View. Click on the slide to select it. If you have additional slides, hold down the Ctrl key and click on each one in turn, or, to select adjacent slides, hold down the Shift key and click on the last one.
3. Choose Edit, Copy or click the Copy button on the Standard toolbar.
4. Switch to the presentation into which you wish to insert the slides, and switch to the Slide Sorter View.
5. Click on the slide before the slide to be inserted.

6. Choose Edit, Paste or click the Paste button. The slide appears in its new location.

Including Special Effects

PowerPoint allows you to create transitions between slides, animate individual slide objects, add music and sounds to slides and objects, and even have hidden slides to answer anticipated audience questions. These effects can draw an audience's attention in ways that a paper-based presentation cannot.

Adding Transitions

Using the Slide Transition dialog box, you can make the slides shift more smoothly from one to the next by adding transitions such as fades, wipes, and dissolves. When you play the slide show, these effects will govern how one slide transforms into the next.

You can also choose to advance from slide to slide manually, or create timings for an automatic slide show. In the latter case, the slide show will proceed from one slide to the next automatically, without your needing to do anything.

You can also add sounds in this dialog box. However, you will probably not want to do so, since you can only use the more limited .WAV files rather than the entire tunes that you can add with the animation effects discussed below.

TIP: Use one transition for all slides, or at most, two. If you start using too many different transitions, the audience's attention will be distracted from your point.

To create transitions, do the following:

1. Open the presentation and switch to the Slide Sorter View.

2. Select the slides to which the transition will apply. Choose Edit, Select All to select all the slides in the presentation. Alternatively, select the specific slides to which you wish the transition applied by clicking on the first one, then holding the Ctrl key and clicking on additional slides.

NOTE: Transitions and other effects are only applied to selected slides.

3. Choose Tools, Slide Transition or click the Slide Transition button on the Slide Sorter toolbar. The Slide Transition dialog box shown in Figure 15-18 will appear.

4. Choose Effect, then select which type of transition you would like to use. If you have design elements in the background of each slide, a transition like Dissolve keeps the background steady while only dissolving the text.

5. Click on one of the three speeds (Slow, Medium, or Fast) to see what the transition does.

6. Repeat steps 4 and 5 until you find the transition you want to use.

7. Choose to advance manually—Only on mouse click—or Automatically. If you choose an automatic advance, specify the number of seconds to pause before the advance.

8. Choose OK when you are done.

9. Play the presentation as described above to test the transitions.

PART IV POWERPOINT

Figure 15-18.
Transitions govern how one slide moves into the next

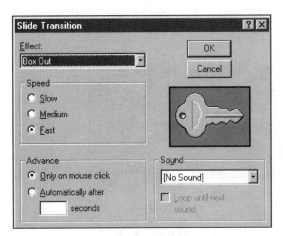

Animating Slide Objects

PowerPoint allows you to add transitions to any object on the slide—not just to the slide itself. These objects can be titles, bullets, text, clip art, charts, sounds, or even videos. You can also program objects so that they appear after a certain time, or in sequence after other objects have appeared.

To animate slide objects, do the following:

1. Open the presentation and click the Slide View button.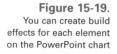

2. Move to the slide containing the object you wish to animate, and select the object.

3. Choose Tools, Animation Settings. You will see the Animation Settings dialog box shown in Figure 15-19. This dialog box will have different options depending on the type of object selected.

4. Choose animation options for the object:

   • You can choose the *build effect* for each object. These effects determine the order, timing, and manner in which individual objects appear on your slides. For instance, you might specify that a graphic appear five seconds after the text, and fade into the slide.

   • If the selected object is a series of bullets, you can choose how the sequence of bullets appear. For example, the next bulleted item can appear when you click the mouse, or automatically after a specified number of seconds. You also have the option to dim previous items in a bulleted list by

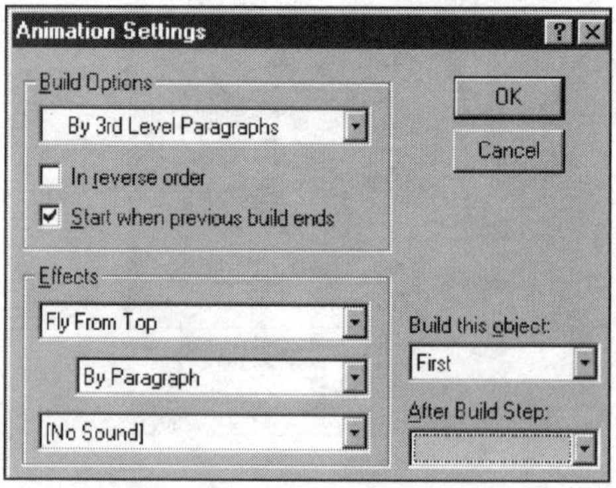

Figure 15-19.
You can create build effects for each element on the PowerPoint chart

Animation Settings

Build Options

By 3rd Level Paragraphs

☐ In reverse order
☑ Start when previous build ends

OK

Cancel

Effects

Fly From Top

By Paragraph

[No Sound]

Build this object:

First

After Build Step:

> **CAUTION:** You can also add a sound, but this sound will occur for each bullet and can be distracting. If you use sound, use it very sparingly, perhaps for the concluding slide.

displaying them in a different color after the focus shifts to the next item.

- If you have multiple animated objects, add a build order—that is, the order in which objects on the slide should appear—by choosing Build This Object. For instance, if you have clip art and a bulleted list, should the clip art appear first or after the list?

5. Choose OK when you are finished.

6. Select other slides and objects and animate them by repeating these steps.

Adding Music

You may find instances where adding music can be very effective in a presentation. You can add sounds to slides and objects in a variety of dialog boxes. Office 95 also provides several very nice melodies that can be inserted in presentations as sound objects.

To insert a sound object, do the following:

1. Open the presentation.

2. Switch to Slide View and move to the slide you wish cue the music.

3. Choose Insert, Sound. You will see the Insert Sound dialog box shown in Figure 15-20.

4. Navigate to the folder where the sound files are stored—often \windows\media—and choose the sound file you would like to play during the presentation.

5. The music object appears as a small box in the center of the slide. Move it to the side and size it so it is a small, unobtrusive vertical line.

6. With the sound object still selected, choose Tools, Animation Settings. You will see the Animation Settings dialog box.

Figure 15-20.
You can select from a number of different melodies for your presentation

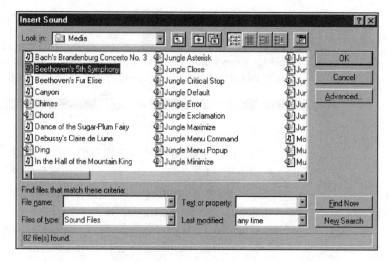

TIP: Canyon and Passport are two upbeat melodies you might consider.

7. Choose Play Options and select Play. The More button becomes active.

8. Choose More. You will see the More Play Options dialog box shown in Figure 15-21.

9. Select Continue Slideshow, Play In Background.

10. Select Stop after. Specify during how many slides the melody should continue (usually the total number of slides in a slide show).

Figure 15-21.
The More Play Options dialog box allows you to create background music for a slideshow

11. Choose OK to return to the Animation Effects dialog box, then choose OK again to return to the slide.

Including Hidden Slides

On occasion, you can anticipate that your audience may ask a question that requires you to show a slide that is not in your main presentation. If you're smart, you'll create such slides and keep them on hand for the right opportunity. These are called hidden slides. To create a hidden slide:

1. Display the slide in the Slide View.
2. Choose Tools, Hide Slide.

To display a hidden slide, run the slide show as you normally would. When you need to display a hidden slide, right-click anywhere in the slide you are displaying. Choose Go To, Slide Navigator, and pick the slide from the list of slides displayed.

Taking Your Show on the Road

With PowerPoint, you can even take presentations with you when you travel. The PowerPoint Viewer even allows you to show a presentation on a computer that not have PowerPoint. To help you get your presentation from here to there, you can use PowerPoint's Pack and Go Wizard.

Using the Pack and Go Wizard

To pack up a presentation and transport it to another computer, use the Pack and Go Wizard:

1. Open the presentation in PowerPoint.
2. Choose File, Pack and Go. You will see the first window of the Pack and Go Wizard, shown in Figure 15-22.
3. Choose Next. The second screen asks you which presentations you want to pack. If you want to pack the open presentation, choose Next. Otherwise, select Other Presentations, then browse to find the presentations you need, then choose Next.
4. Choose where you want the presentation to go. If it is the default Drive A, choose Next. Otherwise, browse to find the proper location.

How Should You Display a Presentation on Another Computer?

Consider these situations when taking your show on the road:

- If the other computer has PowerPoint, you can use it to show the presentation. Otherwise, you can use the viewer included with PowerPoint.

- If the other machine is running Windows 3.1, you can only show a PowerPoint presentation by using the viewer. You cannot see it using an earlier version of PowerPoint.

- If you use the viewer, you can show slides and highlight them using the highlighter tool. You cannot navigate to specific slides, show animation effects, or build slide elements such as bullets.

In short, use PowerPoint whenever you can on the destination machine to show a presentation. If you can't, show the basic presentation; you just won't have a lot of the fancier features at your disposal.

Figure 15-22.
The Pack and Go Wizard helps you compress presentations and move them to a different computer

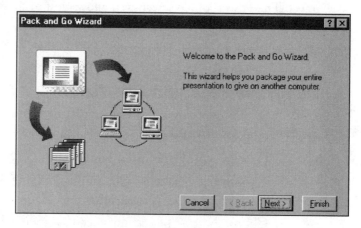

5. In the next step, choose whether to embed linked files and TrueType fonts. You will probably want to embed linked files, since these data files won't otherwise be available in the presentation. If you have only used standard Windows fonts, and

TIP: The Pack and Go Wizard will copy the file to multiple disks, if needed. You will be prompted to insert disks as additional ones are needed.

the destination machine is also running Windows 95, you will not need to embed the fonts. Choose Next to continue.

6. You are asked if you want to include the PowerPoint viewer. If the destination machine does not have PowerPoint, check this box. (You must use the PowerPoint viewer if the destination machine is running Windows 3.1 rather than Windows 95.)

7. Choose Finish. The Wizard will copy the necessary files to the destination you specify.

Unpacking the Presentation

When you're ready to show a presentation, you will need to unpack the presentation on the other computer. To do so:

1. Insert the first disk containing the packed presentation.

2. In Windows Explorer, display the files on that disk.

 TIP: You may wish to create a separate folder to contain all the presentation files.

3. Double-click on the PNGSETUP program. You will see the Pack and Go Setup dialog box shown in Figure 15-23.

4. Type in the name of the destination drive and folder, then choose OK.

Figure 15-23.
You can specify the folder in which you unpack the presentation

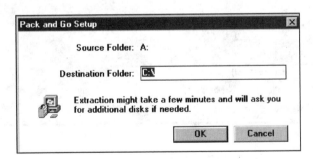

> **CAUTION:** Be careful! This process overwrites any files
> of the same name in the destination folder.

5. You are asked if you want to run the slide show now. Unless
   you do, answer <u>N</u>o. The process is complete, and the presentation is in the destination directory.

Showing the Presentation

After you've unpacked the presentation, you are ready to show it on
the remote computer. If you have PowerPoint, you will open the presentation and show it as usual. Otherwise, you will show the presentation with the PowerPoint viewer. To do so:

1. Open the Windows Explorer, and navigate to the directory
   containing the copy of the PowerPoint presentation.

2. Double-click on the PPTVIEW application. You will see
   the Microsoft PowerPoint Viewer dialog box shown in
   Figure 15-24.

3. Double-click on the presentation to run it.

Figure 15-24.
The PowerPoint
viewer allows you to
view a PowerPoint
presentation on any
machine running
Windows 95 or
Windows 3.1

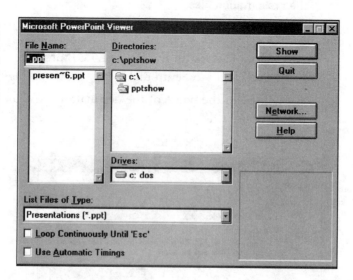

PART V

SCHEDULE+

CHAPTER 16

ORGANIZING YOUR DAY WITH SCHEDULE+

IN THIS CHAPTER

- Creating a Schedule+ Data File
- Familiarizing Yourself with Schedule+
- Making Personal Goals
- Prioritizing and Tracking Your Activities
- Maintaining an Electronic Appointment Book
- Printing Your Schedule+ Data

For many of us, the most important problem we face in our office is the struggle for organization. As one management consultant says, "Good results without good planning comes from good luck, not good management."

Does this apply to you?

- Have you forgotten to return phone calls this week?
- Do you procrastinate and put off important responsibilities?
- Are you swamped with administrative trivia?
- Are you late for meetings?
- Is it difficult for you to set priorities?

If so, then this chapter's for you. While Office 95 can't solve every time management problem, it provides a set of tools that you can combine with time management principles to give you a good start at getting organized and staying organized.

Creating a Schedule+ Data File

Creating a Schedule+ data file is as simple as opening Schedule+ for the first time. The entire Schedule+ data file is saved together— "to-do" items, calendar events, and contacts.

When you open Schedule+ for the very first time, it will ask for your *profile*. Your profile is merely a description of who you are and a list of the Microsoft Exchange services to which you are subscribing, like Fax Exchange or MSN.

To create your Schedule+ data file, do the following:

1. Choose Start from the Task Bar, then select Programs, Schedule+. If Windows 95 is installed for several different users to use the same computer, you may see the Choose Profile dialog box.

2. Select the appropriate profile, then choose OK. The Microsoft Schedule+ dialog box will appear.

3. Choose "I want to create a new schedule file," then click OK. You will see the Select Local Schedule dialog box.

4. Type a filename for your new schedule, then choose Save.

5. You will see the Schedule+ main screen. Click on the Contacts tab. The empty contact list appears, and you're done!

Schedule+ to the Rescue!

Sandra Conner has her own business, teaching a system of movement called the Alexander Technique to musicians, actors, and body therapists. She has to constantly return phone calls from potential new clients, plan and publicize workshops, and register participants, collect tuition and pay bills, and make sure she's on time for her classes and private appointments. In addition, she and her husband have to coordinate the responsibilities of raising their two children. If Sandra isn't organized, her business and personal lives fall apart!

When Sandra started her business, she marked her phone calls on whatever scrap of paper was near the phone, and tried to remember her daily tasks and appointments. You can imagine how well that worked! She graduated to a daily planner system, and that worked fairly well. It taught her the rudiments of planning and kept her organized, but she didn't like having to maintain a paper-based contact management system when her computer was becoming a central part of her business. That is why she started using Office 95 and Schedule+ to organize her day.

Now Sandra keeps her appointments electronically. She can quickly schedule recurring weekly classes with a few clicks of her mouse. If a student cancels she can quickly delete the appointment from her electronic appointment book without messy scratch-outs. Her computer even alerts her to upcoming meetings!

Sandra also finds it easy to keep track of the tasks involved in designing, promoting, and conducting a workshop. She enters all the things she needs to do for a workshop in Schedule+, and then displays them by priority to see what she must do first each day, or by project to get an overview of what must still be done. Since incomplete tasks are automatically carried to the next day, she doesn't deal with a cluttered paper-based to-do list any more, and she can search her electronic to-do list and appointment book for items pertaining to specific individuals.

When she's on the road, she takes a fresh printout of her daily planner, monthly calendars, and phone list. Ten minutes in the morning suffices to keep her organized and on track for the entire day.

PART V   SCHEDULE+

Exploring Schedule+

If you're new to Schedule+, it's worth your while to take a few minutes exploring it. You should be aware of three things:

- What Schedule+ can do for you
- The different Schedule+ views
- How to move to specific dates

What Schedule+ Can Do for You

Schedule+ is a powerful individual and group time management tool. For individuals, Schedule+ provides the ability to:

- Set your personal goals, and link tasks to those goals
- Create a prioritized task list, carrying incomplete tasks over to the next day
- Keep a calendar of appointments, with optional alarms
- Maintain a database of contacts, and link tasks and appointments to those contacts
- Sort and group tasks, appointments, and contacts in a variety of ways
- See your appointments and tasks in several different views, like the Daily view shown in Figure 16-1

Figure 16-1.
Schedule+'s Daily view shows your appointments and active tasks, as well as a monthly calendar

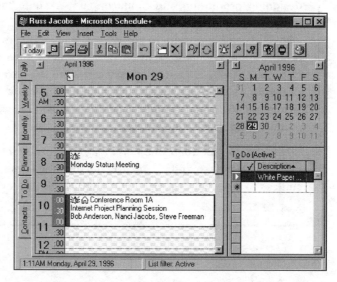

Figure 16-2.
Schedule+'s Planner
view shows times
you have meetings,
as well as the
attendees for the
selected meeting

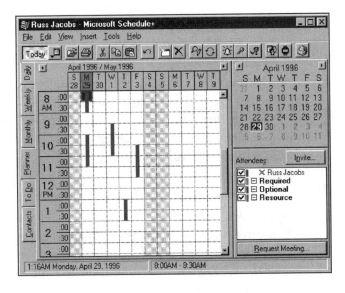

- Print tasks, appointments, and contacts in a number of formats

In addition, when you install Schedule+ to work with a group—called *group enabled mode*—you can:

- Allow others to view your calendar
- View others' calendars
- Find compatible free time and schedule meetings with others on your network, as shown in Figure 16-2

To see how to use Group Enabled mode features, see Chapter 18.

Schedule+ Objects

With Schedule+, you will create and maintain several types of objects:

- **Tasks** A task is something that you need to do such as product you need to produce, a duty or service you need to perform, an errand, or a phone call. They may be associated with a project or a person. Tasks may or may not have a specific due-date, but usually do not have a specific start-time. If they do, they would be an appointment rather than a task in Schedule+. Thus, if you have arranged to make a telephone call at a specific time, it would be an appointment, whereas if you merely must call someone whenever you can, it's a task.

- **Appointments** An appointment is a personal obligation to be somewhere or do something at a specific time on a specific

PART V SCHEDULE+

date, for a certain duration. Needing to attend a sales presentation, having a business lunch, or teaching a class would be examples of appointments.

- **Meetings** A meeting is like an appointment, but it is a group-related event rather than a personal event. When several people use Schedule+ to find a free time and put it on their respective calendars, they are scheduling a meeting. In contrast, if you are making a sales call on a client who is not part of your organization and doesn't use Schedule+, you are making an appointment, since you are only making an entry into your own calendar, not theirs.

- **Events** An event is an appointment that occurs on a specific day, but not at a specific time. An event may be an all-day occurrence, such as a convention or conference. It may also be an anniversary or birthday that you wish to be reminded of.

- **Contacts** A contact is a person about whom you wish to save information, such as their name, address, and phone number. You can maintain both business information (fax number, e-mail address) and personal information (spouse name, birthday) on your contacts, and assign them to categories. You can also link your contacts to tasks, meetings, appointments and events.

Schedule+ Views

Schedule+ offers over a dozen different views of your goals, tasks, appointments, and contacts. The ones you use most often—the active views—are accessed by clicking on tabs on the left of your Schedule+ window. Others can be added as you need them. For instance, you can access the Daily, Weekly, Planner, To Do, and Contacts views from the Monthly view shown in Figure 16-3 by clicking on the appropriate tab.

CAUTION: Schedule+ uses the word *tab* to refer both to views and to the tabs at the left of the Schedule+ window used to select views.

Figure 16-3.
Switch between different views by clicking on the appropriate tab at the left of the Schedule+ window

View tabs

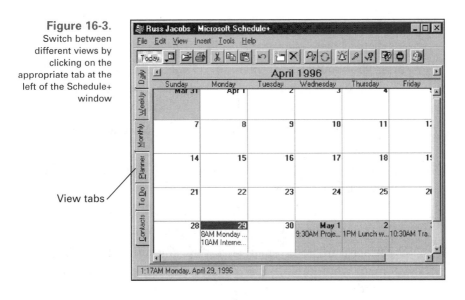

Selecting Tabs

You can choose which views will appear as tabs at the left of your Schedule+ window. This helps you customize Schedule+ for the way you work. To customize your view:

1. From the Schedule+ main window, choose <u>V</u>iew, T<u>a</u>b Gallery. You will see the Tab Gallery dialog box shown in Figure 16-4.

2. Select a view in the A<u>v</u>ailable Tabs list box. You will see what it will look like in the Preview window, along with a

PART V   SCHEDULE+

Figure 16-4.
The Tab Gallery dialog box allows you to choose which views will be displayed as tabs in the main Schedule+ window

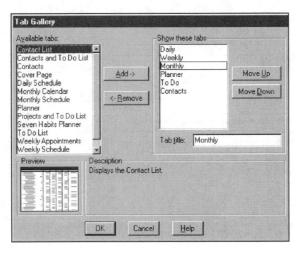

description of it in the Description area at the bottom of the dialog box.

3. If you would like to include the selected view as a tab in the main Schedule+ window, choose Add. The tab is added to the list of tabs in the Show These Tabs list box.

4. Repeat steps 2 and 3 until you have selected all the tabs you desire.

5. To remove a view, select it in the Show These Tabs list box and choose Remove.

6. To change a tab's order, select it in the Show These Tabs list box and choose Move Up or Move Down.

7. When you are finished, click OK. You return to the Schedule+ main window, and your selected tabs appear at the left of the window.

Moving between Dates

Schedule+ offers several different tools for moving between dates, depending on the view you are using. The Daily view shown in Figure 16-5 shows these tools.

Figure 16-5.
Schedule+ provides many ways of moving between dates

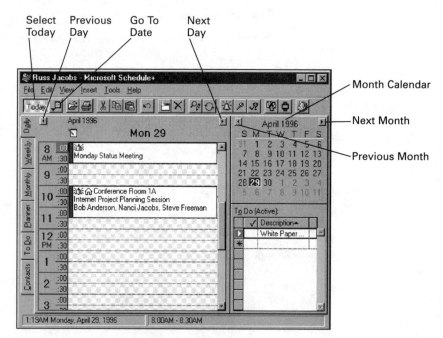

> **TIP:** If you don't see the Today button, the toolbar is probably not displayed. Choose <u>V</u>iew, <u>T</u>oolbar to display it.

These tools include:

- **Select Today button.** This button takes you to today's date. If you are in a Weekly or Monthly view, you will see the week or month containing today's date. In the Monthly view, the current day's date is highlighted.
- **Go To Date button.** This button displays a monthly calendar. If the month you wish to go to is displayed, double-click on the date to which you wish to go. If it is not, use the Next/ Previous arrows at the top of the window to scroll to the correct month, and double-click on the date. This button is especially useful in the Weekly views where there is no monthly calendar included in the display.
- **Previous and Next arrows.** Daily, weekly, and monthly views include Next and Previous arrows under the toolbar that will take you to the next day, week or month.
- **Go To command.** If you choose <u>E</u>dit, <u>G</u>o To or press Ctrl + G, the Go To dialog box will appear. You can type a specific date when using this function.

Organizing Your Day

When you read any books on time management, you find two things. First, most authors have a gimmick or "hook" to make their approach unique. Second, when you get past the gimmicks, most authors agree on some basic principles. These include:

- Have clear goals
- Prioritize your activities
- Minimize interruptions
- Learn to delegate
- Get and stay organized
- Stop procrastinating

> **TIP:** Put Schedule+ in your Startup folder so it opens when you start your computer. When you've finished using it, minimize Schedule+ rather than closing it. Having it readily available will encourage you to use it to its full potential.

Schedule+ can help you with several of these important time management goals, including making personal goals, setting priorities, being on time, and getting organized.

Prioritizing and Tracking Your Activities

Once you know where you're going, the next step is to figure out how to get there. Two important aspects of this are prioritizing your activities—"putting first things first"—and tracking your tasks so that you can gauge your performance.

Tasks, if you remember, are To Do items that are not bound to a specific date and time. If they occur at a specific date and time, Schedule+ regards them as appointments, and they are put on your appointment calendar.

The 1-2-3 Priority System

One of the most important steps in becoming organized is learning to separate the essential from the trivial. To do this, you will want to create and use some type of priority system. There are probably as many priority systems as there are authors of time management books, but the simple 1-2-3 system works pretty well for most people.

The 1-2-3 system organizes tasks around three priorities:

- **Priority 1** items must be worked on today, or some consequence will happen. Priority 1 items have a deadline, and that deadline is today. Examples of Priority 1 items include a completing a personnel evaluation that is due today, returning a phone call to your boss, or helping your daughter with her homework that's due tomorrow. The list of Priority 1 items should be short—it should be no longer than the items you really think you can do today.

- **Priority 2** items are ones that you want to do today, but do not absolutely have to do today. Priority 2 items are the ones you will work first on if you finish your Priority 1 items. Examples of Priority 2 items include starting work on a report due next week, paying your monthly bills, or initiating a call to a prospective client. The list of Priority 2 items should also be fairly short.

- **Priority 3** contains items that you don't want to forget to do, but probably won't get to today. Priority 3 items might include starting work on a project that is due next month, cleaning the gutters of your house, or making a follow-up call to an old client you haven't spoken to in a while. While your Priority 3 list can get fairly long, you need to review it daily and promote items to Priority 1 or 2, or eventually eliminate them if you aren't going to do them.

Maintaining the To Do List

Your To Do list is maintained in Schedule+; however, you can insert a task into your To Do list either from Schedule+ or directly from the Office Shortcut Bar (which will probably be visible on top of your other applications).

Inserting a Task from Schedule+

You can insert a task from whatever tab of Schedule+ happens to be open. This makes keeping your to-do list up to date a snap. To insert a task from Schedule+:

1. Press Ctrl + T or choose Insert, Task. You will see the Task dialog box shown in Figure 16-6.

2. Type a description for your task.

TIP: You can also click the Add New Task button on the Standard toolbar if you are on the To Do tab.

PART V   SCHEDULE+

Choosing a Priority System

While the 1-2-3 system is one of the oldest and best known priority systems, you may find that other systems meet your needs better. Some others to consider include:

- Dynamic 1-2-3 System: This system uses the same priorities, but allows these priorities to dynamically change each day. If you have scheduled an administrative workday at home, many items that have sat in Priority 3 for weeks may graduate to Priority 1 or 2, and since you're out of the office, many Priority 2 calls and tasks are demoted to Priority 3 for the day. Similarly, if you have an integrated home/business task list, weekday Priority 1 and 2 tasks dealing with business may have No Priority on the weekend, and your home tasks may be promoted to Priority 1 or 2.

  If you keep Schedule+ open all day, your 1-2-3 system may be even more dynamic—items can move to Priority 1 as others are done, or Priority 1 and 2 items may move to Priority 3 as you find your time to do things shortening.

- 1-2-3-4 system: This system breaks down Priority 3 tasks into two groups. Priority 3 is Nice If Time Is Available, and Priority 4 is Not Now. This system is handy for people who must keep track of future tasks that they know won't be worked on in the near future, but that they wish to be able to see for planning purposes.

- Letter/Number system: Instead of giving tasks priorities such as 1, 2 or 3, you can give tasks priorities like A1, A2, A3, B1, B2, B3, etc. This type of system was formerly used to group tasks by project. For instance, home-related tasks might be H1, H2, H3 and business tasks B1, B2 and B3. Since Schedule+ allows you to record the projects that tasks are associated with, most people will not use this priority system.

- Unique Priority system: In this system, you can only have one item that is Priority 1, 2, 3, etc. If a new item is created as Priority 1, the former Priority 1 item "bumps" down to Priority 2, the former Priority 2 becomes Priority 3, etc. This system works well for people who prefer to focus on one task at a time. Schedule+ does not support unique priorities, however.

Figure 16-6.
You can insert tasks
when you are in
Schedule+ by
pressing Ctrl + T

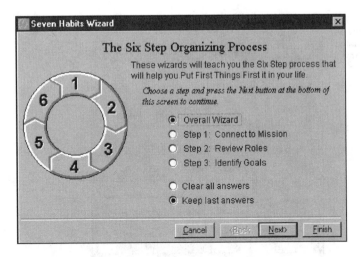

TIP: **You can create a new project by typing a new name
in the Project drop-down list box.**

3. If you track tasks by projects, choose the program associated
   with the task from the Project drop-down list box.

4. Give the task a priority in the Priority box.

5. If you wish to maintain more information on a complex task,
   click the Status tab. The Status information, displayed in
   Figure 16-7, will become visible.

6. When you have finished entering information about your
   task, click OK. The new task is stored in your task list.

NOTE: **Your task will appear on every daily calendar
starting with today's until you mark it completed. If you
wish to schedule a task for the future, you can type an
ending date, and then mark how many days prior to that
date you wish to have the task start appearing on your To
Do list. If you specify an end date, you will also have the
option of setting a reminder for a specific number of days
before the start date. When you open Schedule+, any
reminders you have set will appear in pop-up windows.**

Figure 16-7.
The Status Tab allows you to maintain detailed information about complex tasks

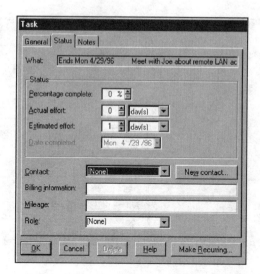

 TIP: If you enter the name of a person from your contact list (described later in this chapter) you link the task to that person. Later, you can display tasks associated with a given person.

Tasks you create will be displayed in a variety of Schedule+ views. The view that provides the most information on your To Do list is the To Do view, shown in Figure 16-8.

Figure 16-8.
The To Do view shows you all your tasks at a glance

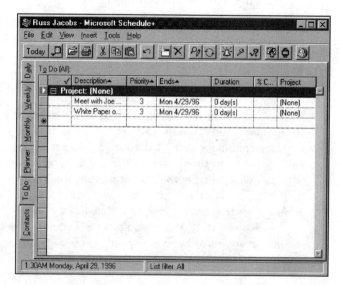

Inserting a Task from the Shortcut Bar

You can also insert a task from any Office 95 application by using the Shortcut Bar:

1. With the Office Shortcut Bar displayed, click the Add a Task button.
2. If Microsoft Exchange is installed on a computer that several people use, you may be asked to verify your name.
3. You will see the Task dialog box. Add the task as described in the procedure above.

Maintaining To-Do Items

To maintain your To Do list, you will want to be able to mark items as completed, delete items, and edit them.

- When you complete a task, you can mark it complete by clicking in the leftmost column of the To Do view (the column with a check mark above it). A check appears in the column, and the task is struck through with a line.
- You can delete a task by clicking anywhere in the line and pressing Ctrl+D; or choosing Edit, Delete Item.
- You can edit a task by scrolling until you can see the appropriate column and clicking in the cell containing the information and editing it appropriately. Alternatively, you can click anywhere in the line, press Ctrl+E to display the Task dialog box and edit the task from within this dialog box.
- You can mark a task as private by selecting the task and choosing Edit, Private. If you are using Schedule+ in Group Enabled mode, others will not be able to see your private items.
- If you have set an Active Range (i.e., a due date) for a task, you can set a reminder by choosing Edit, Set Reminder; or you can make the task a recurring task as described below.

Creating and editing tasks is only part of using To Do lists, however. The other aspect is *reporting*—being able to see the tasks that are associated with particular projects, persons, or priorities.

> **Using Schedule+ in Group Enabled mode is discussed further in Chapter 19.**

TIP: You can also find specific tasks by choosing Edit, Find as described below.

If it would help you to see your tasks associated with persons or projects, you will want to create a tab for the appropriate view. Using the Tab Gallery as described previously, add tabs for Projects and To Do List and/or Contacts and To Do List. When you click on the appropriate tab, you will see a list of your projects or contacts at the top of the window, and the tasks associated with that project or contact at the bottom of the window, as shown in Figure 16-9.

You can also see tasks grouped by priority—one of the best ways to keep yourself organized during the day. To group tasks by priority:

1. Click the To Do tab to see all of your tasks listed together.
2. Choose View, Group By. The Group By dialog box will appear.
3. In the Group tasks by drop-down list box, choose Priority, and ensure that the priorities are Ascending. Your Group By dialog box looks like the one pictured in Figure 16-10.
4. Click OK. You will see your tasks grouped by priority.

The only problem with displaying your tasks in this way is that Schedule+ may display every task you have ever done. To prevent this, you will probably want to display only your *active* tasks. Active tasks are ones that either (a) have no due date, (b) are between their starting and due dates, or (c) were completed today. To show your active tasks:

Figure 16-9.
You can quickly view projects and the tasks associated with them to help organize your work

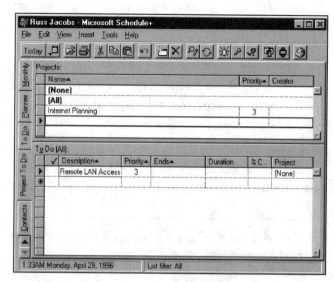

Figure 16-10.
Schedule+ allows
you to group tasks
by any of the fields
maintained in the
task list

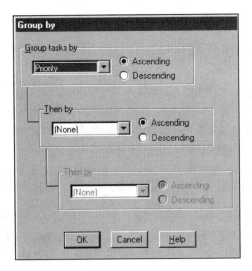

1. Choose <u>V</u>iew, <u>F</u>ilter, Ac<u>t</u>ive. Only your active tasks are displayed.
2. Choose <u>V</u>iew, <u>F</u>ilter again. Ensure that <u>I</u>nclude Tasks With No End Date is checked or unchecked, depending on whether you wish to see these tasks.

Being on Time

If you never have the time to be on time, Schedule+ can help. With Schedule+ you can maintain an appointment calendar, and (most importantly) set alarms to remind you when you need to leave! You can even set recurring appointments for staff meetings or other regularly scheduled events. To effectively use an electronic appointment book, you need to be able to:

- Create, edit, and delete appointments
- Set alarms (reminders)
- Move to specific days and view appointments
- Find specific appointments

Maintaining an Electronic Appointment Book

Schedule+ allows you to easily create appointments, as well as edit and move them when your plans change.

Creating Appointments

To create an appointment:

1. Open Schedule+ and press Ctrl+N, or choose Insert, Appointment. Alternatively, if the Shortcut Bar is displayed, click the Make an Appointment button from within application you are using. You will notice the Appointment dialog box shown in Figure 16-11.

2. Enter a description for the appointment, and a starting and ending time and date.

TIP: Schedule+ has a handy feature for scheduling all-day appointments like conferences (i.e., events). Click the All Day check box.

---

3. To set an alarm, choose Set Reminder. When this box is checked, you have the opportunity to specify how many minutes, hours, or days beforehand you wish to be reminded of this appointment.

TIP: You can set a reminder several days before an all-day event. This can help you remember materials that must be prepared for a conference. You can also use this feature to remind you several days in advance of an important birthday or anniversary, allowing you time to buy a present.

Figure 16-11.
You can add appointments from anywhere in Windows by clicking the Add an Appointment button on the Office Shortcut Bar

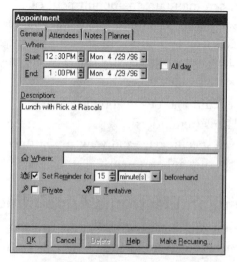

4. If you do not want others to be able to see this appointment, check the Private box.

5. To "pencil in" the appointment, check the Tentative box.

6. Click the Notes tab to add optional notes to the appointment.

7. If desired, click the Planner tab to see how this appointment fits into your week.

8. When you are finished, click OK. Your appointment is added to your Schedule+ appointment book.

TIP: **To invite others to this appointment (i.e., create a "meeting"), you can click the Attendees tab.**

Editing Appointments

The most useful ways to see your appointments are often in the Daily, Weekly, or Monthly views, although several of the other views also show your appointments. In the Weekly and Monthly views, you will only see the first few characters of your appointment. To see the entire appointment or to edit it in any view:

1. Select the appointment by clicking on it.

2. Press Ctrl + E or choose Edit, Edit Item.

3. To delete it, press Ctrl + D or choose Edit, Delete Item.

TIP: **You can also edit or delete an item by right-clicking on it and choosing the appropriate option.**

You can move an item with the mouse in the Daily or Weekly views by dragging the blue bar at the top or left of the item to a new time or date.

You can extend or shorten the appointment by positioning the mouse pointer at the bottom of the item until a double-arrow becomes apparent, dragging up or down to shorten or lengthen the timespan.

Alternatively, in any view you can select the item choose Edit, Move Item. You will then see a dialog box enabling you to specify the new date and time for the item.

Scheduling meetings is discussed in Chapter 17.

PART V SCHEDULE+

You can also cut, copy, and paste an appointment just as you would any other object in Windows, by selecting it and choosing Edit, Cut, or Copy. You can then paste it multiple times by moving to the appropriate date and choosing Edit, Paste.

Creating Recurring Appointments

Schedule+ allows you to enter recurring weekly meetings or monthly appointments once, and then reminds you before each one. Even if you teach a Tuesday and Thursday class each week, you can easily put it on your calendar as a recurring appointment.

TIP: You can also create an annual event like a birthday or anniversary by choosing Insert, Annual Event. Alternatively, you can specify a birthday when you create contact information for a person.

To create a recurring appointment:

1. Create a new appointment or edit an existing one as described above.

2. In the Appointment dialog box, choose Make Recurring. You will see the Appointment Series dialog box shown in Figure 16-12.

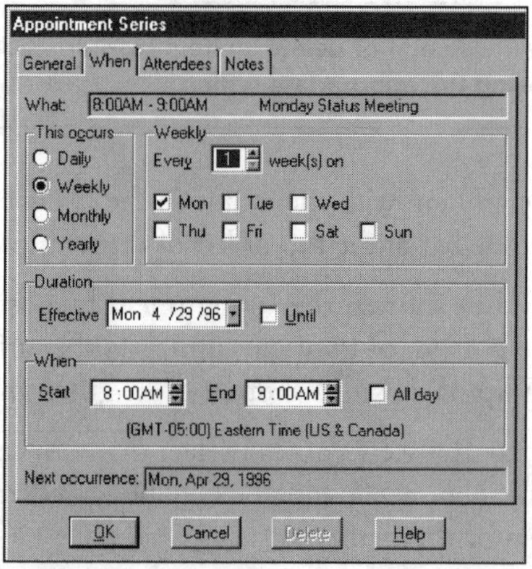

Figure 16-12.
You can easily schedule weekly or monthly meetings by choosing Make Recurring from the Appointment dialog box

Appointment Series
General   When   Attendees   Notes
What: 8:00AM - 9:00AM   Monday Status Meeting
This occurs / Weekly
○ Daily   Every 1 week(s) on
● Weekly
○ Monthly   ☑ Mon ☐ Tue ☐ Wed
○ Yearly   ☐ Thu ☐ Fri ☐ Sat ☐ Sun
Duration
Effective Mon 4 /29 /96 ▾   ☐ Until
When
Start 8 :00AM ⬍   End 9 :00AM ⬍   ☐ All day
(GMT-05:00) Eastern Time (US & Canada)
Next occurrence: Mon, Apr 29, 1996
OK   Cancel   Delete   Help

3. Choose whether the appointment occurs daily, weekly, monthly, or yearly.

4. Depending on which you choose, you can then specify the daily, weekly, monthly, or yearly options that appear in the dialog box. For example, for a Tuesday and Thursday class, you would choose Weekly, specify Every 1 Week, and ensure that Tuesday and Thursday were checked.

TIP: The first time you use the Recurring feature, click on Daily, Weekly, Monthly, and Yearly. Examine the options that are associated with each.

5. Set the duration of the recurring event. By default, the Effective date will be today's date.

6. If the recurring event has an end date, check the Until box and specify the ending date. For instance, to teach a fall semester 1996 class, you might specify 9/1/96 as the effective date and have the appointment recur until the end of the semester, 12/15/96.

7. The starting and ending time will be carried over from the original appointment, if you specified the times. You can change them in the dialog box if you like. The resulting sample appointment can be seen in Figure 16-13.

PART V SCHEDULE+

Figure 16-13.
You can even create a complex appointment that occurs twice a week for a specified range of dates

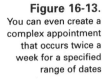
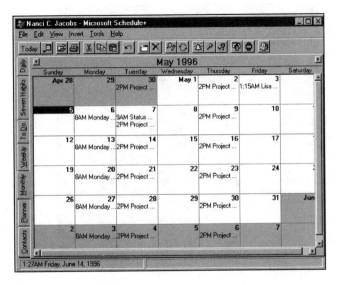

> **TIP:** If you delete a recurring appointment, you will be asked whether you'd like to delete all the appointments or just this instance.

8. When you are finished setting options, click OK. You return to the Schedule+ view you were in, and the appointments appear in your calendar.

Finding Specific Appointments

One great advantage that electronic appointment books have over their paper counterparts is your ability to quickly search through them to find past or future appointments. In fact, your search is not restricted to appointments. You can search through any or all items you have entered into Schedule+, including tasks and contacts. This can be very handy when you need to document phone conversations or meetings months after you've forgotten their exact date and purpose.

To search for a specific item:

1. Choose Edit, Find. The Find dialog box, shown in Figure 16-14, will appear.
2. Type the text for which you'd like to search in the Find What box.

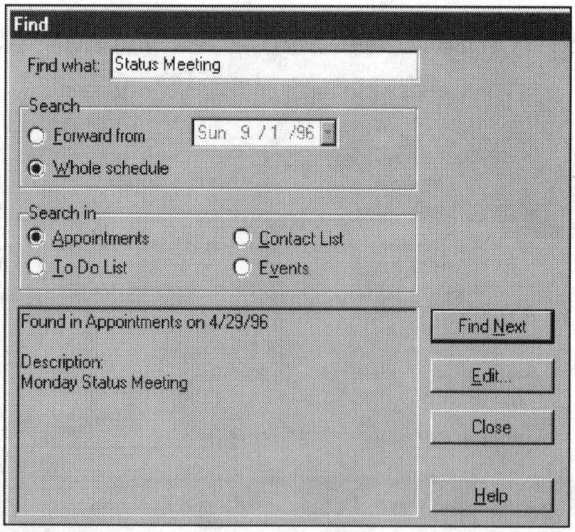

Figure 16-14.
You can search through Schedule+ to find past or future appointments, events, tasks, or contacts

3. If you'd like to restrict your search to specific dates, choose <u>F</u>orward From and specify the first date for your search.

4. Choose <u>A</u>ppointments, <u>T</u>o Do List, <u>C</u>ontact List, or E<u>v</u>ents.

5. Click <u>S</u>tart Search. The first object that meets your search criterion will appear in the dialog box.

6. Choose Find <u>N</u>ext to find the next object meeting the criterion or choose <u>E</u>dit to go to the object that was found.

Taking 10 Minutes Each Morning

In *The Organized Executive*, author Stephanie Winston discusses what she calls the TRAF system for getting organized each morning. Using the TRAF system can reduce the load of paper on your desk by 80 percent. Winston says that there are only four and one-half things you can do with a sheet of paper:

- *T*hrow it away
- *R*efer it to someone else
- *A*ct on it
- *F*ile it

Reading the paper only counts as one-half of an option since after you read the paper you still have to do one of the other four things with it. When you're done, your Act pile is often about 20 percent the size of the original!

You can integrate the TRAF method with Schedule+ by using this 10-minute routine each morning:

1. In the To Do view of Schedule+, mark off all the tasks you finished yesterday. If you printed your To Do list and calendar yesterday, add any tasks you wrote on the printout as new To Do items in Schedule+. Switch to the Daily, Weekly, or Monthly view and add any appointments you wrote on your printout to Schedule+ as well.

2. Gather all papers from your In-Box, Today Box, and Someday Boxes into a pile squarely in the center of your desk. (If you don't have a Today Box and a Someday Box, don't worry. You'll be making them in the next steps.)

3. In the 7-Habits Planner view, review your personal goals, and ensure that the important things aren't slipping away, pushed out by administrative trivia.

4. Quickly go through your papers, and sort them into Priority 1 (must do today), Priority 2 (would like to do today if possible), and Priority 3 (do when time's available). Ensure that each paper has a task associated with it in your To Do list.

TIP: If a paper is priority 3 for 10 consecutive days, consider referring it, tossing it, or filing it, since you probably aren't going to act on it!

5. Review phone calls you need to make, including people you called and for whom you left messages yesterday. In your To Do view, ensure that each phone call you must make is added as a task in your To Do list, and prioritize them as 1, 2, or 3 just as you do other tasks.

6. In the Daily view, look at your daily appointments and meetings. Determine the amount of time left over after you attend these appointments, including travel and preparation time. Based on your experience, factor in some minutes or hours for incoming calls, drop-in visitors, or interruptions of different sorts. The remaining time is what you have left for tasks.

7. Based on the time you have available, switch to the To Do view and re-prioritize your tasks. Ensure that you do not schedule more priority 1 tasks than you have time for. Be ruthless! You won't forget the other tasks—they're still there in Schedule+.

8. Put Priority 1 papers in a tray or drawer that will be your Today Box. Put Priority 2 papers on top of Priority 3 papers, and put them in a similar area that will be your Someday Box.

9. Print out your daily calendar and slip it into your portfolio or binder, if you'll be away from your desk.

This method can be a great time saver. By investing 10 minutes of preparation, you ensure that your daily activities are aligned with your personal goals and work priorities, and that you have organized your actions for the rest of the day.

Printing Your Schedule+ Data

Printing your Schedule+ calendar is very simple. You can print it in several attractive formats to meet your personal needs. To print your calendar:

1. Choose File, Print. The Print dialog box shown in Figure 16-15 will appear.

2. Select each calendar type in turn and click the Preview button to see how it will look.

3. If you are printing on a special paper, such as calendar pages made by Avery or Filoflex, choose Paper Format and pick the appropriate paper type.

4. Choose the date range to print by selecting Starting and inputting the starting date. Choose For to select a number of days, weeks, or months to print.

5. If you wish to change the paper orientation from Portrait to Landscape, or use two-sided printing (provided that your

PART V   SCHEDULE+

Figure 16-15.
You can print your
Schedule+ calendar
and task list in a
variety of formats

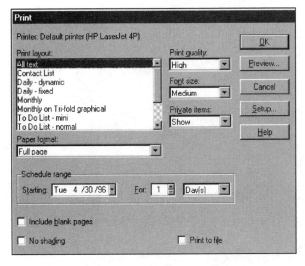

printer supports a duplex feature), you can click <u>S</u>etup and make these changes.

Choose <u>O</u>K when you are done to print your calendar or To Do list.

Making It Work for You

In this chapter, you've learned how to use Schedule+ to get organized and stay organized. Now it's time to begin making these solutions work for you:

1. Think about the different ways of prioritizing your activities each day, and decide which one works best for you.

2. Transfer your To Do list to Schedule+ and make a commitment to try using Schedule+ for two weeks.

3. Print out your calendar, To Do list, and contact list and keep them with you this week.

4. Try the TRAF system this week and then assess what benefits you've derived from it.

CHAPTER 17

MAINTAINING A CONTACT MANAGEMENT SYSTEM

IN THIS CHAPTER

- **Entering Contacts**
- **Arranging Your Contact List**
- **Linking Contacts to Tasks and Appointments**
- **Exchanging Data with Other Applications**

The database most commonly used in the office is a contact management system. While office needs differ, there is often a common requirement for tracking clients, customers, students, or prospects.

In this chapter, you'll learn the tools you need to maintain your contact management system in Schedule+ and import your data into Schedule+ from other applications, as well as how to plan for your contact management needs.

Planning for Your Needs

Finding the best database solution for your needs depends on what you need to know about your contacts. Ask yourself:

- What information do I need to maintain about each client or contact?
- What activities do I need to track?
- How might I need to sort or filter my data? (This will determine what fields you need. Should you break the name into first and last name? Should you break the address into city, state, and ZIP code?)
- How will I get in touch with my contacts? How many phone numbers do they have? Do I need their e-mail address? Home address?
- What personal information do I want to keep? Birthdays? Spouses/partners? Children? Interests?
- Do many of them have assistants or others in the same office who need to be tracked?
- Do I want to track phone calls? Link to-do items or calendar events?

After you answer these questions, you are in a position to know which fields you want to maintain in your Schedule+ contact list.

Your Schedule+ contact management system provides an easy way to interface with Word, and link to your appointment calendar and to-do list. To maintain a contact management system in Schedule+, you'll need to know how to accomplish several things:

- Enter and edit contact information
- Sort, filter, and group your contacts
- Import data from other contact management systems
- Export data to Excel or Access

Using a Contact List

There are several ways to enter contacts, depending on where you are in Microsoft Office. You can enter a new contact whether you are in

Should You Maintain Your Contact List in Schedule+, Excel, or Access?

The answer depends upon your needs. Use Access when:

- You have a large database with thousands of records.
- Many customers are from the same company and you want to store company information separately so you don't have to enter it again for each individual from that company. Access allows you to maintain company information in a separate table from information on individuals, then link them together.
- Several people will be accessing the database simultaneously.

Sometimes, your needs won't be that great. Excel may be appropriate for you if:

- You prefer not to use Access because of either its complexity or the need to learn *yet another* application.
- You expect to have between 500 and 1,000 contacts. Schedule+ may start operating too slowly at the high end of this range.
- You need custom categories and the ability to display your information easily in a variety of ways.
- You want to use shortcuts for data entry, like the ability to copy a business address from one contact to another.
- You want to be able to filter your data easily (e.g., by company or ZIP code) or analyze it geographically and display it using charts and maps.

For many people, the simplest solution is best. Schedule+ is a good call when:

- You have only a few hundred contacts or fewer
- You want to reduce the number of applications you need to use.
- You want tight integration between your contact list, to-do list, and Calendar, since Schedule+ maintains them all in the same program.
- You want the ability to use the Address button in Word to immediately bring an address into your letter

You may also want to consider keeping your contact list in more than one format. For instance, you could maintain your list in Excel and periodically import it into Schedule+ for use in Word letters, or maintain it in Access and analyze it in Excel.

Schedule+, Microsoft Word, or anywhere that you can see the Shortcut Bar.

If you are in Schedule+, choose Insert, Contact; or click on the Insert New Contacts button on the Schedule+ toolbar (when the Contacts tab is on top). You will see the Contact dialog box shown in Figure 17-1.

If you are in Word, click on the Insert Address button. You will see the Select Name dialog box shown in Figure 17-2. Specify that names are to be shown from the Schedule+ Contact List. Choose New to add a new name. The Contact dialog box will appear.

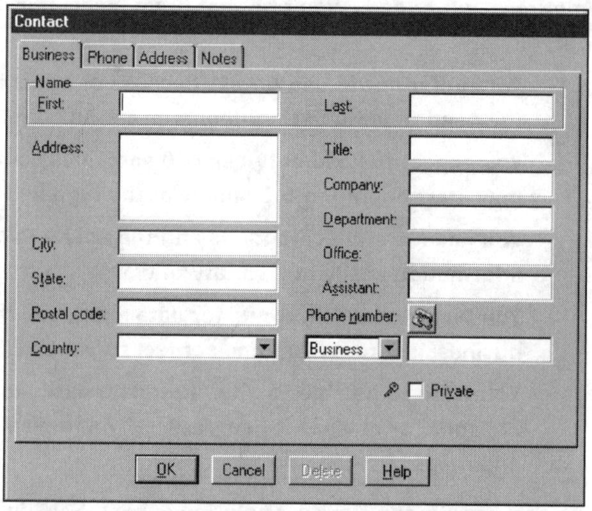

Figure 17-1.
You can enter new contacts from the Shortcut Bar or the Insert menu

Figure 17-2.
You can add new contacts after clicking the Insert Address button in Word

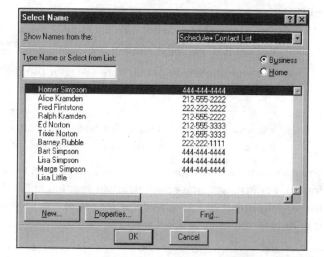

If you are at the Microsoft Office Shortcut Bar, click on the Add a Contact button. You will see the Contact dialog box.

Entering Contact Information

Once you have accessed the Contact dialog box, you can enter information about your new contacts. As you can see in Figure 17-1 above, there are four tabs in the Contact dialog box: Business, Phone, Address, and Notes.

The Notes tab of the Contact dialog box provides four blank fields for you to use as needed: User 1 through User 4. You may wish to store information including the contact's e-mail address or a category (client, lead, friend) in these fields. You may want to use the Notes field for directions, hours of operation, or other helpful information about your contact.

TIP: In Word, you can select records based on information in these fields when you use your contact list as a merge data file, which is another good reason to think about how you might want to use them in Schedule+.

Viewing and Editing Existing Contacts

To see contact information, click on the Contacts tab in Schedule+. The contacts view shown in Figure 17-3 will appear. Depending on how many contacts are in your list, you may need to wait a few seconds for the list to sort itself. (The default sort is by last name.)

You can view a particular contact in either of two ways. You can either move the scroll bars to the right of the contacts list, or type the contact's last name in the Go To box.

If you wish to go to a contact and only know their first name or company, you can do so in one of two ways. First, you can choose Edit, Find and search for their record.

Second, you can click on the field name button at the top of the contact list to re-sort the list immediately by first name, company name, or any other field. When you do this, the Go To box changes from In Last Name to the field you select. You can then type the first name or company name in the Go To box.

Figure 17-3.
The Contacts
view shows you
a sorted list of
your contacts

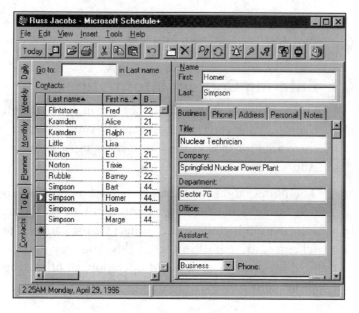

To edit an existing contact, go to the Contact view and select the appropriate record. Use the Business, Phone, Address, Personal, and Notes tabs to access the information to be changed. When you edit the information and select another record, your changes are saved.

Arranging Your Contact List

Schedule+ has limited capabilities for data manipulation. You can sort and group your contact list, but you can't select or filter records.

Sorting Your Contacts

You can sort your contact list by any of three different fields; for instance, you may wish to sort it first by company name, then last name, then first name.

To sort your contact list:

1. Open Schedule+ and click on the <u>C</u>ontacts tab. You will see your contact list.

2. Choose <u>V</u>iew, <u>S</u>ort. The Sort dialog box in Figure 17-4 will appear.

Figure 17-4.
You can sort your
Schedule+ dialog
box by three
different fields

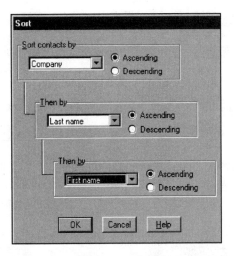

3. Choose the field you wish to sort your list by in the Sort Contacts By box and specify whether you want it sorted in ascending or descending order.

4. In case of ties, choose a second field in the Then By box.

5. If you have a tie in both the first two fields, choose a third field in the last Then By box.

6. Choose OK. Your list will be sorted as specified.

Grouping Your Contacts

You can also group your contacts by a specified field. For instance, you may want to group them by state or by company, as shown in Figure 17-5.

To group your contact list, do the following:

1. Open Schedule+ and click on the Contacts tab. Your contact list will be displayed.

2. Choose View, Group By. You will see the Group By dialog box as in Figure 17-6.

3. Choose the main field by which you wish to group your list in the Group Contact By box.

4. If you would like a subgrouping, choose the secondary criterion in the Then By box.

5. Choose OK. Your list will grouped as you specify.

PART V SCHEDULE+

Figure 17-5.
You can group your
contacts by any field in
the Contact List

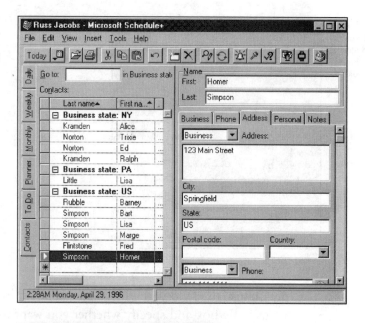

Figure 17-5.
You can group your
contacts by any field in
the Contact List

Figure 17-6.
Three levels of
grouping are possible
in Schedule+

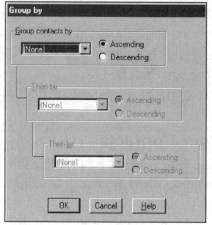

To remove the grouping, use the same procedure. Choose "(None)" as
the field to group the contacts by.

Linking Contacts to Tasks and Appointments

Schedule+ has the ability to create appointments and tasks that are
related to the people in your contact list. When you create an appoint-

ment or task that is related to a person, its description becomes the person's name and organization, and any notes you have on the person are copied to the notes text box of the appointment or task.

Moreover, you can see all the tasks that are related to a specific person by using the Contact And To Do List tab.

To create a task or appointment that is related to a contact, do the following:

1. Click on the Contacts tab in Schedule+, then scroll down to the appropriate contact.

2. With the contact selected, choose Insert, Related Item.

3. Choose either Appt. From Contact or Task From Contact as needed. The description of your appointment or task will be the name of your contact. In the case of a task, you will also find that the contact's name appears in the Contact box under the Status tab of the task.

> **CAUTION:** Creating a linked appointment does not schedule a meeting with the selected person.

You can also create a link from a new or existing task to a contact:

1. Create a new task or edit an old one.

2. From the Task dialog box, click on the Status tab.

3. Use the drop-down Contact list to select the appropriate contact with whom you wish to link the task. The contacts will be listed by company name or first name, rather than by last name, so it may be difficult to find the contact right away.

> **TIP:** You can link a task to an appointment or vice versa by choosing Insert, Related Item from the task or appointment.

Selecting tabs is discussed in Chapter 16.

Scheduling meetings is discussed in Chapter 18.

Creating and editing tasks are described in Chapter 16.

PART V   SCHEDULE+

Exchanging Data with Other Applications

When you first start using Schedule+ to manage your contacts, you may want to transfer previously-existing contact management data from another application. You may also need to export your data if you want to use your Schedule+ contact list in an Excel or Access database. Both importing and exporting data are easy with Schedule+.

Importing Data

Schedule+ can import data that is stored in a comma-separated value (CSV) file. These files can be produced by most personal information managers, spreadsheets, and databases, including Excel and Access. Schedule+ uses an Import Wizard that walks you through the steps to import your data.

To import data from a CSV file:

1. Open Schedule+ and choose File, Import, Text. You will see the first step of the Text Import Wizard.

2. Provide the filename of your CSV file and choose Next. Notice the first lines of the file.

3. You are asked if the first line contains field names. Respond Yes or No, then choose Next.

4. You are asked which delimiters are used in the file. If it is a CSV file, a comma separates the fields and the character used to surround text fields is a quote ("). Choose Next after you select your *delimiter* (a fancy term for the character that denotes the beginning and end of a field).

5. You are asked to specify what type of data is being imported. Select Contact List and choose Next.

6. You are asked to select a type for the fields in this step.

7. Unless the field name of your fields match a field name in Schedule+'s contact list, you will see "IGNORE THIS FIELD" to the right of the CSV field name. For each of these fields, click on "IGNORE THIS FIELD." You will see a drop-down list, from which to choose one of the fields in the Schedule+ Contact List to map the CSV file's field with. Repeat this process for each field in the CSV file.

8. Choose Finish. The CSV file is imported into your Schedule+ Contact List.

Exporting Data

You can also export data from Schedule+ to a CSV file, so that other programs such as Excel and Access can use them. To do so:

1. Open Schedule+. Choose File, Export, Text. The Text Export Wizard will appear.

2. Select Contact List and click the Next button. Create a CSV file by choosing Comma as the character to use between fields, and a quote (") as the character to surround text fields. Choose Next to continue.

3. In the third Wizard screen, choose not to export text containing carriage returns as one line, but choose that you do want to export field names on the first line.

4. Choose Next. The next step allows you to choose which fields to export, as shown in Figure 17-7. Click the Add All button to export all fields, or select each field to be exported and click Add to add it to the list of fields to be exported.

5. Provide the filename of the location to which to export the text, then click Finish. The contact list will be exported to a CSV text file.

Figure 17-7.
You can export any or
all of your Contact List
fields to text files

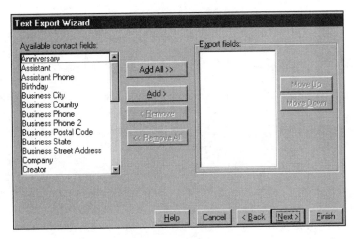

PART V SCHEDULE+

CHAPTER 18

WORKING ON A NETWORK AND ON THE ROAD

IN THIS CHAPTER

- **Setting Access Permissions and Viewing Others' Calendars**
- **Scheduling Meetings**
- **Strategies for Working Away from the Office**
- **Synchronizing Calendar Files**

Schedule+ can do more than help with your personal organization at your desktop. When you use it on a network, it can be used to schedule meetings with others. If you have a laptop, you can use it as a powerful organizational tool while you are on the road. When you return, you can synchronize the laptop and desktop versions of your Schedule+ file.

If you work with Schedule+ on a network, the first three sections of this chapter are for you. If you work with Schedule+ on both a laptop and desktop, read the last section.

Working with Schedule+ on a Network

When you work with a number of people on a network who also use Schedule+ to maintain their calendars, you can schedule meetings electronically. This enables you to see when others are free and short-circuits the laborious process of telephone tag that scheduling often entails.

Schedule+ also permits you to allow other people access to your calendar, task list, and contact list. This offers many possibilities for teams to work together electronically, including the ability to:

- Allow team members to know where everyone is by viewing each others' calendars
- Permit people to delegate authority to maintain their calendars to others
- Allow supervisors to see their subordinates' task lists, and even add items to them
- Schedule the use of resources such as conference rooms or electronic equipment

Working in Group-Enabled Mode

When you use Schedule+ on a network for scheduling meetings, you are working in *group-enabled mode*. In this mode, the schedule file is stored both in a personal folder and in the group's post office. In *stand-alone mode,* the schedule is stored only in your personal folder. Schedule+ will automatically detect whether you are connected to a network, and will open in group-enabled or stand-alone mode as appropriate.

The functions discussed in the first part of this chapter assume that Schedule+ is in group-enabled mode. You can tell whether you are in group-enabled mode by choosing <u>T</u>ools. If <u>M</u>ake Meeting is one of the options, you are in group-enabled mode.

Working with Resources

A very handy way to use Schedule+ for meeting scheduling is to create Schedule+ files for resources such as meeting rooms, projectors, or other places or items whose use needs to be scheduled.

These resources actually become "users" on your network. Since they have their own Schedule+ file, they can be scheduled like any other user. The only difference between a resource and another user is that a resource has an *owner*—a person who has permission to allow the scheduling of the resource, and who is automatically notified of requests for that resource.

To create resources, do the following:

> **Creating Schedule+ files is discussed in Chapter 16.**

1. Request your network administrator to create a separate network user for the resource you wish to schedule.
2. Log on to your network using the UserID of the resource.
3. Open Schedule+ to create a new Schedule+ file for that resource.

Setting Access Permissions and Viewing Others' Calendars

When you work with others, it is often convenient to see their appointments and, on occasion, their tasks. Schedule+ allows you to determine how much access others will have to your calendar, and to view those parts of others' Schedule+ files that they have given you permission to see.

Working with another person's Schedule+ file requires two things. First, they must give you permission to access the Schedule+ file. Second, you must open that file.

Setting Access Permission

The first step in allowing others to work with your Schedule+ files is to determine your *access permissions*—how much of your Schedule+ file you wish others to be able to see and/or modify.

First set the access permissions for the *default* user. This is the minimum access that everyone else on the network has to your file. Then

Table 18-1. Access Permissions in Schedule+	
Permission	**Meaning**
None	Other users have no rights to the Schedule+ object. They cannot even look at your calendar or contact list.
Read	Other users can view the object. They can see your calendar or contact list.
Create	Other users can view the object and create new records. They cannot modify or delete existing records, however. They can create new appointments or add people to your contact list.
Modify	Other users have full rights to the object. They can view your calendar, create new appointments, and change or delete existing ones.

give additional access to other specific people on your network. For instance, the CEO may allow everyone in the organization to see her calendar, but only allow her executive secretary to set her appointments.

You can set access permissions separately for each of the four types of Schedule+ objects: appointments, contacts, events, and tasks. For each object, you may set permissions is specified in Table 18-1.

In addition, you can specify that another person should receive notification whenever your presence is requested at a meeting. For instance, if the "user" is actually a resource, the owner of the resource will probably want to be notified of a request for the scheduling of that resource.

Schedule+ provides preprogrammed user roles to enable you to provide permissions at once for appointments, contacts, events, and tasks, as well as appropriately specifying whether the user will be notified of meeting requests. These user roles are outlined in Table 18-2.

TIP: The most common access permission used in organizations is giving others the ability to view your calendar, but not to change it.

Table 18-2. User Roles in Schedule+

User Role	Meaning
None	No permission for any object; user does not receive meeting requests
Read	Read permission for all objects; user does not receive meeting requests
Create	Create permission for all objects; user does not receive meeting requests
Modify	Modify permission for all objects; user does not receive meeting requests
Delegate	Modify permission for all objects; user receives meeting requests
Modify	Read permission for all objects; user does not receive meeting requests
Owner	Modify permission for all objects; user does not receive meeting requests (same as the Modify role, but often used for resources, since the terminology is more appropriate)
Delegate Owner	Modify permission for all objects; user receives meeting requests (same as the Delegate role, but often used for resources, since the terminology is more appropriate)
Custom	No permissions for any object; the user role switches to Custom whenever you make changes to any individual object

To set access permissions, do the following:

1. Choose Tools, Set Access Permissions. The Set Access Permissions dialog box shown in Figure 18-1 will appear.

2. Click the Global tab and determine whether you will allow overlapping appointments, allow others to schedule recurring appointments for you, and how many months of your calendar you wish to make available to others.

3. Click the Users tab to set access permissions. The default user is selected. Choose the user role you wish for all others in your organization. If none of the selections meets your needs, choose Custom, then set the exact level of permission you wish to have for your appointments, contacts, events, and tasks.

4. After you've set this basic level of access, you can set a greater level for specific persons or groups within the organization.

PART V SCHEDULE+

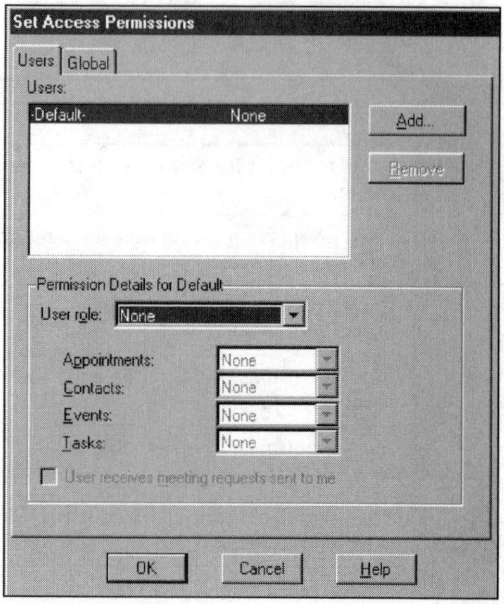

Figure 18-1.
You can determine which parts of your calendar others on your network can access

Figure 18-2.
You can provide additional access permissions to specific persons or groups

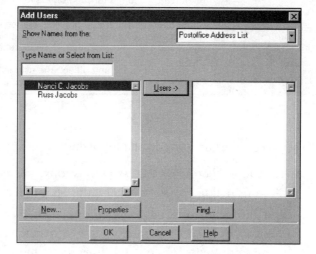

To do so, click <u>A</u>dd, then choose <u>S</u>how Names from your Postoffice address list. You will see the Add Users dialog box shown in Figure 18-2.

5. Double-click on the appropriate users or personal distribution lists, then choose OK. You will return to the Set Access Permissions dialog box.

6. Set permissions for these persons just as you did the default permissions.

TIP: When you are going on vacation, consider giving permission to a selected coworker, allowing him or her to respond to your e-mail. This really depends on your organizational culture, however, since this allows another person the ability to read *all* mail directed to you, and respond in your name.

7. Continue adding new persons and setting permissions for them as needed by repeating steps 4 through 6.

8. When you are finished, click OK.

Viewing Others' Calendars

Access to others' calendars can improve the ability of your workgroup to coordinate projects. Consider the following ideas:

- Create resources (meeting rooms or office equipment, for example) as users on your system and give everyone the Create user role for them. Then anyone can see when a given interview room is available, or schedule a meeting in a common conference room.

- Create a user for a group that needs to respond to requests as a team—for instance, a Help Desk. If all members of the Help Desk staff have full access to the Help Desk user, people from other departments could send requests for assistance as tasks for the Help Desk user. Members of the Help Desk team could then periodically check the task list for the Help Desk user and appropriately respond to inquiries.

- Create a user for the department as a whole, and put the organization's internal phone list or external client mailing list in its contact tab.

All of these suggestions use Schedule+ to enhance your work team's productivity.

To view another person's calendar:

1. Choose File, Open, Other's Appointment Book.

2. Select Postoffice Address List in the Show Names From The box. The Open Other's Appt. book dialog box, shown in Figure 18-3, comes into view.

Figure 18-3.
You can view the calendars of other people who are in your post office

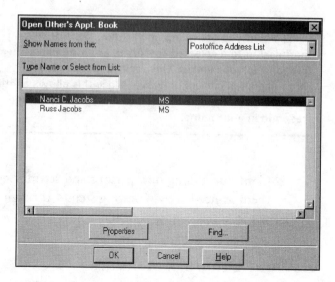

 TIP: The last four calendars you have opened appear at the bottom of your File menu. To switch easily between your calendar and that of your colleagues or groups, open the File menu and choose one of the four calendars at the bottom of the menu.

3. Double-click on the appropriate calendar. The calendar is opened, and you will see the Daily tab showing the other person's schedule.

Scheduling Meetings

Once people in your office use Schedule+ to maintain their appointment calendars, you can schedule meetings electronically.

Electronic scheduling requires that everyone in your office maintain their calendar in Schedule+. This is sometimes a problem in offices, where one or two senior staffers prefer not to use computers, or insist on maintaining their schedules in their paper-based calendar systems.

The effort, however, is often worth the trouble it takes. There are several advantages to an office when everyone uses Schedule+ for their calendar. The obvious one is that meetings can be scheduled and rescheduled electronically, with Schedule+ searching everyone's calendars for free times.

Additionally, managers can gauge their staff's activities better by being able to look at everyone's calendar from their desktop. The reverse is also true. Many organizations like having top executives' calendars open to all employees, so that people know when the CEO is in the office or out of town.

When Schedule+ is used for scheduling, meeting rooms can be reserved as other "participants" in the meeting. Resources such as notebook computers and projection systems can also be defined as "users" of the e-mail system, and scheduled for meetings.

It is a change at first, as everyone moves from paper to electronic calendars. This move often needs to be mandated from the top, and won't happen until senior executives start keeping their own calendars in Schedule+. The organizational benefits almost always outweigh the transitional pains, however.

To schedule meetings, you will need to be able to send meeting requests, and respond to ones you receive.

Sending a Meeting Request

To schedule a meeting, you will send a meeting request to all participants you wish to have at the meeting. You can even attach a copy of your agenda or other relevant documents to it. To do so:

1. Open Schedule+ and click the Meeting Wizard button. The first step of the Meeting Wizard will appear, as shown in Figure 18-4.

2. Choose the types of options you want to specify for your meeting: required attendees, optional attendees, a location, and resources needed for the meeting. Choose <u>N</u>ext when you are finished.

3. If you have chosen Required Attendees, you will pick the required attendees in the next step, as shown in Figure 18-5. If you like, you can type in the names of your attendees, separated by semicolons. Alternatively, click <u>P</u>ick Attendees and choose to show names from the Postoffice Address List. You'll see a dialog box listing names, as shown in Figure 18-6. Double-click on each attendee's name, then click OK to return to the previous dialog box. Choose <u>N</u>ext when you are done.

Figure 18-4.
The Meeting Wizard allows you to schedule meetings with others in your office, automatically finding free times and attaching your agenda or other documents for attendees

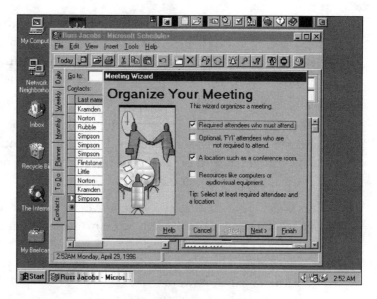

Figure 18-5.
You can type attendees' names manually or select them from a list

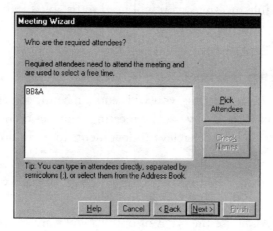

4. If you have chosen Optional Attendees, you will pick the optional attendees in the next step, in exactly the same way that you pick the required attendees. Choose Next when you are finished.

5. If you have chosen to specify a location, you will pick the location in the next step. This presumes that you have defined one or more locations as resources on your system, as described above. You pick a location in exactly the same way that you pick required or optional attendees. Choose Next when you are finished.

Figure 18-6.
You can select
from anyone on
your Postoffice list

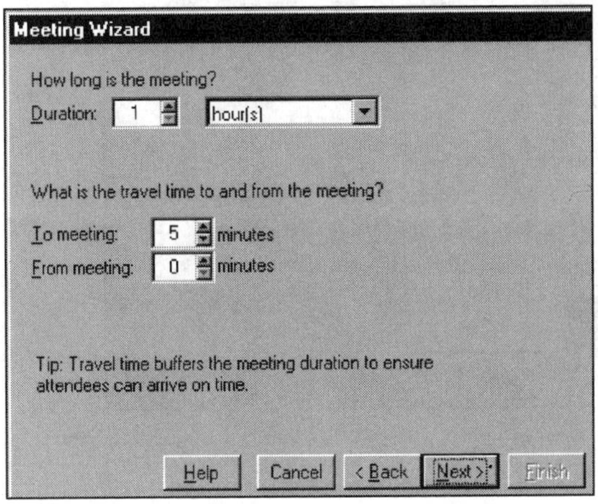

Figure 18-7.
You should specify
both the duration of
the meeting and
required travel time
to allow appropriate
scheduling

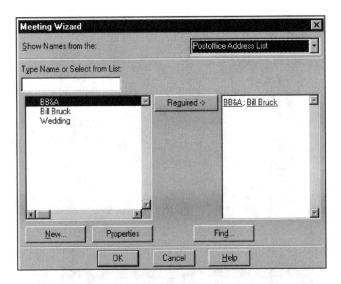

6. If you have chosen to specify other resources, you will specify these in the next step. Again, this presumes that you have defined one or more other resources, as described above. You pick a resource in exactly the same way that you pick required or optional attendees. Choose <u>N</u>ext when you are finished.

7. In the next step, specify the duration of the meeting and necessary travel time, as shown in Figure 18-7, then choose <u>N</u>ext.

8. Input the acceptable meeting times and days, as shown in Figure 18-8, then choose <u>N</u>ext.

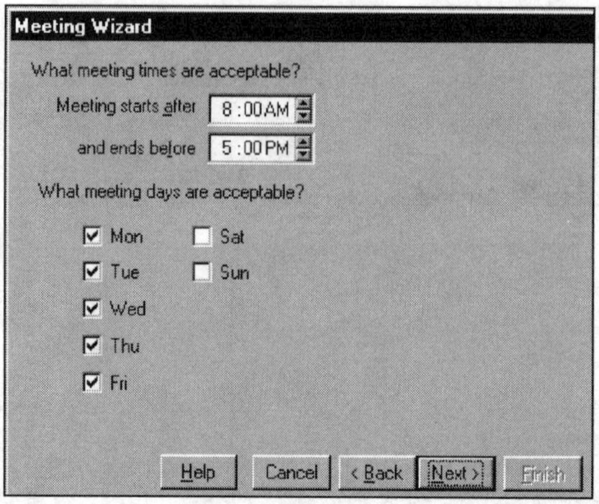

Figure 18-8.
You may specify both the acceptable times of day and days of the week for your meeting

Figure 18-9.
The Meeting Wizard shows you busy and available times for all participants, allowing you to pick a time when everyone is free

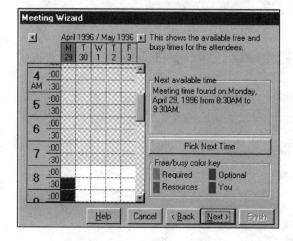

9. If you included optional attendees, you will be asked if their schedules should also be checked for free time. Respond <u>Y</u>es or N<u>o</u>, then choose Next.

10. You will then see the available free times for attendees, shown in Figure 18-9. Use the scroll bar and previous/next buttons to find an acceptable time and date for the meeting, then click in the free time. Alternatively, you can click the Pick Next Time button repeatedly until you find a time you prefer.

11. You see a grid displaying colored lines where attendees, locations, and resources have conflicts. Times when everyone is free are displayed without lines. The first free time is dis-

played in the Next Available Time box, shown in Figure 18-9. Choose the best time in either of two ways. Use the scroll bar and previous/next buttons until you see an acceptable time and date for the meeting in the grid, then click in the grid in the free time. Alternatively, you can click the Pick Next Time button repeatedly until a time you prefer is listed in the Next Available Time box. Click Next, then click Finish. You will see a Meeting Request form like the one shown in Figure 18-10. It will send participants an e-mail request for their attendance at the meeting.

12. Insert a subject for the request, along with any message you would like to include.

13. You might also want to attach an agenda or other documents to the meeting request that participants should review. To do so, click the Attach File button. The Attach dialog box will become visible.

14. Navigate to the file(s) you wish to include. Select them, then choose Open. Repeat this step for all the files you wish to attach to the meeting request. You'll return to the Meeting Request dialog box.

15. Click the Send button to send the message to participants.

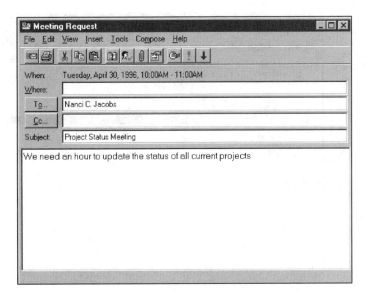

Figure 18-10.
The Meeting Request form is sent to participants to allow them to put the meeting on their calendars

Responding to a Meeting Request

Meeting requests will appear in your In Box. To respond to a meeting request, do the following:

1. Click the View Mail icon on the Schedule+ toolbar. MS Exchange will open and you'll see the Inbox - Microsoft Exchange window, as shown in Figure 18-11.

2. Open the Inbox folder. You'll see any incoming mail on the right side of the window, including any pending meeting requests. Meeting requests are envelopes with a clock on them.

3. Double-click on a meeting request icon to open the Meeting Request dialog box shown in Figure 18-12.

4. Before accepting or declining the meeting request, you may now take the following actions:

   • Read the message. It's considered good form!

TIP: Choosing Tentative marks this as a tentative meeting in your appointment book. It also notifies the sender of its tentative nature. Use this option if you don't know whether you will definitely attend the meeting or not.

Figure 18-11.
You accept or reject appointments from the Inbox - Microsoft Exchange window

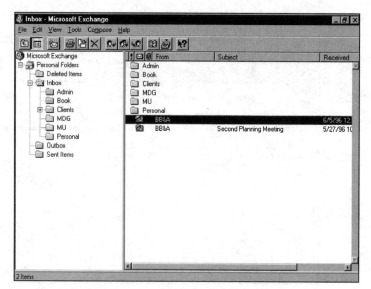

Figure 18-12.
You may accept, decline, or tentatively accept meeting requests, or view your schedule to see if it's a good time for you

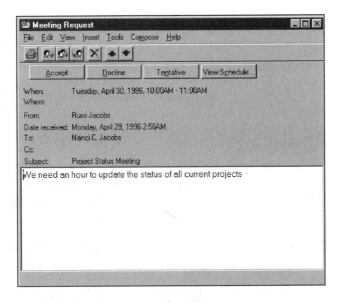

Figure 18-13.
Your response to the meeting request is written at the top of the Meeting Response dialog box

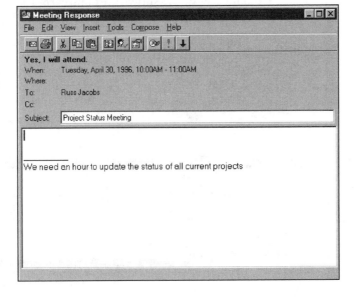

- Choose View Schedule. This opens Schedule+ so you can look at what else you have scheduled for that day, as well as see the tasks you must accomplish.

5. Choose one of the following: Accept, Decline, or Tentative. A Meeting Response dialog box, such as the one shown in Figure 18-13, will appear.

6. Write any message you wish in response, then click the Send button. The response is returned to the sender. In addition, when you accept or tentatively accept a meeting request, the meeting is entered on your Schedule+ calendar and, if appropriate, marked as tentative.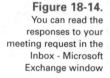

Tracking the Status of Meeting Requests

When a meeting participant responds to a meeting request, you receive e-mail to that effect. After you've read your e-mail, the information on whether or not the participant is coming is transferred to your Schedule+ calendar.

To read responses to your meeting request, do the following:

1. Click the View Mail icon on the Schedule+ toolbar. MS Exchange opens, and you'll see the Inbox - Microsoft Exchange window shown in Figure 18-14.

2. Click on the Inbox folder in the In list of folders on the left of the folder list. You'll see any responses to your meeting request on the right side of the window.

3. Double-click on the appropriate response to read it. You'll see the Meeting Response dialog box shown in Figure 18-15.

Figure 18-14.
You can read the responses to your meeting request in the Inbox - Microsoft Exchange window

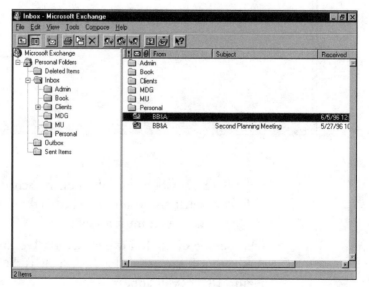

Figure 18-15.
Responses you
receive to your
meeting request
appear as e-mail

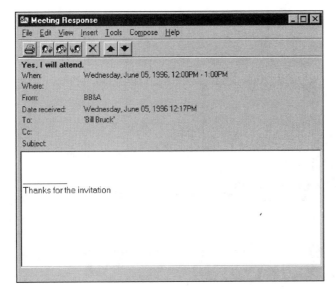

When you close the dialog box, the response information is transferred to your calendar.

Once you have looked at your meeting responses and the information is transferred to your calendar, you can easily see the status of your meeting:

1. Open Schedule+ and click the Daily, Weekly, or Monthly tab.

2. Move to the appointment and double-click on it in order to edit it.

3. Click the Attendees tab. The Appointment dialog box will appear, as shown in Figure 18-16. Decide who the required attendees are and who are optional.

4. To invite others to your meeting, click Invite Others. You can then send them an invitation just the same way as you did to the first group.

5. To see everyone's schedule, click the Planner tab. You will see the free and busy times for all your meeting participants.

6. To see what a participant is doing that conflicts with your meeting, double-click the line that represents their busy time. You will see a pop-up window with their name, and an arrow at the right of the window.

Figure 18-16.
You can track who has accepted, declined, and tentatively accepted your meeting request by editing the appointment in Schedule+

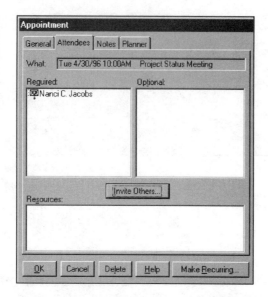

Figure 18-17.
If you have sufficient access rights, you can see the conflicting appointments that other participants have

7. Click on the arrow. If you have sufficient access rights, you will see the appointment they had previously scheduled, as shown in Figure 18-17. If you don't have read access to their calendar, or if they have marked the appointment as private, you will see the word "Busy."

8. Click <u>O</u>K when you are finished. You'll return to the main Schedule+ window.

Strategies for Working Away from the Office

All this may sound good while you're at your computer, but what about when you aren't? By simply making printouts and taking them with you, you should never lose track of information about your tasks, schedules, and contacts.

Printing from Schedule+ is discussed in Chapter 16.

To stay organized away from your computer, make a printout of your daily calendar, calendars for the next few months, your task list, and your contact list. Either print them on plain paper and keep them in small binder, or print them on planner size paper if you use paper-based organizers like Day Planners or Day Timers.

To make sure you don't lose track of things when you're away from your computer, using your paper-based organizer, consider the following tips:

- *Keep your printout with you at all times* when you're away from the office. If you don't do this, the whole scheme falls apart.
- As you accomplish tasks, *mark them off your daily calendar printout.* If new tasks occur to you, write them down on the printout.
- Feel free to make new appointments, or change and delete old ones. Just be sure to *mark down the changes on the monthly calendar printouts.*
- *Add information on new contacts* to your contact list printout.
- *Each morning, transfer information* about tasks, appointments, and contacts to Schedule+ (if you have access to a computer and Schedule+), then reprint your daily calendar.
- Each week, or when your monthly calendars are looking messy from penciled in changes, *make new printouts of them as well.* Similarly, print out your contact list every three months or so.

Keeping Your Calendar Synchronized

You will also want to keep your calendar up-to-date if you are using a laptop computer while you are on the road. You can do this by synchronizing the copies of your calendar that are on your laptop and desktop computers. You will update your calendar differently depend-

PART V   SCHEDULE+

TIP: Even if you *only* use a laptop, if you are on a network you will want to synchronize your calendar with the network so that others can schedule meetings with you.

ing on whether you are working in group-enabled mode or in stand-alone mode.

Updating a Group-Enabled Calendar

When you work in group-enabled mode, there is a master copy of your calendar on the server, and a copy of the calendar on the computer you are using to log on to the network. If you log on to the network with both a desktop and a laptop computer, this means that there are actually three copies of your calendar.

If you are operating in group-enabled mode, your calendar will update itself automatically. When you connect to the network with your laptop and open Schedule+, you will be asked if you want to synchronize your calendar. This ensures that the schedule file in the post office and on the laptop have the same information. Once you have updated your laptop calendar in this way, you can disconnect from the network and go on the road, secure in the knowledge that you have your latest appointments, To Do items and contacts with you.

TIP: Once you've disconnected your laptop from the network, don't use Schedule+ on your desktop, because then it (not the laptop) will have the latest schedule information.

When you return, connect to the network again with the laptop and enter Schedule+. Synchronize your calendar when asked. This updates the post office copy. Then you can disconnect the laptop. Finally, turn on your desktop computer and open Schedule+. Synchronize this computer when asked. The latest version of your schedule file is now brought from the post office onto the desktop, and you're all set to go to work.

Updating a Stand-Alone Calendar

To update your stand-alone calendar, you will need to copy your calendar file from the source computer to the destination computer. The source computer is the computer on which you have been working; the destination computer is the computer on which you *will be* working. Thus, when you finish working on your desktop and are ready to work on your laptop, the source is the desktop and the destination is the laptop. Conversely, when you are moving from working on your laptop to your desktop, your source is your laptop and the destination is the desktop.

Update as follows:

1. On the source computer, open Microsoft Explorer, and navigate to the folder holding your schedule file. This is usually the Schedule folder under the MSOffice folder.

2. Highlight your schedule file. It is often named Schedule. Choose Edit, Copy to copy the schedule file to the Clipboard.

3. If the disk drive for the destination computer is visible in the Explorer (e.g., if it is on a laptop connected to a network) navigate to the appropriate folder on the destination computer's drive. Otherwise, navigate to the A drive.

4. Choose Edit, Paste to copy the file from the Clipboard to the destination drive or directory.

If you copied the file to a floppy, you will need to follow a similar procedure to copy it from the floppy to the appropriate folder on the destination computer.

PART V   SCHEDULE+

PART VI

ACCESS

CHAPTER 19

CREATING A SIMPLE DATABASE

IN THIS CHAPTER

- **Becoming Familiar with Access**
- **Creating a Database**
- **Adding and Editing Data**
- **Finding Records**
- **Filtering Data**
- **Printing Reports**

Access 7 provides an extremely powerful, yet easy-to-use database that will serve your needs well when you require more computing power than is offered by Excel.

In this chapter, you will learn the basics of using Access to create a variety of databases, as well as how to enter, edit, and find data in existing databases.

Reviewing Database Concepts

A *database* is simply a systematic organization of data. Traditionally, databases are organized using *fields* and *records*. A record is all the information about one item. In a Rolodex, for instance, everything related to one person is on a single card, so the card is the record. A field is an item of information. Three fields in a Rolodex would include the name, phone, and address.

Common office database applications often need a more complex structure than this. A database often requires several related collections of fields and records. For this reason, Access uses the term *table* to refer to this matrix of records and fields.

Many databases require several tables, linked together, to accomplish office tasks. For instance, you may need to store information about telephone calls in your contacts database. Any given person (record) in the contacts table may have zero, one, or a hundred telephone calls related to them. Access provides ways to link tables easily. For example, each box inside the Relationships window in Figure 19-1 represents a table. Items listed below the table name in each box are fields in that table. The lines connecting fields from different tables show where the links are located.

A database program that can only accommodate databases consisting of a single table is called a *flat-file database*. A program (such as Access)

Figure 19-1.
Access can link tables to form complex databases

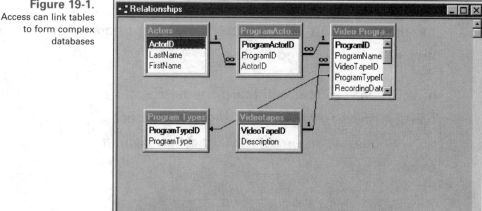

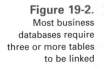

Figure 19-2.
Most business
databases require
three or more tables
to be linked

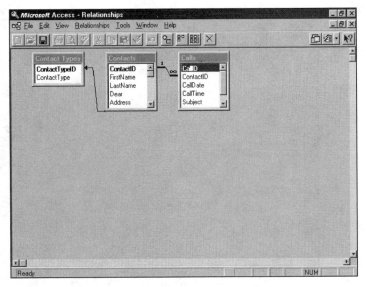

that can create two or more tables that are linked is called a *relational database.* Most business applications require the creation of relational databases. For instance, a contact management system may consist of three different tables: the Contacts table including names and addresses; a Calls table recording the time, date, and subject of each call; and a Contact Types table to store the category of each contact, as shown in Figure 19-2.

Understanding Access Objects

Access can use six different types of objects to create relational databases. All the objects for a given database are saved in the Access database file. These objects include:

- Tables
- Queries
- Forms
- Reports
- Macros
- Modules

Figure 19-3.
Access databases can
contain six different
types of objects

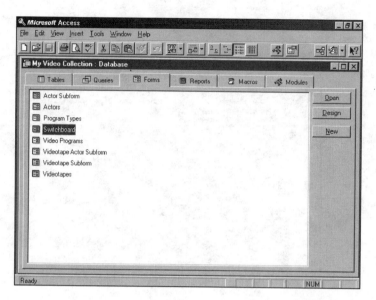

When you open an Access database, you may see the database's database window, shown in Figure 19-3. It has tabs for each of the six types of objects the database may include.

NOTE: **Many sophisticated databases hide the database window when they are started, and instead show you a form containing buttons to do common database tasks. Such a form is called a** *Switchboard*.

Tables

A *table* is the fundamental building block of an Access database. All databases must have at least one table, since this is where the data are stored. A very simple Access database might consist of one table and no other objects. Such a simple database table looks very much like an Excel worksheet:

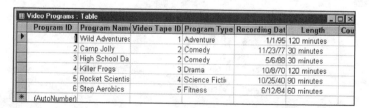

Queries

A *query* is a subset of data in the Access database. It may include an action that is performed on that data.

The most common type of query is a *selection query,* which displays a subset of data, selected and sorted using the criteria you specify. A simple selection query might be all the contacts with the last name of "Smith."

A more complex query can include data from several tables. For instance, a two-table contact management database might include the fields shown in Figure 19-4.

A query might ask for all phone calls made by each sales representative. The names of sales representatives come from one table, while the names of the people called come from the other, as shown in Figure 19-5. An even more sophisticated query might select just the calls made by one sales rep during the last month.

The product of a selection query is a subset of the database tables, called a *dynaset.* The dynaset looks like a regular table, as you can see in Figure 19-5. However, it's dynamically generated every time it is displayed, using data that actually reside in various database tables.

While the word *query* is often used generically to refer to selection queries, queries can also affect data. Queries are used to modify

PART VI ACCESS

Figure 19-4.
A two-table database often uses an ID field to link the tables together

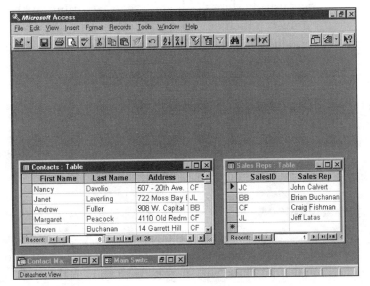

Figure 19-5.
Queries can contain data from two or more tables

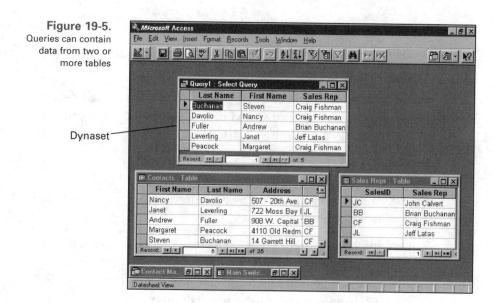

Dynaset

information (e.g., increase all prices by 6 percent), archive data (e.g., save all 1995 invoices in a separate file), or delete data (e.g., delete all men's clothing products).

Forms

A *form* is used for data entry or display. Forms can be displayed in two different ways: the Form View and the Datasheet View. The Form view usually shows only one record at a time, as shown in Figure 19-6. Forms can include fields from more than one table, and they can also contain calculated fields that are updated depending on what you put in other fields.

Reports

A *report* is used for summarizing data. Reports can be formatted to present data attractively, and usually include subtotals or other summary calculations, as shown in Figure 19-7.

Macros

A *macro* is used to automate tasks in Access, and makes the database more user-friendly. Macros are often attached to buttons that appear on forms. Thus, you might have a button that prints a monthly sales

Figure 19-6.
Forms are used for viewing and editing data

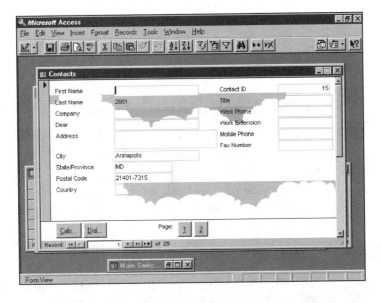

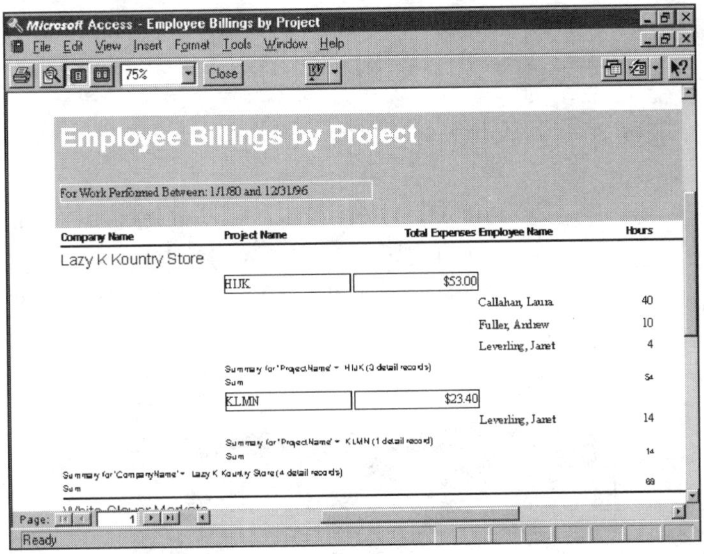

Figure 19-7.
Reports are used to present summary information about a database in an attractive manner

report, a button that deletes the current record, or a button that takes you back to the main database menu.

Modules

Most common database tasks can be accomplished by using the commands available in simple macros. On occasion, however, you may need to program a complex macro using Visual Basic. In this case, you will be creating a *module* that contains the programming code.

Becoming Familiar with Access

Now that you understand basic database concepts and are familiar with the six types of objects used in Access, it may be useful to become familiar with the basics of using Access. The following sections will show how to start and exit Access, open and close databases, and use the Database window.

Starting and Exiting Access

The Shortcut
Bar is
introduced
in Chapter 2.

The first thing you need to learn in order to use Access is how to start and exit the program. To start Access:

1. Click on the Access button on the Microsoft Programs Shortcut Bar.

2. The Microsoft Access dialog box shown in Figure 19-8 will appear. To create a new database, choose Blank Database or Database Wizard. To open an existing database, choose Open an Existing Database.

Figure 19-8.
When you first open Access, you are given the choice creating a new database or opening an existing one

NOTE: If the Shortcut Bar is not available, you can also open Access by clicking on the Start button, then choosing Programs, Microsoft Office, Microsoft Access.

When you are finished using Access, you can close it by choosing File, Exit or double-clicking on the Control icon at the left of the title bar. Closing Access will automatically close any open database. You will not be prompted to save your work, because the database is automatically saved on the disk as you work.

NOTE: Access database files are saved differently than Word, Excel, or PowerPoint files. Each time you add or edit a record in an Access database, the change is recorded on the disk. Thus, if you lost power or your computer were turned off suddenly, the only information you would lose is changes you were making to an individual record.

Opening and Closing Database Files

Access is not like other Office applications, in one important respect. You can only have one file open at once. If you open a second database, Access closes the first one.

Open an existing database as follows:

1. To open a database when you first start Access, choose Open an Existing Database from the Microsoft Access dialog box, make sure that More Files is highlighted, and choose OK. If you are already in Access, choose File, Open Database or click the Open button. The Open dialog box shown in Figure 19-9 will appear.

2. Navigate to the folder containing the database, then double-click on the desired database.

When you are finished with the database, you will often close it by exiting Access. You need not save your database, as changes to it are saved to the disk automatically as you work.

Figure 19-9.
The Open dialog box
performs the same
functions as other file-
management dialog
boxes in Office 95

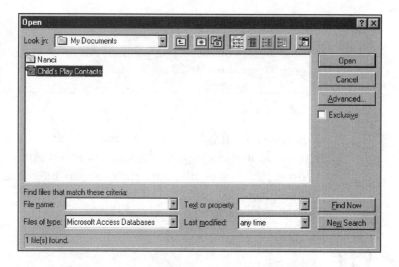

If you want to close the database but remain in Access, choose File, Close. However, you will not usually need to do this, because if you either create a new database or open a different database, the open database will be closed automatically.

Understanding the Database Window in Access

When you open a database in Access, you will normally see a switch-board containing choices for using the database. Often, the switch-board will have all the choices you need. When, however, you wish to create or edit tables, queries, and reports, you will want to switch to the Database Window—a window that lists all the objects in your database—like the one shown in Figure 19-10. From the Database

NOTE: If you are using a database created with an Access Wizard, you will see a dialog box containing a menu of choices such as the one in Figure 19-11. This dialog box is often called the Main Switchboard, and it appears instead of the Database window. If you see a Switchboard and want to access the Database window, choose the Window command. The window at the bottom of the menu that has the same name as your database will be the Database window for that database.

Figure 19-10.
The Database window lists all the objects in the database

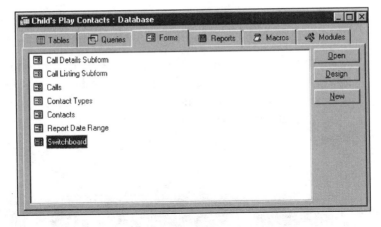

Figure 19-11.
Sometimes you will see a Switchboard rather than a Database window when you open a database

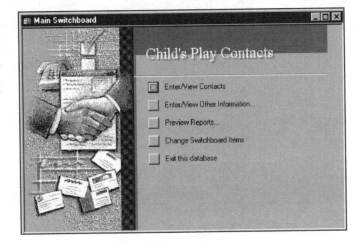

window, you can click on the appropriate tab to see the tables, forms, queries, macros, or modules that comprise the database.

Opening and Closing Database Objects

To open an Access object such as a table, form, or query, do the following:

1. Open the database.

2. If you do not see the Database window, navigate to it as described above.

3. Select the tab for the object you wish to open.

4. Double-click on the object.

Access objects appear as windows, complete with title bars and Maximize, Minimize, Restore, and Close buttons, as shown in Figure 19-12.

You can usually move the object, resize it, or close it just as you would any other window in Windows 95. You can even open multiple objects as windows within Access. If you do so, you may find that they partially or totally obscure each other, as shown in Figure 19-13.

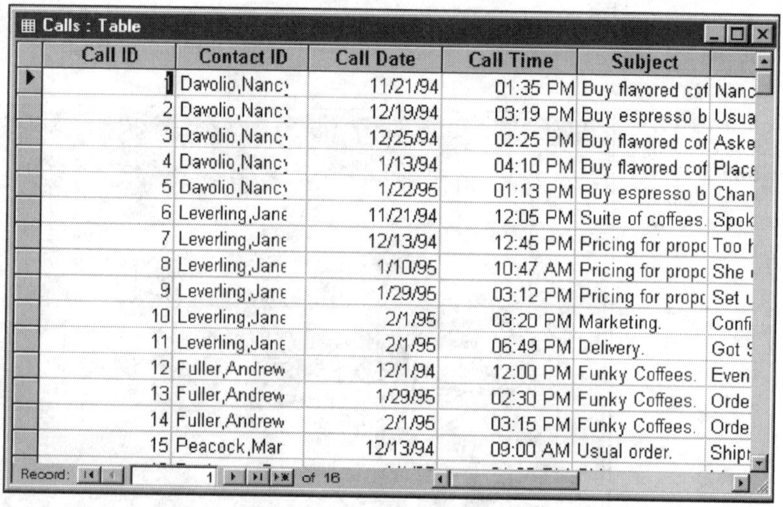

Figure 19-12.
An Access table is a window that has standard features such as maximize, restore, and close buttons

Figure 19-13.
You can open multiple objects within Access

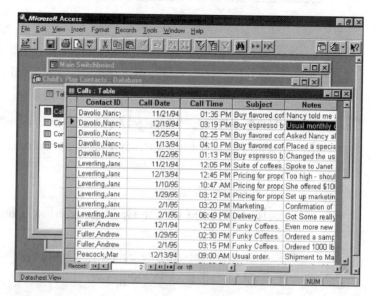

> **NOTE:** When you create custom data entry forms, or forms such as the Main Switchboard, you can set many attributes to govern the way the form is displayed. Some of these attributes hide the title bar of the form; others hide the Maximize, Minimize, Restore, and Close buttons. If you see a form that does not have these buttons, you will not be able to work with it as you do other windows in Windows 95.

Switch from one object to another by clicking in a visible part of the object window. This makes the window active and puts it in front of any other windows. If you cannot see a window, choose Windows from the menu, then select an object from the bottom of the menu that lists all open objects.

Displaying a Hidden Object

Occasionally, an object may be *hidden* so that it doesn't appear on the Windows list. Often, the Database window will be hidden from casual users, when the database designer prefers that they use the Main Switchboard or other menu system that has been designed to make the database user-friendly.

If you wish to make a hidden window active, do the following:

1. Open the database.
2. Choose Window, Unhide. If you cannot choose Unhide, then there are no hidden windows in your database. Otherwise, you will see the Unhide Window dialog box:

3. Double-click on the window to be unhidden.

Creating a Database Using Wizards

The easiest way to learn about Access is to create a simple database, then add and edit records, filter them, and print a simple report. Database creation used to be a complex process, but the Access Wizards make creating databases a snap. To help you learn about Access, we'll use the example of making a contact management database.

Hands On: Creating a Contact Management Database

The easiest way for the average user to create a contact management database in Access is to use a Wizard:

1. Open Access. The Microsoft Access dialog box will come into view.

2. From the Microsoft Access dialog box, select Database Wizard to create a new database, then choose OK.

3. Choose the Databases tab. You will see the New dialog box shown in Figure 19-14, with icons for available database templates.

4. Double-click on the Contact Management icon. The File New Database dialog box will become visible.

5. In the File Name box, give the new database a name and

Figure 19-14.
You can create a new database with a Wizard when you open Access

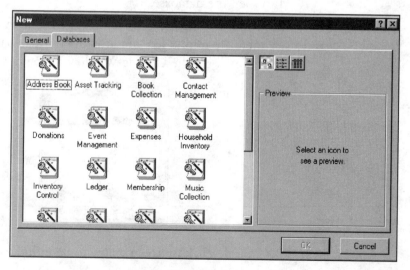

Figure 19-15.
You can select from
predefined fields you
wish to include in your
new Access database,
or add new fields for
your particular needs

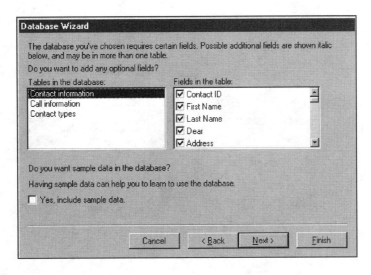

choose Create. The first step of the Database Wizard will
appear.

6. Choose Next to continue. You will see the second screen of
   the Database Wizard. The Wizard will create the three tables
   shown in Figure 19-15 for the database, and you can see the
   fields that will be created in the Contact Information table.

7. If you wish to alter the fields created by the Wizard, select
   any additional optional fields you wish to include in the
   Contact Information table. These appear in italics towards
   the bottom of the field list. Fields in normal type are
   required; you cannot deselect them.

8. Select the Call Information table and ensure that all fields
   are selected for this table, then similarly select all the fields
   for the Contact Type table.

9. Check Yes, Include Sample Data to help you learn to use the
   new database. Choose Next when you are finished.

10. In the next Wizard screens, choose the styles you wish to use
    for the screen display and printed reports (see Figure 19-16),
    and enter **Child's Play Contacts** as the title for the database.

11. Choose Finish at the last screen. After a minute or two, the
    database is created and ready for use.

You will find that you can create most of the common types of databases you need by using Wizards, just as you created the Contact

Figure 19-16.
You can choose from
a variety of attractive
formats for your
Access database.

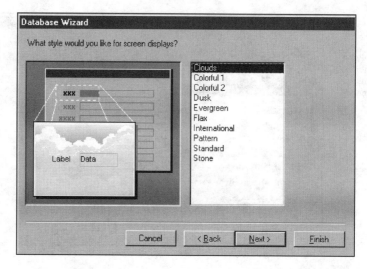

Management databases. Access provides Wizards to create 22 common databases.

Use the Wizards whenever possible. Creating a database from scratch can be a time-consuming and complex process, and the results will not be nearly as attractive as when you use one created with a Wizard.

Using a Database

To effectively use an Access database, you'll want to be able to add new records, navigate through the database, edit and delete existing records, select specific records, and print reports.

Adding Records

Adding a record to a database is easy when you use a data entry form. Access Wizards build these forms for you—which is one reason to use a Wizard to create a database. Often, the forms will even have data

NOTE: You can also add records directly to the tables in which Access stores the data, just as you would add information to the last row of an Excel database.

validation rules built into them, so you cannot enter invalid responses. When you add a record using a form, the table or tables on which the form is built are automatically updated.

Hands On: Adding Records to the Contact Database

To add a new record, follow these steps:

1. Open the Contact Management database. The Main Switchboard, as shown in Figure 19-17, will appear.

2. Choose Enter/View Contacts. You will see the Contacts form showing the first record displayed in Figure 19-18.

3. Click the New Record button. You are at a new, blank record.

4. Enter data in the various fields. Use the [Tab] key to move to the next field, or [Shift] + [Tab] to move to the previous field. Alternatively, you can click in the next field with the mouse.

5. Notice that a warning appears if you enter an invalid phone number, such as one with letters or too few digits.

6. When you are finished, click the Add Record button and add a second record.

7. When you are done, close the contacts form by clicking the Close button. You'll return to the Main Switchboard.

Figure 19-17.
You can add contacts, view them, or print reports from the Contact Manager main switchboard

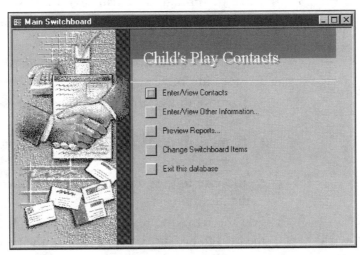

Figure 19-18.
The Contacts form
allows you to enter,
edit, or select contacts
to display

New
Record

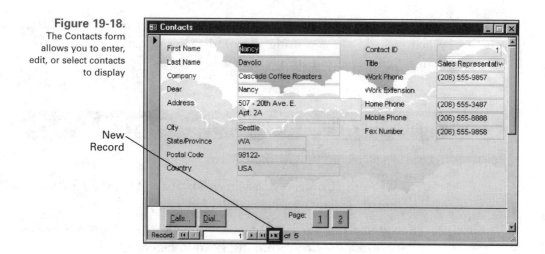

Navigating in a Form

Once you have created a database and entered data, you can easily move from record to record within a data entry form, in order to view or edit a record, as follows:

1. Open Access, and open the desired database. You will see the Main Switchboard.

2. Open the desired data entry form. You will see a form such as the Contacts form in Figure 19-19. At the bottom of the form, the current record appears, along with the number of records in the database.

3. Navigate through the database to the desired record as follows:

   • To move to a blank new record at the end of the database, click the New Record button.

   • To move to the first record of the database, click the First button.

   • To move to the last record of the database, click the Last button.

   • To move to the record before the current one, click the Previous button.

   • To move to the next record after the current one, click the Next button.

4. Edit the active record, if desired, by tabbing to or clicking on the field to be edited, then changing the necessary information.

Figure 19-19.
Access forms have navigation buttons allowing you to move from record to record

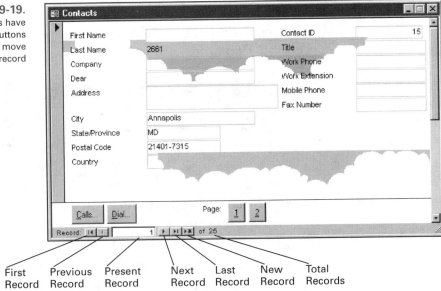

First Record | Previous Record | Present Record | Next Record | Last Record | New Record | Total Records

TIP: You may find it easier to navigate to a specific record if you sort the database first. To do so, click in the field by which you wish to sort, then click the Sort Ascending or Sort Descending button in the toolbar.

5. When you are finished viewing or editing records, close the form. You return to the Main Switchboard or Database window.

Finding a Specific Record

While navigating through the database as described above works for small databases, it is less useful when the database contains hundreds of records. In this case, you will probably want to go directly to the record you need to look at or edit.

To find a specific record using a data entry form, do the following:

1. Open Access, and open the desired database. Either the Database window or the Main Switchboard will become visible.

2. Open the desired data entry form.

3. Tab to or click in the field you wish to search in.

4. Choose <u>E</u>dit, <u>F</u>ind or click the Find button. You will see the Find dialog box:

5. Type the information for which you are looking, such as a contact's last name.

6. Choose Sea<u>r</u>ch and specify whether to search the whole database, or just the records before or after the present record.

7. Choose Matc<u>h</u> and specify whether the whole field should match the search string, or the search string should match any characters in the field.

8. Choose Find Fir<u>s</u>t. The first record matching your criteria is displayed. If this is not the correct record, choose <u>F</u>ind Next until you arrive at the desired record.

9. Close the Find dialog box when you have found the appropriate record.

TIP: Remember that you can sort the database so that other records with the same company name, state, etc. are grouped together.

Switching between Form View and Datasheet View

Depending on how an individual form has been created, you may be able to view it in two modes: Form View and Datasheet View. The Form View shows one record at a time. The Datasheet View shows a table that resembles an Excel worksheet. To switch between Form View and Datasheet View, do the following:

1. Ensure that the desired data entry form is open.

2. Choose <u>V</u>iew, Data<u>s</u>heet to switch to the Datasheet View, or

click the down arrow to the right of the Form View button and select Datasheet View:

You will see the records in a table format.

3. To return to the Form View, choose <u>V</u>iew, <u>F</u>orm; or click the down arrow to the right of the Form View button, then choose Form View.

Using Filters

You can also choose to see a subset of the records, such as customers from New York, by using filters. There are two types of filters that you can easily access from the Contact form, whether you are viewing it in Form View or Datasheet View.

Although it is certainly not necessary, you may find it more useful to look at filtered data in the Datasheet View, since you get a better picture of the number of records that meet your criteria.

The first is the Filter by Selection filter. This filter is used when you are in a record and want to find similar ones. For instance, you may be in the record for a person from Washington state, and want to see others from that state. In this case, do the following:

1. Navigate to a record of a person from Washington state.

2. Click in the State field where you see WA.

3. Click the Filter by Selection button. If you are in the Form view, notice that the total records indicator shows the total number of records meeting the criterion, and the word "(Filtered)" on the status line, as shown in Figure 19-20.

Alternatively, you can use a more sophisticated filtering process: Filter by Form. To do this, use these steps:

1. Open the appropriate form.

2. Click the Filter by Form button. You will see the Filter

Figure 19-20.
You can filter all records that are similar to the active record by using the Filter by Selection button

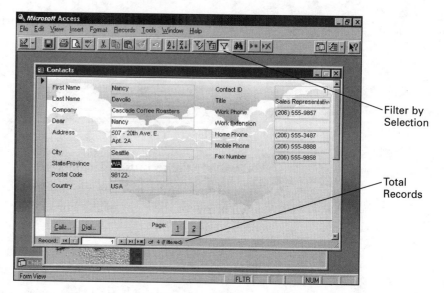

Filter by Selection

Total Records

Figure 19-21.
You can set multiple filter criteria by using the Filter by Form function

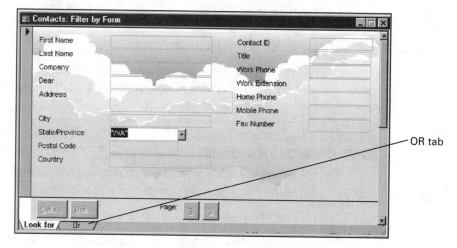

OR tab

by Form window shown in Figure 19-21.

3. Click the first field on which you wish to filter. Notice the down arrow that appears at the right side of the field.

4. Click the down arrow. You will see all the values the field has in the table. For example, you would see a list of all states in which your contacts live. Choose the appropriate value.

5. If you would like the selected records to meet both the original

criterion *and* an additional criterion, select the appropriate field and value on the same line. For instance, you may want to select all people with the last name Smith *and* the state of Virginia.

6. If you would like the records to meet the original criterion *or* an additional criterion, click the OR tab, then select the appropriate field and value. For instance, you may wish to select records from Virginia *or* Maryland.

7. Click the Apply Filter button. You'll return to the Datasheet or Form View and see only the records meeting the filter criteria.

8. When you are finished looking at filtered records, remove the filter by clicking the Remove Filter button.

Printing Reports

Databases created with Wizards come with predesigned reports that provide useful summary information. For instance, the Contact Database comes with an alphabetical contact list and a weekly call summary.

Reports can be previewed on the screen, then printed after you ascertain that the correct report is visible.

Print reports created by the Database Wizards as follows:

1. Open the appropriate database.

2. If you see a Main Switchboard such as the one in the Contact Management database, choose Preview Reports or make whatever other choice is provided for reports. A list of available reports will come into view. Click on the report you wish to preview.

3. Alternatively, if you see the Database window, click on the Reports tab, highlight the appropriate report, and choose

NOTE: Wizards are provided to create many different types of databases. Each database's main switchboard varies slightly from the others.

PART VI ACCESS

Figure 19-22.
You can preview
reports before printing
them out

Print

Zoom

Page
Navigation
buttons

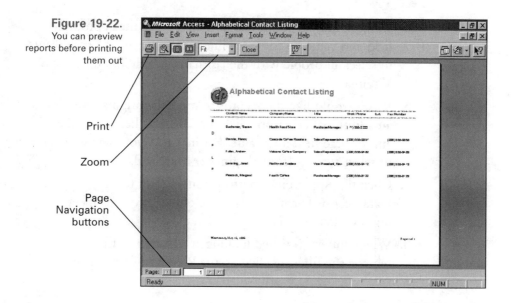

Preview.

4. In either case, you will see the report on the screen. Maximize the report window, if desired, by clicking the Maximize button. Your report appears similar to the one in Figure 19-22.

5. Scroll through the report, if desired, using the scroll bars to the right and bottom of the screen, or use the page navigation buttons at the bottom of the screen.

6. Click the Zoom button to magnify the report, if desired.

7. Click the Print button to print the report.

8. Click the Close button to return to the Main Switchboard.

CHAPTER 20

CUSTOMIZING YOUR DATABASE

IN THIS CHAPTER

- **Creating and Editing Database Tables**
- **Querying Your Database**
- **Using Custom Forms**
- **Creating Reports**
- **Replicating Your Database**

While the databases produced by the Database Wizards may satisfy your needs initially, you will soon find yourself wanting to store more information, select data in different ways, create forms that make data entry easier, and create reports from your data in new ways. You don't have to be a custom programmer to meet these needs.

They can all be accomplished with the help of Wizards provided by Access 7. If you are familiar with using a database, you'll be able to add to your skills and learn to make modifications to the database by following the Hands-On tutorials in this chapter. You'll even learn how to make a copy of the database that you can use while traveling away from your main computer!

Creating and Editing Database Tables

You will find that databases created with a Wizard are adequate for most, but not all, tasks. Sometimes, you will need to add tables to your database or modify existing tables.

For instance, you may wish to categorize your contacts. To do this, you would modify the contacts table by adding a field called Category.

You might also want the data entry form to provide a drop-down list of categories from which you can pick. In this case, you will need to create a drop-down list box in the data form, and a small table containing the possible category values.

When you create a table, you may need to specify how it relates to other tables. For instance, the Contact Management database stores information about the calls you make. You may make several calls to a person in the database; thus, several different records in the Calls table will relate to one person in the Contacts table. This type of relationship is called a *one to many* link.

You can see the relationships in the Contact Management database by clicking the Relationships button, as shown in Figure 20-1.

Creating Tables

There are two ways to create tables for a database—manually and with the Table Wizard. A simple reference table is the easiest to create. If the table has links to other tables, however, you will want to use the Table Wizard.

Creating Tables Manually

To create a simple table, such as one containing values to be used in a drop-down list box, follow the steps below—which, in this example, create a table in the Contact Management database.

Figure 20-1.
You can see the links between tables in the Contact Management database

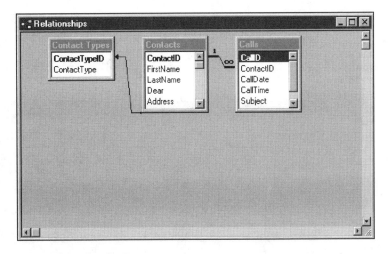

Hands On: Creating a Simple Table

1. Open the Contact Management database in Access. You will see the Main Switchboard.

2. Choose <u>W</u>indow, Contact Management: Database to return to the database's main window.

3. Click the down arrow to the right of the New Object button and select New Table from the list. You will see the New Table dialog box pictured in Figure 20-2.

4. Highlight Design View and click OK. You will see the Table1: Table dialog box shown in Figure 20-3.

5. Type **Category** in the first row of the Field Name column and press [Enter]. You will see Text as the data type, and a number

Figure 20-2.
The New Table dialog box provides several different choices for creating Access tables

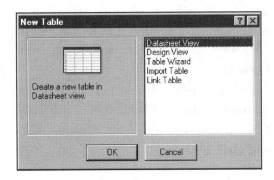

Figure 20-3.
The Design View
allows you to create
a new table and
specify properties
for each field

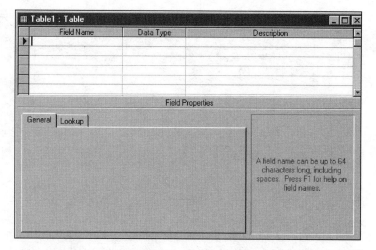

Figure 20-4.
The options at the
bottom of the dialog
box depend on the
type of data specified

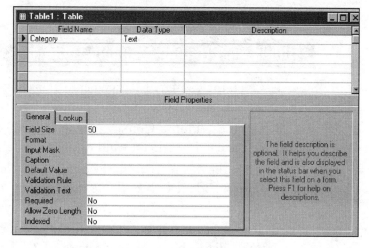

of options appear in the General tab at the bottom of the dialog box, as shown in Figure 20-4.

6. The default options are suitable, and this is the only field our
   table needs to include. In other tables, you might need to add
   additional fields, and change the data type or properties of the
   fields as they are added.

7. Click the Primary Key button to have Access automatically maintain the table and sort it by category.

8. Click the Save button, give the table the name **Categories**,
   and click OK.

9. Switch to the Table View by clicking the Table View button. Add category names, pressing Enter after each one.

10. When you are finished, close the table. You will return to the database main window.

Using the Table Wizard

If you need to create a more complex table, you may wish to use the Table Wizard. The Table Wizard allows you to build a new table based on any of over a dozen templates of commonly used tables—and will link the new table to existing tables automatically.

For example, you might want to create another table in the Contact Management database that would track visits made to clients—similar to the table that tracks calls.

Hands On: Using the Table Wizard

1. Open the Contact Management database in Access. You are at the main switchboard.

2. Choose <u>W</u>indow, Contact Management: Database to return to the database's main window.

NOTE: Steps 1 and 2 may not be necessary if you kept the database window open.

3. Click the down arrow to the right of the New Objects button and select New Table from the list. The New Table dialog box pictured in Figure 20-5 will appear.

4. Highlight Table Wizard and click OK. You will see the Table Wizard shown in Figure 20-6.

5. Highlight Tasks in the Sample Tables list. You will see the sample fields for the Task table.

6. Click the Select All button to select all the fields. They appear in the Fields In My New Table window.

Figure 20-5.
The New Table dialog
box provides several
different choices for
creating Access tables

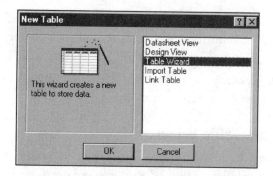

Figure 20-6.
The Table Wizard
allows you to create a
new table based on
table templates

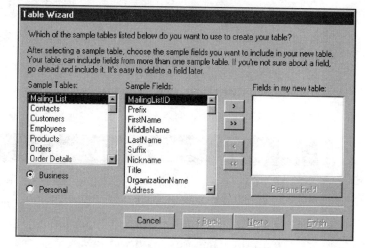

7. Highlight the TaskDescription field and click Rename Field. The Rename Field dialog box will appear.

8. Rename the field **VisitDescription** and click OK.

9. You also need a field for the ID of the contact you will be visiting. To insert this, highlight the Contacts sample table. You will see the Contacts fields in the Sample Fields window.

10. Highlight ContactID and click the Add Field button. This field will be added to the field list.

CAUTION: If you want to insert a new field, it must not have any spaces or special characters in the name.

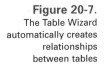

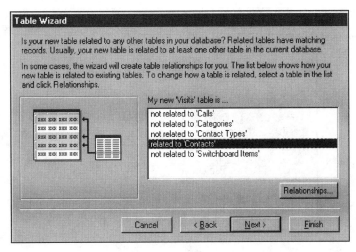

11. Click Next. Change the name of the table to Visits, and check "Yes, set a primary key for me."

12. Click Next. You will see the Table Wizard screen shown in Figure 20-7.

13. Since you are using the same ContactID field as exists in the Contacts table, a relationship will automatically be created between these two tables. Click Next to move to the next step.

14. Choose whether you want to modify the table, enter data directly in it, or have the Wizard create a form for you and choose Finish. The new table is complete.

Modifying the Table Structure

When you design a database, you often don't know exactly what data you need to maintain. Therefore, you may need to modify the structure of a table by adding or deleting a field, or changing a field's properties. You can modify the table structure as follows:

1. Open the Access database.

2. Go to the Main Window and click the Tables tab.

3. Highlight the table to be edited and choose Design. You will see the table in Design View, as shown in Figure 20-8.

Figure 20-8.
Design View allows
you to add, delete,
move, or edit fields

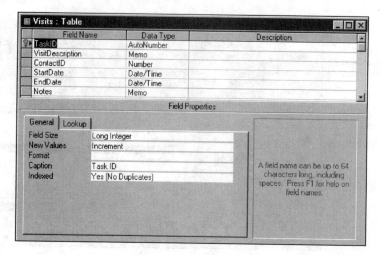

4. To delete a field, highlight the field row by clicking the box to the left of the field, press Del, and confirm the deletion if asked.

TIP: Use the Undo button in case you delete the wrong row.

5. To insert a field, highlight the field row below the one to be inserted by clicking the box to the left of the field, and press Ins. You will see a new, blank row. Enter the field name, data type, and properties.

6. To move a field, highlight the field row by clicking the box to the left of the field, point to the white arrow to the left of the field, and drag it up or down in the field list.

7. To edit a field, click in the field name, type, or description cell, and edit or retype the information. Common data types include:

- **Text** for text or numbers that don't require calculations, such as phone numbers or social security numbers

- **Memo** for long fields like notes or comments fields that will not need to be sorted

- **Date/Time** for dates and times

- **Currency** for currency values

- **AutoNumber** for unique IDs—this field increments automatically when you input a new record
- **Yes/No** for true/false, yes/no, or other binary values

8. To edit a field's properties, click in the field. The properties for that field will be displayed at the bottom of the dialog box. Edit field properties as needed. Some of the more commonly used field properties include:

- **Field Size:** For text fields, enter the length of the largest text string you need to hold. For numeric fields, enter integer, long integer (if you will have values over 32,000), or single for decimal numbers.
- **Format:** For text fields, "(<)" forces all characters to lowercase, "(>)" forces them to uppercase. For date, number, and currency fields, use the drop-down list box showing the available formats.
- **Default Value:** If you want a default value that the user can replace (if necessary), enter it here.
- **Validation Rule:** Use this to ensure the data meet your specifications. For instance, to make sure the text data is one of a series of choices, enter it like this: **="DC" or "MD" or "VA"**. To make sure the numerical data is greater than (>), less than (<), equal to (=) or not equal to (<>) a value, enter it like this: **>50**.
- **Validation Text:** The text a user should see when a validation rule is violated.

TIP: Press the Help key F1 **while the insertion point is in any property to see information about options.**

Querying Your Database

As explained in the last chapter, a query is a subset of data in the Access database. The most common type of query is a *selection query*. A selection query displays a subset of data from one or more tables, selected and sorted using specified criteria.

More complex queries may include actions, such as looking for duplicates, archiving, deleting, or updating data.

PART VI ACCESS

The product of a selection query is a *dynaset.* A dynaset looks like a regular table, but is regenerated every time it is displayed, using data that actually resides in various database tables.

When you create a custom data entry form or a report, you can base it on any table in the database. You can also base it on any query. Queries can thus be very powerful ways to create custom reports that look only at selected subsets of a database.

To make a simple selection query, do the following:

1. Open the Access database. Navigate, if needed, to the main window.

2. Click the down arrow to the right of the New Objects button and select New Query from the list. You will see the New Query dialog box pictured in Figure 20-9.

3. Choose Simple Query Wizard and click OK. You will see the first step of the Simple Query Wizard, shown in Figure 20-10.

4. Choose the table or query on which the new query will be based, and select the appropriate fields. Choose Next.

5. In the second step of the Simple Query Wizard, give the query a name and be sure to select Modify the Query Design.

6. Choose Finish. The query in design mode will appear.

7. Click in the criteria line of each field you wish to select by, and enter a criterion, as shown in Figure 20-11:

   • For a text field, enter the value to which it should be equal. For instance, to pick all contacts from Washington State you would type "WA" in the Criteria line of the StateOrProvince column.

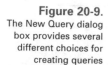

Figure 20-9.
The New Query dialog box provides several different choices for creating queries

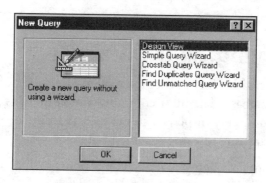

Figure 20-10.
You can base a query
on any or all fields
from tables and
queries in a database

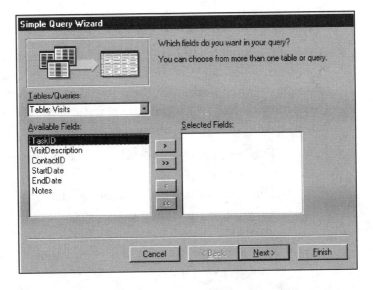

Figure 20-11.
The design mode
allows you to enter
selection criteria
for a query

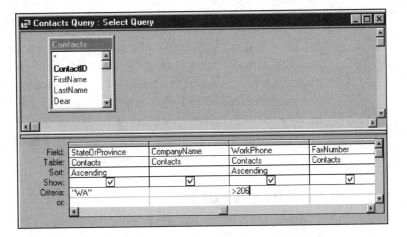

- For a numeric field, enter an operator such as =, <, or >, and the value you will compare it with. For instance, to see all contacts in the 206 aea code you would type **>206** in the Criteria line of the WorkPhone column.

8. Click the Save button to save the changes in the query.

9. Click the Query View button to see the results of the selection.

10. Close the query when you are finished.

Using Custom Forms

One of the most helpful aspects of using an Access database is the ability to create and use custom forms for data entry and viewing. These forms can contain default values, drop-down list boxes, and validation rules for text that help speed data entry and prevent mistakes. Access forms have several other advantages:

- They can be used both with Access databases and Excel worksheets
- They can contain data validation rules
- They can include drop-down lists, check boxes and other data entry aids
- Several people can enter data simultaneously into Access databases via forms

In order to use forms effectively, you need to be able to create them, edit them, and add form objects (such as drop-down lists) to them.

We'll use a specific example of a in the next sections. It will be based on the Contact Management database discussed in Chapter 19. This example will teach you the basics of creating forms that have data validation, formatting, and objects such as drop-down list boxes. You will be able to easily adapt this lesson to the creation of your own Access forms. If you want to follow along, you can create the necessary database in Access by referring to Chapter 19.

Creating a Form

The easiest way to create forms in Access is with the Form Wizard. The Wizard walks you through the steps necessary to make an attractive form based on a table or query, containing the specified fields.

Hands On: Creating a Custom Form

To create a form based on the Contacts table of the Contact Management database, follow these steps:

1. Open the Contact Management database in Access. You will see the main switchboard.
2. Choose Window, Contact Management: Database to return to the database's main window.

3. Click the down arrow to the right of the New Objects button and select New Form from the list. You will see the New Form dialog box pictured in Figure 20-12.

4. The drop-down list box at the bottom of the dialog box will ask on what to base the form; choose Contacts.

5. Select Form Wizard and choose OK. You will see the first step of the Form Wizard.

6. Choose the fields Contact ID through PostalCode, as shown in Figure 20-13. Select each field individually and then click on the right-arrow button to move it to the box on the right. Click on <u>N</u>ext.

7. Choose <u>C</u>olumnar as the preferred layout and click Next. Choose Clouds as the style for the form and click Next again.

Figure 20-12.
The New Form dialog box provides several different choices for automatically creating Access forms

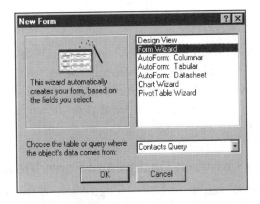

Figure 20-13.
The first step of the Form Wizard allows you to specify the fields you wish to include in the form

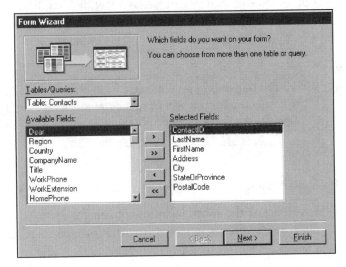

Figure 20-14.
The Form Wizard
creates a finished
form with the
specified formatting

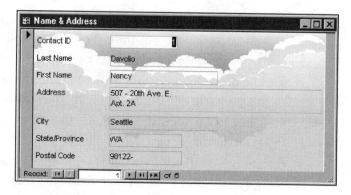

8. In the last step, give the form the title **Name & Address** and choose Finish. You will see the completed form, as shown in Figure 20-14.

Editing a Form

An Access form created with a Wizard is handy, but it is limited in its usefulness. The power of Access forms comes from your ability to edit them by moving and sizing objects, adding fields, formatting data, allowing users to select options from drop-down boxes, and checking data validity.

Switching between Design and Form View

To edit a form, you must be in Design View. If the form is already open, you can switch to Design View by clicking the Design View button. You will see the form in Design View, as shown in Figure 20-15.

> **NOTE:** Depending on what you designing (tables, queries, or forms) the button will have a different name (i.e., Table View, Query View, or Form View).

Switch back to Form View by clicking the Form View button.

If you are at the Main Window of the database, you can edit a form by clicking the Forms tab, selecting the form to be edited, and choosing Design.

Figure 20-15.
The Design View enables you to add, delete, and move form objects, as well as set their properties

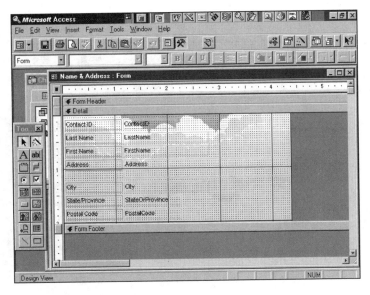

Selecting, Moving, and Sizing Objects

The most basic editing skills are selecting, moving, and sizing objects. To do so, follow these steps:

1. Ensure the form to be edited is open in Design View.

2. Select objects as follows:

   - To select one object, click on it. You will see the small squares called *handles* around the selected object.

   - To select several objects, click on the first one. Then hold down the Shift key and click on the next ones. You will see handles around all selected objects.

   - To select a group of objects that are near each other, move the mouse pointer until it is above (or below) and to one side of the objects, *and not on top of any other object.* The mouse pointer should appear as a white arrow. Click and drag a rectangle around the objects to be selected and release the mouse button. All objects in the rectangle will be selected.

3. To deselect objects, click on another object or on a blank area of the window.

 TIP: To delete an object, select it then press the Del key.

Figure 20-16.
To move an object, the
mouse pointer must be
on the edge of the
object but not on a
handle, and the pointer
must look like a hand

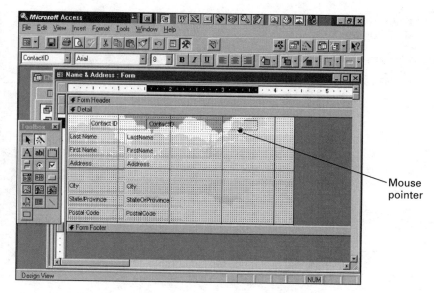

Mouse
pointer

4. To move objects, select them and move the mouse pointer to an edge of the object(s), but not on a handle, *until the mouse pointer looks like a hand,* as shown in Figure 20-16. Drag the object(s) to their new location.

5. To size an object, drag one of its handles until the object is the size you prefer. You can also size the form itself by moving the mouse pointer to the edge of the form, until it is a double-headed arrow. Then you can resize the form's width or depth.

Figure 20-17 shows the Contact form made wider, and with its objects rearranged.

Adding Drawing Objects

There are several types of objects that can be added to the Access form. Some are connected to fields, such as text boxes, drop-down boxes, combo boxes, check boxes, or option buttons. Others are not, such as text labels, lines, and graphic shapes. We can call the latter "drawing objects" because they improve the appearance of the form, but not necessarily its functionality.

To add a drawing object, follow these steps:

1. Ensure the form to be edited is open in Design View.

Figure 20-17.
You can resize objects
or even the form itself

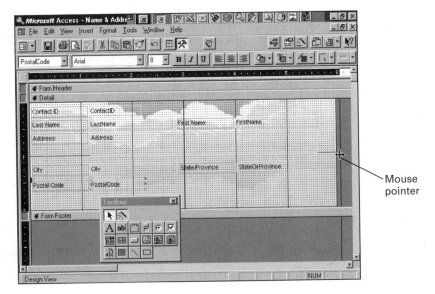

Mouse
pointer

2. If the Toolbox is not open, click the Toolbox button to open it. The pointer changes to reflect your selection.

3. Drag the drawing object you want from the toolbox to the area of the form where it should appear. Drawing objects include:

- **Label** for adding text to the form

- **Image** for inserting clip art

- **Line** for drawing lines

- **Rectangle** for drawing squares and rectangles

4. Move or size the object to its exact position, as described above. The Name & Address form, with additional drawing objects, can be seen in Figure 20-18.

Adding Fields

You may someday need more information in your database than you originally anticipated, and will want to add a field to the table on which the database was built. If you have already created a data entry

PART VI   ACCESS

Figure 20-18.
You can add lines, rectangles, images, and labels to a form to improve its appearance

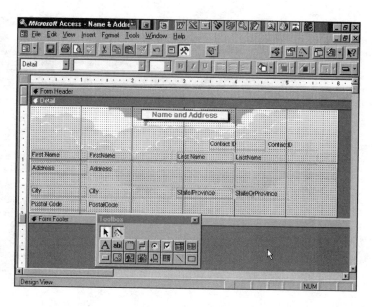

form, you will then need to add this field to the form. You can do so as follows:

1. Make sure the form to be edited is open in Design View, and the field exists in the table or query.

2. Click the Field List button. A window with a list of available fields will appear:

3. Drag the field you want to add from the field list window to the spot on the form where you wish it to appear.

4. Move and size the field box as needed.

5. Reset the tab order (so that when you press the Tab key, you will move from field to field logically) by choosing View, Tab Order. You will see the Tab Order dialog box shown in Figure 20-19.

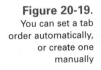

Figure 20-19.
You can set a tab order automatically, or create one manually

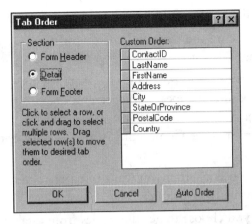

6. Choose Auto Order and click OK. The tab order is reset in a logical progression based on the location of fields on the screen. Click OK when you're done.

Adding a Combo or List Box

You can add a Combo Box or List Box to the form that enables you to pick values for a field from a predefined list. This can be a very effective way to ensure that relatively untrained personnel enter data correctly, since they must pick items from a list rather than typing them without guidance.

The items on the list can either be typed directly when you create the combo or list box, or can be based on items that exist in another table. In general, the latter will provide more flexibility, since you can add or remove items by editing the table more easily than redesigning the form. If you are working with an Excel database and using an Access form, however, you should type values directly.

To create a combo or list box, follow these steps:

1. Create the table containing values for the combo box, if you will be selecting values from a table.

2. Ensure the form to be edited is open in Design View.

3. Open both the field list window and the toolbox.

4. If you are replacing a field that already exists on the form, select the field and press ⌦Del to delete it.

5. Click on the field to be made into a combo or list box.

6. Click on the Combo Box tool or the List Box tool.

7. Move the mouse pointer to where the top-left corner of the box should appear and click and drag to the bottom-right corner. When you release the mouse button, you will see the first screen of the Combo or List Box Wizard, shown in Figure 20-20.

8. Choose whether you want to enter values or obtain them from a table or query and choose Next.

9. If you choose to get the values from a table or query, you will choose the appropriate table or query next. Otherwise, type the values you want in the combo box in the second step and choose Next.

10. If asked, specify that you wish to store the value chosen from the box in the database (as opposed to using it later), and choose Next.

11. Give the box a name then choose Finish.

12. Resize and move the box as needed.

13. Choose View, Tab Order. You will see the Tab Order dialog box.

14. Choose Auto Order. The tab order is reset to a logical progression based on the location of fields on the screen.

Figure 20-20.
A Wizard guides you through the steps of making a combo box or a list box

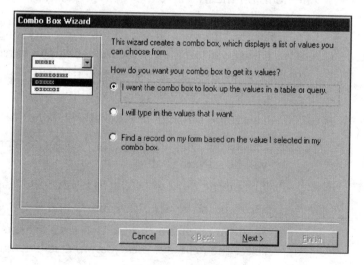

Formatting Data

You can also specify how the data in a form should be formatted when you enter it, by changing the properties of the field. To do so, follow these steps:

1. Ensure the form to be edited is open in Design View.

2. Double-click on the field object whose format you wish to change and click on the Format tab. The properties text box shown Figure 20-21 will appear.

3. Click the Format box and enter the desired format. Some of the more common include the following:

   • To force text to be uppercase, use (>)

   • To force text to be lowercase, use (<)

   • If the field is a number or date, use the down arrow at the right of the Format box to see a list of formatting choices

TIP: Press F1 when you are in the format line to obtain Help about the various text, number, and date/time formats.

4. Close the Properties window when you are finished.

TIP: You can set the format for a number of fields at once by selecting them and displaying the Properties window.

PART VI ACCESS

Figure 20-21.
You can specify the formatting a field should have

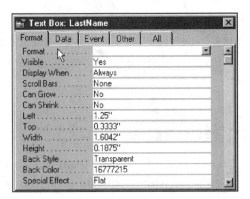

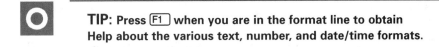

Figure 20-22.
You can set data validation rules from the properties window, along with text that appears if the rule is violated

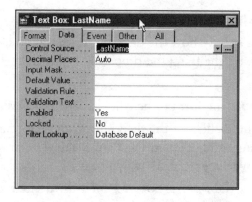

Checking Data Validity

One of the most powerful features of Access forms is their ability to check data as it is entered against specified rules. For instance, you could ensure that a refund amount is less than $1,000, or that the department name entered is not misspelled.

Create validation rules as follows:

1. Ensure the form to be edited is open in Design View.
2. Double-click on the field to prompt the properties window.
3. Click the Data tab. The properties window looks like the one in Figure 20-22.
4. Click the Validation Rule box and enter the data validation rule:
   - To make sure the text data is one of a series of choices, enter it like this: **="DC" or "MD" or "VA"**
   - To make sure the numerical data is greater than (>), less than (<), equal to (=), or not equal to (<>) a value, enter it like this: **>50**
5. Click the Validation Text box and enter the text that appears in a dialog box when the rule is violated, e.g., **State must be DC, MD, or VA.**

Creating Reports

With Access's Report Wizard, you can print out a summary of your data with ease, complete with subgroupings and totals, sorted to your specification.

To create a report, follow these steps:

1. Open the Access database. Navigate, if needed, to the main window.

2. Click the down arrow to the right of the New Objects button and select New Report from the list. The New Report dialog box pictured in Figure 20-23 will appear.

3. Choose the table or query upon which the report will be based in the drop-down list box at the bottom of the dialog box.

4. Highlight Report Wizard and click OK. You will see the first step of the Report Wizard shown in Figure 20-24.

Figure 20-23.
The New Report dialog box provides several different choices for creating Access reports

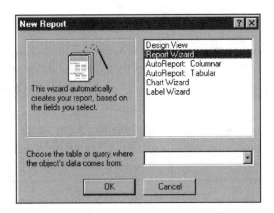

Figure 20-24.
You can choose fields for a report from several tables and queries

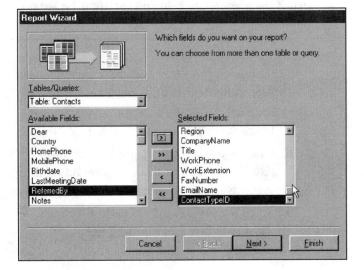

Figure 20-25.
You can group the data by one or more fields automatically

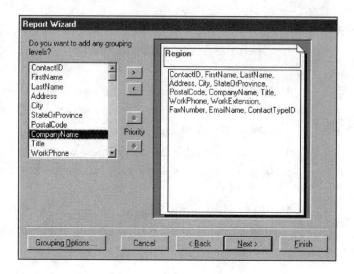

5. Choose the fields you would like to include in the report. You can also select additional fields from related tables or queries. Choose Next. The next step of the Wizard, as shown in Figure 20-25, will appear.

6. If you would like to group the data, select the field(s) by which you wish to group. Choose Next when you are done.

TIP: You can group by first letter—e.g., the first letter of clients' names—by choosing Grouping Options after you select the appropriate field and choosing 1st letter as the Grouping Interval.

7. Choose up to four fields by which you wish to sort the report. Select the field(s) and specify ascending or descending order for each. Choose Next when you are done. You will see the layout dialog box shown in Figure 20-26.

8. Choose the layout you prefer, previewing each choice in the window at the left of the dialog box. Pick Portrait or Landscape as the orientation of the report. Choose Next.

9. To pick a style for the report, preview each one on the left of the dialog box and choose Next.

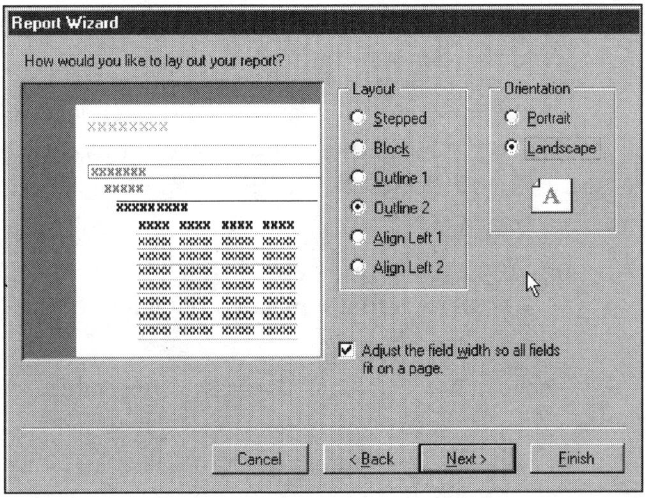

Figure 20-26.
You can choose from a
variety of layouts and
Access will ensure that
all fields fit on one page

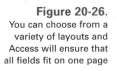

10. Give the report a title and choose Finish. The report is previewed on the screen.

11. Click the Close button to return to the Design View of the report and close the Design View to return to the Main Window.

You can preview and print reports as follows:

1. From the Main Window, click the Reports tab to see a list of reports.

2. Double-click on the desired report to preview it on the screen.

3. Click the Print button while the report is in Preview mode to print it.

Replicating Your Database

You can work on an Access database while traveling and keep it synchronized with the main copy. Your coworkers can even continue to work on the copy at the office and all of you can add, remove, and edit records. The secret is *database replication.*

Database replication is a process that makes it possible to make copies of a database and synchronize the changes that people make in the different replicated copies of the database. There are just a few things to understand when replicating a database:

- One copy of the database is the replication master. You can only make structural changes to this copy and these changes are replicated to the other copies whenever they are synchronized.

- You cannot undo a replicated database. (You could export all the objects in a replicated database to a new, nonreplicated database, however.)

- When you make a database replicatable, you add some fields to it that you may never see. These fields keep track of changes different people make to the database, and help with its synchronization.

- When you work on a copy of the database, you will have all the power and functions of a regular Access database, except that you can't change its structure.

Creating a Replicated Database

To create a replicated database, follow these steps:

1. Ensure that the Briefcase icon appears on the laptop screen. If it does not, you will need to install this Windows component. (Also, close Access if it is open.)

2. Open Windows Explorer and size it so that you can see the Briefcase icon on the desktop.

3. Navigate to the Access database file.

4. Choose the database you wish to replicate, and drag it to the Briefcase icon. You are asked if you are sure you want to continue.

5. Respond Yes. You are asked if you want to make a backup copy of the database (since you cannot undo the replication operation). Answer yes or no, depending on your needs. You will see the Briefcase dialog box in Figure 20-27.

6. Normally, you will make the original copy of the database the master copy with the ability to make design changes. Select the appropriate copy and choose OK. The replication process is complete.

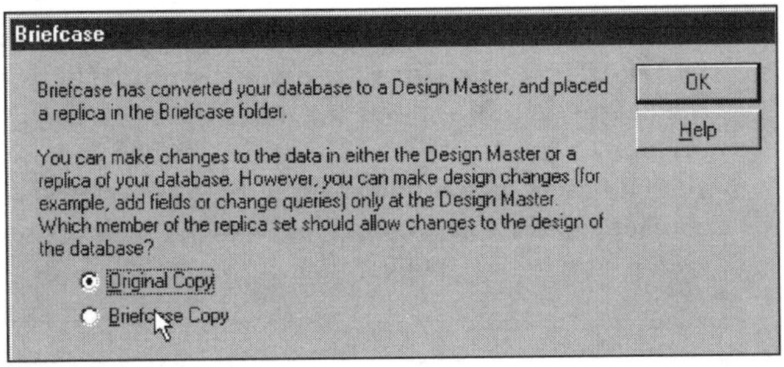

Figure 20-27.
You can assign either
copy of the replicated
database the right to
make changes in the
database design

> **Briefcase**
>
> Briefcase has converted your database to a Design Master, and placed
> a replica in the Briefcase folder.
>
> You can make changes to the data in either the Design Master or a
> replica of your database. However, you can make design changes (for
> example, add fields or change queries) only at the Design Master.
> Which member of the replica set should allow changes to the design of
> the database?
>
> ⊙ Original Copy
> ○ Briefcase Copy
>
> OK
> Help

To use the database while you are on the road:

1. Open the Briefcase from the laptop.
2. Double-click on the Access database in the Briefcase. Access will open, and you can work on the database.

Synchronizing Database Copies

To synchronize the database copies, connect the laptop to your desktop and follow these steps:

1. Double-click the Briefcase icon.
2. Select the database file you want to synchronize.
3. Choose Briefcase, Update Selection. You will see the Update My Briefcase dialog box shown in Figure 20-28.

Figure 20-28.
Updating the briefcase
synchronizes copies of
replicated databases

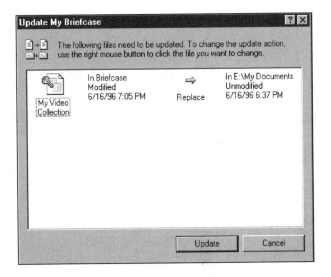

> **Update My Briefcase**
>
> The following files need to be updated. To change the update action,
> use the right mouse button to click the file you want to change.
>
> My Video Collection
> In Briefcase
> Modified
> 6/16/96 7:05 PM
> ⇒ Replace
> In E:\My Documents
> Unmodified
> 6/16/96 6:37 PM
>
> Update   Cancel

NOTE: If you have edited the same record in both copies of the database, you will not see any message during the synchronization. When you open the database, however, you will see a message stating that you need to resolve the conflict. Follow the prompts and choose which copy of the record should be retained.

- If one of the copies was not edited, you will be prompted to replace the unchanged one with the edited one
- If both copies have been edited, you will be prompted to merge the two databases

4. Choose <u>U</u>pdate. Deleted records are deleted from both copies of the database, new records are added, and edited records are changed.

PART VII

APPLICATION ISSUES

CHAPTER 21

CREATING AN ELECTRONIC FILING SYSTEM

IN THIS CHAPTER

- Creating and Organizing a Filing System
- Organizing Electronic Folders
- Using File Properties
- Purging Outdated Files
- Moving Old Files into a New Filing System
- Finding Files

Can you imagine an office that needed to file thousands of documents each year, and did so by throwing them all in a big box? What if everyone in the office used cryptic abbreviations for each file folder, and then came up with their own system for organizing these folders in their own filing cabinets?

Everything would probably work fine, until the time came to find something. People would probably remember where recently stored files were, but if the person who named the file was on vacation or if the file was stored six months ago, the situation would be nearly hopeless.

It's amazing how many organizations that have systematic and logical paper-filing systems haven't gotten around to designing similar systems for their electronic files. You've probably heard someone in your office say, "Where is that file I was working on last month? I can't remember exactly what I named it, but I know it's here somewhere."

Case Study: The Economics Department

A university Economics department hadn't improved their electronic filing procedures since they began to use PCs, even after they began using a network.

The system administrator did not encourage use of the network for filing documents, since it would consume too much valuable disk space. No one had ever trained staff in electronic filing and floppy disks were still the primary storage medium. Files were named rather creatively, depending on who saved them. Temporary workers and assistants were not trained to use an electronic filing system.

After one too many files was lost, a consultant was called to assist with a reorganization. These were some of the changes the consultant made:

- The filing process was redesigned. Staff were taught principles of electronic filing and a filing system was devised, consisting of logical folders and filename conventions.

- Staff were trained to use Explorer to create and delete folders; find files by date, filename, or text; move files into their new folders; and rename them as needed.

- The filing system was established on a shared drive accessible to both faculty and staff. Adjunct faculty were even able to call and access the system from their homes.

- A main folder was created for each course, with subfolders for all syllabi and for each professor. Professors were encouraged to file handouts, lectures, and other materials they wanted to share with other teachers on the network.

An important part of an overall office solution is having a well-organized electronic filing system. Office 95 provides just the tools you need to make one and maintain it.

Getting Organized

The goal of a filing system is to ensure the integrity of files maintained in it, and to allow for files to be easily accessed by appropriate persons. Electronic filing systems have the same goals as paper ones in this regard. The only difference is the tools available to accomplish them.

When you create an electronic filing system with these goals in mind, you will probably want to answer the following four questions:

- How should you organize files?
- How can you easily find files?
- What needs to be done to maintain the filing system?
- How can file security be ensured?

Organizing an electronic filing system requires you to make a plan. Planning, in this case, implies answering the following questions:

- Which files should be saved, and for how long?
- In what medium should the files be saved?
- What determines the organizational structure of your file system?
- Do you need a file-naming system, and if so, what should it be?

You'll learn how to answer these questions as you read this chapter, and then how to use Office 95's file management tools to the organize your file system.

Choosing Files to Save

The most basic decision you must make when you create a filing system is whether to save a given file and, if so, for how long. Some files may not need to be saved at all. For example, there may be no reason to save transmittal letters that just say "enclosed please find . . ." or short memos to office staff.

Other files may also have a limited "shelf life." For instance:

- Early drafts of a report or proposal may be deleted when the final version is approved
- Documents relating to a client may be able to be put in storage when the relationship with the client is over
- Correspondence and memos may be eventually archived

When you create an electronic filing system, you should consider the lifetime of different types of documents. A good filing system helps you to identify documents that can be deleted or archived, allowing you to purge your drives quickly and safely. For instance:

- If report drafts all have the word "Revision" in them (e.g., "Roche Report Revision 06"), you can quickly search for all files with the word "Revision" and then delete those you no longer need.
- If documents relating to a specific client are stored in their own folder, you can quickly move the contents of the entire folder to a floppy or tape backup for storage.
- If letters and memos are stored in their own folder, you can sort the files in that folder by date, then quickly select all files up to the target date and move them to a floppy or tape backup.

Deciding Where to Save Data

There are three basic choices in saving files: a floppy disk, a local hard drive, or a network drive.

Floppies have the advantage of being portable. Conceptually, they are easy for many people to use, since they can save all documents on a particular subject on a floppy. They are slow, however, and unless you save your information to a second floppy, you will lose your data if the floppy disk fails.

The local hard drive has the advantage of holding the equivalent of hundreds of floppies. In addition, it stores information much more quickly than storing it to floppies. However, a hard drive has limited space, and you can't add hard drives to your system indefinitely. In addition, data stored on local hard drives is not automatically backed up, unless you take active steps to do so.

Where Should You Store Data When Using a Network?

- If you store files on floppies, you will not be able to easily build on your previous work, readily combine old documents, or use scrap documents. Don't just store files on floppies because you're used to doing things that way.

- Files that can be used by a workgroup should be stored on the network.

- If local hard drives are not customarily backed up, important files should be stored on the network. Network access and passwords should be set up to provide security for these files.

Network drives have the same advantages as local hard drives. In addition, data on network drives are usually backed up automatically by the system administrator. However, the limit of a network storage device can be reached rather quickly if dozens of people are saving their data on it. Although it is not necessarily true, many users believe their data are safer from prying eyes if stored on a local hard drive rather than a network drive.

Creating a System to Name Files

Whether you work alone or with others, one key to finding files is to name them systematically. There are two guidelines to keep in mind when creating a file-naming system: the length of the name and how it will be alphabetized.

Using Short Filenames

Just because Windows 95 allows long filenames, you're under no obligation to make them as long as possible. Although it seems counter-intuitive, doing so can make files harder to find. The profusion of characters can fill up the screen, and your eye can't easily spot the significant words that identify the desired file.

In addition, some operating systems including certain versions of Novell NetWare do not support long filenames. If you are working on such a network, or exchanging files with people on one, you may wish to consider keeping your filenames to eight characters or less.

Starting with Nouns

When you have just a few files in a folder, names aren't as important. You can find what you want without much trouble. Consider, however, how your folder will look when it is full of files. At that point you'd better have a system.

Office 95 applications arrange your files in alphabetical order as they are saved. Use this to your advantage, just as you do with a paper-filing system. One of the best ways to do this is to avoid filenames starting with articles or adjectives; start with nouns, instead. Imagine trying to find these files:

- My Yearly Budget
- Thursday's memo to Frank Ross about Xircon
- First presentation to Xircon
- A response to Molly Harrod

Now that you know which sorts of filenames to avoid, here are some tips for choosing filenames that won't get lost:

- Coordinate filenames with your electronic folder system
- Alphabetize as you want files grouped—if you want to see all memos together, name the file "Memo - ABASCO #1." If you want to see client files together, name the file "ABASCO - memo 1."
- Use the most important noun first

Thus, to name a memo to Frank Ross at Xircon, consult first with your electronic folder system. If the file is in a memos folder, you do not need to indicate that it is a memo in the filename. Similarly, if it is in a Xircon folder, you need not have Xircon prominently in the filename.

Assuming the files are stored in a general folder, decide how you want the files grouped. Do you want all memos to be together, then all letters; or do you want all Xircon documents together, then those for other clients?

Finally, decide which noun is more important, not which one happens to come first. The last name of Ross may be more important than Frank in this case.

Using the example, suppose you have a general folder for and you want to see all Xircon files together, then the file types (memos, letters, etc.), then the recipient, then a number. In that case, you might name the file:

Xircon Memo Ross, Frank 001

Note that the filename is kept short, rather than cluttering the screen with:

Xircon Corporation - Memo To Ross, Frank - Number 001

The result should be a file-naming system that groups files logically and allows the eye to travel over the directory to find the required file.

A well-designed file-naming system can be explained easily, allowing temporary employees to learn it quickly and maintain the continuity of your files. You could give the following instructions to someone learning to use the file system featured in our example:

- Filenames consist of four parts, divided by spaces. No hyphens or other separators should be used.
- The first word(s) are the name of the company. Do not include "Inc.," "Ltd.," or the like.
- The next word is the document type, which should be letter, memo, proposal, report, or document (used for any other file).
- The next words are the recipient's name, in the format *Last-name, Firstname.*
- Finally, end the filename with the next three-digit number. The first document of this document type to this recipient is numbered "001."

Try out your instructions on one or two people. You may need to revise them, since what seems clear to you may not be as easily understood by someone else. After you refine it, give it out to staff and follow up when people do not follow the naming convention.

A file is the organization's work product, not the individual's. If you use a file-naming system that only you understand, then no one else can find your files when you're sick or on vacation.

Organizing Electronic Folders

What were called directories in Windows 3.1 are folders in Windows 95. The reason for this change is that an electronic filing system oper-

PART VII APPLICATION ISSUES

ates under the same logic as a paper-filing system. Create an organized folder system by keeping the following guidelines in mind.

Work from the Top Down

Whenever you create a filing system, you create it from the top down. In a paper-filing system, the top level is the filing cabinet. Then comes the file drawer, the hanging file, and the manila file.

If you are working on a network, the top level of the filing system is the network drive on which your data is stored. On most networks, the drive determines the accessibility of your files. Thus you should start by storing all files that are needed by workgroup members on a drive and folder (directory) to which they have access. Obviously, if you are working in a standalone system, this doesn't apply to you.

The next level of file storage should be a main data folder. If you are storing data on a drive that also has programs on it, it's probably not a good idea to have the top level (root) directory trashed up with a bunch of folders referring to clients or projects. Consider having one folder in the root directory named "Docs" or 'Files," and place all your

---

The Filing Doctor Is In

Q: Shouldn't data files be stored in a folder under the application folder?

A: This is a practice from the Middle Ages of computing, when applications couldn't read each others' formats, and default directories were often the program directory (gasp!). Thus, WordPerfect documents might be stored in \WP51\DOCS, Word in \WINWORD\DOCS, etc.

There's no particular reason to store files in folders under the folder containing their application, and it takes more time navigating through the folder structure to get there.

While using Office 95, you should try to stop thinking in terms of programs, and start thinking about projects. Create filing systems appropriately, by storing all files relating to a certain activity in the same folder, no matter what application produces those files.

folders holding data in this central folder. Alternatively, use the default My Documents folder as your central folder.

Create a Sensible Filing System

Your paper-filing system is probably arranged to facilitate the work you do. If you are in a law office, your main files may be arranged by case number. In a sales department, they might be grouped by client. In an engineering shop, they may be organized by project. Subfolders, when possible, should be organized the same way in each main folder.

A legal office, for example, might organize their files by case number, then common document type (letters, pleadings, briefs, etc.). File-names for letters might specify the letter subject and attorney, since the case number is given by the folder.

A university department might organize files by course, then common document type, with the professor's name specified in the filename.

Consider Folder Size and Path Length

When you are creating folder systems, it is also important to think about how many documents will be in each folder. Remember the paper-filing system. If you have 500 manila folders, each having one to three pieces of paper, you should consolidate. If you have three folders, each having 500 pieces of paper, you should consider dividing them up.

In an electronic filing system, you want to avoid having lists that contain screens full of items. Whether the list is a list of folders or a list of files, it can get somewhat confusing.

On the other hand, you also want to avoid extraordinarily long paths, such as H:\files\legal\cases\10030\smith\letters\1995\April\. Other-wise, you will spend an inordinate amount of time navigating to the correct directory!

The best filing systems are no more than three or possibly four levels deep. At each level, they have half a screen to a full screen's worth of folders, and each final-level folder has less than a hundred files, so that they can all be seen on a couple of screens.

You can create fewer or more levels of folders by coordinating the folder structure with your filenames. Take the case of a small, one-attorney law firm. If the total number of documents associated with a given case is under 50, the documents may reasonably be put in one folder labeled with the case number (or client name), and document names which have "memo," "letter," "pleading," "brief," or "other" in them. Conversely, if most cases have 100 to 500 documents, it might make more sense to always create main folder with five subfolders whenever a new matter is opened, and store all memos in the Memo subfolder instead of having "memo" in the name.

Using File Properties

You may also wish to take advantage of Office's File Properties dialog boxes to associate descriptive information with your files. If you choose File, Properties in Word, Excel, or PowerPoint, you will see a properties dialog box such as the Presentation Properties dialog box shown in Figure 21-1.

This dialog box allows you to view and save standard information about your file, including its title, author, subject, manager, company, category, keywords, and comments.

You can even create customized fields that allow you to store document properties unique to your business. For instance, a law firm might want to store the client matter number used for all paper docu-

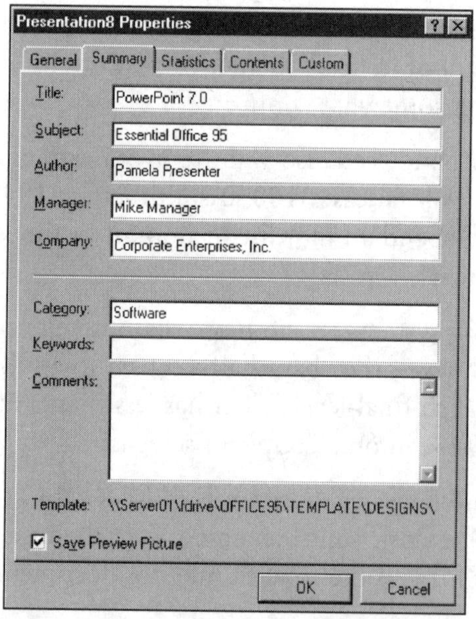

Figure 21-1.
You can save descriptive information with your Word, Excel, or PowerPoint file, enabling you to easily find files by title, subject or keyword

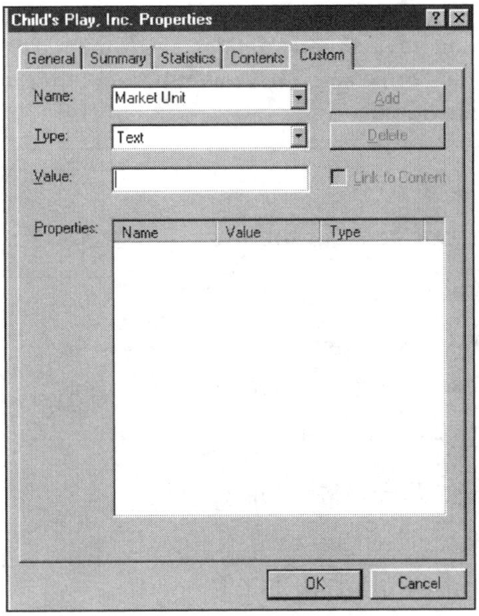

Figure 21-2.
You can create
customized fields to
store properties
unique to your
enterprise

ments relating to a case. A university might want to store the course number that class-related documents are for. Create customized fields as follows:

1. Choose File, Properties in Word, Excel, or PowerPoint. A properties dialog box will become visible.

2. Click the Custom tab. You will see the custom tab of the properties dialog box, such as the Excel worksheet Properties dialog box shown in Figure 21-2.

3. To add a new custom property, type its name in the Name box or choose from predefined names by clicking the down arrow at the right of the box.

4. Select the type of information, as text, date, number, or yes/no.

5. Enter a value for the field. Alternatively, if you would like to link the field to a bookmark in Word, a named cell in Excel, or a selected bullet in PowerPoint, check Link to Content. The Value box is replaced by a Source box, and you can select the appropriate source.

6. Choose Add. The new field is added to the field list.

If you are going to use the file properties, you will probably want to prompt users to fill them out whenever they save a document.

TIP: You must have already defined the bookmark, named the cell, or selected the bullet before entering the Properties dialog box.

In Word, you can do so as follows:

1. In Word, choose Tools, Options.
2. Click the Save tab.
3. Choose Prompt for Document Properties.

In Excel or PowerPoint, follow these steps:

1. Choose Tools, Options.
2. Click the General tab.
3. Choose Prompt for File Properties.

Managing Files

Once you've established filing system, you can start saving new documents in it with ease. You will find, however, that you still have two file management issues: how do you purge outdated files, and how do you move your existing files into the new system you created?

Purging Outdated Files

A well-organized filing system will have folders containing documents that, by their nature, can be purged after a set amount of time passes. For instance, you may decide every six months you will purge your correspondence or memos folder of files that are over one year old.

You can easily purge or archive outdated files from an Open File dialog box in Word, Excel, or PowerPoint. One of the best ways to do this is to sort your files by date. You can then easily see which old files you can archive or delete:

TIP: You may wish to archive these files to a tape backup or floppy disk rather than purging them completely.

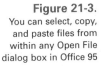

Figure 21-3.
You can select, copy, and paste files from within any Open File dialog box in Office 95

Details

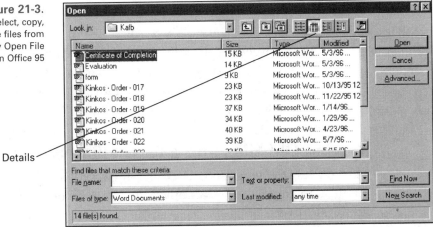

1. Click the Open button. The Open dialog box, as shown in Figure 21-3, will appear.
2. Click the Details button, if necessary, to see your files along with their editing date.
3. Click the Modified header to sort your files by date.

TIP: Clicking the Modified header again changes the sort order from ascending to descending. Clicking the Name header changes the sort order back to filename.

4. Select all files with a specific word anywhere in their filename, if desired, by typing the word in the File Name box and choosing Find Now. You will see a list of the appropriate files.

TIP: You can delete all files relating to a completed project by searching for the project name, assuming that you put that project name in the filename of all its related files.

5. Select adjacent files to be archived or deleted by clicking on the first file, holding down the (Shift) key, and clicking on the last file.

PART VII APPLICATION ISSUES

6. Delete the selected files by right-clicking on them, then choosing <u>D</u>elete from the shortcut menu.

7. Alternatively, cut the selected files to the Clipboard by choosing <u>E</u>dit, Cu<u>t</u>. Navigate to the destination drive and/or folder, then choose <u>E</u>dit, <u>P</u>aste to finish moving the files to their new destination.

Moving Old Files into a New Filing System

Most offices have an existing electronic filing system, or at least existing files. To create a new electronic filing system, you need to know how to do several things:

- Create and maintain folders
- Select groups of files
- Move files into appropriate folders
- Rename files

Creating and Maintaining Folders

You can create new folders directly from your Office 95 applications, as follows:

1. From Word, PowerPoint, or Excel, choose <u>F</u>ile, Save <u>A</u>s. The Save As dialog box will appear.

2. Navigate to the folder that will contain the subfolder you wish to create.

3. Click the Create a New Folder button. You will see the New Folder dialog box:

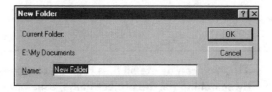

4. Type the name of the new folder and choose OK. Your new folder is created.

To delete or rename a folder, right-click on it from any Open or Save dialog box, then choose either Delete or Rename.

> **CAUTION:** If you delete a folder, the folder and all its files are moved to the Recycle Bin, but they are not marked as having come from any folder in particular.

Selecting Files

There are several ways to select the files you will move into your new folders. If you are lucky enough to be able to recognize them by their filenames, the process is a snap! To select a number of adjacent files, click on the first one, then hold down the [Shift] key and click on the last one.

TIP: Don't hold down the mouse button when you move between the first and last file. Click on the first, let up the mouse button, then [Shift]-click on the last one.

If the files are not adjacent, click on the first file, then hold down the [Ctrl] key and click on the next one. Continue to hold down the [Ctrl] key and click on additional files until they are all selected.

If you want to create archive directories of old letters or memos, you will probably want to select files earlier than a certain date. The easiest way to do so is by using Windows Explorer:

1. Open Explorer.
2. Choose Tools, Find, Files or Folders. The Find: All Files dialog box shown in Figure 21-4 will appear on the screen.
3. Specify the drive and folder in which the files are located, and whether or not Explorer should search in subfolders.
4. Select the Date Modified tab. The dialog box resembles the one in Figure 21-5.
5. Select Find all files created or modified between, and enter the date range to be searched.
6. Choose Find Now. The files between the target dates appear at the bottom of the Find: All Files dialog box.

PART VII APPLICATION ISSUES

Figure 21-4.
Search for files with a specific name in a general location

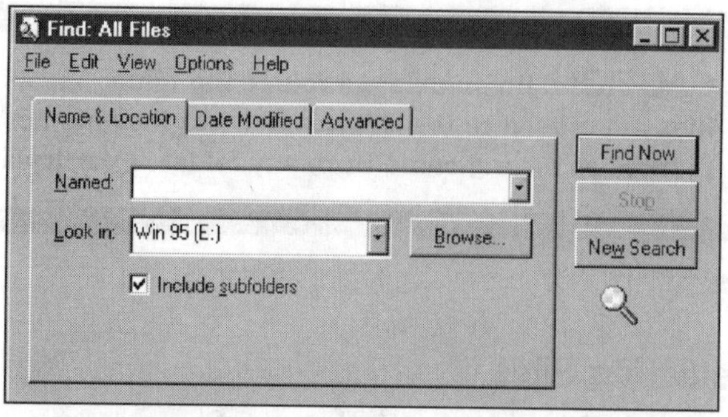

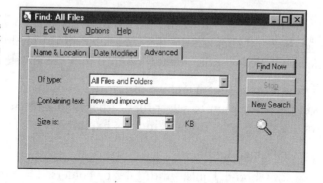

Figure 21-5.
You can select files that were last edited in a specific date range

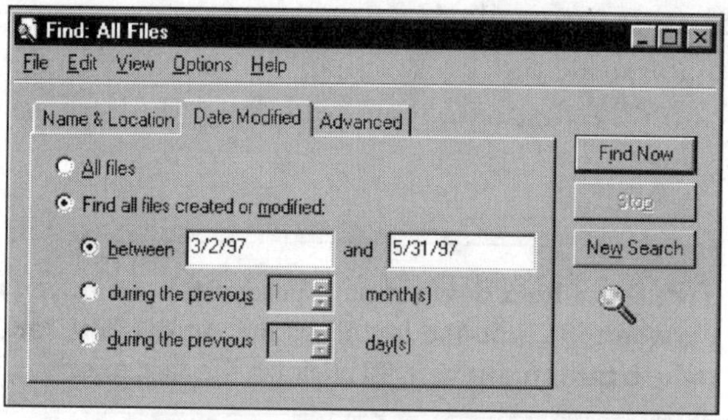

Figure 21-6.
You can search for files containing specific text to assist you in creating a new filing system

Sometimes, you will need to select files based on their subject matter, but the filename is not descriptive enough to be helpful. In this case, you can search files for specific text, as follows:

1. From Explorer, choose Tools, Find, Files or Folders. You will see the Find: All Files dialog box.

2. Specify the drive and folder in which the files are located, and whether or not Explorer should search in subfolders.

3. Select the Advanced tab. The Find: All Files dialog box shown in Figure 21-6 will appear.

4. Restrict the search to Microsoft Word files or the file type for which you are searching, then type the text to be located.

5. Choose Find Now. The target files appear at the bottom of the Find: All Files dialog box.

Moving Files

In Windows 95, you can move files with a cut-and-paste operation. This method works with Office 95 applications as well as Windows Explorer. You may often want to move files with your Office 95 application so you do not need to open Windows Explorer as an additional application. To do so:

1. Select the appropriate files from any Open or Save dialog box, as described above.

2. Choose Edit, Cut to cut the files to the Clipboard, or Edit, Copy to copy the files.

3. Highlight the folder to which you wish to move or copy the files. Choose Edit, Paste to paste the files to the new folder. If you cut them, notice that they are no longer in the old folder.

Alternatively, if you are in Explorer's main window, you can move selected files by dragging them to any visible folder in the All Folders window located on the left, as shown in Figure 21-7. If you hold

Figure 21-7. You can move or copy selected files by dragging them to a folder in the All Folders window

Dragging from this folder . . .

. . . to this subfolder

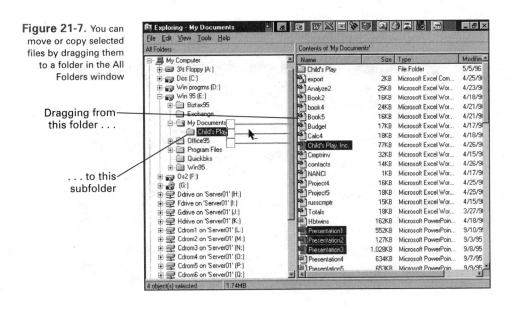

down the Ctrl key while you drag the files, you will copy rather than move them.

Finding Files

Finding files efficiently consists of two somewhat different skills: The ability to navigate quickly to where files are located, and the ability to find lost files.

Using Shortcuts to Navigate through Folders

You can use the Look In Favorites feature along with the My Documents folder to create a system for quickly navigating to your most often used files. Look in Favorites is an icon on Open File dialog boxes listing folders and files identified as ones often used, as shown in Figure 21-8.

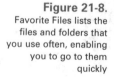

Look in Favorites is particularly effective when it is used in conjunction with appropriate folders. Consider the following ideas:

- Store all files that you might use every week in the My Documents folder. Always keep this folder in the Favorite Files list.

- Keep a minimum number of files in the My Documents folder. Purge it of documents that become outdated or are used only occasionally, and move these into other folders in your filing system.

Figure 21-8.
Favorite Files lists the files and folders that you use often, enabling you to go to them quickly

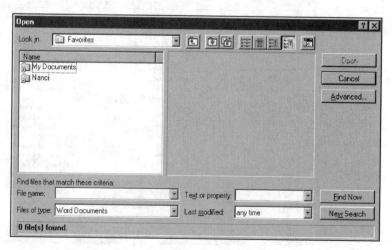

- If you are working on a special project, put the project folder in your list of Favorite Files. When the project is complete or no longer takes much of your time, remove the folder from this list. (The folder will, of course, still be in your filing system.)

- If you have a top-level folder (such as "Docs") under which all your other data files are stored, have it in the Favorite Files list.

- Put up to ten of your most often used files in the Favorite Files list—even if they are in a folder that is listed there. Then you can navigate to them very quickly.

- If there are folders in which you save files often, such as a correspondence folder, include it in the Favorite Files list, since you want to be able to navigate quickly when saving as well as when opening files.

- Keep the Favorite Files list short. You should be able to almost instantly spot the folder or file you want from this list.

This filing system stores folder names in Favorite Files, rather than files. It will then take two mouse clicks to access your most often used files rather than the one mouse click it would take if all the files are stored directly in Favorite Files.

The real advantage of storing folder names in Favorite Files is to prevent the list from getting so large that you have 50 to 100 items in it, forcing you to spend more time navigating this list than you would by clicking a second time on a folder within Favorite Files.

To add an item to Favorite Files:

1. Click the Open button to access an Open File dialog box in Word, Excel, or PowerPoint.

2. Select the folder(s) or file(s) you wish to add to your list of favorites, or move to the folder you wish to add to the list.

3. Click the Add to Favorites button. You will be prompted to add the current folder or selected items to the favorites list.

4. Choose to add the folder or selected items. Your choice is added to your list of favorites.

To see your list of favorites, click the Look in Favorites icon from any Save or Open dialog box. You will see a list of folders and/or files, which really represent a special type of *link* called a Shortcut to these files. The files are actually stored in whatever directory you originally put them.

You can remove a file or folder from the Favorites list without actually removing it from the disk:

1. From a Save or Open dialog box in Word, Excel, or Power-Point, click the Favorites icon. You will see the Favorites list.

2. Select the folder(s) or file(s) to be removed from the Favorites list.

3. Press the [Del] key. You will be asked if you want to send the item(s) to the Recycle Bin.

4. Confirm this by responding Yes.

What is being sent to the Recycle Bin is not the file or folder itself, but only the *link* or reference to the file that is stored in the Favorites subfolder of the Win95 folder.

Finding Lost Files

How often have you needed to search for a file that you know is on the disk, but you can't remember the name? With Office 95, finding lost files is a snap. Just do the following:

1. Click the Open button to access an Open File dialog box in Word, Excel, or PowerPoint.

2. If you know you're in the right folder, and you know any words in the filename, type them in the File Name box, then choose Find Now.

3. If you know you're in the right folder and you don't know the filename, but you know a term or phrase that would be found in the document or one of its properties (like title or keywords), type the words in the Text or Property box and choose Find Now.

4. If you don't know in which folder the document is located, choose Advanced and select options as follows:

   • Choose the disk or folder that probably contains your file by typing its name in the Look In box.

   • Alternatively, click the down arrow and browse to find the appropriate disk or folder. Make sure that Search Subfolders is checked if you don't know the exact location of the file.

- Set one or more search criteria by selecting the Property (document text, title, keywords, creation date, size, etc.), then selecting the Condition (includes, greater than, between, etc.), then typing in the Value (text, date, etc.). You can use more than one criterion in your search.
- If you would like to match all word forms ("drive" would include "driving"), choose Match All Word Forms.
- To restrict the search to match the case of the search strings, choose Match Case.

5. Choose Find Now to conduct the search. The files meeting the search criteria will be listed in the Open File dialog box.

TIP: If desired, you can save searches that you use repeatedly by choosing Save Search after you enter the search criteria. Saved searches can be reused by choosing Open Search.

Putting the Filename in a Footer

You can avoid a lot of wasted time spent searching for files if you will start putting the path and filename on the footer of documents. Even better, put the footer in the template upon which new documents are made, and they'll be there automatically. In Word and Excel the procedures are somewhat similar. Since most people don't have hundreds of presentations, as they do Word documents and Excel worksheets, it is usually unnecessary to do this in PowerPoint.

Documenting Names in Word Footers

In Word, you can put your document name in a footer as follows:

1. Open the appropriate file or template.
2. Choose View, Header and Footer. You will see the header windows, and the Header and Footer toolbar shown in Figure 21-9.
3. Click the Switch Between Header and Footer button. You will see the document footer.
4. Choose Insert, Field. You will see the Field dialog box.

Figure 21-9.
You can put the filename on an identifying footer for Word templates, then all documents will be easy to identify

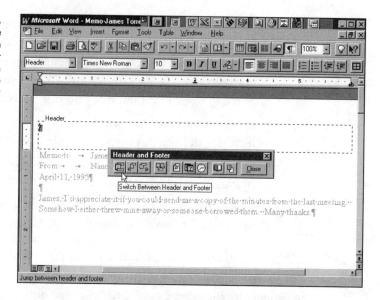

Figure 21-10.
You can add the system path to the filename to help you identify the location of files

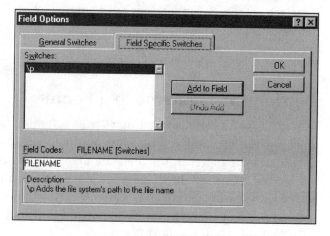

5. Choose (All) in the <u>C</u>ategories list, then select FileName in the Field <u>N</u>ames list.

6. With FileName highlighted, choose <u>O</u>ptions. You will see the Field Options dialog box.

7. Select the Field Specific Switches tab. The options shown in Figure 21-10 will become visible.

8. The /p switch is already selected. Choose <u>A</u>dd to Field to use this switch.

9. Choose OK to return to the Field dialog box and choose OK to return to the document footer.

10. Format the footer by making the font smaller, if desired, then choose <u>C</u>lose to return to the main editing window.

Documenting Names in Excel Workbooks

To insert an identifying footer in an Excel workbook or template, do the following:

1. Open the appropriate workbook or template.

2. Choose <u>F</u>ile, Page Set<u>u</u>p and ensure you are in the Header/Footer tab. You will see the Page Setup dialog box shown in Figure 21-11.

3. Choose C<u>u</u>stom Footer. You will see the Footer dialog box with boxes for the left, center, and right side of the footer.

> **NOTE**: You should use the custom footer rather than the predefined footer with the filename. If you use the predefined footer, the name is entered as text, and will not update to reflect changes in the filename. This is particularly important when putting identifying footers in templates, because the workbook based on the template will indeed have a different name than the template.

Figure 21-11.
You can put identifying footers in Excel workbooks or templates

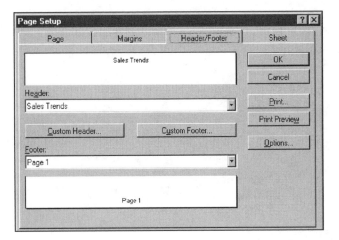

4. Click in the appropriate box and click the Filename button, followed by the Sheet button to insert the filename and sheet name in the footer.

5. Choose OK twice to return to the main editing window.

CHAPTER 22

CUSTOMIZING TOOLBARS AND SHORTCUT BARS

IN THIS CHAPTER

- Displaying Toolbars
- Adding and Removing Buttons from Toolbars
- Creating Toolbars
- Using Shortcut Bars

As you've read through this book, you have undoubtedly seen how toolbars make virtually every task easier and quicker. You've also seen how Shortcut Bars enable you to open applications easily, even when you are working in another program.

To make full use of Office 95, you will want to be able to work with these tools and modify them to suit the way you work.

Working with Toolbars

Toolbars provide quick access to commonly used functions in all Office 95 applications. Because they are such time-savers, it is worth ensuring that the shortcuts you need are on tools that are visible as you work.

Toolbars in Word, Excel, Access, and PowerPoint can be customized. You can show multiple toolbars, choose where on the screen they will be displayed on-screen, and change the buttons that appear on them.

NOTE: Schedule+ also has a toolbar, but your only option is to display or hide it; you cannot customize it. When you are using Binder applications, you can use and move toolbars, but you cannot modify them. The remaining discussion refers to toolbars in Word, Excel, Access, and PowerPoint.

Binder applications are discussed in Chapter 23.

Displaying Toolbars

When you first open Word, Excel, Access, or PowerPoint, you will see one or two toolbars by default. You can easily hide the default toolbars, display others in their place, or display as many toolbars on the screen as you want. Be careful, however: your editing window can become so cluttered with toolbar buttons that you won't easily find the one you need—defeating the role of the toolbars, which is to provide a quick shortcut to often-used features. In addition, the editing window becomes smaller so you see less of the file you're working on.

To display toolbars:

1. Right-click on any visible toolbar. You will see a shortcut menu, like the Word menu shown here:

CAUTION: Left-clicking on a toolbar activates the button on which your pointer is resting. Be sure to right-click on the toolbar to display the shortcut menu.

Figure 22-1.
You can also toggle the display of toolbars using the Toolbars dialog box

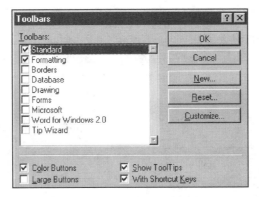

2. Click on any toolbar that has a check mark to remove the check mark and hide the toolbar.

3. Click on any toolbar without a check mark to make it visible.

If no toolbar is visible, you can display a toolbar in a different way:

1. Choose View, Toolbars. You will see the Toolbars dialog box shown in Figure 22-1.

2. Check or uncheck toolbars to determine whether or not they will be displayed.

Although using the Toolbars dialog box is less efficient, it is the only way to make toolbars visible if there are none appearing on the screen.

Moving Toolbars

Toolbars can appear above, below, to the right, or to the left of the main editing window, or as a free-floating toolbar, as shown in Figure 22-2.

> **NOTE:** If a toolbar has a button that includes a text box, like the Font button on the formatting toolbar, you cannot move it to the right or left of the screen in Excel. In Word and PowerPoint, any toolbar can be moved to the right and left of the screen. Buttons with text boxes appear as regular buttons; when you click them they open a dialog box allowing you to choose options.

PART VII APPLICATION ISSUES

Figure 22-2.
Toolbars can be moved to any edge of the editing window, as well as being free-floating toolbars

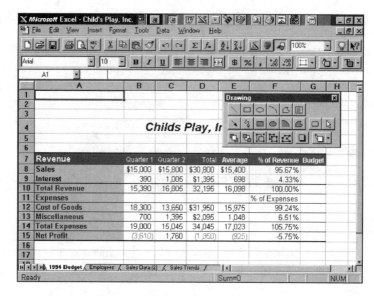

To move a toolbar:

1. Position your mouse pointer in the toolbar but not directly on a button: point to an area between the buttons, above the buttons, or below them.

2. Click and drag the toolbar. It will move as you drag with the mouse.

3. Move the toolbar toward an edge of the editing window. It assumes the appropriate vertical or horizontal shape and "sticks" to the edge of the window. Microsoft refers to this as "docking" the toolbar.

4. Alternatively, move it to the middle of the editing window to create a floating toolbar.

5. Resize a floating toolbar by dragging on its edge or corner, as you would any other window.

Managing Toolbars

To make full use of your toolbars, you will want to put buttons on them for the features you use most and specify how they should appear in the application. You may even want to create new toolbars for specific tasks.

Adding, Removing, and Moving Buttons

You can add buttons to any toolbar for a range of specific functions within Office 95 applications. To do so, follow these steps:

1. Ensure that the toolbar to which you wish to add a button is visible.

2. Right-click on the toolbar, and choose Customize. The Customize dialog box will appear, as shown in Figure 22-3. The categories on the left resemble the menu structure, although they are slightly different.

NOTE: Word and Excel call this the Customize dialog box. PowerPoint and Access call this the Customize Toolbar dialog box.

3. Click on the desired category and notice that a range of buttons appears in the Buttons area.

4. Click on a button to see its description appear at the bottom of the dialog box.

5. To add a button to a toolbar, drag the button from the dialog box to the desired toolbar.

Figure 22-3.
You can add buttons
to any visible toolbar

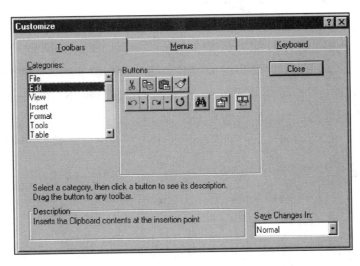

6. To remove a button from the toolbar, merely drag it from the toolbar to the main editing window when the Customize dialog box is visible.

7. To move a button from one location on a toolbar to another, drag it from its original location to its destination.

Changing the Appearance of a Toolbar

You can change the appearance of the toolbars in three ways: specifying whether they should appear in color, the size of the buttons, and whether you wish to see ToolTips appear when you point to a button.

To customize a toolbar's appearance:

1. Right-click on any visible toolbar, then choose Toolbars. The Toolbars dialog box will appear.

2. Choose Color Toolbars to specify whether the little color elements that some buttons have should display in color or not.

3. Select Large Buttons to specify that large buttons be displayed. Unless you have problems seeing the ordinary ones, don't select this. You won't be able to see as many buttons on the screen, and some of the buttons on the standard toolbars won't be visible.

4. Select Show ToolTips to display the little yellow help prompt that pops up when you hold your mouse pointer on a tool for a few seconds.

5. Choose OK. Your preferences become permanent settings, until you change them by repeating this procedure.

You can also change the graphic image that appears on a toolbar button:

1. Display the toolbar containing the button whose image you want to edit.

2. Right-click on a toolbar and choose Customize from the shortcut menu.

3. Right-click on the toolbar button that you want to edit.

4. Choose Edit Button Image from the shortcut menu. You will see the Button Editor dialog box shown in Figure 22-4.

5. You can now edit the individual pixels that make up the button's image:

PART VII APPLICATION ISSUES

Figure 22-4.
You can edit the graphic image that appears on a button

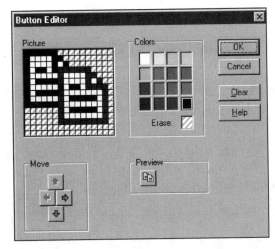

- Click on the color you wish to use, then click in the image to add pixels of that color.
- Click on the Erase button, then click in the image to erase pixels.
- If you cannot see the entire image in the Picture window, click on one of the four Move buttons to see hidden parts of the image.
- You can see how the button looks in its actual size in the Preview window.

Creating and Deleting Toolbars

You can create entirely new toolbars that contain the tools you will use for specific purposes. For instance, you might want to have a toolbar called "Correspondence" in Word that contains only the tools you use in writing letters:

To create a new toolbar:

1. Right-click on any visible toolbar and choose Toolbars. You will see the Toolbars dialog box.

2. Click <u>N</u>ew. The New Toolbar dialog box will appear:

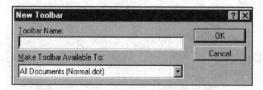

3. Give the new toolbar a descriptive name and click OK. The new toolbar you've created is a small floating toolbar that looks something like a button:

You'll also see the Customize dialog box.

4. Add buttons to the new toolbar as described above.

> **TIP:** You can delete a customized toolbar from the Toolbars dialog box by highlighting it and clicking the <u>D</u>elete button. (You cannot delete the default toolbars, however.)

Working with Shortcut Bars

The Shortcut Bar that you have been using to open Office 95 applications is actually a special type of toolbar. Many of the procedures you have learned for modifying toolbars also work with Shortcut Bars, although some procedures are slightly different.

Although we usually speak of *the* Shortcut Bar, there are actually several Shortcut Bars, just as there are several toolbars in Word, Excel, Access, and PowerPoint. Unlike regular toolbars, however, only one Shortcut Bar can be visible at once. The default one—the Office Shortcut Bar—is what we usually refer as the Shortcut Bar.

If you use multiple applications, you may wish to learn how to manage Shortcut Bars, so you can access applications and commonly used files efficiently. You can display them, move them, change their appearance, add and remove buttons from them, and create a new one. You will also learn how to make the Office 95 Shortcut Bar appear automatically when you start Windows, if this doesn't already occur.

Displaying the Shortcut Bar Automatically

When you first open Windows, you may see the Shortcut Bar at the top of the screen. If you don't, this doesn't necessarily mean that it isn't there. It may be in Auto Hide mode, so that it doesn't get in your way when you don't need it. Move the mouse pointer to the top of the screen, then to each of the other three sides. If the Shortcut Bar pops up, it's in Auto Hide mode. You'll learn how to control this attribute below. If it doesn't appear, then Windows is not set to load it automatically.

To have Windows load your Shortcut Bar automatically, place it in the Windows Startup Group:

1. Click on Start and choose Settings, Taskbar. You will see the Taskbar Properties dialog box.

2. Click the Start Menu Programs tab. The dialog box looks like the one in Figure 22-5.

3. Click Add. The Create Shortcut dialog box will become visible.

4. Click Browse to bring up the Browse dialog box.

5. Navigate to the folder containing the Shortcut Bar application—usually \Msoffice\Office. The application you are looking for is named Msoffice, as shown in Figure 22-6.

Figure 22-5.
You can make the Shortcut Bar appear automatically when you start Windows by putting it in the Startup Group

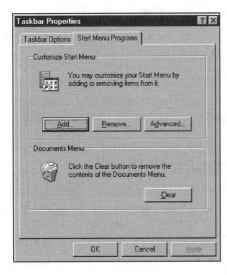

Figure 22-6.
The Shortcut Bar is the application called Msoffice in the \Msoffice\Office folder

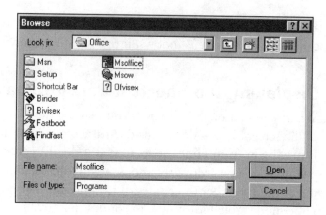

6. Double-click on the Msoffice icon. You'll return to the Create Shortcut dialog box and see the full path and filename of the Shortcut Bar application.

7. Click Next.

8. You are asked to select a folder in which to put the shortcut. Double-click on the \Programs\Startup folder.

9. When asked to give a name for the shortcut, enter a descriptive name such as **Shortcut Bar**.

10. Click Finish. When you start Windows the next time, the Shortcut Bar will appear.

Moving Shortcut Bars

The Shortcut Bar can appear above, below, to the right, or to the left of the main editing window—even as a free-floating toolbar, as shown in Figure 22-7.

Moving your Shortcut Bar is exactly the same as moving any other toolbar. The procedures for doing this is detailed earlier in the chapter.

Managing Shortcut Bars

To make full use of Shortcut Bars, put buttons on them for the features you use most and specify how they should appear on your desktop.

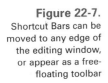

Figure 22-7.
Shortcut Bars can be moved to any edge of the editing window, or appear as a free-floating toolbar

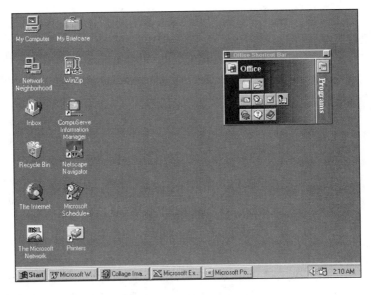

Adding, Removing, and Moving Buttons

Once you've set your display options, specify which buttons appear on the Shortcut Bar. You can easily add buttons to a Shortcut Bar as follows:

1. Right-click on the Shortcut Bar icon at the left of the Shortcut Bar, then choose Customize and click the Buttons tab, as in Figure 22-8.

Figure 22-8.
The Customize dialog box allows you to add buttons to a Shortcut Bar

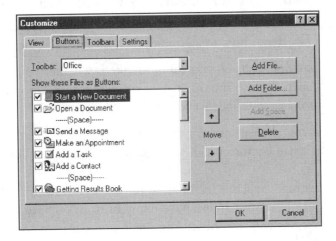

PART VII APPLICATION ISSUES

2. Check or uncheck buttons to add or delete them from the Shortcut Bar. Buttons can do several different things:

   • **Open an Office 95 application.** When the Office toolbar is selected, you can select any of the Office 95 application to be included on the Shortcut Bar.

   • **Perform an Office 95 task.** You can also perform selected Office 95 tasks, such as adding a contact, appointment, or task by selecting the appropriate icon.

   • **Open a file.** You can add a non-Office 95 program by choosing <u>A</u>dd File, navigating to the desired file, and double-clicking on it. You can even add a data file, and the Shortcut Bar will open that file in its appropriate application.

   • **Open a folder.** A shortcut button can open a folder, such as the Control Panel. You can also open a folder containing data files. Double-clicking on such a file will open the appropriate application.

3. To remove a button from the Shortcut Bar, remove the check mark from the appropriate icon in the Customize dialog box.

4. To move a button from one location on a Shortcut Bar to another, highlight it, then click one of the Move buttons. You can also add a space before the button by highlighting the icon in the Customize dialog box and selecting <u>A</u>dd Space.

Changing the Appearance of a Shortcut Bar

There are a variety of display options you can set for Shortcut Bars. They determine, to a large degree, how your Windows desktop looks.

The first decision you should make is whether you want the Shortcut Bar to fit onto the title bar of the active application or be a separate toolbar that appears over or above the application window.

If you choose Auto Fit to Title Bar Area, the Shortcut Bar will appear as small buttons on the title bar of the active application, as shown in Figure 22-9. This is convenient if you only have a few buttons, because the icons for other applications are always visible, small, and out of the way. If you have many buttons on your Shortcut Bar, these buttons will start obscuring the document name on the title bar and make the screen look cluttered.

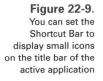

Figure 22-9.
You can set the Shortcut Bar to display small icons on the title bar of the active application

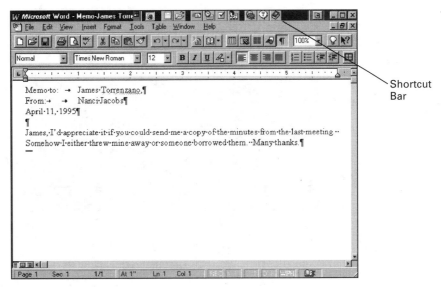

Shortcut Bar

An excellent option if you are not using the Auto Fit feature is to use the Auto <u>H</u>ide option. This option makes the Shortcut Bar disappear a second or two after you are no longer pointing at it. It reappears as soon as you move the mouse pointer towards the edge of the screen where the Shortcut Bar is located.

The only problem with this approach is that no matter which edge of the screen you keep the Shortcut Bar, there are reasons that you will need to bring the mouse near that edge. For instance, if the Shortcut Bar is at the top of the screen, you may inadvertently pop it up when you attempt to click the minimize button. With practice, however, you'll find yourself doing this less and less, and it isn't too much of a problem.

If you don't use the Auto Hide option, the Shortcut Bar will be a toolbar above the title bar of the active application. Even when the application is maximized, the toolbar won't extend to the top of the screen, as shown in Figure 22-10. This can be problematic since it makes the editing window that much smaller, which many users do not like.

Figure 22-10.
When you keep the Shortcut Bar on top, it appears above the title bar of the active application

PART VII APPLICATION ISSUES

Figure 22-11.
The Customize
dialog box allows
you to set Shortcut
Bar appearance
attributes

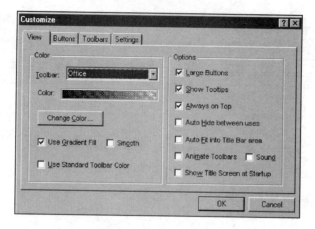

To customize your Shortcut Bar:

1. Right-click on the Shortcut Bar icon at the left of the Shortcut Bar and choose Customize.

2. Click the View tab. You will see the Customize dialog box shown in Figure 22-11.

3. If you wish your buttons to appear on the Title Bar of the application, choose Auto Fit into Title Bar Area. Large Buttons will become unchecked (even if it was checked), and the Auto Hide Between Uses option will become unavailable.

4. Deselect the Show Title Screen at Startup option to prevent the display of the Microsoft logo at startup. Unless you are particularly enamored by looking at advertisements for Microsoft, you will probably want to uncheck this option.

5. Select Change Color to specify the color of the toolbar. This option is only relevant when you are using large tools. You can pick a different color for each toolbar to help you quickly identify it, and use a gradient fill or a solid fill for the Shortcut Bar.

6. Choose Show Tooltips to display the small yellow prompts when you rest the mouse pointer on a button. There's no reason not to have this checked; it can be helpful as you put more and more tools on the Shortcut Bars.

Using Multiple Shortcut Bars

You can use several Shortcut Bars, although you can only display one of them at a time. A useful way to use several Shortcut Bars is to have all your Office 95 applications on one Shortcut Bar, along with non-Office 95 applications you use frequently. Have another Shortcut Bar for Control Panel functions. A third Shortcut Bar can contain files you frequently access. A final one can have personal applications you use less frequently, but want to be able to access with the convenience of a Shortcut Bar.

To activate additional Shortcut Bars:

1. Right-click the Shortcut Bar button, then choose Customize and click the Toolbars tab. You will see the Toolbars tab shown in Figure 22-12.

2. Put a check mark by all the Shortcut Bars that you intend to use.

When several Shortcut Bars are active, you will see icons for each of them at the right and/or left side of the toolbar. Clicking on any of the specific Shortcut Bar icons activates the selected toolbar, as shown in Figure 22-13.

Figure 22-12.
The Toolbars tab allows you to activate multiple toolbars

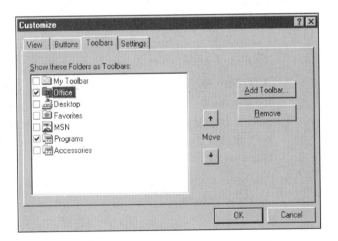

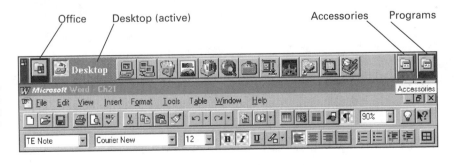

Figure 22-13.
You can switch from one Shortcut Bar to another by clicking on the different Shortcut Bar icons

Creating and Deleting Shortcut Bars

To create a new Shortcut Bar, use this procedure:

1. Right-click the Shortcut Bar button, choose Customize, and click the Toolbars tab.

2. Click the Add Toolbar button. You will see the Add Toolbar dialog box shown in Figure 22-14.

3. Create a blank Shortcut Bar by choosing Create a New, Blank Toolbar Called, then entering the new Shortcut Bar's name.

4. Alternatively, choose Make Toolbar For This Folder and specify the name of the folder, or use the Browse button to select a folder. If you choose this option, the files and programs in it will appear as button options, and you can select any or all of them to be added to the Shortcut Bar.

5. Add and remove buttons to the new Shortcut Bar, as described above.

CHAPTER 23

USING THE OFFICE 95 BINDER

IN THIS CHAPTER

- Introducing the Microsoft Binder
- Making a Binder
- Using Binders
- Using Binder Templates

Computers offer new and wonderful ways to be unorganized. Not only can we lose important papers in our filing cabinets, but we can lose them in our computers, too! The problem becomes even more pronounced when we work on a project that involves several files. For instance, a divisional report may be based on four branch spreadsheets, the division spreadsheet, the PowerPoint briefing, and the report itself written in Word.

There's nothing worse than taking work home or on the road, and realizing that you've forgotten one essential file!

To help solve this problem, Office 95 includes an application called Microsoft Binder. You can think of Binder as an electronic three-ring binder in which you store all your related files, including Word documents, Excel worksheets or charts, or PowerPoint presentations.

Introducing the Microsoft Binder

The term for a document, worksheet, chart or presentation in a binder is a *section*. Thus, if a binder has three sections, this means that it has three Word documents, Excel spreadsheets/charts, and/or PowerPoint presentations in it. Technically, a binder can not contain a Word "file," since a binder is saved as a single file, no matter how many sections it has.

Looking at the Binder Window

The Binder is more than a storage device, however. The Binder displays a modified version of Word, Excel, or PowerPoint, depending on what section is active, as you can see in Figure 23-1.

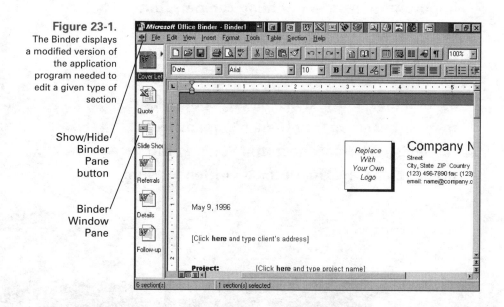

Figure 23-1.
The Binder displays a modified version of the application program needed to edit a given type of section

Show/Hide Binder Pane button

Binder Window Pane

When you use the Binder to organize your work, you never have to open an application. The Binder does it for you, opening applications as they are needed. There are four differences between the normal version of the application and the Section Application that Binder opens for you:

- The Title Bar of the Binder application window says Microsoft Binder, rather than Microsoft Word, Excel, or PowerPoint.
- There is a section of the editing window called the Binder Window Pane that shows icons for sections in the Binder.
- A Show/Hide Binder Pane button replaces the Word, Excel, or PowerPoint control button to the left of the File menu. This button toggles the display of the Binder Window Pane.
- There is a new menu item—the Section menu—to the left of the Help menu item.

Learn more about Word, Excel, and PowerPoint templates in Chapters 5, 13, and 14.

The Binder offers additional functionality as well. You can create Word, Excel, and PowerPoint templates and save them in your Binder as a Binder template. All new Binders are based on templates, just as new Word, Excel and PowerPoint files are. You will usually use a blank Binder template. However, you can automate the preparation of documents related to repetitive projects by creating Binder templates.

You can also use binders effectively in work groups. Binders saved in shared directories can be accessed by many people simultaneously. Several people can even work on a Binder away from the office simultaneously.

Determining Whether to Use a Binder

A binder may or may not be right for you, depending on your needs. Advantages of using a binder include the following:

- All related documents are kept together in one large file. You cannot inadvertently lose one or leave it behind.
- You can store all the documents related to any project in one file to archive them together.
- Using a Binder makes it easy to transfer documents to your briefcase or a shared folder for group access.
- Binders can be saved as templates, so that users can easily open all the needed files for their projects.

- When you use a binder, you don't have to think about the application you're using and can concentrate on your work, instead.

On the other hand, a Binder has certain characteristics and limitations that may not suit your work style. These include:

- Only certain types of files can go into Binders. These include Word documents, Excel worksheets and charts, and Power-Point presentations or graphics. If you are using other types of files, you're out of luck.

- A binder does not integrate with the In Box folders to provide one spot where everything related to a project can be stored, including e-mail, incoming faxes, and the like.

- If you have lots of documents, selecting them from a single row of large icons on the left of the screen may be less convenient than using the Open dialog box.

- If a document is stored as a section of a binder, it will not appear in the list of files when you use Explorer or Open File dialog boxes.

- Many people are more used to performing application-oriented work, i.e., starting a program, then opening the appropriate file.

So which one's for you? You might pick a trial project—something you are doing that uses files from two or more applications, and uses less than six files. Try using the binder and see how it works. If you don't like it, you can always unbind the sections and save them as stand-alone files again!

Creating a Binder

It's easy to create a Binder to store related files. You merely need to create the new Binder, add or create the sections that should go in it, and save the file.

Creating a Binder File

To create and save a new Binder file, do the following:

1. Click the Binder button on the Programs Shortcut Bar. By

CAUTION: Usually, you can start the Binder when other applications such as Word, Excel, or PowerPoint are open. Occasionally, however, if you are in a dialog box in the other application, you will see an error message when you open a Binder that uses that application. The application will terminate, and you may lose data.

TIP: Alternatively, you can start the Binder by choosing Start from the Task Bar, then choosing Programs, Microsoft Binder.

default, you are in a new, blank binder that contains no sections (files), as shown in Figure 23-2.

2. Add new sections to it or retrieve documents into it as described below.

3. Save the Binder by choosing File, Save Binder. The Save Binder As dialog box shown in Figure 23-3 will become visible.

4. Navigate to the folder of your choice, give the Binder a name, and click Save. All the associated Word documents, Excel

Figure 23-2.
When you click the Binder button you are taken to a new, empty Binder

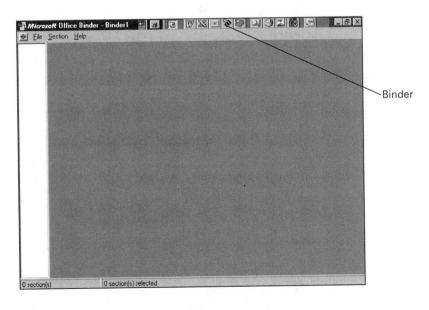

Binder

PART VII   APPLICATION ISSUES

Figure 23-3.
When you save your Binder, all associated documents, worksheets and presentations are saved together in one file

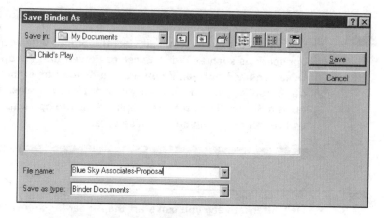

Figure 23-4.
You can add new Excel, PowerPoint, or Word files as sections of the Binder

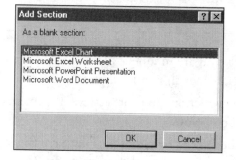

worksheets, and PowerPoint presentations are saved together in one file.

Adding Sections to the Binder

Once you've created a new Binder, you will want to add sections to it. There are two basic ways to do this: create a new section, or incorporate an existing Word, Excel, or PowerPoint file into your Binder.

Creating a New Binder Section

To create a new, blank section of your Binder, do the following:

1. Choose Section, Add. The Add Section dialog box shown in Figure 23-4 will appear.

2. Select the type of section you wish to add. Binders can contain any or all of four different types of files: Excel worksheets, Excel charts, PowerPoint presentations, and Word documents.

3. Choose OK. You will see a new file in the special version of the application you choose—the Binder Application.

Including an Existing File in a Binder

Often, you will create a Binder after the fact. You may already have several related files when you decide to make a Binder to keep them together. In this case, you will want to include existing files in a Binder.

To do so:

1. In Microsoft Binder, choose Section, Add from File. You will see the Add from File dialog box.

2. Navigate to the appropriate folder, then double-click on the file you wish to add. You will see the icon for the selected file at the left of the Binder Application window, as shown in Figure 23-5. The names that appear under the icons are the names of the sections; they used to be the filenames.

It's vital to understand exactly where these imported files exist and how they are saved, so that you won't inadvertently lose your work.

When you include an existing file in a binder, the information exists in two places. It is still there on your disk as a stand-alone file. It is also in the Binder as part of the Binder file. Thus, if the file Worksheet1 is

Figure 23-5.
Icons for files which are included in the Binder appear at the left of the Binder Application editing window

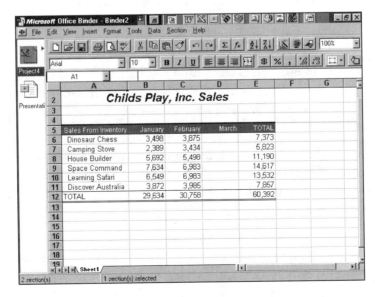

imported into Binder1, when you save it, the worksheet exists both as Worksheet1 and as part of the Binder1 file. It is not the case that the file exists in just one place, with a link pointing to it from the Binder.

The reason this is so important is that you can easily work on both versions accidentally, depending on how you open them. If you open Excel and look in your folders, you will see Excel worksheets, including Worksheet1. You will not see Binder1 (which includes a copy of Worksheet1).

Similarly, if you open your Binder and choose File, Open Binder you will see only Binder files such as Binder1 (which includes Worksheet1), and you will not notice a stand-alone Worksheet1.

Thus, it is very easy to accidentally work on two different versions of a worksheet or other Binder document. The usual solution is to make a practice of only keeping a file in one place. If you include it in a Binder, you may wish to delete it from the disk.

> File management tasks are described in Chapter 21.

Using Binders

To use Binders, you need to know how to open and close them, switch between sections, and use the special features of the Binder Applications. You will also want to be able to unbind sections from your Binder on occasion, to save them as stand-alone documents.

Opening and Closing Binders

To open an existing binder, start Binder and choose File, Open Binder. The Open Binder dialog box shown in Figure 23-6 will appear. The only files that will be listed are Binder files. Navigate to the appropriate folder, then double-click on the Binder you wish to open.

You can close the Binder by choosing File, Close. Closing the Binder file also closes the Binder application. Similarly, if you have a Binder open, and choose File, New Binder or File, Open Binder, it opens a second copy of the Binder program.

Thus, the Binder operates differently than other Office 95 applications. In Word, Excel, and PowerPoint, you can open multiple documents and switch between them with the Windows menu (or by pressing Ctrl + Tab). You can close a document and the application

Figure 23-6.
The Open Binder
dialog box displays
all the Binders you
have saved

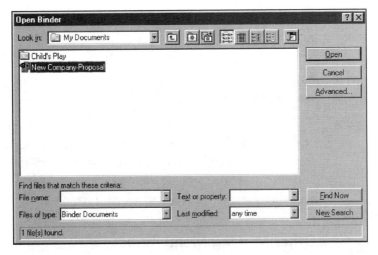

stays open. The Binder application can only have one Binder file open
at once.

Switching between Binder Sections

As you work, you may sometimes want to see the icons representing
all sections in the binder. Other times, you will prefer to have a wider
editing window.

To switch between binder sections:

1. Display the binder Window Pane.
2. Use the binder section scroll bars until the section you wish to
   see is displayed.
3. Click on the desired section.

TIP: If you can't see the entire name of a section, rest the
mouse pointer on the name until it expands.

Using Binder Applications

You will use the Binder version of Excel, PowerPoint, and Word
exactly as you do their stand-alone counterparts, with a few
exceptions.

The Missing Window Menu

Normally, you can open several different files in Excel, PowerPoint, or Word, and switch between open files using the Window menu. Binder applications do not have the Window menu choice, and you can only have one file open in the Binder application.

This is not really a shortcoming, however, since you can still have several Word documents in the same Binder. Instead of being multiple files within Word, they are multiple sections in the Binder. To use another Word document, merely display the Binder Window Pane, and click on the appropriate Word section.

Other Missing Menu Items

Similarly, on the File menu, you won't find entries for New or Open. The File refers to the Binder file—not the Word document. Thus, on the File menu, you will see options for New Binder and Open Binder—which operate on the entire Binder file as a whole. Similarly, there is no option to save your Word document in the File menu.

A Word document in a Binder is a *section*. Thus, to create a new Word document, include an existing one, or save the Word document along, you use the Section menu, not the File menu.

The Section Menu

The Section menu shown in Figure 23-7 allows you to perform the file-management operations on individual sections that are usually found in the File menu.

You can create new sections, open existing stand-alone documents into the Binder as new sections, delete sections, rename sections, duplicate sections, or even rearrange sections using this menu.

Note that the Print command exists on both the File and Section menus. File, Print Section allows you to print any or all sections at once; Section, Print is used to print the active section.

Unbinding Sections

You can also unbind a section, and save it as a stand-alone file:

1. Open the section to be saved.

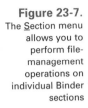

Figure 23-7.
The Section menu allows you to perform file-management operations on individual Binder sections

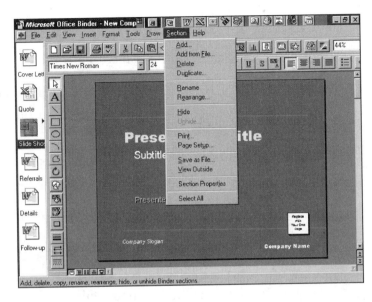

2. Choose Section, Save as File. You will see the File Save dialog box shown in Figure 23-8. Note that the file type is no longer a Binder file, but an application file, and that the default name references the Binder file name.

CAUTION: Unbinding a file saves a copy of it in a stand-alone file. It also exists in the Binder. Be careful that you don't inadvertently work on multiple copies of the same file. You should *seriously* consider deleting the Binder section after you save it to a stand-alone file.

Figure 23-8.
You can unbind a section and save it as a stand-alone file

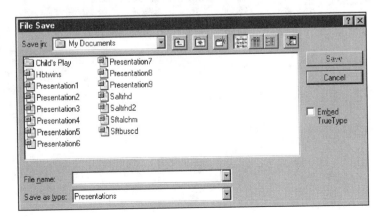

Using Binder Templates

A Binder template is like any other Binder file. It can contain various sections based on different applications. The only difference is when you open it, it opens as an unnamed Binder. Binder templates are used to quickly provide you with the skeleton of documents needed to perform common tasks, such as creating a letter or an invoice.

Office 95 comes with several Binder templates that can be used for template ideas. You will also want to be able to make your own Binder templates.

Using Existing Binder Templates

To use an existing Binder template, do the following:

1. In Microsoft Binder, choose File, New Binder. The New Binder dialog box will become visible.

2. Click the Binders tab to see the Binder templates shipped with Office 95. You will see the New Binder dialog box shown in Figure 23-9.

3. Double-click on the template you wish to use.

You can experiment with the templates in the Binder folder. For instance, the Client Billing Wizard creates an invoice, cover letter, and other documents, while the other templates provide the skeletons of

Figure 23-9.
Office 95 ships with several predefined Binder templates

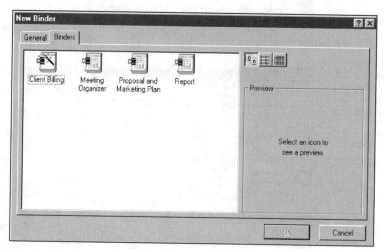

documents that are useful for organizing meetings, making a proposal and marketing plan, and creating a report.

Creating New Binder Templates

The good news is that you can use one of the existing Binder templates, customize it for your own use, then save the customized Binder file back as a Binder Template yourself. Alternatively, you can create entirely new Binder Templates.

To create a Binder template:

1. Open an existing Binder or create a new Binder—either using the Blank Binder template or one of the other Binder templates shipped with Office.

2. Add sections to the Binder as needed. Keep in mind that you are creating a framework for another document.

3. Include *boilerplate* text in your Word documents. This is prewritten text that should appear every time the template is used.

4. Create worksheets that have appropriate headings and formulas, but allow users to enter data.

5. When you are finished, choose File, Save Binder As. You will see the Save Binder As dialog box.

6. Choose Binder Templates in the Save as Type box. Notice that the active folder switches automatically to the Templates folder.

7. Double-click on the Binders icon to move to the Binders subfolder.

8. Give your new Binder template a name and choose Save. Your new template will appear with the other existing templates in the Binders tab whenever you create a new Binder.

CHAPTER 24

LINKING OFFICE 95 APPLICATIONS

IN THIS CHAPTER

- **Adding Objects to Word Documents**
- **Creating Equations, WordArt, and Organization Charts**
- **Using OfficeLinks**

Now that you're familiar with individual Office 95 programs, you can start leveraging this knowledge by using them together to create powerful, persuasive documents that integrate features from different applications.

The most common way this is done is by incorporating objects—like worksheets, charts, diagrams, and clip art—into a Word document.

Another common task is to use the stand-alone applets (small applications in Office) and Excel add-ins to create objects like equations, organizational charts, and WordArt.

Finally, many Office 95 applications utilize OfficeLinks to enable you to work on the same data in more than one application. For instance, you can publish an Access report in Word, or present Excel data with an Access report.

Adding Objects to Word Documents

Many Office 95 users add worksheets, charts or drawings to their documents.

Other elements that can improve the effectiveness of reports include drawings, diagrams, clip art, equations, and organizational charts. These elements are called *objects*, and can be created by using other Office 95 applications. Existing objects can also be imported from Excel or PowerPoint.

These elements are called objects because they have special properties. When you click on them, black squares called *handles* will appear on their sides, as shown in Figure 24-1. These handles allow you to move and size the object, as discussed later.

Figure 24-1.
Objects have handles allowing you to move and size them

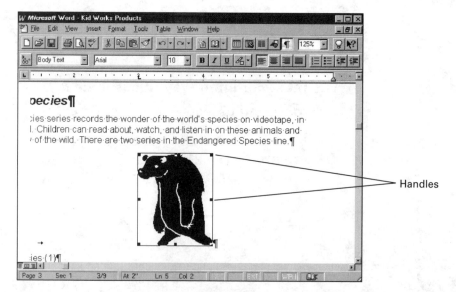

You can create Word objects in a number of ways:

Creating worksheets is discussed in Chapter 8.

- Use Excel to create worksheets for reports
- Charts can be created in Excel, PowerPoint, or directly in Word
- Drawings and diagrams are made using PowerPoint
- Equations, WordArt, and Organization Charts are created using Office applets

Using PowerPoint is discussed in Chapter 14.

The creation of these objects is discussed in the next section.

Creating Objects

You can create objects such as equations and charts in Word or other Office applications by using applets. Applets exist for creating organizational charts, equations WordArt, and possibly other objects depending on how your computer is configured.

To create an object in a Word document:

1. Open the appropriate document in Word.
2. Click at the document position where you wish the object to appear.
3. Choose Insert, Object. You will see the Object dialog box.
4. Select the Create New tab (or option button), if needed. You will see the items that you can access via Word.
5. Double-click on the appropriate item. The item may open inside Word, like the Equation Editor pictured in Figure 24-2. Alternatively, you may see the item open in its own window.
6. Create the object (covered in detail later on).
7. Click on the Word editing window, outside the border of the object. The application will close and you will see the object in the document, similar to the finished equation shown in Figure 24-3.

Excel worksheets are often included in Word documents. For this reason, there is a button on the Standard toolbar to help you create a worksheet in a Word document:

1. Open the appropriate Word document and position the insertion point where you would like the worksheet to appear.

Figure 24-2.
You can create
equations by using
the Equation Editor

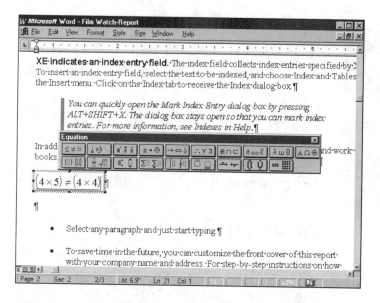

Figure 24-3.
A finished equation
appears in the
document when you
click outside the border
of the equation object

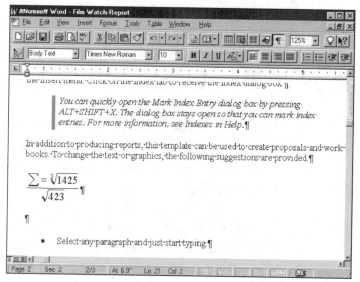

2. Click the Insert Microsoft Excel Worksheet button. You will see a drop-down matrix or grid like the one in Figure 24-4.

3. Drag the mouse pointer to highlight the appropriate number of rows and columns. A small worksheet appears in the Word document and the Word menu items change to Excel menu items, as shown in Figure 24-5.

Figure 24-4.
You can create an
Excel worksheet inside
a Word document

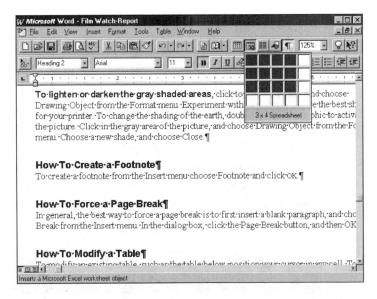

Figure 24-5.
Word's menus change
to Excel menus to help
you create a worksheet
in Word

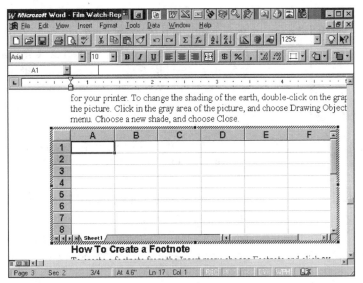

4. Enter the worksheet data using Excel commands, then click
   outside the worksheet boundary to return to Word.

You will be able to use all the functions of the application used to create an object within Word. For instance, if you create an Excel worksheet, you will see the worksheet in a small window in the Word
document, and you can use all the commands you could normally use
in Excel as you create it.

Importing Objects

You can import an existing object such as an Excel worksheet into the report in two ways. You can *embed* the worksheet or *link* it to the report.

Embedding the worksheet is like making a copy of it. If you change the original worksheet in Excel, the copy of it in Word does not change. Linking, on the other hand, is a more dynamic process. It is like putting a pointer to the worksheet in the Word document, rather than importing the worksheet itself. When you change the original worksheet using Excel, it automatically changes in the Word document as well.

When to Embed, Link, or Create Objects

Should you embed or link existing objects such as Excel worksheets in a report, or create them from scratch?

- If you are making a small worksheet with calculations, create it from a new file. By doing this, you will open an Excel window inside Word, and all Excel's functions will be available to you.

- If someone else is creating the Excel worksheet, or if the worksheet is used by other applications such as PowerPoint, create it as a stand-alone document and embed or link it to Word.

- If you are writing a draft report based on data that will change, link it rather than embed it.

- To ensure that the worksheet doesn't get separated from the document (assuming you're not using a binder), embed it rather than link it.

- To ensure that the data doesn't change once it's finalized, embed it rather than link it.

- You can display selected cells of an embedded worksheet, but if the worksheet is linked, you must display the entire worksheet. If you only want to display selected summary cells, you must embed the worksheet.

- If you write frequent reports and use the same table with updated data, link it rather than embed it.

The most common way to import an object is by using the *cut and paste* method. You can import objects from Excel or PowerPoint into Word in this way, or even link text from one Word document to another. For instance, a proposal template could have a link to biographical statements or corporate capability statements, ensuring that every new proposal has the latest statements in it.

To import an object into a Word document, do the following:

1. Open the source application such as Excel or PowerPoint, and select the object to be imported.

2. Choose Edit, Copy to copy the object to the Windows Clipboard.

3. Switch to the Word document and click where the object should appear.

4. Choose Edit, Paste Special. You will see the Paste Special dialog box.

5. To embed the object, click Paste. To link it, click Paste Link. You will have a choice of formats in which to embed or link the object. Unless you are an advanced user, you shouldn't change the default format that Word chooses.

6. Choose OK to embed or link the object.

NOTE: You can also import objects by dragging and dropping them, just as you move or copy text within a Word document. To do so, resize both the Word and the source application window, until you can see both of them on the screen (or tile both windows). Select the object in the source application. To embed it, drag it into the Word window, and drop it where it should go. To link it, hold down the Ctrl key while you drag-and-drop it.

Editing Objects

Once you have brought an object into a Word document, you can delete it, move it, resize it, or edit it. You can do any of these as follows:

1. Select the object by clicking on it. Handles will appear around it.

2. Edit the object as follows:

- To delete the selected object, press the [Del] key.
- To move the selected object, click the mouse inside the object and drag it to its new destination.
- To resize the selected object, drag one of its handles. The object will be resized. Drag a corner handle to maintain the object's proportions.
- To edit an *embedded* object, double-click on it.

When you edit an object, one of two things may happen, depending on the application that created it. First, the application may open in its own window, with the object inside it. You can edit the object using all the features of that application, then choose File, Exit. (Depending on the application, the exit command may be worded slightly differently.) When you exit the source application, the object in the Word document will reflect the editing changes.

Depending on the object source, double-clicking on an embedded object may instead change the Word menu and toolbar to the menu and toolbar of the source application. You still see the surrounding Word text, but you can edit the object in place, since the commands of the source application have replaced the regular Word commands. To finish in-place editing, click anywhere in the Word document outside of the object.

If the object was linked, you should not attempt to edit it in this way. Instead, open the source application, then open the appropriate file and edit it. When you save the file and return to Word, you will see the changes you have made.

Adding Captions

Word allows you to add captions to objects automatically. This is helpful in reports, because you can both reference figures in the text, and create a list of figures for the reader.

To insert captions automatically whenever an object is added to any report, you will want to modify the report template. Alternatively, to insert captions automatically in the current report, modify the report itself.

To modify the template or report to add captions, do the following:

1. Open the template or report to be modified.

2. Choose Insert, Caption. The Caption dialog box shown in Figure 24-6 will appear.

3. By default, there are labels for figures, tables, and equations. To add a new label for a list of exhibits, maps, or diagrams, choose New Label. You will see the New Label dialog box.

4. Type the new label, then click OK to return to the Caption dialog box.

5. When you have made labels for the different types of objects you will use, choose AutoCaption. You will see the AutoCaption dialog box shown in Figure 24-7.

6. Click the file type that you wish to have auto-captioned. Select the appropriate label type in the Use Label text box. Choose OK when you are finished. You'll return to the main editing window.

Whenever you insert an object of the selected type, a caption will be inserted into the document automatically: e.g., "Figure 1." You can add text after the caption that describes the object: e.g., "Figure 1 - Profits for 1995." This text will be included in any list of figures you create.

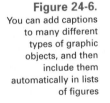

Figure 24-6.
You can add captions to many different types of graphic objects, and then include them automatically in lists of figures

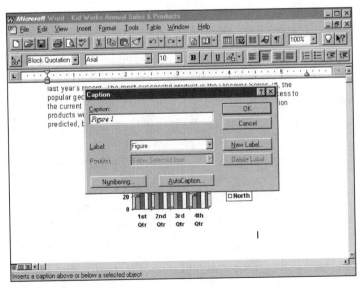

Figure 24-7.
The AutoCaption dialog box allows you to associate different types of objects with different label types

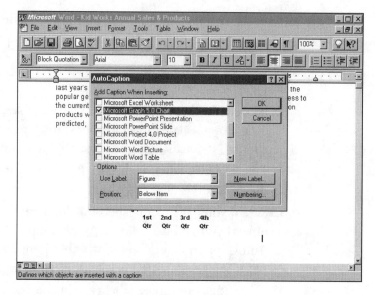

Using Applets to Create Objects

You can create a variety of objects using Office 95 *applets*—small applications that can be run from within Office 95 programs. Applets are provided for creating objects such as equations, WordArt, and organization charts.

Creating Equations

Office 95 makes creating even complex equations into an easily mastered procedure, once you learn a few tricks of the trade. To create an equation, do the following:

1. Open the Word document or PowerPoint slide where you want the equation to appear.

2. Move to the point in the document or presentation where you want the equation to appear.

3. Choose Insert, Object, and select Create New, if is not already selected. The Object dialog box will appear.

4. Double-click on Microsoft Equation 2.0. You will see the appropriate application or applet. The Equation Editor for Word is pictured in Figure 24-8. In PowerPoint, you will see an Equation Editor window that provides equivalent functions.

Figure 24-8.
You can create
equations that open
inside a Word
document by using the
Equation Editor

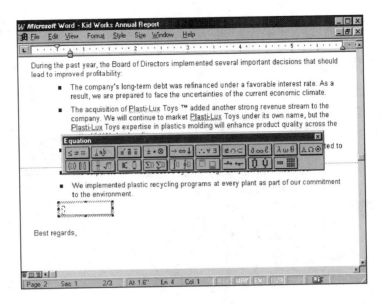

5. Create the equation using these guidelines:

   • Click the toolbar buttons to show drop-down menus of functions and variables.

   • To insert a function such as a square root or division, choose the appropriate function. You will see the function in the equation. Insert the values for the function inside the dashed box that appears with the function, like the one shown in Figure 24-9.

   • Insert functions and groupings such as parentheses before adding values, working from the larger units to the smaller units. For instance, to create the equation in Figure 24-10, first create the largest unit—a division. In the dashed box under the division, create the square root. In the dashed box inside the square root, create the parentheses. Inside the parentheses, you can then type **a+b**. To the right of the parentheses, you can then type *2. In the dashed box above the division, you can then insert the lambda character (L).

6. Finish the equation in Word by clicking in the editing window, outside the border of the object. In PowerPoint, close the Equation Editor window. The applet closes and the object in the document appears, as in the example of the finished equation shown in Figure 24-11.

PART VII   APPLICATION ISSUES

Figure 24-9.
Put values inside the
dashed box that
appears when you
insert a function

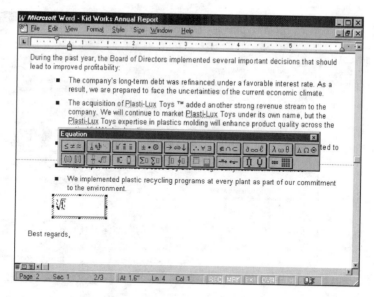

Figure 24-10.
When creating
complex formulas,
insert functions first,
working from the
largest to the
smallest

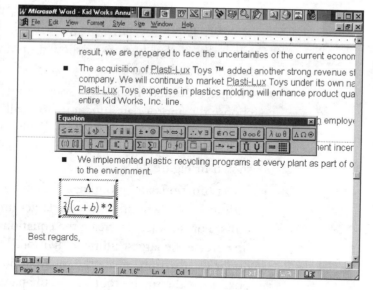

Creating Organizational Charts

You can easily create organizational charts that can be inserted into
Word or PowerPoint documents. To create an organizational chart, do
the following:

1. Open the appropriate Word document or PowerPoint slide.

Figure 24-11.
The finished equation appears in the document when you click outside the border of the equation object

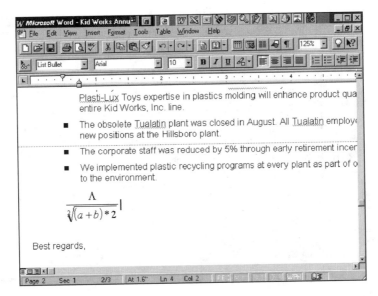

2. Move to the point in the document or presentation where you want the chart to appear.

3. Choose _I_nsert, _O_bject, and select Create _N_ew, if is not already selected. You will see the Object dialog box.

4. Double-click on MS Organization Chart 2.0. The Microsoft Organization Chart window will appear.

5. Create the organizational chart as follows:

   - To insert a name, title, or additional line of information, click on the appropriate box and replace the sample text.

   - To add a subordinate to a position, click the Subordinate button, then click the manager's box to whom the subordinate reports. Add coworkers, managers, and assistants in a similar manner.

   - To delete a box, click it and press Del.

   - To add text to the chart, click the Text button and then click where the text should appear and enter it.

   - To change the box style, select the appropriate boxes by choosing _E_dit, _S_elect, All. Choose _B_oxes, then choose C_o_lor, Shado_w_, _B_order Style, Border Co_l_or, or Border Line St_y_le.

Figure 24-12.
You can create organizational charts using MS Organization Chart 2.0 inside a Word document or PowerPoint slide

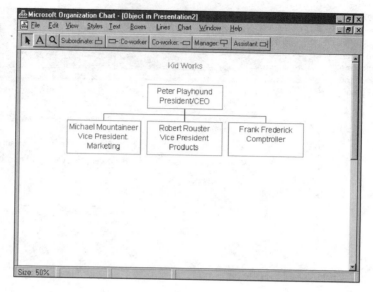

- To change the lines between boxes, select the appropriate lines. Choose Lines, then choose Thickness, Style, or Color.

- Change the style of an organizational chart by choosing Styles, then picking the type of chart from the drop-down menu.

6. When you have finished making an organizational chart (Figure 24-12 shows an example), choose File, Exit. You will be prompted to update the Word document or PowerPoint chart with the new organizational chart.

Using WordArt

You can enhance Word documents or PowerPoint slides with attractive titles and logos, by using WordArt and following these steps:

1. Open the appropriate Word document or PowerPoint slide.

2. Move to the point in the document or presentation where you want the WordArt to appear.

3. Choose Insert, Object and select Create New, if is not already selected. You will see the Object dialog box.

4. Double-click on Microsoft WordArt 2.0. The menu bar will

Figure 24-13.
You can create
WordArt using
Microsoft WordArt
2.0 that opens inside
a Word document or
PowerPoint slide

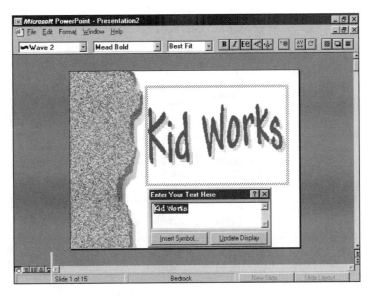

change, followed by a WordArt window similar to the one shown in Figure 24-13.

5. Type the text you wish to use in the WordArt window, then choose Update Display. Your text will appear in the large display window.

6. Choose the font you wish to use from the Font drop-down list.

TIP: WordArt usually looks better with a simple font.

7. Choose the shape you wish to use from the Shape drop-down list.

8. Experiment with the other buttons on the toolbar to change the rotation of letters, their spacing, color, or shadow effects.

9. When you are finished making the WordArt object, click on the Word or PowerPoint editing window, outside of the WordArt box. You will see the WordArt in the document, along with the normal Word or PowerPoint menus.

PART VII APPLICATION ISSUES

Using OfficeLinks

Using Office 95's OfficeLinks technology, you can work with data from one application inside another. You have already been introduced to this type of function in other chapters:

- In Chapter 7, you learned how to bring addresses from Schedule+ into Word documents
- In Chapter 10, you learned how to import Access databases in Excel
- In Chapter 14, you learned how to bring Excel worksheets, Excel charts, and Word documents into PowerPoint presentations

Now, you'll learn three other ways to link Office 95 applications:

- Using Access forms and reports in Excel databases
- Analyzing Access data in Excel
- Publishing Access reports with Word

Creating Access Forms and Reports in Excel Databases

Sometimes, you may prefer to keep a database in Excel, but you need the data validation or other sophisticated features offered by Access. You can satisfy both needs by using Access forms and reports with an Excel database.

Creating Access Forms

To create an Access form for use with an Excel database, do the following:

1. Open the appropriate database in Excel.
2. Choose <u>D</u>ata, <u>A</u>ccess Form. You will see the Create Microsoft Access Form dialog box. Choose to create the form in a <u>N</u>ew database and choose OK.

TIP: You need to be on the header line of the data. If you've skipped lines at the beginning, the Access form can't see the data.

Creating
Access forms
is discussed in
Chapter 20.

3. Access opens, using the Excel database as its data source. You will see the Form Wizard. Create the form as needed. (This process can take a lot of time.)

4. Use the data form to enter the data.

5. Close Access when you are done.

You will see a View Access Form button on the worksheet. This button can be used for future data entry by using the linked Access database.

Creating Access Reports

Creating
Access reports
is discussed in
Chapter 20.

To create an Access report for use with an Excel database, do the following:

1. Open the appropriate database in Excel.

2. Choose Data, Access Report. You will see the Report Wizard.

3. Create the report as desired.

4. Close Access when you are done.

A View Access Report button will appear on the worksheet. This button can be used whenever you wish to preview or print a report using the linked Access database.

Analyzing Access Data in Excel

While Access is a very powerful database, for data analysis, nothing beats Excel. You can easily convert an Access table or query into an Excel worksheet using OfficeLinks, to further analyze data.

To do so, follow these steps:

1. Open the appropriate database in Access.

2. Navigate to the Tables or Reports tab of the Main Window, and highlight the table or report you wish to analyze with Excel.

3. Click the down arrow to the right of the OfficeLinks button and choose Analyze It with MS Excel.

4. Excel opens, and the table or query appears in a new Excel workbook.

5. Perform data analyses on the Excel worksheet. Do not make changes to the data, as these will not be reflected in the Access database.

Publishing Access Reports with Word

Access offers an excellent reporting capability. However, you may wish occasionally to use Word for Access reports. You may want top utilize Word's superior formatting features or when you want to include the Access report in the body or appendix of a longer Word report.

To convert an Access report into a Word document, do the following:

1. Open the appropriate database in Access.

2. Navigate to the Reports tab of the Main Window, and highlight the report you wish to publish in Word.

3. Click the down arrow to the right of the OfficeLinks button and choose Publish It with MS Word.

4. Word opens, and the report appears in a new Word document, as shown in Figure 24-14.

5. Save the document, or cut and paste the information to an existing Word document in which you wish it to appear.

Figure 24-14.
You can publish Access reports as Word documents

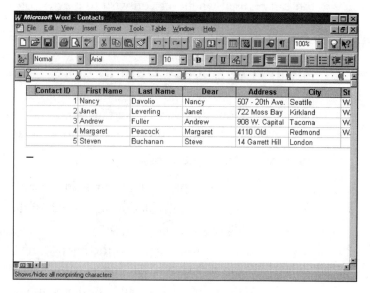

CHAPTER 25

GETTING YOUR MESSAGE OUT

IN THIS CHAPTER

- Conducting a Simple Mail Merge
- Merging from Other Databases
- Selecting Recipients
- Sending E-mail
- Sending Faxes
- Creating Personal Distribution Lists

Old software programs allowed you to broadcast your message to many people by creating a mass mailing using the mail merge feature of a word processor. Office 95 offers more options. Not only can you send a mass mailing, but you can also send faxes, post e-mail, and even publish messages on the Internet.

What's the best way to use Office 95 to send a message? Consider the following options:

- If the appearance of your message is of paramount importance, print it on high-quality paper stock and mail it. A mailing has one other advantage—it is an artifact that can be shared, stored, or posted. The disadvantage of creating a mailing is that it is much more expensive than other forms of document transmittal. Not only is there postage to consider, but the expense of paper and the time required to prepare and send the mailing can add up. Good candidates for mailings include newsletters and schedules that might be seen by more than one person, announcements, invitations, or coupons.

- If the content of the message is more important than its appearance, and you do not need to persuade the audience to pay attention to it, you may wish to use a fax or e-mail transmittal instead of a mailing. The advantages of these methods are that they are fast, cheap, and can be repeated many times with very little effort. The disadvantage to faxes and e-mail messages is that people may pay less attention to them. Good candidates for fax or e-mail transmittals include messages that are tabulated and don't require a response (such as a petition or a letter of support), informative material (sales promotions, for example), or the distribution of intraoffice business information, (such as updates on a project).

- If you wish to broadcast a message then engage the recipient in an on-going dialog, e-mail or Internet publishing are effective methods to send your message. These methods of communicating allow readers to respond to your message and offer the opportunity to create an ongoing relationship with potential customers or clients.

- If you would like to broadcast a message to an unknown but potentially interested audience, consider publishing it on the Internet. The advantage to this method is its relative low cost and wide audience. The disadvantage is that you are not targeting specific recipients, and you don't know who actually reads it. General announcements and resource lists are good candidates for this sort of message.

Electronic publishing is discussed in Chapter 26.

Best of all, you don't need to choose between these solutions. Use all four ways to get your message out!

Case Study: University Sales

Increasingly, universities have recognized the need to sell their services. They can no longer afford to sit back and wait for students to knock on their door.

I recently consulted with a mid-sized university in a major metropolitan area and explained how Office 95 could assist them to broadcast their message. A number of recommendations are currently being implemented—do any of them apply in your organization?

- The university recognized that many prospective students use the Internet and attractive Web pages have been created to sell the university to prospective students. (You'll find out more about using the World Wide Web in Chapter 26.)

- The admissions office maintains a database of prospective students on a mainframe with proprietary software. This database periodically updates departmental databases stored in Access. Department chairs send out a series of personalized and customized mailings to prospective graduate students.

- A fax group is maintained of high school guidance counselors from the 20 high schools that send the most students to the university, as well as an e-mail group for those counselors who have access to e-mail. Announcements of events and speakers that might be of interest to high school students and/or the counselors themselves are routinely posted.

- When new programs are developed, a response is solicited from high school guidance counselors who are on the e-mail list. The university tries very hard to generate dialog with these counselors, who often refer students to the university.

Saying It with a Mailing

Sometimes, nothing but a mailing will do. When this is the case, you should make your best effort to insure that the letter, newsletter, or announcement is as attractive and personal as possible. Word's Mail Merge feature will help you to generate mailings. To be able to use this feature effectively, you need to be able to do several things:

- Conduct a simple mail merge to make a form letter or mailing labels

- Send the message to appropriate people on the mailing list
- Send messages to mailing lists maintained in Schedule+, Excel, Access, or mainframe computers

Conducting a Simple Mail Merge

In Word, performing a mail merge is a three-step:

1. Identify or create a Main Document—a form letter.
2. Identify or create a Data Source—the mailing list for the mail merge.
3. Conduct the merge.

The data source is associated with the main document, so that field names in the data source (e.g., name, address, etc.) can be used in the main document. That's why, as you'll see, you'll go back and forth between the data source and main document during the merge process.

These three steps underlie all the variations of mail merges. To learn them, we'll do two of the most common types of merges: creating form letters and creating mailing labels.

Merging with Form Letters

Let's start by creating a simple form letter and mailing list, and merging them. To create a form letter, do the following:

1. Create a new document, or open a sample letter that you want to convert into the form letter.
2. Choose Tools, Mail Merge. You will see the Mail Merge Helper dialog box shown in Figure 25-1.
3. Choose Create, Form Letters. You are asked if you want to create the form letter in the active window, or in a new window.
4. Choose Active Window, unless you have another document already open in the active window. If the form letter is already open in the active window, Word will convert it into a merge Main Document.

The Mail Merge Helper dialog box remains open, and you are ready for the next step of the mail merge.

Before typing or editing the text of a form letter, you need to create or specify a data file, since you will be using fields from this data file in

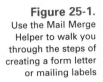

Figure 25-1.
Use the Mail Merge
Helper to walk you
through the steps of
creating a form letter
or mailing labels

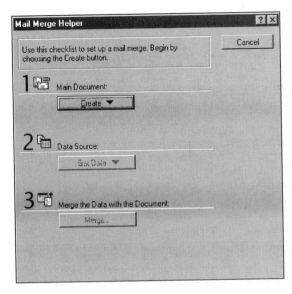

the form letter. When you finish making the form letter, the Mail
Merge Helper is still open, and the prompt at the top of the helper
indicates that the next step is to choose a Data Source. In our first
example, we'll assume you are going to create a data source, rather
than open an existing one. You can do so as follows:

1. From the Mail Merge Helper dialog box, choose Get Data,
   Create Data Source. The Create Data Source dialog box
   shown in Figure 25-2 will appear.

2. Scroll through the field list and remove any fields you don't
   need by highlighting that field and pressing the Remove Field
   Name button.

3. Add any new fields that you do need.

4. If you would prefer to add the data fields in a different order,
   highlight the one to be moved and click the Move Up or
   Down button.

5. Choose OK when you're done. You will see the Save As
   dialog box.

6. Give the data source file a name and choose Save to save it.

When you have finished creating the data source file, you are asked
whether you want to edit the data source or edit the main document.
You can do either first, but we'll edit the data source:

PART VII   APPLICATION ISSUES

Figure 25-2.
Word helps you
create a new mailing
list by listing
common field names
from which you can
choose, or you can
add your own

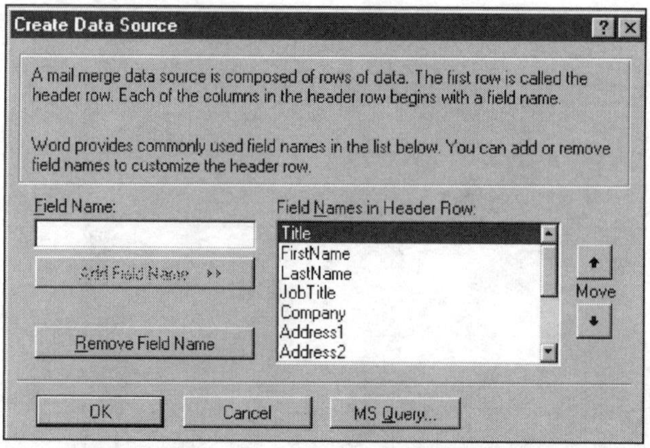

Figure 25-3.
Word's Data Form
allows you to easily
add, edit, or delete
records from the
mailing list

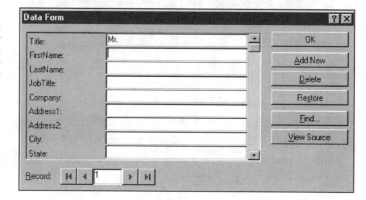

1. Choose Edit Data Source. You will see the Data Form dialog box shown in Figure 25-3.

2. Add records, choosing Add New to add each new record.

3. When you are finished, choose OK. Word takes you directly to the form letter.

When you've finished editing the data source, you return to the form letter. The Mail Merge toolbar is visible to help you write it, as shown in Figure 25-4.

Compose the form letter as follows:

1. Write the text of the letter.

2. Place the insertion point wherever you wish to insert a merge field, and click the Insert Merge Field button. You will see a list of the field names you created.

Figure 25-4.
The Mail Merge
toolbar provides an
easy way to insert
fields in a form letter

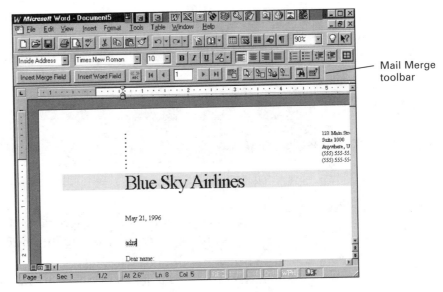

Mail Merge
toolbar

3. Click on the one you wish to insert. For instance, you might type **Dear** with a space after it, then click on Insert Merge Field, then click on the FirstName field, and finally type a colon. What you will see in the form letter is "Dear «FirstName»:"

4. Save the document.

The final step in the process is to merge the form letter with the data file. To do so:

1. From the form letter, click the Mail Merge Helper button. You will see the Mail Merge Helper dialog box.

2. Choose Merge. The Merge dialog box will appear, as shown in Figure 25-5.

3. Choose merge options as follows:

   • Specify the destination of the merge as a new document, the printer, or e-mail recipients.

   • If the records are in sequence, you can specify which records are to be merged by number.

   • You can opt to print blank lines or not. This can be especially useful when some addresses have one line and others have two.

Figure 25-5.
The Merge dialog
box allows you to
select which records
will be merged, and
allows you to skip
blank lines in the
data file

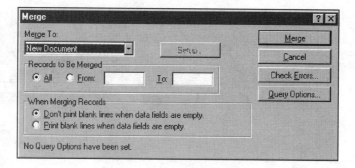

- Set query options to choose specific data file records for the merge based on criteria, as described below.

4. When you're finished selecting options, choose Merge. Word merges the form letter and mailing list and sends the output to the new document or printer, as you specified.

Creating Labels

You can also create mailing labels by using a similar procedure:

1. Create a new document, and choose Tools, Mail Merge. You will see the Mail Merge Helper dialog box.

2. Choose Create, Mailing Labels.

3. You are asked if you want to create the mailing labels in the active window, or in a new window. Choose Active Window.

4. Before creating the mailing labels, you need to create or specify a data file, since you will be using fields from this data file to create the mailing labels. You will see the Mail Merge Helper again, and the prompt at the top of the helper indicates that the next step is to choose a Data Source. Accordingly, choose Get Data, Create Data Source.

5. Scroll through the field list and remove the fields you won't need for the mailing labels. Choose OK when you're done. The Save As dialog box will appear.

6. Give the mailing list a name and choose Save to save it.

7. You are asked whether you want to edit the data source or edit the main document. Choose Edit Data Source.

8. Add records, choosing Add New to add each new record.

9. When you are finished, choose OK. You will return to your blank mailing labels main form, with the Mail Merge toolbar visible.

10. To create the mailing labels, click the Mail Merge Helper button. You will see the Mail Merge Helper dialog box.

11. Choose Setup. You will see the Label Options dialog box shown in Figure 25-6.

12. Pick the type of labels you're using by choosing the correct Label Products, then choosing the Product Number for the labels you are using.

13. Choose OK. The Create Labels dialog box shown in Figure 25-7 will appear.

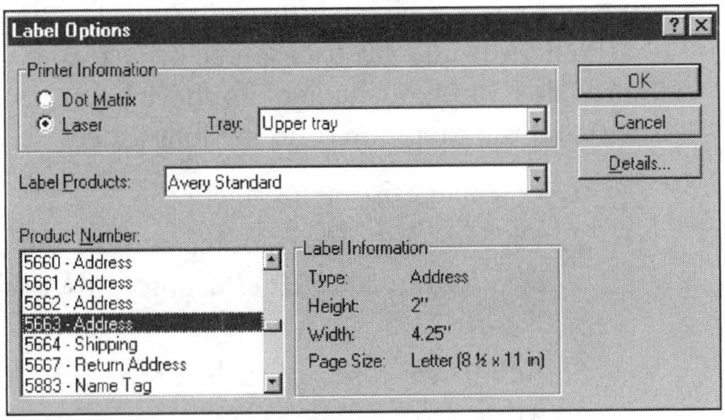

Figure 25-6.
Word will automatically set up paper for the type of labels you specify

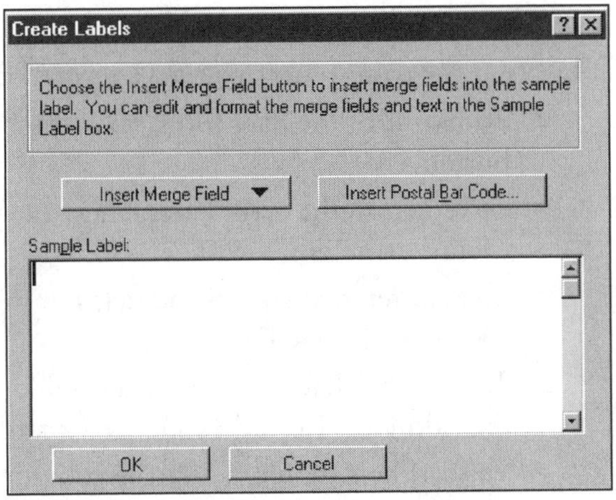

Figure 25-7.
You can insert fields and custom text on each label, along with a USPS Bar Code

14. Choose Insert Merge Field to put merge fields in the label. Add spaces, punctuation, and new lines as needed, along with any text that should go on the label.

15. Choose OK after the fields have been. You will return to the Mail Merge Helper dialog box.

16. Choose Merge to conduct the merge. You will see the Merge dialog box.

17. Set merge options as needed, then choose Merge. Word merges the mailing labels and mailing list, and sends the output to the new document or printer, as specified.

Editing the Data Source

While it's easy to create a merged document when you are creating a new form letter and data source, working with existing form letters and data sources can be a little confusing. The first thing you may need to do is to edit the data source by changing, adding or deleting records after you have made it. To move between a form letter (or labels) and the data source, do the following:

1. Open an existing form letter.

2. Click the Edit Data Source button. You will see the data form used to enter data records, as shown in Figure 25-8.

3. Add new records using the procedure above.

4. Alternatively, to see the data source file, choose View Source. You will see the document with the data source, arranged as a Word table, as shown in Figure 25-9.

5. From the data source, you have several options:

   • To return to the data form, click the Data Form button.

   • To return to the form letter, click the Mail Merge Main Document button.

   • To add, remove, or rename fields in the data source, click the Manage Fields button.

   • To add or delete a record in the Table, click the Add New Record or Delete Record button.

   • To sort the data file, select the column to be sorted by clicking at the top of the column, when the mouse pointer

Figure 25-8.
You can switch between the data form and the data source file to edit the data in a table

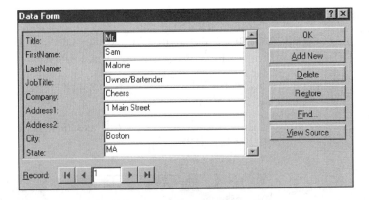

Figure 25-9.
Data sources are maintained in Word tables, and can be directly edited in this mode

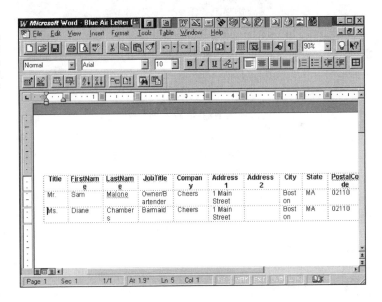

is a black down arrow. Sort the data by clicking the Sort Ascending or Sort Descending button.

Merging from Other Databases

In many offices, address lists are maintained in other applications, then they are brought into Word for mass mailings. You have great flexibility in Word, including the ability to directly merge Word documents with databases maintained in Schedule+, Microsoft Exchange, Excel, and Access. In addition, you can convert a variety of other database formats into Word tables, or merge via text files, as described next.

Merging from the Address Book

If you maintain contacts in a Schedule+ Contact List, you can merge it directly into the Word form letter as follows:

1. Access the Mail Merge Helper and specify the main document as described above.

2. Choose Get Data, Use Address Book. The Use Address Book dialog box will appear:

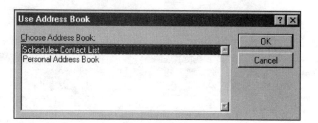

3. Choose to use the Schedule+ Contact List, then choose OK. You may be asked to specify a profile or user name, depending on how Windows is configured. Your address book will then be converted into a Word data source file (e.g., a table).

4. Proceed by setting up or editing the Main Document. You may wish to select specific records from the data source file, as described below. When you are finished, conduct the merge.

> **NOTE:** Since you are creating a Word document containing the address book, future changes you make in Schedule+ or Microsoft Exchange will not be reflected in this data source file. You need to re-create it when it is to be used again.

Merging from Excel

If you maintain a database of contacts in Excel, it is also easy to merge it with a Word document, as follows:

1. Access the Mail Merge Helper and specify the main document as described above.

2. Choose Get Data, Open Data Source. You will see the Open Data Source dialog box shown in Figure 25-10.

Figure 25-10.
You can directly merge with Excel worksheets by specifying them from the Open Data Source dialog box

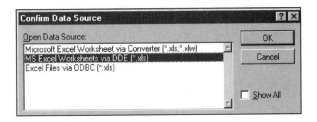

3. Make sure that Select Method is checked. In the Files of Type drop-down list, choose MS Excel Worksheets.

4. Double-click on the Excel workbook you wish to use. You will see the Confirm Data Source dialog box shown here:

5. Choose Microsoft Excel Worksheet via Converter. This method is much quicker than the DDE method, since Office does not need to open Excel. Moreover, you can import any sheet in the workbook using this method. If you have not loaded this converter, however, you will need to choose MS Excel Worksheets via DDE (Dynamic Data Exchange).

Loading Office 95 components is discussed in Chapter 1.

The Excel database will be linked to Word, and you can edit the main document and insert appropriate fields from the Excel database, then conduct the merge as described previously.

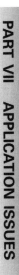

PART VII APPLICATION ISSUES

Merging from Access

Merging from an Access table is just as easy as merging from an Excel workbook, and follows much the same procedure:

1. Access the Mail Merge Helper and specify the main document as described above.

2. Choose Get Data, Open Data Source. The Open Data Source dialog box will appear.

3. Make sure that Select Method is checked.

4. In the Files of Type drop-down list, choose MS Access Databases, then double-click on the Access database you wish to use. You will see the Confirm Data Source dialog box shown here:

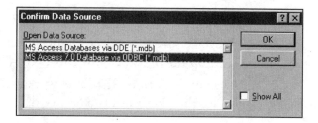

5. Choose MS Access 7.0 Database via ODBC (Open Database Connectivity) if it is available. This is much quicker than the DDE method, since you do not need to open Access.

6. You will see the Choose Access Tables dialog box. Double-click on the appropriate table or query.

The Access database will be linked to Word, and you can edit the main document and insert appropriate fields from the Access database, then conduct the merge as usual.

NOTE: Word also supports Paradox, dBASE, and FoxPro database formats. Use the method above to utilize files from these applications as the data source.

Merging from the Mainframe

You may occasionally need to merge data from another data source, such as a mainframe database, or another database not supported by Word. This is a simple procedure, as long as the other database can provide its data in a comma separated value (CSV) format, such as:

"John Appleby","242-9990","PFC"

"Shirley McCann","294-9490","LtCol"

To perform a merge with a file such as this, ask your database administrators to provide you a file in a CSV format, then merge with it as follows:

1. Access the Mail Merge Helper and specify the main document as described above.

2. Choose Get Data, Open Data Source. The Open Data Source dialog box will appear, as shown in Figure 25-11.

3. Choose Select Method.

4. In the Files of Type drop-down list, choose Text Files, then double-click on the file you wish to use. You will see the Confirm Data Source box shown here:

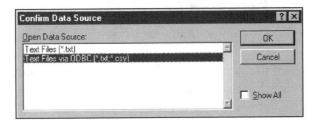

5. Select Text Files (*.txt) as the data source type, then choose OK. After a few moments, the CSV file will be opened and linked to the Word document.

You can edit the main document and insert appropriate fields from the CSV file, then conduct the merge as usual.

There are two common problems, however, when importing a CSV file:

- There is no header row, and the first row of data is used for field names

Figure 25-11.
To merge a CSV file,
be sure to click on
Select Method

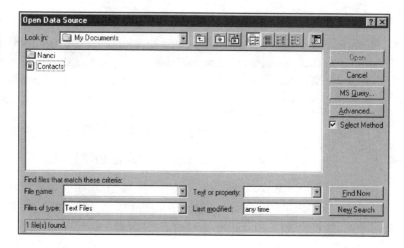

• The other database may "lump" desired fields together into one: for instance, first and last name

The easiest way to fix these problems is to import the CSV file into Excel and modify it there, then save the resulting file as an Excel workbook.

Selecting Recipients

One of the best ways to conduct a mailing is to use an existing database. When you do this, however, there will often be more names in the resulting data file than you need, and you will need to select specific records for the. Moreover, you may with to sort the records— either by last name or by ZIP code.

Sorting Records

To sort records as you merge them, do the following:

1. Create the form letter and specify the data file as described above.

2. From the main document, click the Mail Merge Helper button. You will see the Mail Merge Helper dialog box.

NOTE: A data file must be attached to the merge file.

Figure 25-12.
You can sort
records by up to
three different
fields while you
conduct the merge

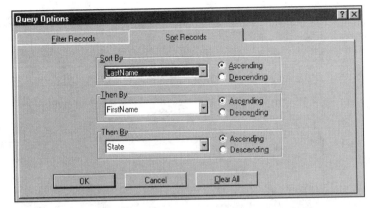

3. Choose Query Options and make sure the Sort Records tab is chosen. The Query Options dialog box shown in Figure 25-12 will appear.

4. Select the name of the field to Sort By, choosing it from the drop-down list, and choose Ascending or Descending.

5. If you would like to specify a field to sort by in case of ties (e.g., two people with the last name of Smith), select the name of the field in the Then By box.

6. Choose OK when you are done. You'll return to the Mail Merge Helper and can complete the merge as desired.

Selecting Records

You can also select records using a similar procedure:

1. From the main document, click the Mail Merge Helper button. The Mail Merge Helper dialog box will appear.

2. Choose Query Options and ensure that the Filter Records tab is chosen. You will see the Query Options dialog box shown in Figure 25-13.

3. Select the name of the field to use as the criterion by choosing it from the Field drop-down list.

4. Choose the comparison type, then type in the value to compare it to. For instance, for all records from VA you would choose "=" as the comparison type and type **VA**.

5. Add additional criteria on other lines, specifying them as AND or OR criteria.

Figure 25-13.
You can select records
meeting multiple
criteria from whatever
data source you are
using for the merge

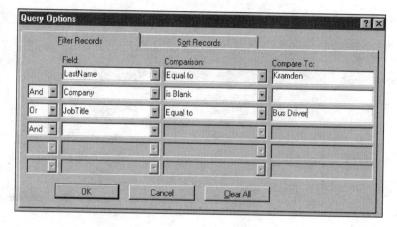

6. When you are finished, choose OK. You return to the Mail Merge Helper and can conduct the merge as described previously.

Getting the Word Out Electronically

While a mass mailing can be a time-saver, it is nothing compared to the efficiency of sending messages electronically via fax or e-mail. For instance, you can write someone a note, then fax or e-mail it directly from Word. Alternatively, you can send faxes and e-mail to a group of people all at once when you send it to a personal distribution list that you define. This list can contain both e-mail and fax addresses. Your message will be sent to each person using the right medium.

Sending an Electronic Message

Using Office 95, you will be able to send documents electronically with ease. When you send a file to someone, Microsoft Exchange automatically sends it via fax or e-mail depending on which type of address you have for them. Thus, the method for sending faxes and e-mail is exactly the same.

In order to send faxes electronically, you will need a fax modem attached to your computer or accessible via your LAN (Local Area Network). You'll also need to install the Microsoft Fax service as part of Microsoft Exchange.

NOTE: Any file that can be printed using Windows 95 printer drivers can be sent via fax or e-mail. Thus, you can send Word documents, Excel spreadsheets, Access reports, or PowerPoint presentations. You could even fax or e-mail a Schedule+ monthly calendar if you like.

Installing Microsoft Exchange is discussed in Chapter 1.

In order to send e-mail, you will need to be attached to a network running an e-mail system, or have a modem and dial-in access to a provider offering e-mail service.

To send a fax or e-mail from Word, Excel, PowerPoint, or Access:

1. Choose File, Send. Depending on how Exchange is configured, you may be asked for your profile name, then you will see the New Message dialog box shown in Figure 25-14.

2. Click the To button. You will see a list of persons in the Personal Address Book.

3. If the person to whom you are sending the message is already in the Personal Address Book, double-click on his or her name, otherwise add them to the Personal Address Book.

4. Click OK. You return to the New Message dialog box.

5. Click the Send button. The message is sent. If it is a fax, the fax server will appear in the upper-left corner of the screen as the fax modem dials the number and sends the fax.

Figure 25-14.
When you choose File, Send, the file on which you are working becomes an attachment to an Exchange message

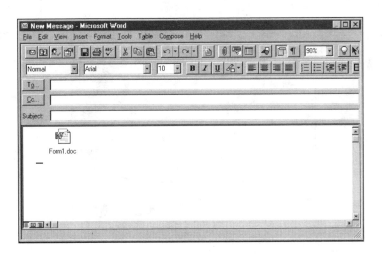

Adding a Name to the Personal Address Book

If the recipient is not in your personal address book, you can easily add him or her. To do so:

1. Access the New Message dialog box as described above, then click To. You will see the Address Book dialog box showing all the current entries.

2. Click the New button. The New Entry dialog box will appear, as shown in Figure 25-15.

3. If you send messages to the recipient via fax, choose Fax, then enter the necessary information in the New Fax Properties dialog box.

4. Otherwise, if you send them messages via e-mail, pick the appropriate entry such as Microsoft Mail or Internet Mail. Enter the information in the appropriate dialog box.

5. Click OK. The person is entered into the address book.

Creating a Personal Distribution List

If you send messages to the same group of people repetitively, it can very useful to create personal distribution lists in the personal address book. These lists can contain the names of people to whom you regularly send faxes, e-mail, or a combination of both. For example, you could create a list called Politicians that includes your congressman, your senators, and the President.

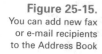

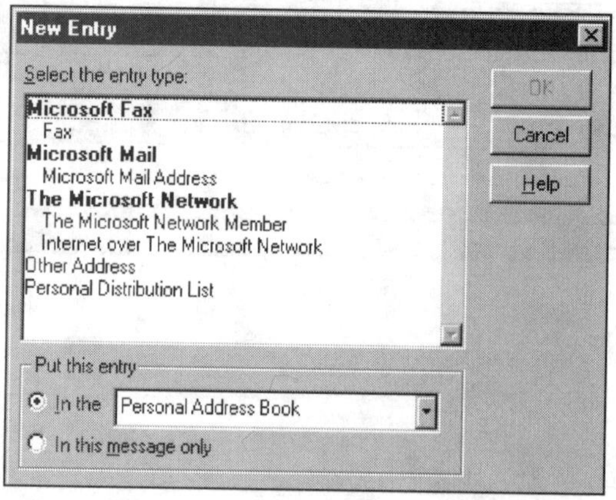

Figure 25-15.
You can add new fax or e-mail recipients to the Address Book

You create a personal distribution list in the same way that you create other new entries in the Personal Address Book:

1. Access the New Message dialog box as described above, then click T<u>o</u>. You will see the Address Book dialog box showing all the current entries.

2. Click the <u>N</u>ew button, then choose Personal Distribution List from the New Entry dialog box. You will see the New Personal Distribution List Properties dialog box shown in Figure 25-16.

3. Give the distribution list a name, then click the Add/Remove <u>M</u>embers button. You will see the Edit New Personal Distribution List Members dialog box, showing you a list of names from the Personal Address Book.

4. Double-click on the names of all persons to be included in the new distribution list.

5. Click OK when you are done.

6. Choose OK in the New Personal Distribution List Properties dialog box to return to the Address Book.

You will see the new distribution list as a bold entry in the address book. You can use it as you do any other entry in the book.

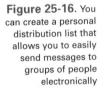

Figure 25-16. You can create a personal distribution list that allows you to easily send messages to groups of people electronically

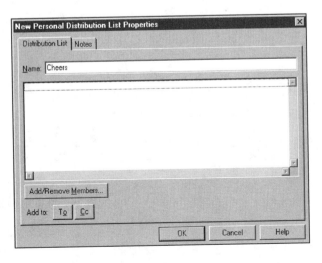

CHAPTER 26

PUBLISHING DOCUMENTS ELECTRONICALLY

IN THIS CHAPTER

- **Writing for an Electronic Audience**
- **Using Word's Internet Assistant**
- **Creating a Home Page on the World Wide Web**
- **Putting PowerPoint Slideshows on the Web**
- **Putting Excel Worksheets on the Web**

Electronic publishing is coming of age, both locally and via the Internet. More and more organizations are saving money by publishing corporate documents on their network. Microsoft refers to this process as *local Web publishing*. (Local Webs are also called *intranets*.)

Other companies are finding that they can transmit their message via the Internet's World Wide Web. They produce Web pages that provide corporate information, details on services or products, and even include ways that customers can order items or communicate with the company via e-mail. Individuals are getting on the electronic bandwagon, too. Electronic job hunts and résumés published on the Internet are becoming common in technology-related fields.

See Chapter 1 for instructions on how to download and install the Internet Assistants.

Microsoft has made it easy to publish Office 95 documents on the World Wide Web with its Internet Assistants. These are free add-ons to Word, PowerPoint, Excel, Access, and Schedule+ that automatically convert Office 95 files for publication on the Web.

NOTE: Office 95's Internet Assistants are available free from Microsoft Office's home page. They are not provided with Office 95 itself.

Understanding Web Publishing

Office 95's Internet Assistants help you create Web documents from all Office 95 applications, then publish them on the World Wide Web for the entire world to see.

Before making your first Web document, it's important to learn some about some basic terms, such as the World Wide Web, HTML, URLs, and Web browsers.

The World Wide Web

The *World Wide Web* (also referred to as the *Web*) is a global network of computers that people can connect to from anywhere in the world. These computers display a specific type of document, called a *Web page,* that can contain formatted text, pictures, sound files, and animation.

Web documents are connected to each other by links, similar to the links in the Windows Help system between a subject and related text. In the Windows Help system, certain terms (usually specially formatted) link you to other documents or places in the current document. Similarly, Web documents have links to other Web documents.

There is no hierarchical organization of Web documents. They are not organized in a central index or table of contents, as you find in other types of Internet spaces, such as Gopher—where there is a menu of choices, leading to submenus, leading to further submenus. The Web is merely a collection of Web pages that are linked and cross-linked to other pages on the Web.

HTML

HTML stands for HyperText Markup Language. It was designed so that a variety of different computers, all of which save documents in unique formats, could publish complex documents on the Web.

HTML documents are plain-text documents. That is, they contain no special formatting. Instead of using complex codes to format text, they use tags. A *tag* is simply angle brackets with text inside them. For instance, to make a word appear in boldface, an HTML document uses the <b> tag, as in "This is <b>bold</b> text."

You don't need to know HTML codes to publish documents on the Web, since the Internet Assistants convert text from Word, Excel, PowerPoint, Access, and Schedule+ formats into HTML.

URLs

URL stands for Uniform Resource Locator. It's a fancy name for the address and filename of a document on the Web. Actually, URLs contain more information than this, but thinking of them this way will help you understand the concept. Examples of URLs include:

http://www.microsoft.com

http://www.primapublishing.com

http://www.tmn.com/Community/bruck/home.html

We can dissect these URLs to understand them by their component parts:

- **http:** stands for HyperText Transfer Protocol. It tells the Internet server that the document will be a Web document in HTML format. The **//** always follows this.

- **www** indicates that the file is on a computer that is a World Wide Web server.

- **tmn** or **microsoft** is the name of the organization owning the server. If the organization has more than one server, the server's name appears before the organization's name: e.g., www.purple.tmn.com. (People who name servers have a unique sense of humor.)

- **com** indicates that it is a commercial organization. You will also see "edu" (education), "mil" (military), "gov" (government), and "org" (organization), for U.S.-based servers. Internet servers in other countries use a country code in place of the organization type code, such as "au" for Australia, "ca" for Canada, "de" for Germany, "jp" for Japan, "pe" for Peru, etc.

- **/Community/bruck/**, if present, indicates the directory on the server that contains the file.

- **home.html**, if present, indicates the specific file. (UNIX, the operating system used on most Internet servers, allows longer filename extensions than Windows does.) Internet Assistant saves files as .htm files, rather than .html; Internet servers recognize either one as an HTML document.

Web Browsers

A *Web browser* allows you to view Web pages. It converts HTML tags to a more readable format. Instead of seeing "bold," you see the text in boldface. Similarly, codes for horizontal lines, bulleted and numbered items, headers, and special alignment are converted into text and graphics with the appropriate attributes. More sophisticated Web browsers also allow you to download files, print them, mark favorite Web locations, and save a history of sites you've visited. Windows-based, graphical Web browsers also allow you to see graphics, play sounds, and watch videos that are included with Web documents. Advanced Web browsers, such as Microsoft Explorer 2.0 or Netscape Navigator 2.0, support sophisticated features such as tables, forms, scrolling banners, and multimedia programming tools, including Java. You will need one of these browsers to take full advantage of Web pages created by Office's Internet Assistants.

Writing for an Electronic Audience

Writing for an electronic audience requires you to think in new ways. The computer screen is a different medium from paper in several respects:

- The screen holds much less information than a piece of paper
- The eye can't read long paragraphs of text as easily on the screen
- Electronic documents allow you to locate keywords immediately
- Electronic documents allow you to jump instantly to related topics
- Electronic documents can include sound and video clips
- Electronic documents can be interactive, allowing you to fill out forms and send e-mail
- Electronic documents can include "clickable" images that illustrate a process, and allow you to click on an image and see an explanation on the screen

NOTE: Forms and clickable images are not yet supported by the Microsoft Windows 95 and Office 95 tool set.

Hints you might keep in mind when creating electronic documents include:

- **Create a short home page.** The home page is the first document that readers see. Depending on your specific requirements, consider keeping it short. Display a nice heading or graphic, followed by a sentence or short paragraph that will keep the reader interested. Then include a table of contents.
- **Use a two-level table of contents.** One of the better strategies for listing topics on your home page is to show a short table of contents. This should fit on one screen. Each entry can then link to more detailed information on another page.

PART VII   APPLICATION ISSUES

- **Use small graphics.** Not everyone has high-speed access to the Internet. Don't put a full-page graphic on your page that takes one to two minutes to download to the screen; people just aren't patient enough to wait. Use graphics as design elements, and use them judiciously. Keep them small, so they'll download quickly, and remember that not everyone has a browser that displays graphics well, or at all.

- **Use plenty of links.** Links are the heart and soul of the Web. "Paper-oriented" thinking produces a thesis-sized tome, while "electronic thinking" creates scores of small documents, linked and cross-referenced. This allows people to jump between them when they see topics of interest.

- **Change the content or look frequently.** Unless a Web site has a closed, limited readership (say, within a company or organization), it won't attract many repeat visitors if they feel they've already seen it. Most Web documents are designed to be as good-looking and informative as possible so they'll attract the attention of the Web-surfing audience, which delights in discovering new online gems. Any site can look brand new if it changes its content regularly.

Creating Hypertext in Electronic Documents

The major feature of electronic publishing is the use of *hypertext*—a fancy term for *jump terms,* such as the ones in Windows Help screens. When you click on a jump term, you're taken immediately to another place in the document, or even to another document altogether. Hypertext is a way of connecting information stored in different locations.

You cannot create hypertext in Word 7 alone; you also need the Internet Assistant 2.0, which calls it *hyperlinks.* To use hyperlinks, all PCs must be running both applications. This includes the computer on which the links are created and the computer(s) on which the documents with links are viewed.

To create a hypertext link involves marking the destination, then creating the jump term. Before starting, make sure you are running Internet

How Can Hypertext Enhance Electronically Published Documents?

Consider the following ideas:

- The table of contents could be linked to the various parts of the document they reference. When you clicked on "Chapter 11," for instance, you would instantly go there rather than just see the page number on which it begins. Similarly, a list of figures or an index could contain hypertext links.

- Technical terms in the text could be linked to their definitions in the glossary.

- Footnotes referring to other documents could take you directly to those documents.

- Cross-references could take you to the relevant text.

Imagine how different reading this book would be if it were an electronic document!

Assistant 2.0 along with Word 7. Select the Insert menu in Word. If the last entry is Hyperlink, you are running the Internet Assistant 2.0.

Making a Bookmark

To mark the hypertext link destination, first create a bookmark at that point in the document. A *bookmark* is a way of giving names to places in a document. You can use the Go To command F5 to go to any bookmark you have defined.

To create a bookmark, do the following:

1. In the document, click where you want users to jump as they move through the link.

2. Choose Edit, Bookmark. The Bookmark dialog box shown in Figure 26-1 will appear.

3. Give the bookmark a name. It must be one word; use an underscore if you want to indicate a space.

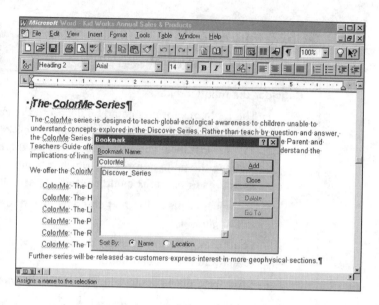

4. Choose <u>A</u>dd to return to the main editing window. The book-mark is there (although you cannot see any indication of this).

Creating a Link

The link is the point in the document where the user can click to jump to the destination. The link can be a jump term, which appears underlined (in blue), or an icon.

To create the link, follow these steps:

1. Create a bookmark for the destination as described previously.

2. Save the document and give it a name. (Documents must be saved for the hyperlink feature to work properly.)

3. Move to the point in the document where you want the link to appear.

4. If the link is to be a jump term, select the appropriate word or phrase. Otherwise, click where the button or icon should appear.

5. Choose <u>I</u>nsert, Hyperlin<u>k</u> and click on the To <u>B</u>ookmark tab. The HyperLink dialog box will appear, as shown in Figure 26-2.

Figure 26-2.
Links can be created
to make jump terms
in your document

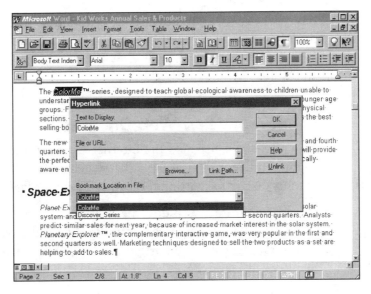

6. If you have selected text, it will appear in the Text to Display box. Otherwise, create a jump term by typing text in this box.

7. If the link is to another document, specify its name in the File or URL box. If it is another document on the Web, enter the document's URL.

8. Specify the bookmark's name in the drop-down Bookmark Location in File box.

9. Choose OK. Your new jump term is underlined.

To use a link, move the mouse pointer to the jump term. Double-click the mouse button. You will jump through the link to the point in the document.

Publishing Word Documents on the Web

Using Word's Internet Assistant, you can convert existing Word documents to HTML format, retrieve and edit documents from the Web, and browse the Web.

PART VII APPLICATION ISSUES

The Internet Assistant operates in two modes—the *Edit View* and the *Web Browse View*. The Edit View is used for creating and editing Web documents; the Web Browse View is a simple navigator for browsing the Web.

Creating a New Web Document

When you have installed the Internet Assistant, the screen looks slightly different than usual—the Switch to Web Browse View button appears on the formatting toolbar, as shown in Figure 26-3.

While you create a Web document, Word is in the Internet Assistant Edit View. The screen looks similar to the regular editing window in Word, except that some buttons (and menu commands) are different, as shown in Figure 26-4.

To create a new HTML document, do the following:

1. Choose File, New. You will see the New File dialog box.

2. Select the HTML template. The Edit View of the Internet Assistant will appear. Notice that the toolbar and menu commands change.

3. Type the text of the document as you normally would in Word. Use Word's editing commands to navigate in the document or move text.

Figure 26-3.
When Word's Internet Assistant is installed, a new button appears on the Formatting toolbar

Switch to
Web View

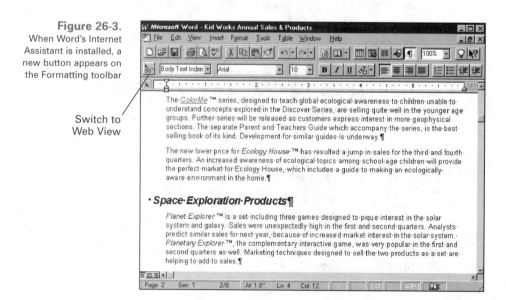

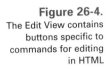

Figure 26-4.
The Edit View contains
buttons specific to
commands for editing
in HTML

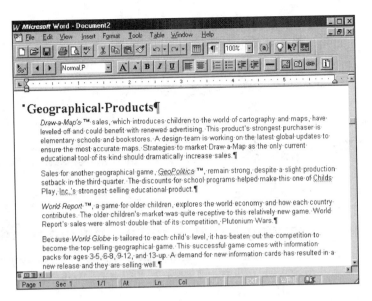

4. Format the document as you normally do in Word, by using the formatting toolbar or the Format menu. Most formatting commands are available, including boldface, italic, left-justify, or center-justify. Formatting commands not supported in HTML, like right-justify, are not available in the menus or toolbar.

5. Create bulleted and numbered lists or insert horizontal lines with appropriate buttons on the toolbar.

6. Use styles that are listed in the style box, such as Heading 1 through 5, to mark section and subsection headings in the document.

7. When you are finished, click the Save button to save your work. Notice that "HTML Document" appears in the Save as Type box of the Save As dialog box.

After the Web document is saved to disk, you can edit it as you would any other Word document. Just remember that it's been saved in a format other than Word:

1. Choose File, Open or click the Open button on the standard toolbar. The Open dialog box lists Word files, not HTML files.

2. Open the Files of Type list box and select HTML Document. Now you can see all the HTML documents in the folder.

3. Navigate to the appropriate folder and double-click on the desired document.

4. Edit the document as desired.

5. Save the document to your disk.

TIP: You can also convert an existing Word document to HTML. Choose <u>F</u>ile, Save As; then choose Save as <u>T</u>ype and specify HTML Document.

Viewing HTML-Equivalent Commands

While you are creating or editing an HTML document in Word, you may wish to look at a complete list of Word commands and their HTML equivalents:

1. Choose <u>H</u>elp, <u>I</u>nternet Assistant for Word Help Topics.

2. Double-click on HTML/Word Equivalents.

3. Double-click on HTML Tags and Equivalent Word Commands. You will see a complete listing of the commands or tags used to create Web documents.

If you would like to see the HTML codes in a document, you can do so as follows:

1. Open the appropriate HTML document.

2. Choose <u>V</u>iew, HTML Source.

3. If asked, answer Yes to save the HTML document. You will see a screen like the one in Figure 26-5, showing you the HTML source codes in the document.

4. Insert any HTML codes you wish to put in manually.

5. When you are finished, click the Return to Edit Mode button on the floating HTML toolbar.

6. If asked, respond Yes to save changes in the HTML document.

Retrieving Documents from the Web

The Internet Assistant does more than merely help you create and edit HTML documents. You can also browse the Web and retrieve documents from it. You can then edit them and save them to your local disk.

Figure 26-5.
You can view the
HTML source codes
of existing Internet
documents to assist
you in learning how
to create Web pages

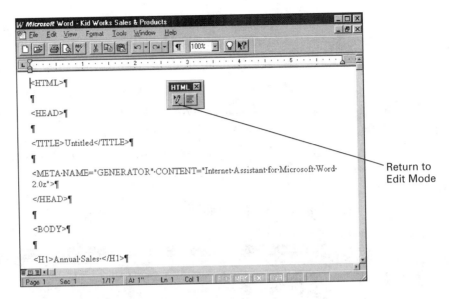

Return to
Edit Mode

NOTE: Current versions of the Internet Assistant do not allow you to upload documents to the Web. Ask your system administrator or Internet Service Provider for instructions on uploading HTML documents from your computer to the Internet.

An easy way to learn about Web publishing is to use the Browse mode to view a Web document with formatting you find attractive and then save it to your local drive. This allows you to view its HTML to see how it was constructed. To use the Internet Assistant to view and retrieve documents from the Web:

1. Click the Switch to Web View button to switch to Browse mode. The toolbar switches to the one shown in Figure 26-6.

2. Click the URL button. The Open URL dialog box will appear.

3. Type in a URL, such as **http://www.microsoft.com**, and choose OK. After seeing the Contacting Host dialog box, the Connect To dialog box will appear, as shown in Figure 26-7.

4. Make sure the default settings are correct, then choose

Connect. After a moment, you will be connected to the Web site specified by the URL you entered.

5. Navigate around the Web in any of several ways:

   • Click the URL button to go to a specific site.

   • Click on hypertext terms or images on Web pages to jump to other documents.

   • Click the Home button to go to Microsoft's home page.

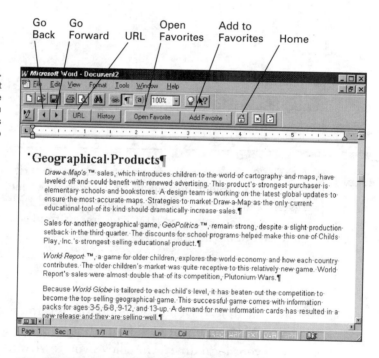

Figure 26-6.
The Internet Assistant provides a simple browser that allows you to open documents from the Web

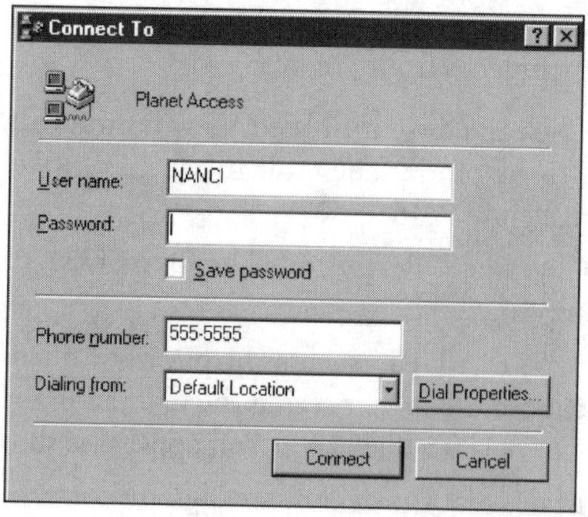

Figure 26-7.
The Connect To dialog box allows you to customize your connection to the Internet

- Click the Go Back button to go back to the last Web page you visited.
- Use the Go Forward button to come back once you've used the Back button.
- Add special sites to a list of favorites by clicking the Add to Favorites button.
- Go to a favorite site by clicking the Open Favorites button, then selecting a site you have previously saved.

6. When you have found a document you wish to save, click the Save button. You will see the Save dialog box. Specify the appropriate folder and filename, and choose Save.

Putting Your Document on the Web

Before you can publish a document on the Web, you will need to do two things:

- Upload the document from your computer to the Web computer
- Set user-access rights for the file on the Web computer

The Internet Assistant cannot assist you with either of these tasks. Various programs allow you to upload a file, but the most efficient way for you to do this should be discussed with your network administrator or your Internet Service Provider (ISP).

Similarly, your administrator or ISP should tell you what user-access rights you should give your files, and whether there are shortcuts that have been established for doing so.

Creating a Personal Home Page

You can create a simple Web page for yourself if you first ensure that the Internet Assistant is installed and you have access to the Web.

Hands On: Creating a Personal Home Page

1. Choose File, New and select the HTML template. You will see the HTML toolbars and a blank editing window.
2. Choose Tools, Options, View and set the Style Area Width to 0.5 inches. Click OK to close the dialog box.

3. Click the Title button and insert a title for the Web page. (This title will appear on the title bar of the browser when you look at the document on the Web.) For now, type something like **Bill Bruck's Home Page** and click OK.

4. Click the Style button and select the Heading 1,H1 style. This style is good for the main heading.

5. Type your name and center it by clicking the Center button. Press [Enter] for a new line.

6. Insert a horizontal rule by clicking the Horizontal Rule button and typing **You can find information on the following topics:**. Press [Enter].

7. Click the Bulleted List button and type some lines like the following:

   • **All about my family**
   • **Bill at work**
   • **Bill at play**

8. Choose the Address style, then type something like **This home page produced by Bill Bruck - bruck@tmn.com**—except replace my name and Internet address with your own. A document similar to the one in Figure 26-8 will appear.

Figure 26-8.
The Internet Assistant quickly produces a simple HTML document that you can publish on the Web

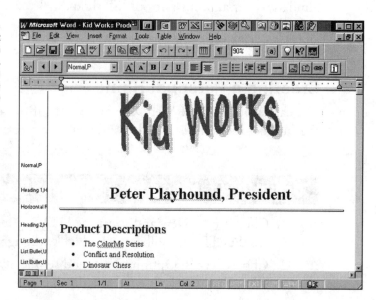

9. Save the document. It will automatically be saved as an HTML document with an .HTM extension.

10. Upload it to the Internet directory and set access permissions as instructed by your ISP. You've published your first Web document!

Adding Graphics to Your Web Page

The most common way to refine a Web page is by adding graphics and links to other Web documents. Graphics can add interest to a Web document and give it visual appeal. Be careful not to overuse graphics, however, because they can take a long time to download. Also, if you rely on them for navigation, people with text-based browsers won't be able to use your site at all.

Graphics must be in the GIF or JPEG format to be suitable for Web documents. Unfortunately, this format is not supported by PowerPoint or PC Paint, so you cannot convert existing clip art using Windows 95 or Office 95 applications. You can, however, download freeware or shareware programs such as CVTGIF.EXE from the Internet or commercial online services, such as America Online or CompuServe. Do a search on the keywords "GIF" and "JPEG" to find such programs. Then convert your bitmap files from TIF, BMP, or PCX formats to GIF or JPEG.

When you've done the preliminary work, you'll be able to include a picture on your Web page, as follows:

1. Open the HTML file in Word.

2. Position the insertion point where you want the image to appear.

3. Click the Picture button. You will see the Picture dialog box shown in Figure 26-9.

4. To insert a picture on your hard drive, click the Browse button and double-click on the GIF or JPEG image you want to include. To insert an image on the Internet, type its URL.

TIP: If you convert an existing Word document to HTML, graphics in the document will be converted to GIF format and saved as separate GIF graphics files, linked to the HTML file you create.

PART VII APPLICATION ISSUES

Figure 26-9.
Add pictures to the
Web page by first
inserting a dummy
picture contained on
your hard drive

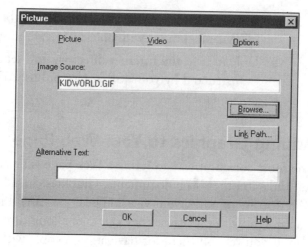

Figure 26-9.
Add pictures to the
Web page by first
inserting a dummy
picture contained on
your hard drive

Publishing PowerPoint Slideshows on the Web

Microsoft has provided two ways to publish a slideshow on the Web. The simpler way is with the PowerPoint Internet Assistant. It creates Web documents that can be viewed with any Web browser, although you lose multimedia or animation effects. The more complex way is with the ActiveX Animation software. This free software creates files that contain all your multimedia and animation effects, but it requires a sophisticated browser to use, and requires that the ActiveX player be downloaded the first time that a slideshow is viewed.

Converting Slideshows to HTML Files

Loading the
Internet
Assistant is
discussed in
Chapter 1.

With PowerPoint's Internet Assistant, you can now publish slideshows on the Web. This is an excellent way to make attractive advertisements for your company, or make presentations that are completely portable. Just log on to the Web from your client's computer and the entire sales pitch will be accessible on their machines!

To do so, use the following procedure:

1. Load the PowerPoint Internet Assistant.
2. Open the desired slideshow in PowerPoint.
3. Choose File, Export for Internet. You will see the HTML Export Options dialog box shown in Figure 26-10.
4. Choose either GIF or JPEG as the graphics format. If you choose JPEG, select the image quality.

Figure 26-10.
You can export a slideshow using either GIF or JPEG graphics

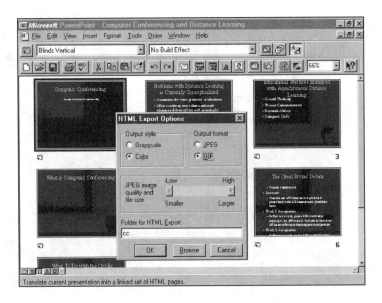

NOTE: If you have both the Internet Assistant and the ActiveX Animation Player loaded, you need to choose <u>F</u>ile, Expor<u>t</u> for Internet, As <u>H</u>TML.

TIP: GIF format may provide slightly greater resolution. With JPEG, however, you can adjust the image quality. Lowering the quality can make files drastically smaller, and thus quicken the downloading time. The quality of most PowerPoint slides can safely be lowered to halfway between the low and midpoint of the scale without affecting their visible quality.

5. Specify a folder for new HTML documents. This can be a folder that does not exist; the Wizard will create it if needed.

6. Wait while the Wizard plays the slideshow, and converts it to a series of HTML documents in the specified folder.

7. Copy all the files to a directory on the Web server.

You can play a slideshow on the Web as follows:

1. Open the Web browser.

2. Enter the URL that includes the directory containing the

Figure 26-11.
The Internet Assistant makes a title slide named index.htm

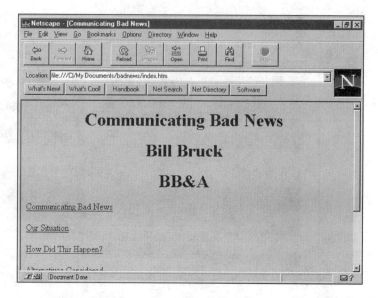

Figure 26-12.
Your slideshow is converted into a series of Web documents

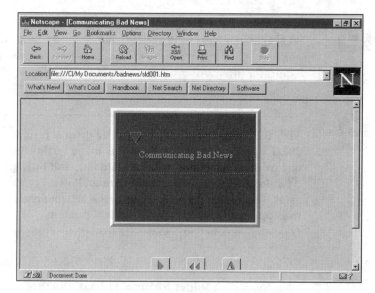

slideshow and the filename index.htm. For instance, if it's in a directory called "slides," you'll enter a URL like http://www.bruck.com/slides/index.htm. You will see a title slide like the one shown in Figure 26-11.

3. Click on the first slide. You will see the slide, with navigation buttons below it, as shown in Figure 26-12.

Figure 26-13.
The Internet Assistant
creates both a graphic
and text version of the
slideshow

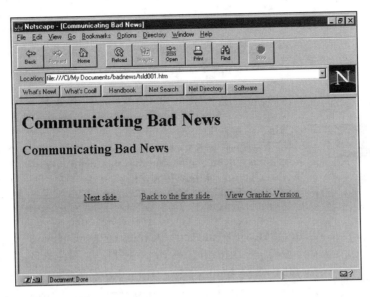

4. If you prefer just to see text versions of the slides, click the Text button. A text version of the slide will appear, as in Figure 26-13.

5. Use the navigation buttons at the bottom of the slide to go from slide to slide. Any speaker notes will be included at the bottom of the slide, and you can scroll down to see them.

When you use the Internet Assistant to convert slideshows to Web pages, each slide becomes a Web page and is downloaded individually when you access it. You lose any animation, sounds, videos, transition effects, and animation. However, the only software needed to view the presentation is the Web browser itself.

Converting Multimedia Slideshows

The second way to publish a presentation is by using ActiveX Animation. This is a separate, free Internet product that can be downloaded from the PowerPoint section of the Microsoft Office Web site. It consists of two parts: the publisher and the viewer. The publisher is a menu item in PowerPoint. When you use it, a slideshow is converted into one compressed file that can be uploaded to the Web site.

PART VII   APPLICATION ISSUES

To view an ActiveX presentation, you need only two things:

- An advanced browser such as Microsoft Exchange 2.0 or Netscape Navigator 2.0
- The ActiveX viewer

> **TIP:** Most ActiveX files are located on Web pages that contain a link to the place where you can download the ActiveX viewer if you do not have it.

When you view an ActiveX presentation, the entire presentation file is downloaded onto the computer. The ActiveX viewer is then run automatically as a helper application from the browser to view the file. All multimedia attributes of the original presentation—including transitions, animation effects, sound clips, video clips, etc.—are retained.

> **CAUTION:** Including sound or video clips in an ActiveX presentation makes the file very large and slow to download.

To convert the slideshow to an ActiveX presentation, do the following:

1. Load the PowerPoint Internet Assistant.
2. Open the desired slideshow in PowerPoint.
3. Choose File, Export for Internet, As ActiveX Animation. You will see the Export as ActiveX Animation dialog box shown in Figure 26-14.
4. Give the ActiveX file a name and choose Save. You'll be prompted to wait as the file is created.
5. Upload the file to the Web site.

Playing an ActiveX slideshow is as simple as following these steps:

1. Use Microsoft Explorer or Netscape Navigator to access the Internet.

Figure 26-14.
You can save your
PowerPoint file as an
ActiveX Animation file

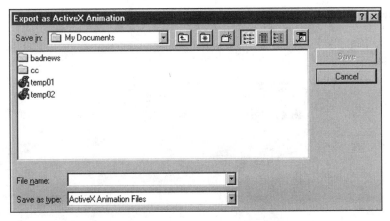

2. Load the ActiveX viewer.

3. Browse to a location containing a link to an ActiveX presentation and click on the link. The file will be downloaded, and you will see the first slide of the slideshow.

4. Click anywhere on the slide or press $\boxed{N}$ to advance to the next slide.

5. Click the right-mouse button or press $\boxed{P}$ to advance to the previous slide.

Publishing Excel Worksheets on the Web

The Excel Internet Assistant allows you to create Web pages from Excel worksheets, as shown in Figure 26-15. You can also incorporate an Excel worksheet into an existing HTML document, such as a Web page created with Word's Internet Assistant.

Creating a Stand-Alone HTML File

A stand-alone file is appropriate if you have a large Excel table and are creating a link to it from another Web page. To create a stand-alone HTML file, use this procedure:

1. Load the Excel Internet Assistant.

2. Open the desired worksheet in Excel.

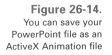

Figure 26-15.
You can publish Excel
worksheets as Web
documents with the
Excel Internet Assistant

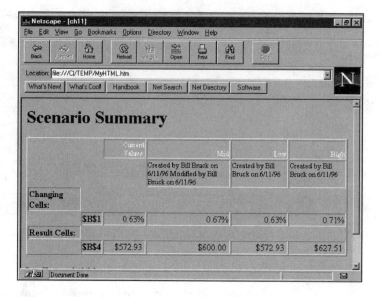

3. Open the Tools menu. If you do not see the Internet Assistant Wizard in the Tools menu, choose Add-Ins, check the Internet Assistant Wizard, and choose OK. It will now be on the menu.

4. Choose Tools, Internet Assistant Wizard. You will see the first step of the Internet Assistant Wizard, shown in Figure 26-16.

5. Select or type the range you wish to convert and choose Next.

6. Select Create An Independent HTML Document and choose Next.

7. Enter the title, header, and footer information for the Web page in Step 3 of the Internet Assistant.

8. In Step 4, choose whether or not to convert the formatting of the worksheet. Not all formatting can be converted into HTML, but the Assistant will convert as much as possible.

9. In Step 5, give the new file a name and choose Finish. Your document will be converted into a Web page.

TIP: You cannot change the formatting of the resulting HTML document with the Excel Internet Assistant. You can, however, open the HTML file in Word's Internet Assistant and modify it, as described previously.

Figure 26-16.
You can specify the range of Excel data you wish to convert to HTML

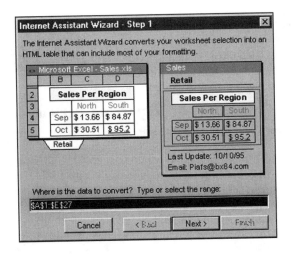

Creating a Table on Another Web Page

If you have a small Excel table, you may wish to place it in an existing Web page. This is a two-step process. The first step is to open the Web document that receives the worksheet and enter a special HTML code in it. This will usually be a document that you create with Word's Internet Assistant. The second step is to use Excel's Internet Assistant to create the table.

NOTE: Word's Internet Assistant supports Word's Table feature, so you may prefer to create the table directly in the Web document with Word's Internet Assistant.

To insert the special HTML code in the Web document, do the following:

1. Open the Web document that will receive the table in Word's Internet Assistant.
2. Place the insertion point where you want the table to appear.
3. Choose Insert, HTML Markup. You will see the Insert HTML Markup dialog box shown in Figure 26-17.
4. Type <!--##Table##--> and click OK. You will see the code as a blue jump term in the document.
5. Save and close the document.

PART VII   APPLICATION ISSUES

Figure 26-17.
Before using Excel's
Internet Assistant to put
a table into an existing
Web page, you must
put a special HTML
code in the document

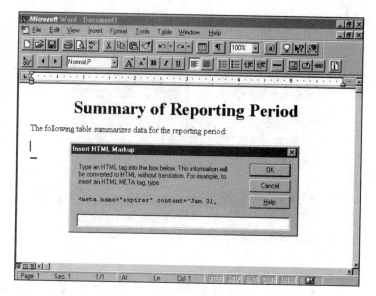

You can now use the following procedure to insert the table in your Web document:

1. Load the Excel Internet Assistant.

2. Open the desired worksheet in Excel.

3. Choose the Tools menu. If you do not see the Internet Assistant Wizard in the Tools menu, choose Add-ins, check the Internet Assistant Wizard, and choose OK. It will now be on the Tools menu.

4. Choose Tools, Internet Assistant Wizard. The first step of the Internet Assistant Wizard will appear.

5. Select or type the range you wish to convert and choose Next.

6. Select Insert the Converted Table To An Existing HTML Document, then choose Next.

7. Enter the path and filename for the Web page in Step 3 of the Internet Assistant, then choose Next.

8. In Step 4, choose whether or not to convert the formatting of the worksheet, then choose Next. Not all formatting can be converted into HTML, but the Assistant will convert as much as possible.

9. A new Web page will be created that contains the contents of the old one, plus the new table. In Step 5, give this new file a name and choose Finish. A new file is created.

Publishing Access Databases on the Web

If you have Access reports that you would like to publish on the Web, you can do so with the Access Internet Assistant, as shown in Figure 26-18. You can also use this Internet Assistant to convert any tables, forms, or queries into Web documents.

To create a Web document from an Access database, do the following:

1. Load the Access Internet Assistant.

2. Open the desired database in Access.

3. Choose Tools, Add-ins, Internet Assistant. You will see the first step of the Internet Assistant for Microsoft Access.

4. Choose Next. You will see the second step of the Assistant shown in Figure 26-19.

Figure 26-18.
You can publish Access reports on the Internet by using the Access Internet Assistant to convert them to HTML documents

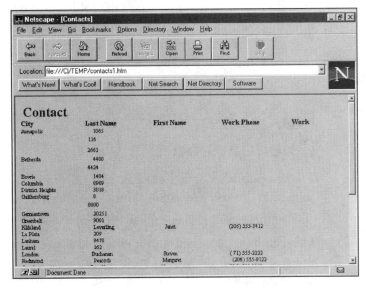

Figure 26-19.
You can choose to publish any report, table, or query in an Access database

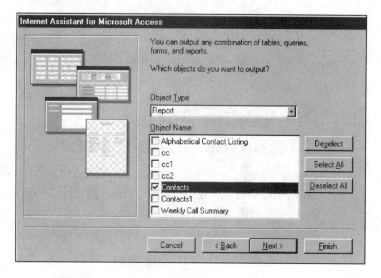

5. Choose Object Type and specify the type of object you will be selecting. Check the specific object you wish to select and choose Next.

6. To format a report or table in an attractive way, select an HTML template from the templates provided in the Assistant and choose Next.

7. In the next step, specify the folder into which the HTML documents will be placed and choose Finish. The relevant HTML documents will be created and saved to the disk in the folder you specify.

Publishing Schedule+ Calendars on the Web

You can publish a Schedule+ calendar on the Web by using the Schedule+ Internet Assistant. You can publish either a full schedule, or merely a list of free and busy times.

This can be especially useful if you keep a calendar showing the availability of a commonly used conference room or the travel schedule of senior management officials. The result is an attractive Web document that looks like the one in Figure 26-20.

Figure 26-20.
You can publish a
personal calendar as
a Web document
with the Schedule+
Internet Assistant

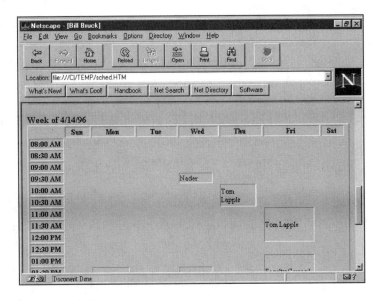

NOTE: Your Internet Service Provider must support
this feature.

To publish a calendar, do the following:

1. Load the Schedule+ Internet Assistant.

2. Choose File, Internet Assistant. You will see the Microsoft
   Schedule+ Internet Assistant dialog box shown in Figure 26-21.

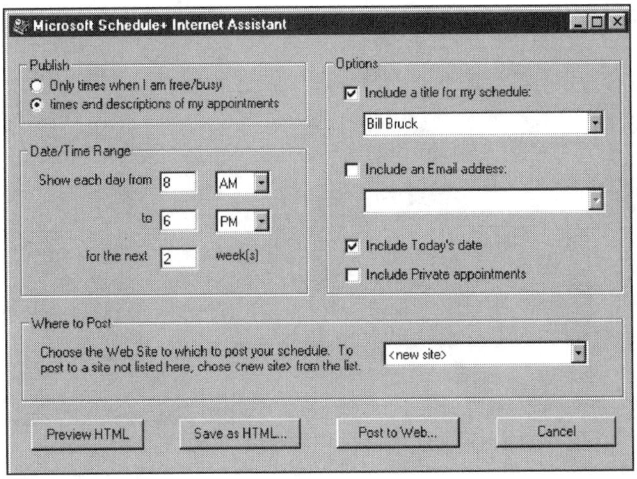

Figure 26-21.
You can publish a
Schedule+ calendar as
a Web page

3. Choose Only Times When I Am Free/Busy to publish just your free/busy times, or Times And Descriptions Of My Appointments to publish your entire calendar.

4. Specify the range of calendar you wish to publish. Indicate any desired title for the Web document and whether or not to include a link to your e-mail address so that readers of the document can contact you directly.

5. Specify the Web site to which you wish to post your calendar, if desired.

6. To see the Web document, choose Preview HTML.

7. To save the Web document on your local computer, choose Save as HTML.

8. To send it directly to the Web site, choose Post To Web.

NOTE: At the time this book went to press, the Schedule+ Internet Assistant was in beta (testing) form. It may have changed since then, or not even be available until Microsoft finishes testing it. As with all aspects of the Internet, sites change their content frequently. For the latest news about downloading and running the Office Internet Assistants, go to the Microsoft Office Web page:

http://www.microsoft.com/msoffice/

INDEX